D1105987

BRECHT'S AMERICA

Miami University, through an arrangement with the Ohio State University Press initiated in 1975, publishes works of original scholarship, fiction, and poetry. The responsibility for receiving and reviewing manuscripts is invested in an Editorial Board composed of Miami University faculty.

BRECHT'S AMERICA

By Patty Lee Parmalee

With a Foreword by John Willett

Published for Miami University by the Ohio State University Press

Library of Congress Cataloguing in Publication Data

Parmalee, Patty Lee, 1940–
  Brecht's America.

  Bibliography: p.
  Includes index.
  1. Brecht, Bertolt, 1898–1956—Knowledge—United States. 2. United
States in literature. I. Title.
PT2603.R397Z79454   832'.912   80-25857
ISBN 0-8142-0307-8

for China Beth Ho Parmalee

Als ich dich in meinem Leib trug
Sprach ich leise oft in mich hinein:
Du, die ich in meinem Leibe trage
Du mußt unaufhaltsam sein.

Ich hab dich ausgetragen
Und das war schon Kampf genug.
Dich empfangen hieß etwas wagen
Und kühn war es, daß ich dich trug.

Doch hab ich im Kampf dich Kleinen
Erst einmal groß gekriegt
Dann hab ich gewonnen einen
Der mit uns kämpft und siegt.

("Wiegenlieder," *GW* 9:431–32)

CONTENTS

Foreword   ix

Acknowledgments   xvii

Introduction. America and the Postwar Generation in Germany   3

One   1920–1922. America Represents Cruel Progress: *In the Jungle* and Its Sources   12

Sinclair, *The Jungle*, 16; Jensen, *The Wheel*, 25; *Other sources,* 35; *In the Jungle* and *In the Jungle of the Cities*, 40

Two   *1924–1926. America as Business: Joe Fleischhacker* and Other Fragments   49

A. Sources and Influences: Pacquet, *Flags*, 50; Tarbell, *The Life of Elbert H. Gary*, 55; Norris, *The Pit*, 58; White, *The Book of Daniel Drew*, 63; Harris, *My Life and Loves*, 68; Mendelsohn, *America: An Architect's Picture Book*, 69; Anderson, *Poor White*, 76; Myers, *History of the Great American Fortunes*, 79.

B. Poems and Fragments: Brecht's Creative Crisis, 83; Brecht's Poetry, 86; *Man from Manhattan*, 95; *The Flood*, 101; *Dan Drew*, 107; *Joe Fleischhacker*, 113

Three   Brecht's Political Development   134

Four   1927–1929. Studying Marx: *Mahagonny* and the Learning Plays   176

CONTENTS

Mahagonny Song Play and *The Rise and Fall of the City of Mahagonny*, 176; *Happy End*, 198; *Flight over the Ocean* and the Learning Plays, 204; Style, 214; Sources, 220

Five   1929–1931. The World Economic Crisis and Brecht's Commitment: *St. Joan of the Stockyards*   225

"Vanished Glory of the Giant City New York," 226; Commitment, 236; *The Bread Store*, 240; *St. Joan of the Stockyards*, 244

Postscript. Exile and Return: Brecht and America after 1933   265

Conclusion. The Old and the New   271

Notes   279

Bibliography   291

Index   299

Foreword

Brecht has always presented a challenge to conventionally minded scholars and critics, for the simple reason that his literary and theatrical genealogy is so unorthodox. As he himself once explained, the German tradition that influenced him was not the recognized classical mainstream, leading from the Enlightenment through Schiller and Goethe to Gerhart Hauptmann and the great bourgeois novelists, but a parallel, semiunderground river whose outstanding rocks are named Grimmelshausen and Lenz, Büchner and Wedekind. If this is true of his dramatic writing, how much harder must it be for traditionalists to stomach all the other multiple aspects of his theater. For theater is almost by definition a ragbag, eclectic, ephemeral art that picks its ideas and influences from all sides, without the least respect for the academic decencies. Indeed, Brecht actually prided himself on being what he called "a thief," remorselessly stealing whatever he found useful in other people's work. What differentiated him, and made him so well worth trying to understand, was his ability to knit the results into a coherent and instantly recognizable whole.

Deeply rooted as he was in Germany—and even in a certain South German provincialism—he represents a specially awkward problem for academic Germanists because of the strong Anglo-Saxon element in his work. For, from very early on, a large part of its ingredients were taken from England and the United States, often in a very odd, and at times perverse, way. This was not an entirely

uncommon phenomenon in the 1920s (which were roughly speaking
Brecht's own twenties too), the early days of the American cinema
and the English detective story, when Nick Carter and Sherlock
Holmes were international mythical figures, echoed as far away as
Moscow in Marietta Shaginyan's "Jim Dollar" thrillers. But Brecht
did not merely parody or copy; he took what seemed to him relevant
in the English-speaking world and used it for objectives of his own.
Looking back now, we can see that England and Ireland were, in the
main, literary influences, providing him with many of his models
and even to some extent penetrating the actual language in which he
wrote. By contrast America, as this book will show, provided
unforgettable images for his poetic fantasy to work on—the "cold
Chicago" of his early writings, greedily sucking in ingenuous families from the flatland; a paradigm of that city/country antithesis
which he felt operating within himself—and at the same time giving
him vivid, undisguised insights into the economic jungle we live in:
something that fascinated him increasingly from the mid-20s on.

Together, too, they gave him much of what Dr. Parmalee aptly
terms his "nonchalant geography." Two maps could be drawn, after
the fashion of those early diagrams of the world as imagined by
Herodotus or Strabo: the world according to Brecht and the United
States according to Brecht. In the one you would have the preposter-
ous India that he acquired largely from Kipling: Haiderabad (*sic*),
Rangoon, Mandelay (*sic*), the South Pandjab (*sic*), Cape Town,
Cooch Behar, and Tibet, with Hongkong (*sic*) not far away; then
Tahiti (lapped by the Gulf Stream), Malaya, and that unknown
country of his diaries where Maori women live in kraals. The second
would center on Chicago and take in Miami and Alaska, Manhattan
and San Francisco, Havana and Oklahoma, Lake Erie and the
savannahs. It would be threatened by all kinds of natural catastrophes, ranging from earthquakes and hurricanes to that ever-
present desert which lurks around in his late Hollywood poems, just
waiting to take over the shining freeways and lush gardens of the
City of the Angels. This new cosmography would quite exclude the
countries where Brecht's deeper interests lay: Germany and, from
the late 20s on, the USSR (though maybe the medieval Georgia of
the *Caucasian Chalk Circle* might figure somewhere in the larger
map). It would include the two towns that he himself saw as successful "poetic conceptions": Kilkoa with its army cantonments some-

where in India, and *The Threepenny Opera*'s ragged, corrupt Victorian London.

The interaction of English and American elements in Brecht's work was quite recently brought home to me by a rereading of his only complete work in novel form, *The Threepenny Novel*, with its London setting. For there are three mutually complementary aspects to this remarkable exercise in fiction, which is itself, of course, a development of the Brecht-Weill *Threepenny Opera* and the film that G. W. Pabst made of it—or more precisely, of Brecht's dissatisfaction with that film. The shady business intrigues that go to make up its rambling story are fairly clearly inspired by those readings in American financial biography of which Dr. Parmalee gives such an intriguing account: Gustavus Myers's splendid three-volume *History of the Great American Fortunes*, for instance (which she virtually rediscovered for us), seems to have provided the idea of selling unseaworthy ships for use as troop transports, and Brecht's refurbished and upgraded Macheath has plainly learned a good deal from the noble examples of Pierpont Morgan and Dan Drew. From the literary point of view the novel reflects English models: not only John Gay, whose *Beggar's Opera* underlies the whole undertaking, but Kipling and the vastly successful 1920s thriller writer Edgar Wallace. Then third, there is the picture of London itself, whose "poetic conception" here could well have been pieced together from recollections of Dickens, the Sherlock Holmes stories, and the illustrations of Gustave Doré (though we do not know how well Brecht knew them) and possibly also from Friedrich Engels's *Condition of the English Working Classes in 1844*. (One of the few points where I am skeptical about Dr. Parmalee's conclusions concerns Brecht's reading of the Marxist classics. Until some scholar goes into the question properly and marshalls all the evidence, I shall question its alleged extent and depth.)

In such ways *The Threepenny Novel* provides a quite characteristic instance of Brecht's ability to pick his material from the most unexpected sources—he would have had no inhibition about marrying Dickens with a hastily-written yellow-bound crime story such as Wallace used to churn out—then turning the whole improbable mixture into an original work of art. But of course his debt to English literature was much more extensive than that. It was grounded in Shakespeare, who to him was certainly the greatest of all dramatic writers, and also embraced his adaptations of Marlowe and Webster; later he based *Trumpets and Drums* on Farquhar and *Señora Carrar's Rifles* on synge. If Kipling gave him his attitude to Imperial India (and to private soldiers), his approach to Chinese and Japanese literature was through the translations of Arthur Waley; *Der Jasager* was indeed a virtually complete translation from one of the Waley *Nō Plays of Japan*, which he and Weill turned into a "school opera"; likewise his "Chinese Poems" are all but one of them taken from Waley's versions. As for the detective novel, he came to see it as a model of what modern writing should be: it posed problems, traced out a rational solution, had little (in those distant days) to do with psychology, played fair with the reader, and altogether fulfilled Brecht's requirements for the art of what he termed "the scientific age." Oddly enough, the kind of story that Brecht had in mind here was not the tough-guy thriller in the wake of Hemingway, which he dismissed as "Hollywood run wild," but the highly artifical crime puzzles of Englishmen like Austin Freeman and John Rhode. Georges Simenon, to him, was a less modern writer than Conan Doyle.

He was avid in his reading of such stories: in 1956 his country house at Buckow had a room lined with paperback crime stories, which he ranked with cigars as his "means of production." Not that he didn't also read more serious works: thus his diary of 1940 shows him reading Macaulay and Arnold, and Boswell's life of Johnson, and when he reads Wordsworth's "She was a phantom of delight," his imagination goes out to an England that is preparing for a possible Nazi invasion. What these gave him was something very unlike the vivid imagery and astounding socioeconomic revelations that he got from America. It was far more a sense of a vastly rich literary tradition, rooted in an England (and an English theater) quite different from that of his own time: an awareness of three centuries' worth of writers who still seemed to be living in the same city and the same age—something that a fragmented country like Germany could not hope to have. What it did not give was an awareness of a complex modern society such as he got from his American reading. In fact, even when he came to visit London in the mid-1930s, his few poems (like "The Caledonian Market" with its Kipling references) are written from an almost antiquarian point of view; London is a city of gaslights and old clothes, with none of that deceptive modernity that is so devastatingly conveyed by his long New York poem.

Look at his actual language, however, and it seems to reflect both aspects of our shared tongue. Expressions like "poker face man" (*sic*; and to begin with, he spelled it "pokker"), "hard-boiled," "k.o.," and such come clearly from this side of the Atlantic; the deeper permeation of his style and syntax (as in the un-German word order of "Als wir kamen vor Milano") and the English-language thinking and writing that went into the long-drawn-out work on *Galileo* and *The Dutchess of Malfi* are due to his more literary readings. A central figure here was his collaborator (from the mid-20s on) Elisabeth Hauptmann, whose role in his early American researches is described by Dr. Parmalee. She had studied English literature and for a time had taught it, and until he went into exile, she acted as his interpreter and adviser where anything to do with England or America was concerned. It was thus she who translated Gay and Waley for him and actually wrote the two English-language "Mahagonny Songs" that were later taken up in the opera; then after Brecht's return to Europe in 1947, she largely resumed her old role, notably in adapting *The Recruiting Officer* as *Trumpets and Drums*. By then Brecht himself could not only read English with apparent ease but also write it, to judge from a translation of the first scene of *Man Equals Man* that is in his handwriting and can be found in the Eyre Methuen edition, fitting almost imperceptibly into the English text of that Kiplingesque play.

Much of this is of course outside the scope of Patty Parmalee's illuminating and highly enjoyable book, which is concerned rather to establish the foundations of Brecht's interest in the United States, then to show the far-reaching use that he made of the insights and images to which it led him. She stops her investigations in 1933—the time of Hitler's accession to power and Brecht's removal to exile—at which point another new book has recently taken over. This is Professor James K. Lyon's *Bertolt Brecht in America*, which has appeared almost simultaneously from the Princeton University Press and retraces Brecht's subsequent real-life experience of the country (his previous knowledge having been based more imaginatively on reading, rumor, picture-books, and the movies). It should do much to clarify Brecht's slightly ambivalent relationships with Broadway, Hollywood, and the American political and theatrical

Left, besides setting out the American angles of *Galileo* and *Arturo Ui* and the four plays actually written here, from *Simon Machard* to the *Duchess of Malfi* adaptation. What will still remain lacking is any full study of the literary influences that came to him from England and (more marginally) Ireland. Some of the relevant information can be found in *Brecht in Britain*, a paperbound publication issued some years back by *Theatre Quarterly* to accompany an exhibition at the National Theatre. James Lyon, once again, has published a short monograph on Brecht's special debt to Rudyard Kipling, and there is a subtle analysis of his treatment of Arthur Waley's translations in Antony Tatlow's *Brechts chinesische Gedichte.*

So much for the context of *Brecht's America.* I read this book in typescript some time ago, and have always greatly admired it. Unlike most of the secondary literature about Brecht that keeps piling up year after year, it is in the first place extremely useful: I have repeatedly had to turn back to my heavily marked up copy to look up references to half-forgotten authors like Gustavus Myers and Bouck White, or extracts from previously unpublished poems by Brecht—for which Patty Parmalee's work is the sole source outside the Brecht Archive in East Berlin. Moreover, it is exceptionally well written; it is actually interesting, to an extent that is rare among academic publications. This because it has so much that is new to communicate, and communicates it with the freshness of discovery. Some of Dr. Parmalee's insights may since have been shared by others, but they remain original and infectious; they are imbued with her own critical yet deeply affectionate feeling for American society, and they have the—by Brecht's own standards— essential merit of being *fun*, a genuine source of enjoyment. To some extent this is the result of her close contact with Brecht's writing and thought, which can perhaps only be properly appreciated by those who have worked with his actual manuscripts and typescripts. For Brecht's writings are not just something finished and fixed, to be published in twenty volumes; they are also a long process of getting there, full of false starts, unrealized conceptions, sidetracks and byways and alternatives, all of which together make up something much greater, tenser, and more imaginative than the final text: a writer in motion.

Once you encounter Brecht in this way, you begin to pay much more attention to his judgments, whether about America itself and its institutions or about the books that he happened to come across and read. As with all great artists, his choices and opinions are often disconcerting; but there is likely to be something inspired about them, and again and again they are worth following up. I myself, for one, am grateful to Brecht, Hauptmann, and Patty Parmalee for, between them, putting me on to Frank Norris's novel *The Octopus*, that epic story of the Southern Pacific Railroad which seems to call out not merely for revival but for a great film director to make a movie of it. (Though less useful to Brecht, it is a far better book than *The Pit*.) Perhaps one day we shall have an annotated list of Brecht's recommended reading, with some of his recorded comments; it would be a lot livelier and more illuminating than the average Students' Guide. Unfortunately such pointers are only really convincing once you recognize the man's genius, and this is something that not all his interpreters help one to do. This again is where the present book is among the rare exceptions: you may or may not like the man who emerges from it, but the genius comes across. Here is a writer getting his insights and imaginative inspiration from far outside his own culture—indeed, very largely from a form of revolt against it: sometimes getting them wrong, yet finally fusing them with all kinds of other opinions and intentions to make something new. About America's meaning for Brecht's theater and his political development Dr. Parmalee is surely right; it contributed something essential at a crucial turning point in his life and work. And this is a fascinating process to watch.

And yet if we look across to Germany, we find a very different, somewhat jaded view of Brecht. For years now he has been thought to have acquired what Max Frisch described as the all-pervading ineffectiveness of classical status, no longer offering any fresh stimulus to the theater and half-smothered on the bookshelves by the ever-increasing weight of academic dissertation. At least this seems to be so in the Federal Republic, and farther East too he is now in a kind of limbo. For whereas once his works were outside the offical canon of Socialist Realist esthetics, and therefore very inviting to the younger generation in the Communist countries, today the gradual liberalization of such standards has made him appear tamely acceptable. It has indeed become a case of a prophet being better honored not only outside his own country but also outside his own camp. There he is a classic, whether of German literature or of progressive socialist art; and it is a moot point that is the more mortifying. Meanwhile, in the Third World countries and in America, England, and Australia, he is still an inspiration and a force, to be felt both artistically and politically, even though the emphasis differs according to what each of those areas is looking for most. He is alive and well, but living away from home.

The lesson of this book, then, is a double one. It shows that a scholarly, investigative approach to Brecht's work does not always have to be stupefying and soporific, provided that the writer is truly interested and stimulated by what she is finding out. That stimulus—which is at bottom an awareness of genius—can sometimes be passed on to the reader, just as it can and should be passed on to the audience by any true staging of the plays. At the same time, however, it does seem that a full understanding of the non-German elements in his writing, however seemingly eccentric, does a lot to help bring it to life. Brecht is not really suited for a plinth in Valhalla as a German classic; he is something much more universal, or at any rate many-sided—a selective, restless explorer with a South German mind but exotic tastes. This is something that the critics in his own country seem to find difficult to accept, to judge from the way in which they ignore the work done on Brecht's non-German aspects by scholars in other parts of the world. It is also very noticeable— and surely not coincidental—that they base themselves much less than their English-speaking colleagues on direct study of his scripts. No wonder that they should have managed to remove him from the interesting mess of real life to some higher and windier cloud up in the eternal sky. Let us hope they lower their heads, read what follows, and feel ashamed.

John Willett

Acknowledgments

Principal thanks are due to the Bertolt Brecht Archive in Berlin, for permission to use the photocopies there of Brecht's unpublished work, for arrangements for me to work there at an inconvenient time, and for permission to quote the unpublished passages that I requested, granted by Helene Weigel.

I would also like to thank the following people in East and West Berlin, who gave generously of various kinds of help: Elisabeth Hauptmann, Helene Weigel, Werner Hecht, Herta Ramthun, Werner Otto, Volker Klotz, Dieter Knaup, Jürgen Werth, and Helfried Rieger.

Apologies, on the other hand, are due to citizens of Canada and Latin America for the use of the word "America" as if it referred only to the United States. At the time of Brecht's early writings, the United States had appropriated the name "America" for itself, and Brecht used it half consciously to refer to the public-relations image the United States propagated of itself abroad: "America" was not so much a geographical region as an ethical concept, as in the "American dream" and the "American myth." It would have been too confusing to try to correct Brecht's usage.

Post script, 1980: In revising this work (originally written 1968–70) for publication, I have added materials that were suggested to me by James K. Lyon and Michael Morley, and made many cuts and changes suggested by Fred Jameson and Reinhold Grimm, who deserve special thanks. John Willett, as always, has been very kind and helpful in many ways. John Fuegi, John Barlow, Verne Moberg, and Virginia Parmalee made additional suggestions that I used, and Darko Suvin and Lee Baxandall were always very supportive. I want to thank Robert Demorest of Ohio State University Press, and the Miami University Editorial Board, for their advice about improving the manuscript and their friendly support; and I especially want to thank Gisela Bahr, my editor at Miami, who deserves more thanks and credit than I can say or than she usually gets. Finally, I would like to mention the pleasure of working in common with the international Brecht "community," through the International Brecht Society; the degree of helpful sharing of tips, ideas, and writings that goes on among the members would have pleased Brecht, who was always such a collaborator and help and inspiration to his fellow creative workers.

I have resisted the friendly suggestion, however, to expand the scope past 1933, since I am interested in exploring the impressions Brecht had of America while he was in Germany, and while he was first developing his Marxist and dramatic theories. The American visit has in the meantime been thoroughly studied by James K. Lyon, and anything I could say would only be derived from his research. For information on the later American works and Brecht's stay here, readers should consult the works by Lyon and Seliger listed in the bibliography.

By now much of the factual matter from my original research has become familiar knowledge, partly because I made photocopies widely available through the International Brecht Society. I am delighted that the general English-speaking public will now have the chance to see all the information about Brecht's interest in America in the context of his developing politics and aesthetics. Even if you already know about Joe Fleischhacker, Dan Drew, and Anne Smith—figures new to most of the Brecht world in 1970—I think you will find their origins and their political results fascinating.

I have added the relevant recent studies of Brecht to the bibliography, and have updated the text to reflect important materials both by and about Brecht that have been published in the last ten years. However, I have taken little information from other critical studies, preferring to leave this a book that reports on my own research and thinking.

Since the time when they graciously agreed to talk with me about

xviii

Brecht's early interest in America, both Elisabeth Hauptmann and Helene Weigel have died. (In the text, all unannotated references to statements by them are based on their interviews with me.) Without either of them, Brecht's work described in the following pages would have been very different from what it was, and so I like to think of publication of this study as a small contribution to their memorial.

All translations are by me.

In the quotations from Brecht's manuscripts, I have retained his idiosyncratic (or bad) spellings, and his use of lower case letters for capitals and spaces for punctuation.

Depending on knowledge of German, the reader can choose to read all quotations in English or German. However, to avoid tedious repetitions in the text, the titles of all Brecht's works and projects are given in English only; there is a list of the German equivalents included in the index.

BRECHT'S AMERICA

Introduction

America and the Postwar Generation in Germany

Nearly everyone who has written about Bertolt Brecht has noted that many of his plays are set in America, and that his America has a strange, mythical quality modeled on Al Capone, boxing, and jazz culture. This study looks in detail at the works Brecht read about America, considering their influence on his picture of America and on his political philosophy, and showing how his interest in America caused changes in his philosophy and in his aesthetics, and how these changes then affected his attitude toward America. Although it is an exhaustive study of all the sources we know about from Brecht's published and unpublished writings, it cannot hope to be definitive, partly because Brecht's letters and journals are not yet all available to the public, partly because we can never know about all the nonliterary influences, such as the fascination of America for postwar Germany; how many children played cowboys and Indians; what Brecht and his friends said to each other about America; to what extent they believed the American dream and to what extent they used it as a posture and literary device.

Even when we have direct evidence that Brecht read a book, describing its "influence" on him is a tricky matter. He was a shameless borrower, and it is easy enough to find anecdotes or metaphors that are simply lifted from the works he read. But we also want to know how he reacted to, and transformed, the *style* of a book; how its *ideas* may have changed his; and how it contributed to his picture of America. We want to know what he may have rejected in it, too, since he had an extraordinary ability to cull the useful from the hogwash. And we may even find ourselves moved to reevaluate some half-forgotten parts of our own literary tradition, on discovering that

3

Brecht found them useful. Likewise, we may possibly see America itself in a new light after learning what it meant to him and how he used its positive and negative features.

Descriptions of the fascination America held for Brecht tend to be very similar:

> The city of Chicago provides a persuasive setting for Brecht's parable, for its immense size and chilling impersonality give the struggle of Shlink and Garga the very cosmic scope Brecht is after.[1]

> In place of a faraway land where human passions reign untrammeled, America here [*St. Joan of the Stockyards*] becomes the center of the capitalist world where all the evils of the system exist in grotesque and exaggerated form.[2]

> Brecht's interest in American cities is also inspired by the coarser texture of American society, its mixture of racial types, its shameless materialism, its idiomatic speech and jazz culture, and, especially, its love of sport.[3]

> So the need for a legend, for escape, is rationalized through a Red Indian America that would astonish that continent, Mahagonny, a world of tomahawks, hurricanes, early film gangsters and gold rush days. Jack London used in character seriousness.[4]

There is no denying that, as these critics and others suggest, Brecht was fascinated by America. There were other countries he liked to write about, such as China, Victorian England, Russia, Finland— seldom Germany—but America appears far more frequently than any other part of the world as a setting for his plays. That he chose "exotic" settings is explained by the desire to make the action on the stage unfamiliar (an aspect of *Verfremdung* or dramatic alienation), but that he chose specifically America so often must be explained by the content of the American image itself. Examining that content and understanding its sources and its influences on Brecht's thinking will be the task of this book.

People who knew and worked with Brecht often mention his preoccupation with the New World. An early schoolmate remembers that Brecht was, earlier than his classmates, an avid reader of Karl May, the Zane Grey of Germany who wrote many Wild West novels. At the age of eleven Brecht was interested in a public reading by Karl May in Augsburg.[5] Elisabeth Hauptmann (Brecht's secretary and almost lifelong assistant) said he had relatives in America, and that he and she collected American recordings together in the twenties. She recalled that the single thin voice against a whole orchestra seemed to them symbolic of the conflict between individual and society in America.[6] "I think I'd like to eat my hat up" ("Ich glaube, ich will meinen Hut aufessen") in *Mahagonny* came from one of these records. Arnold Zweig speaks of a fantastic Chicago in *Im Dickicht der Städte* "which the relentless imagination of the widely-read Brecht had distilled out of manifold reports" ("das sich die unerbittliche Phantasie Brechts, des Vielesers, aus mannigfachen Berichten herausdistilliert hatte")[7]. And Bernhard Reich remembers Brecht's atelier in Berlin around 1925:

> On the long table against the window stood a typewriter, always open and ready for work, lay many folders—they held source materials, mainly newspaper clippings from the Old and especially the New World.

> Auf dem ans Fenster gerückten sehr langen Tisch stand eine jederzeit arbeitsbereit aufgeklappte Schreibmaschine, lagen viele Mappen—sie enthielten Materialien, hauptsächlich Zeitungsausschnitte aus der Alten und besonders aus der Neuen Welt.[8]

Although America is evident mainly in Brecht's early works, he retained the habit of collecting clippings about it till he died; in the Brecht Archive in East Berlin, one can still see many clippings from 1956 (the year of his death) on *The Power Elite*, by C. Wright Mills, from 1954 on Oppenheimer, and many materials and anecdotes on Einstein.[9] He apparently read regularly the *New York Times*, the *Christian Science Monitor*, and the *Saturday Review*. Erwin Strittmatter remembers Brecht's plans just before his death:

> At the end he spoke frequently of his intention to write about Einstein and his "American tragedy." One evening he said, "Ja, how would you put this scene on the stage: Einstein writes that letter full of portent to Roosevelt.—How would you dramatize that? A real problem."

> In der letzten Zeit sprach er häufig von seinem Vorhaben, über Einstein und seine "amerikanische Tragödie" zu schreiben. Eines abends sagte er: "Ja, wie willst du die Szene auf die Bühne bringen: Einstein schreibt jenen Brief voller Tragweite an Roosevelt.—Wie willst du das dramatisieren? Ein echtes Problem."[10]

But it is not necessary to take the word of critics and friends that Brecht was fascinated by America. He himself has demonstrated the fact not only by using America as a setting but by describing often the generation he grew up with, a generation affected above all by World War I and the consequent artistic and political turmoil. He

5

admitted and described his "Americanism" often. In 1920 he wrote in a notebook:

> How this Germany bores me! It is a good, medium-sized country, the pale colors and planes are beautiful in it, but what inhabitants! A degenerate peasant class, whose coarseness however gives birth to no fabulous monster, but only to a quiet bestialization, an obese middle class and a dull intelligentsia! There remains: America!

> Wie mich dieses Deutschland langweilt! Es ist ein gutes mittleres Land, schön darin die blassen Farben und die Flächen, aber welche Einwohner! Ein verkommener Bauernstand, dessen Roheit aber keine fabelhaften Unwesen gebiert, sondern eine stille Vertierung, ein verfetteter Mittelstand und eine matte Intellektuelle! Bleibt: Amerika![11]

At that time (he was twenty-two years old), Brecht seems to have been convinced that America was a kind of promised land for the bored younger generation. In the same year he expressed this sentiment in a poem, "Germany, You Blond, Pale . . . ," that is a paean of hatred to Germany:

> . . . O carrion land, anxiety hole!
> Shame strangles the memory
> And in the youth that you
> Haven't corrupted
> Awakes America!

> . . . O Aasland, Kümmernisloch!
> Scham würgt die Erinnerung
> Und in den Jungen, die du
> Nicht verdorben hast
> Erwacht Amerika!

> (*GW* 8:69)

Later, looking back with some irony, he described the emotions of his generation on discovering America:

> SHORTLY AFTER THE GREAT WAR a new age seemed to us young people to have dawned. listening to the new american music looking at the photographs of the big cities we could no longer doubt: the new age had come greater than any previous one and we were destined to spend our unique life in it. this age didn't seem bathed in sunlight to us this life hardly seemed easy to us on the contrary: of a great hardness and extraordinary boldness. in the image of this creature of our imagination neither injustice nor cruelty bothered us.

> KURZ NACH DEM GROSSEN KRIEG schien uns jungen leuten eine neue zeit angebrochen. anhörend die neue amerikanische musik

6

betrachtend die fotografien der großen städte konnten wir nicht mehr zweifeln: die neue zeit war gekommen größer als jede vorhergehende und wir waren bestimmt unser einmaliges leben in ihr zu verbringen. diese zeit schien uns nicht in sonne getaucht dieses leben schien uns kaum leicht im gegenteil: von großer härte und außerordentlicher kühnheit. im bilde dieses geschöpfes unserer einbildungskraft störte uns nicht ungerechtigkeit noch grausamkeit. (BBA 460,63)

These few unpublished sentences cover all the ground on the subject: the excitement of a new age, the admiration for boldness and largeness, the cultural debt to America, the glorification of toughness, the roots of all this in the war. But looking back, Brecht became critical: it was an imaginary America he had made for himself, allowing him to ignore or to accept injustice and cruelty.

Another time he described his generation of young theater people as not very agreeable in their Americanism and not very effective in their rebellion:

It must have been around the year 1920 that we first caused a public stir. We came swimming in on a big but not very pleasant wave of anarchy, of profiteering in Army materiel, of relativity theory and Americanism. Our friends were young guys who sold the platinum parts of Army telephones or devoured the brochures of Lenin, but our audience was those fathers whom we let be killed on the stage in our plays.

Es müß um das Jahr 1920 herum gewesen sein, daß wir zuerst von uns reden machten. Wir kamen auf einer großen, aber nicht sehr sympathischen Welle von Anarchie, Heeresgutschiebung, Relativitätstheorie und Amerikanismus dahergeschwommen. Unsere Freunde waren junge Burschen, die Platinteile aus Heerestelefonen verschoben oder die Broschüren von Lenin verschlangen, aber unser Publikum waren jene Väter, die wir in unseren Stücken auf der Bühne umbringen ließen. (*GW* 17:974–75)

To understand the appeal of America for these young cultural rebels, it is necessary to have some idea of what they were reacting against. The German defeat in World War I created conditions that polarized German society quickly into radicals of the right and radicals of the left. Fascist and extreme nationalist tendencies appeared very early on the one hand; on the other, most intellectuals were on the left, and among the people who had taken part in the war there was a sort of counter-nationalism, a feeling of extreme antipathy to Germany. This was the period of the Russian Revolution, the Bavarian *Räterepublik* or soviets, the assassination of Karl Liebknecht and Rosa Luxemburg—though Brecht managed to remain remarkably undisturbed by those events when they happened. It was also the period of expressionism, the literary and artistic expression of extremes that produced some of the most thrilling art and poetry of the century and some of the worst, most turgid drama. Expressionism did battle with naturalism, and Brecht eventually did battle with both styles. He was never very enthusiastic about expressionism; he satirized it in his first play, *Baal*, and he later characterized it as "a dull, idealistic wave" ("eine dumpfe idealistische Welle") and a mere phenomenon of inflation that changed nothing.[12] (Nevertheless, he profited greatly, possibly unconsciously, from the expressionist style, which at its best is concise and vigorous.) But then came a period of relative stability after the inflation, when American financing kept Germany on its feet, and a new literary movement began, called *Neue Sachlichkeit* (new objectivity or sobriety). Käthe Rülicke-Weiler describes the background to Americanism and *Neue Sachlichkeit*—two very closely related phenomena:

> With American finance capital's Dawes Plan dollars had flowed to Europe, the great monopolies—in 1925 IG Farben, in 1926 the United Steelworks Inc.—organized themselves anew, the economy was reorganized and began to rise. Technology celebrated triumphs: sobriety, efficiency, the "American way of life" with sport, auto, radio, movies—matter-of-factness in all spheres and relations of life—were popularized.
>
> Brecht too was fascinated for a while by the accomplishments of this advancing technology, but he saw at the same time the sharpening of the contradictions of reality: "Fordism" brought the growth of unemployment along with rationalization and the assembly line; the exploitation of the workers was intensified.

> Mit dem Dawesplan des amerikanischen Finanzkapitals waren Dollar nach Europa geflossen, die großen Monopole—1925 IG Farben, 1926 Vereinigte Stahlwerke A.G.—organisierten sich neu, die Wirtschaft wurde reorganisiert und nahm einen Aufschwung. Die Technik feierte Triumphe: Nüchternheit, Geschäftstüchtigkeit, der "amerikanische Lebensstil" mit Sport, Auto, Radio, Kino—Sachlichkeit in allen Bereichen und Beziehungen des Lebens—wurden popularisiert.
>
> Auch Brecht war eine Zeitlang fasziniert von den Errungenschaften dieser Technisierung, aber er sah zugleich die Verschärfung der Widersprüche der Wirklichkeit: Der "Fordismus" brachte neben der Rationalisierung, dem Fließband, auch das Anwachsen der

8

Arbeitslosigkeit mit sich, die Ausbeutung der Arbeiter wurde intensiviert.[13]

The center of these and all other political and literary movements in postwar Germany was Berlin. And Berlin in the twenties was certainly the single most important influence on Brecht. All the progressive people were attracted to Berlin; it was a cosmopolitan city full of new energy and future, but with a smell of decay as well (best preserved for today in George Grosz's art). The conflict between newness and decadence in the arts was a reflection of the conflict between revolution and reaction in politics. At first this correspondence was expressed as a generation conflict, an extreme rejection of everything the older generation produced: plays by expressionist playwrights used the theme of parricide repeatedly. One influential example was *Vatermord* (*Parricide*), by Brecht's friend Arnolt Bronnen, which Brecht attempted to direct in 1922. But, as Brecht says, the young rebels played these plays to the very fathers they were talking about murdering. Their revolt was an affectation; it was not until it received real political content that it became effective.

However, in Berlin in the early twenties, most of the extremism on the left remained in the arts. Brecht's first contribution too was not in revolutionary politics, even though he was chosen as a representative to the soldiers' soviet in Augsburg in 1918, but in—he hoped—revolutionizing the theater. All his sharp polemics were vented on the bourgeoisie of the theater. Even when he wrote a play with revolutionary new form, he thought of it as a means of revolutionizing ("organizing") the theater: "The theater work *Jungle*, in content a critique, had the formal assignment to organize the theater (that is revolutionize)" ("Das Theaterwerk 'Dickicht', dem Inhalt nach eine Kritik, hatte die formale Aufgabe, Theater zu organisieren [das heißt umzuwälzen]") (*GW* 15:209).

For those Germans who were not political enough to be dedicated either to Germany or to the new Soviet Union, America rushed into the ideological gap. These were a class of people whose life centered around the arts anyway, and everything new in the popular arts and recreation seemed to come from the United States: jazz, Chaplin films, the Charleston, skyscrapers and neon lights, boxing, clothing styles. America's youngness and freshness and confidence were just what the disillusioned young German generation wanted.

9

This cultural need is described by Frederic Ewen, who has written a biography that shows Brecht's development against the background of the German social scene. He writes of postwar Germany that it

> had constructed out of America a fabulous, visionary domain, partly concocted out of reality, mostly built on fantasy. The reality had, of course, been the presence of American troops in Europe, the occupation of German territory, the collapse of President Wilson's dream of a new world and a new Europe, and, not least, the ever-present lure of the American dollar seen as a sort of radiant vision against the background of the nightmarish collapse of the mark. There were also reminiscences of the past, the "American dream" brought to Europe by Walt Whitman; the American West and the Indian, celebrated by Fenimore Cooper and domesticated by Karl May; the grand adventures of the open prairies, buffaloes, cowboys, and not least, the lure of the great American cities with their "Wolkenkratzer"—their skyscrapers. . . .
>
> In those hectic, hysterical days, when Germany was a land that felt enclosed and prison-like, the appeal of "open spaces" was supplemented by the wonder aroused by skyscrapers, the fury and battle of the prize-ring, American boxers, six-day bicycle races, American lingo, American jazz, and Negro spirituals. Nor was Germany alone enthralled by this American invasion. All of Europe was captivated. Add also the "terror" and awe inspired by the American's cavernous, tortuous, labyrinthine cities, with their inexhaustible potentialities for mystery, crime, and adventure. So, in German eyes, appeared New York, Chicago, and San Francisco.[14]

Ewen's description sounds too rhapsodic to be Brechtian, and certainly Brecht was intelligent enough to treat the whole fad with some irony. Americanism was always a role he played consciously, a game that made a close community with his friends. With the exception of a few early poems, America appears in none of Brecht's works as El Dorado; on the contrary.

To determine why Brecht's image of the American dream was tarnished from the beginning, we will presently examine his literary sources. But first, to illustrate how far the cult of America did go among Brecht's contemporaries (including himself), here is a catalogue by John Willett of its expressions in the early twenties:

> A spurious Anglo-Saxon mythology grew up, and Brecht embraced it in his plays and even in his life. Bertolt was Bert, Georg (Grosz) became George, Walter Mehring passed as Walt Merin; Helmut Herzfelde had earlier taken the name of John Heartfield as a deliberate gesture against the war. Sport was the culture of this mythical world, jazz its music, the

According to Gisela Bahr (editor of the early version), Brecht wrote very quickly in the first few weeks, but then work on the play came to a halt.[3] Perhaps the idyllic setting in which he worked (the countryside around his parents' home in Augsburg, complete with swans and chestnut trees [*GW* 18:14]) seemed too unrelated to the themes of alienation, struggle, and the city that he was trying to write about. At any rate, he moved to Berlin in the beginning of November and quickly finished the play there that winter. At first he felt well received in Berlin; the popularity of the just-published "Bargan Lets It Be" helped him meet important literary people. But he was unable to earn any money in that particularly cold winter. By the end of January, he was so undernourished that he had to go to the Charité hospital.

The move to Berlin, and the difficulties Brecht experienced there for the first time, had a large influence on his development. His conception of the city as a jungle came out of his own very real experience: he learned something in Berlin that he was to emphasize throughout his writings, namely, the primacy of the struggle for existence or "first comes eating, then comes morality" ("erst kommt das Fressen, dann kommt die Moral"). Having starved in a cold winter himself, he never felt the scorn that his idealistic do-gooders (personified by the Salvation Army in his plays) feel for poor people who "know nothing higher than the rim of a bowl" (*GW* 2:677).

From that time Brecht identified the coldness of Berlin with the coldness of Chicago. Just before moving to Berlin, he wrote in a letter or his journal, "the great fear of cold Chicago!" ("die große Angst vor dem kalten Chicago!").[4] A letter he wrote from Munich to Arnolt Bronnen in Berlin is probably just one example of familiar use of the word Chicago to refer to Berlin among Brecht's circle of friends: "be nice to cas and show him cold chicago . . . in short, initiate him with piss into the secrets of cold chicago" ("sei nett zu cas und zeige ihm das kalte chikago . . . kurz weihe ihn ein mit pisse in die geheimnisse des kalten chikago").[5]

Chicago became and remained the center of Brecht's interest in America. Bronnen sheds some light on the Chicago mania and its autobiographical nature in his description of the writing of *Jungle:*

> He called it *Garga* then. He called it the inexplicable wrestling match of two men in the giant city Chicago, and in fact the small-towner Brecht never really finished with the problem of the city of millions. But what

13

did the struggle of two men mean, which also kept appearing in Brecht's dramaturgical reflections and conversations? If Garga was Brecht—and he was—:who was Shlink?

The play was written with breakneck speed, it was simply there, and Brecht only needed to write it down. What was this drama after? Bronnen said: "Bert, that's you, but you've come crawling through an underbrush of Rimbaud, Baudelaire and Villon, shreds of you, of them are hanging all mixed up together. What did you want to say?" Brecht said: "The last sentence." It was: "The chaos is used up. It was the best time."

But the chaos was still there. Chicago itself was still there. Maybe write a film, to get rid of this Chicago?

Er nannte es damals *Garga*. Er nannte es den unerklärlichen Ringkampf zweier Männer in der Riesenstadt Chikago, und in der Tat wurde der Kleinstädter Brecht mit dem Problem der Millionenstadt nie ganz fertig. Was aber bedeutete der Kampf zweier Männer, der auch in Brechts dramaturgischen Erwägungen und Gesprächen immer wieder auftauchte? Wenn Garga Brecht war—und er war es—: wer war Shlink?

Das Stück entstand in reißender Schnelle, es war einfach da, und Brecht brauchte es nur niederzuschreiben. Was wollte dieses Drama? Bronnen sagte: "Bert, das bist du, aber du bist durch ein Gestrüpp von Rimbaud, Baudelaire und Villon hindurchgekrochen, Fetzen von dir, von diesen hängen durcheinander. Was wolltest du sagen?" Brecht meinte: "Den letzten Satz". Der hieß: "Das Chaos ist aufgebraucht. Es war die beste Zeit".

Aber das Chaos war immer noch da. Selbst Chikago war noch da. Vielleicht einen Film schreiben, um dieses Chikago loszuwerden?[6]

That Brecht identified so much with this play is important. He felt a simultaneous revulsion and attraction to Chicago/Berlin that the Germans call *Haßliebe*. It was precisely his difficult experience with the big city—the necessity to fight to stay alive—and simultaneously a sense of wonder and respect for technology and progress, that formed his symbolic picture of America when he first started writing about it.

In the edition he prepared for print (1927, *In the Jungle of the Cities*), Brecht removed the most personal passages, so it is harder for the reader of the standard version to realize what Chicago (or America) meant for him.[7] In 1928, in program notes for the Heidelberg production, he continued to downgrade his own identification with America by explaining the use of Chicago as a kind of aesthetic trick. Although the note does not perfectly express Brecht's attitude at the time he wrote the first version of the play, it is a major

14

statement on his use of American settings for purposes of dramatic alienation:

ON JUNGLE

my preference for the american milieu does not come as was often supposed from a penchant for romanticism   this false conception arose from false productions that in turn arose because the theaters assuming I knew america very badly or not at all simply held to the aroma   the aroma was in fact too seductive and I have taken pains to eliminate it   i had chosen america not only for purely aesthetic reasons but from shall we say somewhat imprecisely but understandably political instinct   the point for me was not to emphasize the freedom or offensiveness of certain actions—which could have happened if i had chosen germany as milieu—rather almost everything depended for me on making these actions utterly strange i e conspicuous . . . the device of a background (namely the american) that corresponded by nature with the freedom (or offensiveness) of my types so that [it] would not disturb and distract seemed to me the easiest way to steer attention toward the uniqueness of the actions of contemporary great human types   in the german milieu these types would have become romantic that is ideals in the american they are realities   practically speaking i would have been fully satisfied if the theaters had projected america on the backdrop with ordinary photographs

ZU DICKICHT

meine vorliebe für das amerikanische milieu entspringt nicht wie oft gemeint wurde einem hang zur romantik   diese falsche vorstellung entstand durch falsche aufführungen die wieder dadurch entstanden daß die theater in der annahme ich kännte amerika sehr schlecht oder gar nicht sich einfach an das aroma hielten   das aroma war tatsächlich zu verführerisch und ich habe mich bemüht es abzustellen   ich hatte amerika nicht nur aus rein künstlerischen gründen gewählt sondern aus sagen wir etwas ungenau aber verständlich politischem instinkt   es kam mir nicht darauf an die freiheit oder anstößigkeit gewisser handlungen zu betonen—was geschehen konnte wenn ich deutschland als milieu genommen hätte—sondern es lag mir beinahe alles daran diese handlungen ganz und gar fremd d h eben *auffällig* zu machen . . . durch einen hintergrund (eben den amerikanischen) der der freiheit (oder anstößigkeit) meiner typen von natur entsprach so daß sie [*sic*] nicht störend ablenkte glaubte ich das augenmerk am leichtesten auf die eigenartigkeit der handlungen zeitgemäßer großer menschentypen lenken zu können   in deutschem milieu wären diese typen romantisch das heißt wunschbilder geworden in amerikanischem sind es realitäten   praktisch gesprochen hätte es mir völlig ausgereicht wenn die theater amerika durch gewöhnliche fotografien auf den prospekt geworfen hätten[8]

15

As we will see, Brecht's ideas both on America and on dramatic technique had changed considerably by 1928. We can be certain that in 1921–22 Chicago and America had strong personal—although ambivalent—meaning for him. In fact, for a while he seems to have wanted to include Chicago in the title of the play that became *In the Jungle:* there are five loose pages in the Brecht Archive with handwritten notes from 1921 and 1922 for a play to be called *Chicago* or *The Play of Cold Chicago* or *Cold Chicago.*[9] And even at the end of 1925, he still considered Chicago a principal theme of the play: "That's why you were for the play *Jungle.* . . . You were pleased that cold Chicago is so pleasant to look at" ("Deshalb waren Sie auch für das Stück 'Dickicht'. . . . Sie waren erfreut, daß das kalte Chicago so angenehm anzusehen ist") (*GW 15:75*).

We have some conception already of the phenomenon of Americanism in postwar Germany. And we know that throughout the twenties Brecht was fascinated and horrified by the great cities; he planned a whole series of works on the "Human Migration to the Big Cities."[10] But we find no clue in his autobiographical statements as to why he consistently chose Chicago, rather than, say, New York or San Francisco, to represent both America and the cities.

The reason is simply that the sources for his ideas both on America and on the city are themselves all set in Chicago; they use Chicago as the extreme and therefore the typical, archetypical case of urbanization and the American social and economic system. We will look at these books thoroughly, because they provided most of Brecht's imagery of America; then we will return to *In the Jungle,* to see how Brecht used his sources.

Sinclair, "The Jungle"

The first American book that we know Brecht read, Upton Sinclair's *Jungle,* may have determined his fixation on Chicago, his city imagery, and his picture of America for the rest of his life, regardless of future reading. It is a giant in the "Chicago genre"; it made an impression in both the United States and Germany out of all proportion to its literary value. In the United States it was the direct cause of federal legislation (the pure food laws); in Germany it was translated and published within the same year that it had appeared in the United States, 1906, and (to give an example of its effect) before he ever met Brecht, Paul Dessau had tried to turn it into an opera![11]

On 15 April, 1920 Brecht wrote a review of Schiller's *Don Carlos* for the newspaper *Volkswillen* in Augsburg. It is one of the first examples we know of Brecht's materialism, to be formulated in 1928 (in *The Threepenny Opera*) as "first comes eating, then comes morality." That idea, though certainly not new with Brecht (Büchner had already explored it unforgettably in the very "epic" *Woyzeck*, for instance), is very closely tied up with the development of Brecht's ideas on America.

He begins the review by saying God knows he has always loved *Don Carlos*:

> But recently I've been reading in Sinclair's *Jungle* the story of a worker who is starved to death in the slaughterhouses of Chicago. It's a matter of simple hunger, cold, illness, which will do a man in as surely as if they were appointed by God. Once this man has a modest vision of freedom, then he is beaten down with rubber nightsticks. His freedom hasn't the slightest thing to do with Carlos's freedom, I know that: but I can't take Carlos's oppression really seriously any more. . . . So go see *Don Carlos* . . . (But when you get a chance read Sinclair's novel *The Jungle* too.)

> Aber in diesen Tagen lese ich in Sinclairs "Sumpf" die Geschichte eines Arbeiters, der in den Schlachthöfen Chicagos zu Tod gehungert wird. Es handelt sich um einfachen Hunger, Kälte, Krankheit, die einen Mann unterkriegen, so sicher, als ob sie von Gott eingesetzt seien. Dieser Mann hat einmal eine kleine Vision von Freiheit, wird dann mit Gummiknüppeln niedergeschlagen. Seine Freiheit hat mit Carlos' Freiheit nicht das mindeste zu tun, ich weiß es: aber ich kann Carlos' Knechtschaft nicht mehr recht ernst nehmen. . . . Seht euch also den "Don Carlos" an . . . (Aber lest auch gelegentlich Sinclairs Roman "Der Sumpf".) (*GW* 15:9–11)

Brecht must have taken his own advice and reread *The Jungle* occasionally, because its influence is much clearer in *St. Joan of the Stockyards* (1929–30) than in the early plays. But it certainly determined his picture of America from the beginning. It also had some influence on his political and his aesthetic ideas, as is plain from the *Don Carlos* review. There are insights here that lay dormant through the whole first period of his work, until he was twenty-eight years old and writing on economic themes, using drama for the purpose of unmasking the processes that lie behind suffering and man's inability to attain freedom. Beginning shortly before 1926 but particularly in *St. Joan*, Brecht was concerned to show that simple hunger, cold, and sickness do not in fact come from God but are caused by human beings as agents of a human system. As he puts it in this early review, the worker in Chicago's stockyards does not starve but *is starved*—by someone. And: having read a novel treating these problems, Brecht cannot take the old drama seriously. He also returned to this aesthetic problem in 1926. To be sure, at age twenty-two he was already cursing loudly at the old drama and especially the old way of producing drama (theater); but it was not until about 1926 that he thought of transforming drama so that it could have the function of the novel (called in German "epic," or narrative).

The fact that the principal ideas of Brecht's later development were present in embryo after an early reading of *The Jungle* shows the importance of the book for him, and the fact that he went back to those ideas specifically when writing his best and longest America play, *St. Joan*, shows that he probably associated the book strongly with his conception of America. And well he might, for it is a powerful and memorable indictment of the American system. That is not necessarily to say that it is a well-written book, but it is an important book, important for its documentary value, as Brecht would say. Brecht used works of literature just as he would use history or reference books: as sources of information. It was always the sociological data, seldom the style or tone, that Brecht took from his sources on America.[12] They are all in the naturalistic and muckraking tradition, completely devoid of humor; but even when using the most lurid elements of the source or when without reservation criticizing conditions under capitalism, Brecht wrote with irony and humor—though the irony was often bitter and the humor black. He was irritated almost as much by illogic as by injustice and used a dialectical, superficially humorous, *reductio ad absurdum* kind of logic to demonstrate that a situation was *wrong* (in both the logical and the moral sense). Throughout his works he wanted to promote thought. At no time did he use the naturalist style.

The effect of Sinclair's technique is to produce not primarily thought but horror and nausea. It is a masochistic act to read *The Jungle*: the optimism felt at the beginning by the new immigrants to Chicago's stockyards sinks and sinks into drudgery, then squalor, then degradation, and farther down to misery, then desperation, and yet farther and even farther down. Every disaster is dwelled on, in loving detail, every wound salted and probed. Sinclair is

18

determined to make the reader *suffer*, experience some of the hopelessness of a working man in Chicago. The book is a tour de force in empathetic technique, with an almost pornographic effect on the reader, who finds himself skimming ahead eager to find what worse catastrophes can occur, hardly interested in the "clean" passages. The reader's reaction is similar to the reaction of helpless Jurgis in jail hearing from one of the children about conditions at home:

> "Ona is very sick," Stanislovas said; "and we are almost starving. . . . She won't eat anything, and she cries all the time. She won't tell what is the matter and she won't go to work at all. . . . And then Marija . . . she's cut her hand!" said the boy. "She's cut it bad, this time, worse than before. She can't work and it's all turning green, and the company doctor says she may—she may have to have it cut off. And Marija cries all the time—her money is nearly gone, too, and we can't pay the rent and the interest on the house; and we have no coal and nothing more to eat, and the man at the store, he says—"
>
> The little fellow stopped again, beginning to whimper. "Go on!" the other panted in frenzy—"Go on!"[13]

The impact of this short passage is representative of almost the whole book. After three hundred pages of being forced to feel the situation in his heartstrings and his stomach, the reader cannot make the sudden transition to using his head in the last few pages; the arguments for socialism at the end are simply anticlimactic, tacked on rather than organic. They certainly do not seem to have made any impression on Brecht. Much later (1938?), he attributed Sinclair's inability to show the positive side (i.e., the socialist alternative) to his naturalistic technique, which

> does not permit showing the new humaneness of the class-conscious worker of our age. Upton Sinclair's technique is not too new but too old for such tasks. That is not too little Balzac, but too much Balzac.

> gestattet nicht, die neue Menschlichkeit des klassenbewußten Proletariers unserer Zeit zu gestalten. Upton Sinclairs Technik ist nicht zu neu, sondern zu alt für solche Aufgaben. Das ist nicht zuwenig Balzac, sondern zuviel Balzac. (*GW* 19:316)

Of course, not all naturalism is as depressing as Sinclair's, and Brecht's confrontation with naturalism occupied his whole life; it cannot be summarized as briefly as this. Nevertheless, his fundamental objections to it were apparent from the beginning:

19

stylistically, it was too florid, and ideologically it encouraged fatalism. The positive contribution is, of course, the respect naturalists give to working and poor people as subject matter. Brecht adopted the subjects but transformed the style into one that encouraged activity, optimism, and critical thinking.[14]

In 1920 Brecht was not so interested in the class-consciousness of the working class and would not have criticized *The Jungle* in those terms; in fact, he only praised it. But the book nevertheless failed to interest him in the socialist solution to the situation presented; he seems not to have expressed any interest in socialism until about 1926.

What did interest him in *The Jungle* was the picture presented of a poor immigrant family moving to the New World—and to the city—and having their dreams destroyed. Brecht cared at that time about the life-and-death struggle itself, not its solution, and he cared about Chicago (= America = city) as the setting for the struggle. The picture of Chicago that impressed Brecht so much in *The Jungle* is above all the stockyards, with their utter disdain for any sanctity of life. The meat kings are as ready to kill men as animals. (This is later rendered by Brecht in the figure of Mauler, who in *St. Joan* cannot bear to see cattle killed but orders strikers shot.)

But Jurgis, the young immigrant and focus of the story, is impressed at first not by the inhumanity but by the efficiency of the stockyards. (Such a response is also representative of the reaction by Europeans to the United States in the twenties.) Never before had anyone seen such a concentration of life-energy producing such miracles and monstrosities.

Brecht too was impressed by the mere dimensions of progress in America and in the cities: "the new age had come greater than any previous one" ("die neue zeit war gekommen größer als jede vorhergehende") (BBA 460, 63). And in 1931, in another significant short sketch, he confirmed that the interest of the postwar generation of dramatists was

> the material grandeur of the age, its huge technological accomplishments, the mighty deeds of the big money people. . . . The world as it is should be demonstrated and recognized, its own mercilessness shown mercilessly to be its greatness: its God should be "the God of things as they are."

die materiellen Größe der Zeit, ihre technische Riesenleistungen, die gewaltigen Taten der großen Geldleute. . . . Die Welt, wie sie ist, sollte gezeigt und anerkannt, ihre eigene Schonungslosigkeit als ihre Größe schonungslos aufgewiesen werden: ihr Gott sollte sein "der Gott der Dinge, wie sie sind". (*GW* 15:218)

That is exactly the same kind of fatalistic admiration that Sinclair's Jurgis feels on being shown the stockyards:

To Jurgis it seemed almost profanity to speak about the place as did Jokubus, sceptically; it was a thing as tremendous as the universe—the laws and ways of its working no more than the universe to be questioned or understood. . . . To be given a place in it and a share in its wonderful activities was a blessing to be grateful for, as one was grateful for the sunshine and the rain. (P. 45)

It is the American dream, the dream that young men can by their own efforts reach superhuman heights, always upward, never failing, in a system too marvelous to be understood or questioned. Jurgis, himself young and very strong, is fully in favor of a situation where the strongest survive.

But gradually the full meaning of the law of survival unfolds itself to him and his family. They discover that each of them has got his job through the misfortune of someone else; each is forced to kill or pack diseased meat (and even rats and human corpses); each is subject to serious injury and disease. The rest of the book shows the various members of the family gradually reduced to the state of animals, losing all their "human" values in the fight to survive.

The basic law of Chicago, of the city, and of the industrial system is presented by Sinclair as the law of the jungle: not only the survival of the fittest but also the inexorable perishing of all who become unfit. It is an inhuman law, forcing human beings to behave like beasts of prey. As Jurgis discovers, it is a system that only looks good as long as you have the resources, physical or financial, to stay on top. It is of course the "inhumanity" of capitalism that Sinclair attacks, and Darwinian competition fits well for him as a metaphor for capitalist competition. It is not just a metaphor; Sinclair wishes to say that under capitalism men are actually forced to relate to each other as beasts: each beast has his own family whose right to live he protects by fighting for whatever he can get at the cost of other families. This metaphor informs the whole book, as is obvious from the title.[15]

The idea of calling his Chicago play *In the Jungle* probably came

21

to Brecht in the fall of 1921, when he wrote the first scenes, including one called "Jungle" (literally, thicket) ("Dickicht") and one called "Wooden Structure in the Jungle" ("Holzbau im Dickicht").[16] That is also when he recorded the "epochal discovery that no one had yet described the big city as a jungle" (see above, p. 12); but even as he wrote that, he must have been reminded of Sinclair's *Jungle*, which he read a year and a half earlier. (It is unimportant that *The Jungle* was translated as *Der Sumpf* and that Brecht used the word *Dickicht* not *Dschungel* for the title. Their metaphoric meanings in German are similar.)

However Sinclair does not describe primarily the *city* as a jungle; it is the capitalist system he describes; the city is simply a setting that exhibits the faults of the system to an extreme. For Brecht, at this point and for several years to come, the focal point was the city itself. Therefore, he adopted the conditions of poverty in *The Jungle* for his play, but he did not show their origin. It is clear from the subject matter of Brecht's poems that his fascination with cities began around the time he wrote *Jungle* and moved to Berlin, and that it reached a climax about 1925–26. At the very beginning of his career, he had a certain romantic and almost animistic attachment to nature, evident in *Baal* and early poems; but this quickly gave way to the necessity of dealing with a more modern theme, the cruelty of the cities.

Although it is primary, the metaphor of the city as jungle is not the only impression of Chicago that Brecht gleaned from Sinclair: another very forceful impression was of the *coldness* of Chicago. As we have seen, Brecht used the expression "cold Chicago" to refer to Berlin. In *St. Joan*, Chicago's cold is a major factor in ruining the strike, and it also kills Joan, in scenes similar to Sinclair's unbearable description of Jurgis's family's miseries. The struggle that builds the plot of *In the Jungle* begins and ends with Garga's declaration that Chicago is cold: "The windows are closed, since Chicago is cold, if that amuses you" ("Die fenster sind geschlossen, da Chikago kalt ist, wenn es Ihnen Spaß macht") (p. 15); and "I will carry my raw flesh out into the sleet. Chicago is cold. I'm going into it" ("Ich werde mein rohes Fleisch in die Eisregen hinaustragen. Chikago ist kalt. Ich gehe hinein") (p. 100). And in the notebook that Brecht kept in the fall of 1921, he wrote, "The play is set in an unreal, cold Chicago" ("Das Stück spielt in einem unwirklichen, kalten Chikago").[17]

22

It is not trivial to pinpoint the origins of Brecht's association of coldness with Chicago: it was a strikingly important symbol for him, a large part of his Chicago picture and significant in his plays. Natural cold as a symbol, of course, represents human coldness, unfriendliness, inhumanity. This was certainly part of what Brecht meant when he called Berlin "cold Chicago"—he had a very hard time at first in Berlin finding contacts—and it is a connotation of Garga's "Chicago is cold." Unfriendliness, coldness, is a characteristic of cities in general for those who move there from the country or small towns, as Brecht and so many of his characters did, and so a city known for its cold temperature is an especially good model for The City.

At the same time, the cold also leads human beings to become more "bestial," forces the instinct to struggle for survival nearer the surface; and so it serves to show the competition in the city (and, for Sinclair, in capitalism). Sinclair repeatedly describes the cold in terms of the natural struggle and the animalization of man:

> The blizzard knocked many a man out. . . . When it was over, the soul of Jurgis was a song, for he had met the enemy and conquered, and felt himself the master of his fate. So it might be with some monarch of the forest that has vanquished his foes in fair fight, and then falls into some cowardly trap in the nighttime. (P. 116)

> There came a spell of belated winter weather, with a raging gale, and the thermometer five degrees below zero at sundown and falling all night. Then Jurgis fought like a wild beast to get into the big Harrison Street police station. (P. 201)

Sinclair's Chicago is not only a cold city and a jungle; it is also a corrupt city. Jurgis is introduced to all the inner connections of the politicians and the underworld, a subject that was later to fascinate Brecht and form the basis of *Happy End* and *Arturo Ui*, both also set in Chicago. Elections are won in *The Jungle* by elaborate manipulation of ignorant opinion, of which buying votes is only the most open form; Jurgis himself is hired to carry out this function, thereby betraying his class. He betrays his class again by working as a scab in the strike that is a significant model for the strike in *St. Joan*.

Also important for Brecht's conception of America is the fact that Sinclair's stockyards are peopled entirely by immigrants. Moving from Europe to America is a parallel to moving from the country to the city, which Brecht considered the central theme of his early

23

work. For Brecht, country = backwardness = Old World, and city = progress = America. The American dream is for Brecht the same as the dream of living hard and getting rich fast in the cities. In *Jungle*, Shlink is a Malayan (originally a Chinese) who has become rich in America but still feels inferior because of his race. And the Garga family is presented in the introductory program notes as being French immigrants, but in the text of the play they only mention that they are from the country. (This inconsistency demonstrates the similarity in symbolic meaning between a move from Europe to America and a move from country to city.) The mother was born in the southern states (p. 89); the family comes from the "Alleghani-Gebirgen" (mountains) (p. 99) and from the "Savannah" (p. 109); and Garga tells Marie, "We grew up in the flatlands" ("Wir sind im flachen Land aufgewachsen") (p. 28), meaning they do not understand the ways of the city.

It is important not just for Brecht's conception of America but also for the whole series he built around the "Human Migration to the Big Cities" that the American dream is reversed in *The Jungle*, transformed into the American nightmare. This gullible immigrant family from Lithuania falls for every gimmick; the glittering picture of America in Europe is traced back to public relations stunts performed by the kings of the meat industry to get cheap labor. There is not much left of the land of opportunity when Jurgis has seen it from the bottom; as Brecht later puts it in *Mahagonny*, "Here everything is allowed" ("Hier darfst du alles dürfen") as long as you can pay for it, and if you cannot: you die.

Sinclair is quite specific about what is wrong with the American dream: "If we are the greatest nation the sun ever shone upon, it would seem to be mainly because we have been able to goad our wage-earners to this pitch of frenzy" (p. 198). Sinclair maintains in *The Jungle* that corruption and injustice are inherent in the American, or capitalist, system, and presents rebellion against the system in any form as legitimate, but only rebellion through trade union and Socialist Party organization as effective.

To all these political opinions Brecht returned later, but they did not really impress him in 1920. As we have seen, what excited him about America was not so much the opportunity to "make good" as its symbolization of the new beginning, the rebellion against the decadence of Europe or the decadence of the bourgeoisie—which

24

was Brecht's own rebellion—the progress, the vitality. Brecht embraced jazz and boxing and cigars and casual American clothing and the anti-intellectual, pro-sport, and pro-entertainment attitude that was associated with the growth of the United States.[18] America was confidence and rebirth. America was a slap in the face of the older generation.

Yet in *The Jungle*, America, or Chicago, is an unfriendly backdrop, a place of utmost cold and alienation. This is not a contradiction; Brecht believed that this energetic land was also a merciless one, an impression gleaned partly from *The Jungle*. And it is not an accident that he chose America as the setting for a struggle; he knew it was the land of competition. What did change was his ideological understanding of competition; that it exists he had always known.

Jensen, "The Wheel"

But there are two kinds of struggle in *Jungle*: the struggle of the poor Garga family to stay alive, and the "metaphysical" struggle between Shlink and Garga. This latter struggle, which builds the basic plot of the play, has little to do with class struggle or a social Darwinist society; for Shlink it is the means to overcome alienation and make contact with another man, and for Garga it is the means to assert his freedom and individuality. Chicago would not seem to be a necessary setting for such a story, but it was the obvious choice for Brecht, because it is the setting of the book that served as an immediate model for that struggle. The material struggle of the Gargas is based partly on *The Jungle*; the metaphysical struggle of Shlink and George Garga is based largely on *The Wheel* (*Hjulet*), by the Danish novelist Johannes V. Jensen. It was translated into German under the title *Das Rad* and printed in Berlin in 1908. Brecht himself mentions *The Wheel* as an influence on *In the Jungle* in the 1954 essay "On Looking through My Early Plays." He calls it not a source but an impression (*Eindruck*) (*GW* 17:949). Clearly *The Wheel* is a source for the plot (the struggle) of *In the Jungle*, as Gisela Bahr notes: "What Brecht found in Jensen's novel, and reproduced in the plot framework as well as in some individual psychological characteristics, was the model of a private struggle between two men" ("Was Brecht in Jensens Roman vorfand und im Gerüst des Handlungsverlaufs wie auch in manchen psy-

25

chologischen Einzelzügen nachgebildet hat, war das Modell eines privaten Kampfes zweier Männer").[19] Yet Brecht in referring to *The Wheel* as a source does not mention that aspect of it; he calls it just "J. Jensens Chikagoroman" (*GW* 17:949). And it is a "Chicago novel" to an even greater extent than *The Jungle*; here the city of Chicago itself is virtually anthropomorphized. Chicago is a character—a living presence—in the story.

Brecht used Jensen's Chicago not only as a setting for his text but also as a stage setting for the original production of *In the Jungle* in Munich, May 1923. His early friend H. O. Münsterer recalls the scene:

> The performance began splendidly, but for the Residenztheater audience, shockingly; Cas Neher's scenery, built on the revolving stage, rotated under the street noises of the metropolis waking up on the open stage, and after some hesitation stood still as if by chance at Maynes's lending library. Jensen's *Wheel*, which had very substantially inspired the writing of the play, is also known to begin with the Git-up calls of the Chicago wagon drivers.

> Die Aufführung begann großartig, aber für das Publikum des Residenztheaters schockierend; die auf der Drehbühne aufgebauten Schauplätze Cas Nehers kreisten unter dem Straßenlärm der erwachenden Großstadt bei offener Bühne und standen nach einigem Tasten wie zufällig bei Maynes Leihbibliothek still. Auch Jensens *Rad*, das sehr wesentlich zur Entstehung des Stückes angeregt hatte, wird bekanntlich durch die Git-up-Rufe der Chikagoer Lastkarrenführer eingeleitet.[20]

Münsterer's description makes clear that the production treated the city of Chicago as a significant entity in the play.

There are many similarities between Sinclair's and Jensen's Chicago, and there is one great difference: Jensen loves the city unequivocally. He is a passionate dreamer of the American dream, as is the young poet in the book, Lee.

Chicago is the city that embodies for Jensen the typically American pulsing of life. It is business; action; huge machines; progress. Although man-made, it is so huge that it is out of the control of human beings; behind the perfectly functioning machinery of the city lurks the danger of loss of control, of regression to the primitive. The city is strong and wonderful and *kind*; its breakdown is chaos. Technology is mysterious but marvelous: it protects man from the primeval.

The book opens with pages of description in purple periods; Jensen's as well as Lee's stylistic purpose is to sing the praises of industrial society in the rapturous idiom previously reserved for novels of love and nature or for romantic poems. The flowery style probably amused Brecht. (But he apparently liked Jensen's book just the same; Helene Weigel said he also read the same author's *Madame D'Ora*.) Since the book has not been translated into English and is largely unavailable even in German, I will translate a few long passages from the version that Brecht read, to give an idea of its style.

One example from the opening pages is enough to demonstrate the euphuistic style of the whole book, and it demonstrates Jensen's conception of Chicago as well:

> In the deep gorge between Michigan Avenue and the water the trains of the Illinois Central ran in and out, hundreds of long, heavily laden trains from all regions of America, from the Atlantic to the Pacific Ocean, from the polar regions to the gardens of Florida, a rolling of thousands of wheels, a tone deep and dark and acrid like the air that was saturated with soot and rested heavily over everything. The black ravine was alive with trains, with endless rows of freight cars pushing in crowded confusion, with smoking locomotives; it lay like an endlessly milling pit between the yellow fog walls of Lake Michigan and the copper-red fiery air of the city, which rose like a funeral pyre of stone and metal with its long white cliff banks of towered houses, and which mixed its red vapors and its piercing sulfur smoke with the raw fog of the winter night. Here in this mighty hell thundered the mill that grinds America together and sets its tone, here sang *Grotto*, the old destroyer and lifegiver, here grumbled the *Wheel*.[21]

The wheel is Jensen's symbol of the civilization of Chicago, of progress or technology, and above all of order:

> It was the pulse of the living machines, that are nourished from the coal fires underneath, it was the beat in the heart of the light which sends artificial day through copper arteries under the ice-cold tiles of the street into the main body of the city. Oho, it was the *Wheel* that never rests! It was the Wheel that upheld the possibility of life and the day, here in this rock vein of a city in the middle of the prairie, where only three, four generations ago the redskin struggled on snowshoes in the buffalo's trail across the desolate snow-desert. (P. 13)

Here is the vision of the grandeur of the city that gripped Brecht, too, though Brecht would never have used such rhetoric to describe it. This admiration for progress he did not simply take from Jensen;

his whole generation shared it. It was the generation of *Neue Sachlichkeit*, of glorification of the non-poetic, technical elements of modern civilization. But Brecht also recognized the danger and inhumanity in the modern cities; for Jensen the danger lies only in the possibility that primitive passions and primitive natural conditions may reconquer civilization.

It is that threatened catastrophe of disorder and irrationality that makes a general strike in Chicago so dangerous. Lee's heroic act is to save the city by killing the strike's demagogic leader, Evanston alias Cancer (who is also the man who has him under the spell that becomes a struggle to the death).

The danger to Chicago is expressed in terms of encroachment of cold. In the scheme of the book, Cancer is the destructive force that tries to end human and technological control of Chicago and turn it over to the natural cold:

> Telegraph and telephone will be suspended! The *press* will stop! Cancer wants to cordon Chicago off. Chicago is to be isolated from all four world regions, until silence returns, the silence that prepares God's coming!
>
> Cancer wants to give Chicago to the poor!
>
> Before midnight God will be in Chicago! (P. 237)

Lee has a vision of what it would be like were Cancer's strike to succeed and all the wheels running Chicago to grind to a halt. The vision is a nightmare of the power of cold and natural forces:

> Ice blooms out of the sidewalks and out of the doors of abandoned houses, the entire city turns to stone. Winter marches into Chicago, the north wind in its full biting majesty, and sets up in the streets a fortress of steeply combed snowdrifts, towers the snow up on Masonic Temple, transforms parks and districts into wilderness, fills the Illinois Central gorge, buries all train stations. (P. 239)

and so on—a single periodic sentence designed to create terror of snow and cold.

Lee ends his vision by deciding it must not be allowed to happen. He goes walking by Lake Michigan and there are almost two pages of description of the cracking of the ice in the cold. "And that awakened monstrous images of something in nature that has been subdued and that can rise up again. It was a raw and wild winter night, like a night in the beginning of all existence" (p. 242). In this situation Lee is suddenly overwhelmed by the insight that the high

28

grade of civilization reached by the city is caused by Chicago's need to overcome unusually strong natural forces: "From that followed inviolable property rights, the rights of a creator, which he felt himself called upon to maintain and defend" (p. 243).

Brecht's references in *Dickicht* to trains going to Illinois and to both coasts may well be an echo of the heroic setting in the opening pages of *The Wheel*. Brecht did not care in the slightest whether his geographical bearings were correct, but he wanted the atmosphere of mighty activity and progress that Jensen creates, and he wanted place-names. The geography of the American railroads is confused in *Dickicht*: in the scene "In the Quarry" ("Im Steinbruch"), we hear the "Pacific trains" ("Pazifikzüge") in the background; Garga asks, "What's the noise?" ("Was ist der Lärm?"); and although they are in Chicago, the other answers, "The trains to Illinois" ("Die Züge nach Illinois"). Later when he hears a train above, he says, "That's the Pacific. New York!" ("Das ist der Pazifik. New York!") (p. 23).

Throughout the works that are set in America, especially in *Mahagonny*, Brecht is blithely unconcerned about correctness of detail—and yet he uses many very concrete details. This apparent contradiction comes from the fact that actually the setting in all of his plays has somewhat the character of an allegory; he is not interested in painting a portrait of America but in using the conception people already have of America to reinforce the points he is making in the play. The sprinkling of place-names through the play serves the same purpose as projecting pictures of these places on a screen, as he suggests in "my preference for the American milieu" (see above, p. 15). It does not matter where they are, as long as the audience recognizes them as being America.

This is the early *dramaturgical* function of America: simple dramatic alienation, carrying the action into a strange milieu so it will not be judged with traditional or local criteria. But there is an *ideological* function beginning right with the first American play, *In the Jungle*, and growing in importance later on, of which Brecht himself was not fully aware at first. One way of getting at America's ideological role for him is to notice the way he reacted to Jensen's ideology in *The Wheel*. *The Wheel* is an example of a book from which Brecht took some concrete details and atmosphere that he found valuable, but we can easily see that he totally rejected the ideas. The book is startlingly racist, misogynistic, and anti-working

29

class. Each of these subjects—race, women, and class—gets a treatment in *Jungle* that is not necessary just to show the struggle between Shlink and Garga; perhaps Brecht was moved to include them because of his reaction against Jensen.

The young hero of the book, Lee, wants to convince his millionaire capitalist friend, H. A. Gronau, that America is the great melting pot, the home for all free men. Lee as the Promethean, creative genius envisions himself (presumably through his poetry) making "out of America a home also for the Germans!" ("aus Amerika eine Heimat auch für die Deutschen!") (p. 63). He has a special affinity for the Germans because they help him give America the tradition, the history as promised land, that he wants to create for it: "I want to found an Aryan center here in America—this is after all the discovered land! The wheel of freedom is here, giving energy to as many as want to join it. Here is also the mill hole around which the freed peoples of the world swing" (p. 64). This is something more than the standard American dream. This is exaltation of it and synthesis of it with European traditions into a racist mythology; this is the beginnings of an Aryan Reich on American soil. These immigrants are not at all the same as those in Sinclair's Chicago novel; here they are the master race (and Gronau is a millionaire to boot). "England and Australia, Scandinavia, Germany and Holland and America, they all constitute one empire . . . they are all America . . . everywhere where there are descendants of the old nordic nomadic tribes, America is there, because the land of which the ancients dreamed is America" (p. 25).

This is not the only disturbing aspect of Jensen's ideology of race. There is the explicit racism of Evanston against the Chinese, which may have influenced Brecht's portrayal of Shlink (originally Chinese):

> I had the urge to present myself as the foreign white god from faraway to these four hundred million yellow people, who hate each other to the point of bloodshed. . . . The Chinese doesn't know yearning. He has the other venereal diseases, but yearning is reserved for the white man, especially the Northlander. (P. 194)

There is no sign that Jensen himself rejects such prejudices expressed by his characters; on the contrary, he probably shares them, since Lee, the protagonist (whom he intends to make sympathetic), himself shares them. On the other hand, it is amply

30

clear that Brecht uses the repeated references to race in *Jungle* for characterization, i.e., to expose racism in his characters. In 1928 he writes that it would have been enough to signify Shlink's race on stage with simple yellow paint, and then just to let him behave like an Asian, "that is like a European" ("nämlich wie ein Europäer") (*GW* 17:972).

Any possible doubts about Brecht's attitude toward racial prejudice disappear with the lynching scene. First Garga tells Shlink that there were lynchings that day: "Negroes like dirty laundry on clotheslines" ("Neger wie schmutzige Wäsche an Stricken") (p. 88). Then he has the idea of turning all the men in the bar (who have animal names) against Shlink so he will be lynched. It is ridiculously easy to do; he simply tells them the old story that yellow-skinned men are sleeping with their daughters. He uses all the old clichés that were used to turn white men against black men for a lynching in the American South. Brecht knows exactly the right lines; he may have had a specific source on racism in the United States that we do not know about.

Jensen's attitude toward other races is bad enough, but his attitude toward women is unequivocally reactionary:

> Nature's gender is female, woman is existence itself, and Cancer was man of the masses and traditional type enough to be a woman's equivalent, he had remained just far enough behind in evolution, he was just weak enough in nerve and irresponsible enough a liar so that he, although of the male gender, could stand on a niveau with nature and with woman. Even his fanatic misogyny was only the force with which the female pole of his being removed him from his own, it was one more piece of wenchlike behavior. . . . He was, like woman, a born criminal—but he lacked woman's fertility. (Pp. 295, 296)

The theme of objectification of women plays an important part in Brecht's play, too, but with a very different value attached to it. Unlike his later plays, which treat women as strong, independent, and equal to men, Brecht's early works, including *Jungle*, present women as objects, which is the role literature has traditionally assigned to them. Most women in the early plays are whores; *Mahagonny* and *The Threepenny Opera* are of course replete with them. But Brecht shows he is conscious that society forces women into a role where their only function is to give pleasure to men, regardless of what their wishes may be.

Both Garga's mother, Maë, and his sister, Marie, are strong

characters who understand what is going on. But Maë disappears
after an insult from her husband (she rejects objectification), and
Marie is forced to become a whore. It is one of Shlink's tactics in the
fight to try to get at Garga's emotions by making Marie suffer; Garga
refuses to be upset and uses her in turn against Shlink. They both
use her emotions like pieces in a game. Schlink says, "I burden you
with the fate of your sister. You have opened her eyes to the fact that
for all eternity she will remain an object among [under] men!" ("Ich
belade Sie mit dem Schicksal ihrer Schwester. Sie haben ihr die
Augen geöffnet darüber, daß sie in alle Ewigkeit ein Objekt bleibt
unter den Männern!" (p. 56). Brecht understood the reification of
women very clearly.

Both Shlink and Garga would like to love Marie, but they
subordinate kindness to her to the tactics of their fight; neither can
allow himself a moment of emotion in this completely psychological
battle. Marie sees more clearly than Garga himself that each time he
appears to be winning he is actually losing, because he has degraded
himself, allowed himself to become a little more inhuman. It is a
terrible side-effect of the ruthlessness of the struggle that she must be
sacrificed. In an unusually emotional scene, when Garga has come
out of prison and she has told him what she has become, someone in
the bar calls "Coquettes!" ("Kokotten!") at her and "Vice is women's
perfume" ("Das Laster ist das Parfüm der Damen"). She answers,
with tears running down her cheeks,

> We coquettes! Powder over the face, you can't see the eyes that used to
> be blue. Stink of plague between our legs! The men who do business with
> scoundrels make love with us. We sell our sleep, we live from
> mistreatment, the orphans of our dear lady!

> Wir Kokotten! Puder über dem Gesicht, man sieht die Augen nicht, die
> blau waren. Pestgestank zwischen den Beinen! Die Männer, die mit
> Schuften Geschäfte machen, lieben mit uns. Wir verkaufen unseren
> Schlaf, wir leben von Mißhandlung, die Waisen unserer lieben Frau! (P.
> 82)

Here Brecht is seeing through the tortured eyes of the ruined
woman; he is seeing woman as a subject that has been made an
object by men, not as a creature born only to be an object.

But at least Marie gains financial independence, by demanding
payment for her degradation. The role of whore in Brecht's plays is
an ambiguous one: whores are victims of male society, but they are

also tough and independent, like the Jennys in both *The Threepenny Opera* and *Mahagonny*. Interestingly, the whore seems to have been associated in Brecht's mind with the American or Anglo-Saxon milieu.

There is one aspect of Jensen's ideology that must have angered Brecht even more than his racism and misogyny; that is his treatment of the strike. It is clear that he has no conception whatever of the workers' side of it. He does not know the term "general strike." The strike is utter chaos; he describes it like a war, with shooting and rioting; for him it is the breakdown of order; it is total disaster. The honest workingmen are kept at it against their own interest by Evanston's demagogy: they have no ability to think for themselves. Jensen speaks of the strike as a "destroying power," a "mishap," a "catastrophe." In other words, the mass is as terrifying and dangerous to him as nature, and just as irrational. It never occurs to him that perhaps the strikers should have won; the proper solution is to break the strike and end the chaos.

And in the end Lee himself becomes a capitalist. Although this shift away from his sloppy romanticism must have pleased Brecht, he cannot have been so pleased by the capitalist-aristocratic prejudice of the whole book. He was not a socialist then, but he knew what poverty was like, he knew he hated the bourgeoisie; he had, after all, read another novel about Chicago that made it quite clear why the poor (like the Garga family) suffered. He did not know what he was for, but he certainly knew what he was against. A quick look through the early theater criticism and early political notes shows that he was against the bourgeoisie, the establishment, the rich, the older generation, the nineteenth century, and everything that was old.

In "On Rhymeless Poetry with Irregular Rhythms" (1939), he talks about his style in his early work:

> One must consider the times when I wrote. The World War had just ended. It had not solved the enormous social tensions that had caused it.
>
> My political knowledge was shamefully small then; nevertheless I was aware of great inconsistencies in human social life, and I didn't consider it my task to neutralize in the form all the disharmonies and interferences which I felt so strongly. I caught them up more or less naïvely into the actions of my plays and the verses of my poems. And that long before I recognized their actual character and their causes. It was a matter, as one can see from the texts, not only of a "swimming

against the current" in the form, a protest against the smoothness and harmony of conventional verse, but already of an attempt to show incidents between people as contradictory, raging with struggle, violent.

Man muß die Zeit bedenken, in der ich schrieb. Der Weltkrieg war eben vorüber. Er hatte die ungeheuren sozialen Spannungen, die ihn verursacht hatten, nicht gelöst.

Mein politisches Wissen war damals beschämend gering; jedoch war ich mir großer Unstimmigkeiten im gesellschaftlichen Leben der Menschen bewußt, und ich hielt es nicht für meine Aufgabe, all die Disharmonien und Interferenzen, die ich stark empfand, formal zu neutralisieren. Ich fing sie mehr oder weniger naiv in die Vorgänge meiner Dramen und in die Verse meiner Gedichte ein. Und das, lange bevor ich ihren eigentlichen Charakter und ihre Ursachen erkannte. Es handelte sich, wie man aus den Texten sehen kann, nicht nur um ein "Gegen-den-Strom-Schwimmen" in formaler Hinsicht, einen Protest gegen die Glätte und Harmonie des konventionellen Verses, sondern immer doch schon um den Versuch, die Vorgänge zwischen den Menschen als widerspruchsvolle, kampfdurchtobte, gewalttätige zu zeigen. (*GW* 19:397)

Brecht did not understand the causes, but he knew that there was disharmony. His plays show human events as violent and characterized by struggle. An attempt at harmonious solution by a writer like Jensen simply would not do; there was no harmony, the social tensions that caused the war were still there. For Jensen the conclusion of the struggle has to be to end it and restore order. For Brecht there was no question of restoring order; the nature of contemporary life was struggle.

This could be one reason for his choosing to portray a "struggle per se" ("Kampf an sich"), a fight abstracted from any motivation or context. Realizing that conflict was characteristic of the times but instinctively condemning the values in Jensen's work, he simply avoided values and contexts in *Jungle*. This supposition is supported by a note from 1929, where he says the motivation "our fathers" (the older generation, the bourgeoisie, the nineteenth century) understood is an impossible explanation for today's actions and characters; therefore:

We helped ourselves (provisionally) by not investigating the motives at all (example: *In the Jungle of Cities*, *East Pole Train*), in order at least not to give the wrong ones, and presented the plots as mere phenomena.

Wir haben uns (provisorisch) damit geholfen, die Motive überhaupt nicht zu untersuchen (Beispiel: "Im Dickicht der Städte", "Ostpolzug"), um wenigstens nicht falsche anzugeben, und haben die Handlungen als bloße Phänomene dargestellt. (*GW* 15:197)

And it is in fact only the plot and background, and not the motivation, that Brecht adopted from *The Wheel*. The plot of *Jungle* is a series of phenomena that cannot be explained by traditional values, performed by strange new men with unfamiliar motivations.

Other Sources

There is, however, one aspect of *The Wheel* (besides the setting, the coldness of Chicago) that Brecht clearly and uncritically adopts: the identification of both Lee and Garga with poets. Lee is not only mad over Whitman; he is also a poet himself, in the Byronic tradition of what a poet is supposed to be like: sensitive, excitable, wildly creative, impressionable. Lee is not Whitman, but perhaps he is what he himself—or Jensen—thinks Whitman was. Urged to read his poetry, he fears to bare his innermost self and reads Whitman instead—but with such an evangelical fervor that he might as well be reading his own work.

The way Garga reads Rimbaud is too similar a phenomenon not to have been consciously based on *The Wheel*. His Rimbaud quotations also express himself, or the exotic creature he would like to be: the Tahiti side of himself. He recites Rimbaud when he needs to believe that he is strong:

I will go, and I will come back with limbs of iron, dark skin, rage in my eye. From my face one will think I come from a strong race.

I am an animal, a Negro, but I may have been saved. You are false Negroes.

I don't understand laws, have no morality, am a raw man.

Ich werde hingehen, und ich werde zurückkommen mit eisernen Gliedern, dunkler Haut, die Wut im Auge. Meinem Gesicht nach wird man glauben, daß ich von starker Rasse bin. (P. 99)

Ich bin ein Tier, ein Neger, aber vielleicht bin ich gerettet. Ihr seid falsche Neger. (P. 21)

Ich verstehe die Gesetze nicht, habe keine Moral, bin ein roher Mensch. (P. 21)

This is Baal again, or a trapped man trying to be as free as Baal. It is the vision of the natural man, repeated by Brecht in *Mahagonny*:

Garga dreams of taking his mother with him to the South ("I can fell trees" ["Ich kann Bäume fällen"] [p. 37]) as Paul Ackerman dreams of returning to Alaska, where life was not alienated. But they are both trapped where they are, in the land and age of commercial relations.

The passages Brecht used from *Une saison en enfer* (*A Season in Hell*) are in fact about traveling, about whether to leave Europe or not; they are in their theme as well as their passion appropriate to Brecht's purpose. He had been reading Rimbaud (he names "Summer in Hell" ["Sommer in der Hölle"] as an "impression" along with *The Wheel* [*GW* 17:949]); and he was particularly interested in somehow using Rimbaud's *style*: "After that I occupied myself for a play (*In the Jungle of the Cities*) with the exalted prose of Arthur Rimbaud (in his *A Season in Hell*)" ("Danach beschäftigte ich mich für ein Theaterstück ['Im Dickicht der Städte'] mit der gehobenen Prosa Arthur Rimbauds [in seinem 'Sommer in der Hölle']") (*GW* 19:396). In fact, in the style of *Jungle*, Brecht succeeded to a large extent in achieving a compactness similar to Rimbaud's: apparent non sequiturs burst with meanings that one cannot quite paraphrase (like trying to outguess a déjà vu: it can only be grasped when the next image appears). Perhaps even more than Rimbaud, Brecht wrote compact sentences that are masterpieces of the technique of inevitability; this is what gives them their misleading simplicity and makes them almost impossible to translate without making him seem simpleminded. The technique of choosing only the perfect and necessary words may have come from his study of Rimbaud. At any rate, he wanted to base Garga on him: "George Garga is like A. Rimbaud visually. He is essentially a German translation from the French into the American" ("George Garga gleicht A. Rimbaud im Aussehen. Er ist im Wesentlichen eine deutsche Übersetzung aus dem Französischen ins Amerikanische").[22] And of course the homosexual relationship in *Jungle*, like that in *Baal*, is partly based on Rimbaud and Verlaine.

It is important to know about Brecht's interest in Rimbaud, because otherwise we could not understand why he did not simply use Whitman as the poet model. Both Bernhard Reich[23] and Elisabeth Hauptmann[24] testify that Brecht read and appreciated Whitman while in Berlin; Reich specifies about 1924–25. We do not know whether Brecht's reading of *The Wheel* was his first acquaintance with Whitman, but it is not an insignificant one: there are pages and pages of *Leaves of Grass* printed in the novel in German translation, all of which Lee reads out loud to the bored Gronau family.

We have no direct evidence of the impression the lines quoted in *The Wheel* made on Brecht, because he himself hardly mentions Whitman until very late: once in 1954, once in 1956.[25] The volume of *Auf der Brooklyn Fähre* (*Crossing Brooklyn Ferry*) in his library was printed in 1949. But there is no mistaking the impression of America that Whitman intends to convey. The lines in *The Wheel* are unequivocal praise. This is the America one would like to believe in, bursting with life and creative energy. This is the America of the pioneers; it is the America that Alaska represents in *Mahagonny*; it is the grand vision of a gigantic land and a heroic people. It is the antidote to Sinclair's *The Jungle*, and it is the America Brecht praised in his early poems and for which he longed in stuffy Europe.

These are some of the passages of Whitman's praise for America that Brecht read in Jensen's translation:

Starting from fish-shape Paumanok where I was born . . .
Dweller in Mannahatta my city, or on southern savannas, . . . or a
 miner in California,
Or rude in my home in Dakota's woods, . . . aware of mighty Niagara,
. . . Solitary, singing in the West, I strike up for a New World.

Victory, union, faith, identity, time,
The indissoluble compacts, riches, mystery,
Eternal progress, the kosmos, and the modern reports.
. . . This then is life.

Americanos! conquerors! marches humanitarian!
Foremost! century marches! Libertad! masses!
For you a programme of chants.
Chants of the prairies,
Chants of the long-running Mississippi, and down to the Mexican sea,
Chants of Ohio, Indiana, Illinois, Iowa, Wisconsin, and Minnesota,
Chants going forth from the centre from Kansas, and thence equi-
 distant,
Shooting in pulses of fire ceaseless to vivify all.
Take my leaves America, take them South and take them North,
Make welcome for them everywhere, for they are your own off-spring,
Surround them East and West, for they would surround you.[26]

John Willett says that Whitman had very little influence on Brecht, that "nothing could be more foreign to Brecht than Whitman's egotism and rather hollow rhetoric."[27] But for Brecht,

Sinclair's and Whitman's pictures could both be right: we will see him learning about the system that spoils what could be a great country. Brecht used literary sources for their informational value; Whitman's poetry certainly provided Brecht with an important conception of America, the positive statement of the American dream, full of adventure, robustness, and optimism.

It is essentially the same picture as that presented by Jack London's and Bret Harte's stories of the West, both of which Brecht also read, though it is not clear exactly when. London is quoted in Brecht's notes for *Joe Fleischhacker* (1924–26), and there are three volumes of Bret Harte's *Kalifornische Erzählungen* (*California Tales*, published in Leipzig, no date), with Elisabeth Hauptmann's name in them, in Brecht's library.[28] The Wild West, outlaw, and gold rush themes are clear in *Mahagonny*, but perhaps Brecht read London and Bret Harte even before writing his first American poem, "The Song of the Railroad Gang of Fort Donald" in 1916.[29]

There is also no way of knowing exactly when Brecht read Carl Sandburg and Edgar Lee Masters (*Spoon River Anthology*). Helene Weigel remembered only that they were among the American books Brecht read early. Their influence, if any, was of a general nature, like Whitman's; it is impossible to point to any specific passages or plays that derive from them.

There are two other books in Brecht's library that may have contributed to his picture of America while he was writing *In the Jungle*, though there is no direct influence visible. They are both plays by Upton Sinclair that were published by Malik in Berlin in 1921, and one of them, *Prinz Hagen* (*Prince Hagen*), was performed in Piscator's *Proletarisches Theater* in Berlin in 1920–21.[30] It is a fantasy, set partly in the high society and high finance world of New York, which Richard Wagner's Prince Hagen plans to control through total monopoly. This is possible because of his almost limitless stores of gold from Nibelheim; only death stops him. The play is a clever and biting attack on American capitalism. The ironic position that "morality" takes is particularly close to Brecht's own sensibility. Hagen is thrilled with the discovery of this principle for preventing revolution. He exclaims to his horrified and very Christian tutor:

> And the number of those creatures is a thousand to your one, and the best that is might be theirs if they would take it; but there is Morality!

38

And the poorest of them would starve and die in his tracks before he would touch a bit of bread that was not his own, and he struts about and boasts of it, and calls it his "virtue!" And so the rich man may have what he will, in perfect peace and indifference! By heaven, if that is not a wondrous achievement, I, at least, have never seen one in my life.[31]

This is the kind of dialectical twist Brecht gives not only to the role of the Salvation Army but also to the function of "goodness" under capitalism in nearly every play (most obviously *St. Joan of the Stockyards* and *The Good Person of Sichuan*).

But Sinclair's *Die Maschine* (*The Machine*) is a terrible play, both artistically and ideologically. It is concerned with trying to get one capitalist to stop being a capitalist, and with keeping his daughter's conscience clean. The streetcar king Jim Hegan (= Hagen?), although he loves his daughter, is unable to give in to her pleas that he stop dealing with corrupt politics (Tammany Hall) and the white slave trade; but the play ends happily because the man who told the daughter about her father's sins—called a socialist by Sinclair but actually only a muckraker—declares his love for her and the curtain goes down on their embrace. The play is full of the over-simplifications and reformism that Brecht avoids, but it may have been one stimulus for *St. Joan*: here too the heroine goes to the poor to do unspecified "good works," and insists on finding out the whole truth about exploitation once she has stumbled on a hint of it.

One other work about Chicago that Brecht read at this time seems also to have had a stronger influence on *St. Joan*. In "On Looking through My Early Plays," where he lists Rimbaud and Jensen as sources of "impressions" ("Eindrücke"), he mentions also a collection of letters whose title he has forgotten; they had, he says, a cold and final tone, almost the tone of a will.[32] In a 15 September 1920 diary entry, he mentions a certain Lorimer next to Synge as a source for his studies on using the verb,[33] and in notes on *Galgei* (an early version of *A Man's a Man*), he includes two short quotations from Lorimer.[34] We are indebted to Michael Morley for the literary sleuthing that put these three hints together and resulted in the discovery of George Horace Lorimer's *Letters from a Self-Made Merchant to His Son*,[35] translated into German by O. Oppen in 1905 under the title *Briefe eines Dollarkönigs an seinen Sohn*.[36] All the following information is from Morley's useful article.[37]

Lorimer was the man who made the *Saturday Evening Post* a

success; he became its editor in 1899 and almost tripled its circulation in the next five years. He did this primarily by writing a series of letters that he submitted pseudonymously to the literary editor; in 1902 they were printed as a book that became a best-seller. The letters purported to be advice by the owner of a Chicago meat-packing plant, John Graham, "known at the stock market by the nickname 'The Old Pig Graham' " ("an der Börse unter dem Spitznamen 'Der Alte-Schweine-Graham' bekannt"), to his son Pierrepont "called in intimate circles 'piglet' " ("in intimem Kreise 'Ferkelchen' genannt"),[38] on how to get rich and other moral matters. The style is vigorous, humorous, and hardheaded, as is Brecht's in *Jungle*. The "impressions" that Brecht gained from these letters were, then, partly about the city of Chicago and the nature of capitalism, and partly stylistic. As with *The Jungle*, he did not use the subject matter until much later, but then quite explicitly.

Of the books Brecht read on America before or during his work on *In the Jungle*, *The Jungle* and *The Wheel* had the strongest influence on the play. It is obvious, then, why Brecht chose Chicago for the setting, and what kind of an image he had of that city. Both novels are set in Chicago, and they both portray it as a city of the American dream, yet also as a city of cold, struggle, and cruelty. They both have labor struggles as central themes, but the authors stand on different sides of the barricades. (Lorimer's book too covers similar themes, but it is much more sanguine about the possibility of success in America.) Both novels portray America as a country of immigrants, but with different conclusions about how well off the immigrants are there.

Let us now look at the play itself to see what Brecht did with the impressions of Chicago and America he had gathered.

"In the Jungle" and "In the Jungle of the Cities"

Although *In the Jungle* was written at the height of Brecht's and his friends' cult of Americanism, there is no suggestion that America is a promised land, or a land of unlimited opportunity. It is not a fresh and hopeful beginning to which decadent Europeans can flee; in fact, Garga wants to flee *from* America to Tahiti. Brecht seems to have taken his literary use of America from his literary models and not from the popular conceptions that were current.

Later, in *Mahagonny*, he wrote a satire on what his generation

40

promised itself in America; and in "Vanished Glory of the Giant City New York," he wrote a devastating reminiscence of the short-lived American dream. He could only be so bitter about the dream if it had visited some of his own youthful nights, and he admits quite openly that it did.

But he was not dreaming when he wrote his plays: in the case of *Jungle* he was very wide awake and consciously using the conception of America and Chicago that he found in those works that also served as models for other aspects of the play. The Garga family's poverty, the young women who are driven to prostitution, George Garga's urge for freedom and escape from responsibility for a family, and the subsequent destruction of the family are all elements from *The Jungle*. There they happen in a Chicago that is cold and inhumanly cruel, and makes "beasts" out of human beings. *In the Jungle* paints Chicago as the same cruel jungle. And the dynamics of the battle between Shlink and Garga, Shlink's love for Garga, Shlink's losing because he is the one who *needs* the other, Garga's inability to extricate himself, his idealism, his disgust at Shlink's physical presence and age, the subtleties of the battle that make apparent victories into defeats, the final victory only through murder, and the subsequent flight of the victor from Chicago—all these are from *The Wheel*. There they happen in a Chicago that is the symbol of progress, a city of machines that have gone beyond man's level, but with primeval cold and hungering masses waiting to creep through any weak spot and turn order into chaos: a Chicago whose civilization must protect itself against barbarism and nature. This Chicago is not so explicitly evident in *Jungle* but it is there, in the manipulable passions of the mob that wants to lynch Shlink, in the conception of the American city as a higher form of human organization than the "savannah" or the Old Country, in the omnipresent cold.

Brecht maintains the dominant imagery of the jungle throughout the play. Shlink and Garga retreat into the thicket to fight out their duel like two bucks disappearing for days and fighting to the death. But they are also surrounded by animals fighting each other: the Baboon, the Bear, the Ape, the Worm are the names of some of the characters. A howling is heard throughout the scene where Garga incites the lynchers. Marie cries, "Oh you animals!" ("O ihr Tiere!") at them on discovering that he is dead. Garga experiences the forest

41

as origin of the first men, who are "hairy, with ape's teeth, good animals that knew how to live" ("haarig, mit Affengebissen, gute Tiere, die zu leben wußten") (p. 93). Again and again animal imagery is used to describe people: animals, dogs, vultures, bestialization, elephant, vermin, game, pig, scarab, beast, crocodile skin, animal corpses, lamb, quail, alligators, hedgehog, crabs, beast of prey, flies, menagerie. (Tiere, Hunde, Geier, Vertierung, Elefant, Viecher, Wild, Schwein, Skarabäus, Bestie, Krokodilshaut, Tierleichen, Lamm, Wachtel, Alligatore, Igel, Krebse, Raubtiere, Fliegen, Menagerie.) Brecht makes use of animal imagery in other plays, such as *Drums in the Night* and *Edward*, but in *Jungle* it is more than imagery. The conception implied in Sinclair's title, but only mentioned a few times in his book, is transformed by Brecht into a conceit that informs the entire play.

The animalization of human beings is not only a consistent metaphor throughout the play; it also contains the play's message. In the fight for survival, it is not possible to make real contact with other human beings; Shlink tries and perishes, Garga refuses to try and survives. Hence the emphasis in the play on love (and its impossibility) and on loneliness (and the impossibility of overcoming it). Language cannot reach far enough to reach to other men. Shlink:

> Yes, you wanted the end, but I the struggle, Garga.
>
> And never, George Garga, will there be an end to this fight, never an understanding.
>
> The infinite loneliness of man makes being enemies an unobtainable goal.
>
> Ja, Sie wollten das Ende, aber ich den Kampf, Garga. (P. 97)
>
> Und niemals, George Garga, wird ein Ausgang dieses Kampfes sein, niemals eine Verständigung. (P. 99)
>
> Die unendliche Einsamkeit des Menschen macht eine Feindschaft zum unerreichbaren Ziel. (P. 92)

Garga:

> In the jungle each one is alone.
>
> Why are there no words?
>
> Language is not adequate for communication.
>
> In dem Dschungel ist jeder allein. (P. 66)
>
> Warum gibt es keine Worte? (P. 20)
>
> Die Sprache reicht zur Verständigung nicht aus. (P. 92)

42

Brecht:

> With *Jungle* I wanted to improve *The Robbers* [Schiller] (and prove that struggle is impossible because of the inadequacy of language).

> Mit "Dickicht" wollte ich die "Räuber" verbessern (und beweisen, daß Kampf unmöglich sei wegen der Unzulänglickheit der Sprache). (*GW* 15:69)

The one advance human beings have made over their animal state, language, is not enough to overcome the alienation from each other that results from no longer being in the natural state. They are forced back into the condition of beasts—and yet they are no longer capable of being satisfied by the simple physical life of the beasts. Shlink:

> I have observed animals. They seemed innocent. Love, warmth from close bodies, the one mercy for them in the darkness. The uniting of the organs is the only unity; it doesn't bridge in a human lifetime the separation of their languages.

> Ich habe Tiere betrachtet. Sie schienen unschuldig. Die Liebe, Wärme aus Körpernähe, ihre einzige Gnade in der Finsternis. Die Vereinigung der Organe ist die einzige, sie überbrückt nicht in einem Menschenleben die Entzweiung ihrer Sprachen. (P. 92)

Garga:

> The forest! Humanity comes from here, doesn't it? Hairy, with ape's teeth, good animals that knew how to live. They simply tore each other to pieces, and everything was so easy. . . . and the one that bled to death among the roots, that was the loser, and the one that had trampled down the most woods was the victor!

> Der Wald! Von hier kommt die Menschheit, nicht? Haarig, mit Affengebissen, gute Tiere, die zu leben wußten. Sie zerfleischten sich einfach, und alles war so leicht. . . . und der verblutete zwischen den Wurzeln, das war der Besiegte, und der am meisten niedergetrampelt hatte vom Gehölz, war der Sieger! (P. 93)

Nothing is as simple for human beings as for animals, neither in love nor in battle, because they are cursed with the words for thinking, feeling, and loneliness. All their attempts to raise themselves above the level of the animals only throw them lower. Marie cries, "How they debase us, love and hate!" ("Wie niedrig es macht, die Liebe und der Haß!") (p. 85). And all there is to do after all is to survive. Garga concludes: "But it is not important before God to be the stronger, only the survivor" ("Aber es ist nicht wichtig, vor Gott der

43

Stärkere zu sein, sondern der Lebendige") (p. 100). He must not allow himself to be affected by the destruction of his family or by the murder of his wife, or he will lose. That he loses anyway, by losing his humanity in order to survive, only means that this is an absolutely pessimistic play. You can only win by losing. You are reduced to being an animal, but you cannot enjoy the pleasures of animals.

And yet Garga (or Brecht) regrets the ending of the fight. Brecht told Bronnen the meaning of the play was in words "The chaos is used up. It was the best time" ("Das Chaos ist aufgebraucht. Es war die beste Zeit").[39] Despite all the destruction, there was a kind of hope in the struggle, a hope that something would be born out of it; it was creative in setting all its own rules, ignoring morality. It was a relationship. Life after the fight could only become duller.

Undoubtedly Brecht's remark to Bronnen applied to his or their own life too; this was in fact the last play Brecht wrote in the metaphoric and emotional language that he got from the expressionists and Rimbaud. After this he moved from *Jungle*'s disconnected fragments of free association to crystal clarity in language; the dialectic of ideas, which must be expressed as clearly as possible, became more important for him than playing with dazzling but subjective images.

And so the version of *Jungle* that he put together for print in 1927 has a very different atmosphere: the passions, the love affairs, the personal references are largely gone, and the diction is tight, strict, utterly compact. It is to this revised version that Brecht prefixed the famous admonition to the reader or audience:

> Don't worry about the motives of this struggle, but be concerned with the human stakes, judge impartially the fighting form of the opponents and direct your interest to the finish.

> Zerbrechen Sie sich nicht den Kopf über die Motive dieses Kampfes, sondern beteiligen Sie sich an den menschlichen Einsätzen, beurteilen Sie unparteiisch die Kampfform der Gegner und lenken Sie Ihr Interesse auf das Finish. (*GW* 1:126)

In other words, avoid getting emotionally involved in the fighters' lives, stay coolly detached from their persons and feelings as you would at a sporting match, and use your head to analyze their moves—just as they themselves are doing. This cool, rational approach is consistently reflected by the style of the late version. It is, in a word, non-chaotic. Herbert Ihering, from the beginning Brecht's most faithful supporter among the critics, mourned the passing of the old chaotic style when he read the printed version in 1927:

> Now he has brought the *Jungle* over from the tropical climate of the first, atmospheric versions into the cooler air of an objective fight. . . . The new *Jungle*, the *Jungle of the Cities*, has lost some color and atmosphere. It has won some clarity and concentration. . . . Brecht has used up the chaos. It was his best time, because it provided the pregnant ground for his development.

> Jetzt hat er das "Dickicht" aus dem tropischen Klima der ersten, atmosphärischen Fassungen in die kühlere Luft des sachlichen Kampfes hinübergeführt. . . . Das neue "Dickicht", das "Dickicht der Städte", hat an Farbe und Atmosphäre verloren. Es hat an Übersichtlichkeit und Konzentration gewonnen. . . . Brecht hat das Chaos aufgebraucht. Es war seine beste Zeit, weil sie den trächtigen Boden abgab für seine Entwicklung.[40]

"Chaos"—fascination with the exotic, sinking deep into every vice, rebelling against the stagnation of German society by embracing anarchic and cruel but very alive societies—some time after finishing *Jungle* Brecht did not need it any more. But certainly it was the "best" time of his life; he would never be so free again, because he would never be so completely in rebellion. Of course, as Bronnen hints, "chaos" did continue for a while; the next plays continued to be bitter and apocalyptic visions without a hint of a way out. But the lush, wild language disappeared. It was necessary for a while, and it was beautiful. It is easy to see how Brecht could feel nostalgia for the wild creativity of his youth.

Early articles by Ihering are a valuable contemporary interpretation of the stylistic characteristics of Brecht's "chaotic" rebellion:

> Brecht experiences chaos and decay bodily. Hence the matchless power of the imagery in his language. . . . It leaves out connecting links and tears perspectives open. It has a brutal sensuality and a melancholy tenderness. There is coarseness in it as well as unfathomable sadness; fierce humor as well as plaintive poetry.

> Brecht empfindet das Chaos und die Verwesung körperlich. Daher die beispiellose Bildkraft der Sprache. . . . Sie läßt Zwischenglieder weg und reißt Perspektiven auf. Sie ist brutal sinnlich und melancholisch zart. Gemeinheit ist in ihr und abgründige Trauer. Grimmiger Witz und klagende Lyrik. (1922)[41]

And Ihering's interpretation of the need for this anarchic language is important because it shows the dialectic between the old and the new that produced a Brecht, and that was symbolized for much of Europe by America.

> People cursed the coming generation and failed to sense that it had to fight harder than any other in 100 years . . . for experience itself. . . . Energies were so exhausted that apocalyptic events were accepted like everyday annoyances.

> Man beschimpfte die aufsteigende Generation und fühlte nicht, daß sie schwerer als irgendeine seit hundert Jahren zu kämpfen hatte . . . um das Erlebnis selbst. . . . Die Energien waren so aufgebraucht, daß man apokalyptische Ereignisse wie Unannehmlichkeiten des Alltags hinnahm. (1922)[42]

In 1924 Ihering continued that analysis in a review of *Jungle*:

> War and revolution struck a humanity that was so mechanized by civilization that it could no longer experience elemental events in an elemental way. Drama couldn't begin again where it had broken off. It couldn't deny Americanism, couldn't rub it out. What was necessary, though, was not to see it as a refinement, not as a stage of development, in other words not to refer it back to history again, but to feel it as a new, primitive beginning. The final technical precision of the age could only be artistically productive if it was possible to experience it as barbarism. As prehistory that would be productive for a new spiritual beginning.

> Krieg und Revolution trafen auf eine Menschheit, die durch Zivilisation so mechanisiert war, daß sie elementare Ereignisse nicht mehr elementar empfinden konnte. Das Drama konnte nicht wieder einsetzen, wo es abgebrochen war. Es konnte den Amerikanismus nicht leugnen, nicht weglöschen. Notwendig war aber, ihn nicht als Verfeinerung, nicht als Entwicklungsstufe zu sehen, ihn also nicht wieder historisch zurückzubeziehen, sondern als neuen, primitiven Anfang zu empfinden. Die letzte technische Präzision des Zeitalters konnte nur dann künstlerisch zeugungsfähig werden, wenn es gelang, sie als Barbarei zu erleben. Als eine Urzeit, die produktiv wird für einen neuen seelischen Beginn.[43]

Ihering believed that European humanity had forgotten how to be primitive; it was alienated to the point of complete apathy; it needed to be rejuvenated. Drama was trapped in the same dilemma: the more it tried to be an experience, to awaken feeling, the more it would fade into the background of experiences that an exhausted society was trying to forget.

This is where America came in. America represented the extreme of civilization, of overmechanized experience that one wants to escape, but it was simultaneously utterly primitive; the two are brought together in the word *barbarous*. Hence it was a new beginning, the chance to feel the elemental emotions again—love, hate, fear. This has always been the function of "escape" entertainment in a decadent society: the experience of vicarious emotion. But for Brecht the myth of America meant more. Since he was a creative talent and not just in search of experience, America was only a beginning for him. He saw the mammoth technical development achieved there not only as the furthest extension of Europe's own tendency toward progress but as a qualitatively new stage, the beginning of a new era. Although the Americans had carried civilization even further than the Europeans, they had done it with such confidence, naïveté, and ruthlessness that they were now in the early, barbarous stage of a new culture. The brilliant incarnation of this paradox is the city Chicago as jungle; the most unnatural city becomes a new kind of nature.

For Brecht the dawning of a new age (a theme treated again thoroughly in *Galileo*) is grounds for hope because new experiments can be made, human nature can be changed, new social orders can be attempted. This is where the next stage in Brecht's development actually took him. But right now the positive feeling only came from the newness itself, from the consciousness that history lay ahead, not behind, from the feeling of being young and having a young world to experiment with, rather than being old before one's time in a world afraid to try any more experiments.

This is what Ihering says was the meaning of America for Brecht's development. It is a valuable insight. But we must not forget that neither Brecht nor Ihering thought America was *nice*; on the contrary, it was harsh and cruel. It is the very nature of Chicago that causes the devastating loneliness of man, that makes human language inadequate, that turns men into beasts.

These things can happen in Brecht's plays with the absoluteness they do because of the ruthlessness of his America: in America (Germans supposed) everything is absolute, the great city is the beginning of the new age where stakes are high and passions are laid bare and the most merciless man wins. At the beginning of an age you make your own rules. As we have seen, Brecht always portrayed

Chicago and America as unjust and cruel, even as early as in *Jungle*. But in the beginning there was nevertheless a promise of future in the celebration of the tough new age. Brecht was conscious of social injustice in *Jungle*; he was even critical of racism, poverty, and the use of women as objects. But the negative picture of America is only the background of the play. Fundamental is the gruesome strength of a new kind of man who can sacrifice everything to a metaphysical fascination. The very destruction in *Jungle* is glorious in its uncompromising boldness.

But looking back, Brecht was ashamed of that attitude toward America. To find out what caused him to change his mind, we must again look at his literary sources, and at his next works on America.

Chapter Two

1924–1926
America as Business:
"Joe Fleischhacker" and
Other Fragments

In the years 1924–26 Brecht only completed one original play, *A Man's a Man*, which is set in India, not the United States (though they are not unconnected in Brecht's mind). But for anyone interested in Brecht's ideas of America, these years could merit a small book in themselves. We will limit ourselves to a book-length chapter, divided somewhat artificially, for the sake of ordering this complex material, into two parts. In the first part we examine the many sources, mostly literary, that contributed during this time to Brecht's growing consciousness of the contradictory nature of U.S. society; in the second part we will look at the poems and fragments of plays that he wrote based on this material.

A. SOURCES AND INFLUENCES

Between the writing of *In the Jungle* and the work on the next plays set in America (unpublished fragments from 1924 to 1926), Brecht consolidated his success on the stage, moved permanently to Berlin as the fascists became too oppressive in Munich, began his first team writing (with Lion Feuchtwanger), and began his friendships with the actress Helene Weigel, the boxer Samson-Körner, and his secretary and collaborator throughout his life, Elisabeth Hauptmann. She was a teacher of English literature, and introduced him to much of what he knew of England and America.

He also made the first significant change in his style, the change from the lyricism of *Jungle* to the sober and ironic prose of *A Man's a Man*. Simultaneously with the change in writing style, he began using "epic" staging techniques associated with Erwin Piscator's experimental proletarian theater.

There is no doubt that Piscator was the principal influence on Brecht's staging technique, though not on his literary technique. Plays produced by Piscator were always exclusively intended as agitprop theater and often had small literary merit; Brecht's work was always more subtle and literary—though Piscator planned to produce at least one of the plays (*Wheat*) that Brecht never finished. Brecht, looking back at the twenties, later calls Piscator "without a doubt one of the most significant theater people of all times" ("zweifellos einer der bedeutendsten Theaterleute aller Zeiten") (*GW* 15:237), and "the great master builder of the *epic theater*" ("der große Baumeister des *epischen Theaters*") (*GW* 15:316); he praises Piscator's innovative daring, saying:

> Piscator's experiments burst nearly all conventions. They intervened to bring changes in the dramatist's work methods, the actor's style of representation, and the designer's sets. They aimed at a completely new social function for the whole theater.

> Die Piscatorschen Experimente sprengten nahezu alle Konventionen. Sie griffen ändernd ein in die Schaffensweise der Dramatiker, in den Darstellungsstil der Schauspieler, in das Werk des Bühnenbauers. Sie erstrebten eine völlig neue gesellschaftliche Funktion des Theaters überhaupt. (*GW* 15:291–92)

And Piscator himself relates that Brecht wrote him a letter from exile in the United States suggesting collaboration on a project, because, as Brecht said, major political, anti-emotional theater was unimaginable without Piscator; his words were: "I'd like to say here that in my entire career no one has been as valuable for my artistic development as you") ("Ich möchte Dir hiermit sagen, daß mir kein Mensch in der ganzen Zeit meiner Tätigkeit so wertvoll war in der künstlerischen Entwicklung wie Du").[1]

Paquet, "Flags"

Leo Lania, whose book *Welt im Umbruch* (*World in Transition*) is a valuable "biography of a generation" (as its subtitle says), and who himself wrote for Piscator, recalls that "a new dramatic period, a new style of theater, a new literary direction" ("eine neue dramatische Periode, ein neuer Theaterstil, eine neue literarische Richtung")[2] began with Piscator's production of the play *Flags*

(*Fahnen*) by Alfons Paquet in 1924, in the Volksbühne. *Flags* is an extremely important production in the history of the theater. It was the first play produced by Piscator in the "Piscator style"; it was also the first play to be called "epic theater," which is now identified more with Brecht than with Piscator and which has changed the complexion of twentieth-century world theater. Lania describes the play and the production as follows:

> *Flags* was set in the eighties and dealt with the Chicago anarchists' trial. In a loose succession of scenes Paquet portrayed the rebellion of the workers, the crushing of the strike, the trial against the strike leaders, and their conviction.
>
> A revolutionary drama of workers' life, such as the period of naturalism had already produced in great numbers. But what differentiated this play fundamentally from other drama with similar content was that Paquet wanted to give neither a naturalistic milieu depiction nor a psychological study of different types of workers: without resorting to any kind of poetic creations he let the naked facts speak for themselves. The play had no individual heroes, and no central theoretical problem—it was a dramatized newspaper article.
>
> The production had taken this basic idea of the author's as a leitmotiv. Slides introduced the drama: they showed the photographs of the historical personages. As in the movies, titles between the scenes delivered the mediating text. On both sides of the stage, right and left, stood tablets [screens]; at the decisive points in the plot texts would be projected on these that drew the moral from what was happening. Thus was this "dramatic narrative" intended to appeal not to the emotions but to the understanding of the audience.

> "Fahnen" spielte in den achtziger Jahren und behandelte den Chicagoer Anarchistenprozeß. In einer losen Szenenreihe schilderte Paquet den Aufstand der Arbeiter, die Niederwerfung des Streiks, den Prozeß gegen die Streikführer und ihre Verurteilung.
>
> Ein revolutionäres Drama aus dem Arbeiterleben, wie solche die Periode des Naturalismus schon in großer Zahl hervorgebracht hatte. Aber was dieses Stück von jenen Dramen ähnlichen Inhalts grundlegend unterschied, war, daß Paquet weder eine naturalistische Milieuschilderung geben wollte noch eine psychologische Studie der verschiedenen Arbeitertypen, sondern daß er, auf jede dichterische Gestaltung verzichtend, nur die nackten Tatsachen für sich sprechen ließ. Das Stück hatte keine individuellen Helden, auch kein zentrales geistiges Problem—es war ein dramatisierter Zeitungsbericht.
>
> Die Inszenierung hatte diesen Grundgedanken des Dichters zum Leitmotiv genommen. Lichtbilder leiteten das Drama ein: sie gaben die Photographien der historischen Personen. Zwischentitel lieferten, ähnlich wie im Kino, den vermittelnden Text. Auf beiden Seiten, rechts

und links von der Bühne, standen Tafeln; auf diesen wurde an den entscheidenden Stellen der Handlung ein Text projiziert, der die Lehren aus dem Geschehen zog. So sollte diese "dramatische Erzählung" nicht an das Gefühl, sondern an den Verstand der Zuschauer appellieren.[3]

It is these technical innovations in staging that Brecht always mentions in connection with Piscator: use of film, conveyor belts, elevators, new music and scenery.[4] He never specifically mentions Piscator as an influence on his politics, and Brecht's own theories of the social aspect of "epic" theater come from a later date than his adoption of the technical means from Piscator.

The word *epic* in German refers not only to Homer and to Hollywood extravaganzas, as it does in English, but to all narrative literature, in distinction to drama and lyric. Brecht sometimes says "narrative" ("erzählend") instead of "epic" ("episch"). The subtitle of the printed version of *Flags* (1923) is "a dramatic novel" ("ein dramatischer Roman"); the subtitle of the theater production was "an epic drama" ("ein episches Drama"). Both Piscator and Brecht may have got their use of the term from Paquet; *Flags* was the first epic drama that *called* itself epic. What makes it "epic," is, first, the staging techniques, which allow the kind of commentary on the action that is normally possible for novelists but not dramatists; second, the open form, the "loose succession of scenes" ("lose Szenenreihe") or "dramatized newspaper article" ("dramatisierter Zeitungsbericht"), as Lania calls it; and third, the attempt to expose the social and economic causes of the events shown. "Thus *Flags* represented in a certain sense the first Marxist drama, and that production the first attempt to grasp these materialist forces and make them tangible" ("So stellte 'Fahnen' in gewissem Sinne das erste marxistische Drama dar und jene Inszenierung den ersten Versuch, diese materialistischen Triebkräfte zu erfassen und fühlbar zu machen").[5] So Piscator on his discovery of epic theater.

To a certain extent Brecht had already used the first two techniques in his earliest plays: in songs and open form in *Baal*, and in the newspaper report preceding *Jungle*. In 1926 (about the time that Brecht first started using the term *epic* himself), he claimed his own *Baal* was one of the first examples of epic theather (*GW* 15:133). But it was not until *A Man's a Man*, completed in 1926,[6] that he consistently used the distancing effect of cool and carefully controlled language, and the actors' stepping out of their roles in order to comment on the play. In this play too there are special staging techniques and deliberate avoidance of naturalism (in both language and staging). There is also some attempt at showing economic causes behind the action, as in the little vignette where one soldier asks, "Do they know yet who the war is against?" ("Weiß man schon, gegen wen der Krieg geht?") and the other answers, "If they need cotton, it's Tibet, and if they need wool, it's Pamir" ("Wenn sie Baumwolle brauchen, dann ist es Tibet, und wenn sie Schafwolle brauchen, dann ist es Pamir") (*GW* 1:348). But this imperialist nature of the war is not emphasized; it is hard to judge what the political direction of the play is. The fact is, Brecht started using the techniques of the epic theater before he knew exactly to what end he needed them. That is the case also with his intention to appeal more to the intellect than to the emotions. As early as 1922 Brecht wrote, "I hope I have avoided in *Baal* and *Jungle* a great mistake of other art: its effort to carry the audience away" ("Einen grossen Fehler sonstiger Kunst hoffe ich im 'Baal' und 'Dickicht' vermieden zu haben: ihre Bemühung, mitzureißen") (*GW* 15:62). But this is in rebellion against the sentimental art of the "bourgeoisie"; it remains a *formal* principle, not a means to communicate any particular idea. Brecht's early plays were in rebellion more against the theater than against society.

The early attempts at an "epic" drama in Piscator's theater were not as sophisticated as what Brecht came to call his epic drama. They were closer to the later German "documentary theater" of the sixties: usually without fictionalized plot, presenting a panorama of history rather than concentrating on a few characters, and using for text the actual words of the historical characters. The newspaper-like style of the plays (Lania calls it *Reportage* and says it came from the influence of the American novel, e.g., Sinclair Lewis and Dos Passos[7]) makes for rather dull reading; Brecht was always much more interested in language and used the mock newspaper reports, which he himself prepared, only to clarify the plot to himself. Furthermore, it is probably true, as Ernst Schumacher says,[8] that the dramatists for Piscator's "epic" theater were not really penetrating below the surface of events to social causes and economic processes, but were only using realistic journalism to reproduce the thing in itself, in a new kind of naturalism.

Nevertheless, Piscator had a very strong influence on Brecht.

Brecht cannot help but have seen *Flags*; he even had a copy of the book edition from 1923 in his library.

And *Flags* too is about Chicago—specifically about the Haymarket Massacre in 1886. Here Chicago is again presented as a city torn by class war; this time it is literally a war, a workers' uprising and brutal repression by the state. The atmosphere is very similar to that in Brecht's *Drums in the Night*; but Paquet is unequivocally on the side of the workers in revolt. Again Chicago (and in fact America) is peopled by working-class immigrants. Special emphasis is put on the Germans, who were historically the principal anarchists involved. They, and all the workers, are disappointed by America.

> We thought: a little piece of land, a quiet life in America. And now here we sit.

> The worker has no homeland. He has to create one. My homeland is called the International.

> Bah, the American apples taste like rainwater. . . . What use are flowers that have no scent. Have you noticed that nothing in this land gives real pleasure?

> Wir dachten uns: ein Stückchen Land, ein ruhiges Leben in Amerika. Da sitzen wir nun.[9]

> Der Proletarier hat keine Heimat. Der muß sie sich erst schaffen. Meine Heimat heißt die Internationale.[10]

> Bah, die amerikanischen Äpfel schmecken wie Regenwasser. . . . Was nützen ihm Blumen, die keinen Duft haben. Hast du schon bemerkt, daß nichts in diesem Land einem wirkliche Freude macht?[11]

In fact Paquet's America is unmitigatedly evil—excepting of course those who fight against it. A worker sums up America in an aphorism: "This is a rich country that shoots its workers dead in thanks" ("Dies hier ist ein reiches Land, das seine Arbeiter totschießt zum Dank").[12] The police and courts are absolutely corrupt, interested not in human life but in making Chicago look like a peaceful, prosperous city for the World's Fair. This is all the class analysis that is provided in the play; as Schumacher says, it does not really attempt a serious portrayal of the mechanisms behind the action.

That is what is most "un-Brechtian" about it; its argument is based on emotional identification with the workers, even to the point of involvement in their private lives. The revolt is led by anarchists, without planning or analysis, and Paquet's own attitude toward the revolt he portrays is also unanalytical. It is: romantic. The style of the play is naïve; although it presents a pageant rather than only individuals, it still uses empathy; and its language has no stylization, no distancing from the naturalistic. There are a good many English words in the German text (mark you, citizens, look here, shopkeepers, stairbuilder, etc.), but Paquet has not got Brecht's ear for special associations with words and for slang: these Anglicisms seem gratuitous, stuck in like the many place-names just for a bit of local color. They have perfectly good German equivalents.

And so Brecht was probably not very impressed by the play as literature, only by its staging. But despite its weaknesses the play seems to have impressed people as theater, and it probably helped form Brecht's image of Chicago, pushing him now to identify as class struggle the brutal struggle he had already recognized there. Chicago was still very much with Brecht, now with the addition of the cry of one of Paquet's anarchists in his ears:

> Nothing is as interesting as Chicago. The explosion must come. Our movement was not arbitrary. Only premature. There will be wars. People will be blown up wholesale.

> Nichts ist so interessant wie Chikago. Der Krach muß kommen. Unsere Bewegung war nicht willkürlich. Nur verfrüht. Es wird Kriege geben. Leute werden massenhaft in die Luft fliegen.[13]

Tarbell, "The Life of Elbert H. Gary"

Another book in the library Brecht left when he died is the fascinating *Life of Elbert H. Gary: The Story of Steel*, by Ida Tarbell.[14] Of course, the fact that the book was published in 1925 does not necessarily mean that Brecht read it then. His knowledge of English was slight at that time; usually Elisabeth Hauptmann did his English reading for him, as Bernhard Reich tells us:

> She knew English and provided him with materials: clippings from English and American newspapers and magazines. She had plenty to do, because Brecht's appetite for things American was enormous.

> Sie konnte Englisch und versorgte ihn mit Materialien: Ausschnitte aus englischen und amerikanischen Zeitungen und Zeitschriften. Sie hatte alle Hände voll zu tun, denn Brechts Appetit nach Amerikanischem war ungeheuer.[15]

It is also possible that there are books in his library that he never read at all, but this is not likely to be the case with the few older books he kept from the twenties. At any rate something turned his interest around at that time (1924–25) to economic relations, especially in America. Tarbell's book was likely a factor, either through his own reading or through Hauptmann's.

The Life of Gary reads like a historical novel: it has a plot and a central conflict (will honest Judge Gary be able to retain his Methodist virtues and still do well in business?), and big names in government and finance (notably J. P. Morgan and Teddy Roosevelt) are reduced to likeable folks with definable personalities, yet they are heroes just the same. These are the people who set up the first billion-dollar corporation in history; everything they do shakes the nation and the world. If he read the book when it was published, Brecht was undoubtedly impressed by the bigness of it all; he writes later that one of the main themes of the time was "the construction of a mammoth industry" ("der Aufbau einer Mammutindustrie") (*GW* 15:236).

Although Ida Tarbell is known as a muckraker, there is nothing in this biography to indicate that she had any conception of class struggle. Tarbell reveals herself in this book as a liberal, not a socialist, critical of excesses but approving of progressive and "moral" capitalists like Gary. There are two prominent explicit ideological messages in the book and one implicit one. Implicit is the complete indentification with management's side. Again and again, the workers just do not understand that Gary is trying to keep their interests in mind, that he believes in "cooperation." Gary seems to be the country's first liberal businessman; he realizes at every turn that it is profitable to avoid conflict. Tarbell does nothing to suggest that no matter how many concessions Gary gives the workers, they remain class enemies.

The explicit ideological messages in the book are, first, the value of the pioneer spirit that made America great, combined with Methodist uprightness, and second, the great advantages for business of cooperating with government rather than fighting it. American business ethics are transformed by one man, who is determined to hang on to the Christian virtues even when making money—according to Tarbell's book. In fact, of course, the founders of the great corporations gradually realized they would be incomparably more powerful with government at their service, particularly in foreign investment. Gary may have been especially intelligent and farsighted; Tarbell depicts him as having to fight hard to get this concept through at board meetings.

The glorious pioneer heritage is extolled in the opening two paragraphs of the book, and a dichotomy described that informs many of Brecht's works on America. The pioneers who leave settlements to strike out into uncharted country are the same kind of people who later leave the country to build the great cities and great industries. This is a theme of book after book that Brecht now read on America, and it is the motion he used as the basis of his planned series "Human Migration to the Big Cities." It is the instinct for progress, basic to Brecht's idea of the American character.

Judge Gary the pioneer comes into business at an anarchic, brawling time when patents are stolen, corporate law is just beginning to be written, legal differences produce fistfights in the courtroom, large firms are beginning to consolidate, and individual men control their own destinies and those of their church, community, children, and business. (That is, all the people mentioned in this book are able to control their own destinies; the poor are only present as an occasional irritant.)

But we leave Judge Gary, still running U.S. Steel, with the age of competition behind us. The individual capitalist no longer controls the market; it is the age of the giant corporation, cooperating with the government and the other corporations in the same industry. Speculation has been superseded by planning; stability is the most important goal.

This is the process that is shown in *St. Joan*: at the end of the play Mauler ends his deadly competition and consolidates the meat industry without regard to the workers' interests but with the enthusiasm and cooperation of the other capitalists. Mauler receives from his former competitors the same kind of "trust" that makes it possible for Gary and J. P. Morgan to get many interests together to form the U.S. Steel Corporation:

> Most important, no doubt, was faith in Mr. Morgan's power to make money for everybody who joined—and that was what they wanted. The best of them believed not only in the man, but the process of integration. They believed it inevitable, beyond the power of men to resist.[16]

St. Joan also shows the ostensible moral concerns of the capitalist

57

and the harnessing of religion into the service of enlightened moneymaking, both unconscious themes of Tarbell's book; but *St. Joan* fails to show the tremendous cooptive potential of corporate liberalism, as practiced *par excellence* by Judge Gary in Tarbell's book.

It may have been more Tarbell's characterization of J. P. Morgan than that of Gary that influenced Brecht's creation of Mauler. Brecht's "Pierpont Mauler" is of course meant to sound like "Pierpont Morgan," only more brutal. There is a short scene in *St. Joan* where Mauler's partner and his competitor call him "Pierpy" to get his goat, after having punched him in the chest to prove his heart has feeling (*GW* 2:683). This little bit of psychological rivalry among the giants could have been inspired by a parenthesis in Tarbell's story: "(Judge Reed is very likely to remark that Mr. Morgan always winced when Carnegie called him 'Pierpont')."[17] Carnegie too may have provided part of the character of Mauler, in particular the brilliant tiny vignette where "the meat king and philanthropist P. Mauler" goes to the dedication of the hospitals he founded, guarded by two detectives so he will not be attacked (*GW* 2:671). Tarbell writes of Carnegie, "He was a very rich man. When he died he wanted to leave behind him a reputation not of being the greatest iron master in America, but the greatest philanthropist."[18]

Norris, "The Pit"

Another book that we find in Brecht's library, Frank Norris's *The Pit* (published in English in Leipzig in 1903), ranks with or even above *The Jungle* in the influence it had on him. Bernhard Reich writes of the years 1924–25 in Berlin:

> During this time Brecht read Walt Whitman and Frank Norris. Often Brecht mentioned *Wheat* by Norris with great thoughtfulness. He occupied himself intensely with economic materials.

> In dieser Zeit las Brecht Walt Whitman und Frank Norris. Oft erwähnte Brecht mit tiefer Nachdenklichkeit den "Weizen" von Norris. Er beschäftigte sich intensiv mit ökonomischen Materien.[19]

At the same time as he was working on *A Man's a Man*, Brecht was planning the second and third plays in his projected series "Human Migration to the Big Cities"; the first was retroactively declared to be *In the Jungle*, then were to come *Fatzer*[20] (*The Decline and Fall of the Egoist Johann Fatzer*, a fragment actually written between 1927 and 1930 in *Lehrstück* style) and *John Schlachthacker*, as Reich remembers it. That fragment, renamed *Joe Fleischhacker*, was begun in 1924 and written mainly in 1926. It is based primarily on *The Pit*.

Norris's novel is (by now we expect it) set in Chicago. Like the biography of Judge Gary, it centers its attention on the great capitalists—this time the speculators of the wheat exchange at the turn of the century—not on the repercussions these men's acts have for the masses. However, Norris does occasionally mention the victims, and by implication they are always there, accusing. When he describes the Board of Trade as a generator that sends ever widening circles of influence throughout the country and the world, it is the "little man" who in the end pays.

> Endlessly, ceaselessly the Pit, enormous, thundering, sucked in and spewed out, sending the swirl of its mighty central eddy far out through the city's channels. . . . And men upon the streets of New York felt the mysterious tugging of its undertow engage their feet, embrace their bodies, overwhelm them, and carry them bewildered and unresisting back and downwards to the Pit itself.
>
> Nor was the Pit's centrifugal power any less. . . . Because of an unexpected caprice in the swirling of the inner current, some far-distant channel suddenly dried, and the pinch of famine made itself felt among the vine dressers of Northern Italy, the coal miners of Western Prussia.[21]

For those who have the means, the appeal of gambling proves irresistible, although they sacrifice their friends, love, health, and even life; for those without means, the effect of the capitalists' gambling is disastrous.

The Pit is simultaneously the story of a beautiful but conceited and self-centered girl from small-town Massachusetts—who marries the rich wheat operator Curtis Jadwin in Chicago and then all but loses him to the fascination of speculation—and the story of Jadwin's speculations themselves, ending in his great corner and subsequent ruin—which is what leads him back to Laura and leads her in turn to learn unselfishness. But Brecht was not very interested in the story of the spoiled rich girl who is loved to distraction by three men. What moved Brecht so much was nothing but the economic plot, the drama of the wheat exchange; and that is also where Norris really excels. There could hardly be more dramatic suspense than in his tale of the mundane events in the Board of Trade. And not only are they fascinating like a game or a sporting match, they are also of the most extreme importance for the fate of millions of human beings.

Jadwin, true to the type, comes from a farm in Michigan and has moved to the city, Chicago, where he made his early fortune in real estate. He is portrayed as a strong, large, and good man: he passes the plate in church; he is kindness and generosity itself to Laura and all his friends; he has a huge Sunday School for poor children (of which he is very proud because it is run on such fine business principles as consolidation and streamlining). Jadwin is downright sentimental. And everyone thinks of him as a kind man; it never occurs to himself or Laura to hold him responsible for the reverberations throughout the world that his speculation and crash cause: banks closing, tight money, people losing all their savings overnight.

Jadwin's friend Cressler (who represents Norris's views) explains the evils of speculation to Laura:

> Those fellows in the Pit don't own the wheat; never even see it. Wouldn't know what to do with it if they had it. They don't care in the least about the grain. But there are thousands upon thousands of farmers out here in Iowa and Kansas or Dakota who do, and hundreds of thousands of poor devils in Europe who care even more than the farmer. . . . It's life or death for either of them. And right between these two comes the Chicago speculator, who raises or lowers the price out of all reason, for the benefit of his pocket. . . . Think of it, the food of hundreds and hundreds of thousands of people just at the mercy of a few men down there on the Board of Trade. They make the price. (Pp. 121–22)

It is quite an ingenious, though gratuitous, system. Using statistics on supply and demand and weather, plus their sixth sense, the speculators bet on what the price of wheat will be in the coming harvest, and through their bets they influence the price: the more people buy in expectation of higher prices, the higher the prices rise. This is suggested but incompletely explained in Cressler's speech to Laura; likewise the function of a commodity exchange is never explained. It does not have the function of a stock exchange, which is to provide starting capital for enterprises and to share profits and ownership. Whether commodity exchanges have any truly necessary function at all is doubtful. Hence they are incomprehensible to anyone who is looking for a rational basis in the economy.

60

And it is this incomprehensibility that drove Brecht, who had very little precise knowledge of economics, to search farther and farther for explanations of how the wheat market worked. No one could explain to his satisfaction, because it simply did not make sense.

Jadwin is tempted by an apparent sure deal his broker suggests to him. But once in, he feels the desire to prove how good he is. "Oh, it's not the money," he says, " . . . it's the fun of the thing; the excitement—" (p. 220). His broker has a secret connection in Paris who has tipped them off by coded cablegram that the French Chamber of Deputies will pass a bill for heavy import duties on foreign grains. (Compare in *St. Joan* Mauler's letters from New York about the probability that tariffs will be lowered in the South.) The broker cajoles Jadwin:

> Now here's the chance to make a really fine Bear deal. Why, as soon as this news gets on the floor there, the price will bust right down, and down, and down. (P. 80)

> I'll sell short for you at the best figures we can get, and you can cover on the slump any time between now and the end of May. (P. 81)

It is easy to see how this unfamiliar language, which the speculators take for granted, would have fascinated Brecht, who always wanted to understand and demonstrate how everything *worked*. And it is not simple; why does the expectation of higher prices for wheat sold abroad make the Chicago price sink?

The deal is successful, and Jadwin becomes a big-time Bear; there are hard times throughout the land. But come winter his sixth sense tells him things will change: business is picking up, stocks are booming in New York, and reports predict a very small crop. He talks the broker this time into secretly turning Bull, and starts buying. From now on the whole show is masterminded by Jadwin, the "unknown Bear." (All of this is familiar to any reader of *St. Joan*.)

Suddenly he discovers that 80 million of the 100 million bushels of wheat that will be harvested in May will be bought by Europe, and some speculators have already sold short and will not be able to deliver because there is no wheat to be had. This means—he and his broker are overwhelmed as they realize it—that he can corner the market.

Which is what he does for the rest of the book. He secretly buys up 40 million bushels, so that other investors will have to buy from him at a high price to deliver to him at the former low price. Drunk with the power of shooting the moon, Jadwin cannot let go. Having driven the price up to a dollar, he decides to buy up July shorts, and force two dollars. He becomes nervous, physically exhausted; he never sees his wife, and he is furious at advice. He never makes the two dollars. On the day of crisis, the Pit senses an unprecedentedly large crop coming because of the high price, and it starts to take courage to oppose him. As his broker warns him, he is fighting against the earth itself. This is Norris's grand moment; the author cuts in and explains what has happened:

It was the wheat, the wheat! . . . Almighty, blood-brother to the earthquake, coeval with the volcano and the whirlwind, that gigantic world-force, that colossal billow, Nourisher of the Nations, was swelling and advancing. (P. 357)

For months, he had, by the might of his single arm, held it back; but now it rose like the upbuilding of a colossal billow. It towered, towered, hung poised for an instant, and then, with a thunder as of the grind and crash of chaotic worlds, broke upon him, burst through the Pit and raced past him, on and on to the eastward and to the hungry nations. (Pp. 375–76)

Here natural forces overwhelm man as they threaten to do in *The Wheel*; but they are not man's enemy. Rather they are, if he would only see it, his friend and guide: he must learn not to interfere with them, and not to set up artificial barriers in the way of natural (logical, simple) production and distribution. The wheat is the life force itself, and will have its way. Norris's social criticism is clothed in the ethics of non-interference with nature, his brand of naturalism.

Strangely, though, he speaks of the great city with similar imagery. It is dirty and squalid to be sure, but it is alive. Again like Jensen, Norris writes in rhapsodic prose of the trains roaring and screeching in and out of Chicago as the lifeblood of the city, and the carriages and markets and streets are pure activity—expression of life—and power. Norris renders once more the American dream of infinite confidence and will to progress, of a country without history that knows it will make its history in the future. He chose Chicago as the embodiment of the dream because Chicago was to Americans what America was to Europeans; Brecht, realizing this, again and again used Chicago as the most extreme case of what he meant by Americanism. His picture coincides with Norris's as far as the latter's goes: Chicago is healthy, brutal, arrogant. But Brecht knew of more; he knew of the symptoms of despair that appear in the great cities: prostitution, drinking, violence. He knew that barbarism and decadence coexisted. For a naturalist, Norris writes of remarkably clean-living people; Brecht, who rejected naturalism because it presented the human condition as unchangeable (*GW* 15:207, 173), was nevertheless interested in the outcasts and victims of society, as symbols, as clues to the workings of society.

The poems and fragments of plays Brecht wrote during this period show that he was partly caught up by the image of the city as an irresistible force himself. But for him it was also a very human institution, and the suffering that took place in it was not impersonal but caused by people. That is why the account of men's activities on the wheat exchange, and their far-reaching implications, was what fascinated Brecht in *The Pit*. We know that he found the book extremely important, because the economic processes both in *St. Joan* and in *Joe Fleischhacker* are copied right from Curtis Jadwin's corner.

White, "The Book of Daniel Drew"

We find an even closer example of copying market manipulation—this time the stock market—in Brecht's fragmentary script in the Archive for a play to be called *Dan Drew*. There are frequent references to page numbers in "the book" ("das Buch") in Brecht's manuscript, and notes to himself like "best the scene on page 198 199" ("am besten die scene von seite 198 199"); "JIM TELLS THE STORY 219" ("JIM ERZÄHLT DIE GES-CHICHTE 219"); and "(exactly the conversation on page 195)" ("[genau das gespräch von seite 195"]) (BBA 194, 21, 30, and 18). Nowhere does Brecht give a clue what book he means. Luckily, although she was not sure of the author or title, Helene Weigel was able to remember the translator (Hanns Heinz Ewers) of the biography of Drew that Brecht used (and that she and Brecht found it delightful and gave it to all their friends), and so it was possible to track down *The Book of Daniel Drew*, by Bouck White.[22]

It is a strange book, ostensibly an autobiography written by Drew as old man, but actually a biography written by White in the first person. White claims to have based it on papers of Drew's that may have been intended as notes toward a book, but how much is Drew and how much is White, or whether the whole thing is made up by White, is impossible to tell. In any case, White has done a remarkable job of maintaining Drew's point of view throughout: the picture that emerges is of a drastically uncultured, unprincipled, ambitious, and ostentatious swindler, the kind of man who today would be a stereotyped Texan, but who a century ago was only one of many similar men who controlled the country's wealth. Drew was by no means the biggest swindler, but he was one of the more colorful; and few had such imaginative biographies written about them, revealing with such psychological clarity their devastatingly simple philosophy. At any rate, this was the book that came into Brecht's hands at the end of 1925, and so it is the one he used. Apparently it made such an impression on him that he simply sat down and decided to turn it into a play.

Adapting this book by White is another example of Brecht's rebellion against the bourgeois tradition of legitimate literature. It is not a book of great literary value but rather another "document," a study in psychology and economics. The urge to dramatize the life of this illiterate cattle-driver-turned-unscrupulous-speculator came at the same time and was as "unliterary" as the urge to tell the life of the boxer Samson-Körner. Brecht found the spirit of sport and suspense in the great stock deals intensely dramatic. (In production the stock market scenes in *St. Joan* can be the most effective part of the play. But in *Dan Drew* the stock market scenes, plus the kibbitzing and plotting of which they are the climax, make up the whole play; in the far more complex *St. Joan*, they are contrasted to the workers' poverty and the strike.)

White portrays not only Drew's almost sadistic lack of conscience and his rough and illiterate beginnings as a cattle driver, he also emphasizes Drew's quaint piousness. In the sport of making money, Drew unflinchingly lies, steals, bribes, betrays his friends—and then he goes to church immediately afterward and prays and condemns exactly those sins in others, and is certain he is one of the more moral persons on earth. He even donates money for a theological seminary to perpetuate his name as a religious man. It is almost eerie that he himself never sees the slightest conflict between his religion and his secular life; this is, of course, a comment by White on the church as well as on Drew's somehow naïve capacity for duplicity. (It is strange that Brecht did not take up the theme in *Dan Drew*. All the

64

treatment of religion we ever get from the early Brecht is always incorporated in the Salvation Army.)

In all Brecht's reading on America, Drew comes closest to being like Lorimer's John Graham: somehow appealing, homespun, and humorous despite his ruthless use of capitalism and his self-righteousness. But he also sounds a little like Tarbell's Gary and Norris's Jadwin. A cumulative impression of these rich Americans and their country is forming for Brecht. Chicago as brutal represser of workers' revolt and center of speculation, America as imperialist, America as corporate capitalist, home of the robber barons: these are the very negative impressions Brecht was collecting after writing his first American play. Yet he was still paradoxically charmed by the Americans, to the extent that he was infuriated by some remarks by Bernard Shaw claiming, on the evidence of the monkey trial in Dayton, that Europeans are more civilized than Americans.

The epithets Brecht uses to praise Americans in this outburst are perhaps left-handed compliments, but he clearly intends to say that it is an advantage not to be civilized to the point of apathy as Europeans are. Except for that possible valid point, Brecht's position is quite untenable, and it is interesting only as it reveals his confused state of mind at the time. He is really bending over backward to praise Americans for their bigotry and stupidity in the matter of evolution versus fundamentalism.

> I consider it in any case a great moment for the history of ideas when a busy people like the Americans, through a healthy i.e. strong reaction, makes a meeting with new theories into a real adventure.

> Ich halte es in jedem Falle für einen großen Moment der Geistesgeschichte, wenn ein ausreichend beschäftigtes Volk wie das amerikanische durch eine gesunde, das heißt heftige Reaktion das Zusammentreffen mit neuen Theorien zu einem wirklichen Abenteuer gestaltet. (*GW* 18:26)

He goes on to call the American people "this extraordinarily unbiased people, totally unspoiled by history" ("dies erstaunlich vorurteilslose und von der Geschichte gänzlich unverbildete Volk"). This description is consistently repeated in 1928–30 when he twice again mentions the monkey trial. Once he calls the Americans "a somewhat more healthy people" ("ein etwas gesünderes Volk") (*GW* 15:200); and once he writes that the monkey trial must be considered an important stage in the progress toward Bolshevism,

65

because in it a people showed a strong, healthy reaction to an idea and at the same time a naïve trust in the courts. That a people would let a conflict between religion and science be decided by a criminal court is a clear victory of Bolshevik atheism.

weil in ihm ein Volk eine starke, gesunde Reaktion auf eine Idee zeigte und sogleich das naive Vertrauen auf seine Gerichtshöfe. Daß ein Volk einen Streitfall zwischen Religion und Wissenschaft durch einen Kriminalgerichtshof entscheiden läßt, ist ein klarer Erfolg des bolschewistischen Atheismus. (*GW* 15:160)

This is the same ironic idea in a new political context: here it is clear that Brecht is pleading for common sense, for beliefs determined on the basis of discussion (he delighted in the dialectical dramatic form of a trial) and not just by acceptance. That is not exactly what he said in the early reaction to Shaw. There it was a simple defense of Americanism. In fact, he quite overreacted; the article by Shaw[23] has very little to say about Americans. Shaw is interested in showing that the Bible is full of contradictions and that fundamentalism is a bunch of impractical nonsense. Actually Brecht shared Shaw's opinion on religion; all that can have angered him is Shaw's sarcasm directed at America, which is, granted, heavy-handed:

It doesn't happen often that a single state can make an entire continent ridiculous, or that a single man can cause Europe to question whether America was really ever civilized at all. But Tennessee and Mr. Bryan have made it an event. To us on this side of the Atlantic American civilization was of course always suspicious. The lawbooks of the federated states are museums of childish, temperamental lawmaking, and are defended by traveling Americans with the argument that not even in a dream did anyone ever think of actually applying these childish laws.[24]

But Brecht's angry reaction and overeager defense of the American people are characteristic of this period. He was, simply, ideologically confused. The comment on Shaw goes on to state a position of complete agnosticism on beliefs:

If I were asked what I would prefer: the terrorism of those who don't want to know something or the terrorism of those who claim to know it better, I would prefer the former without hesitation and in every instance.

Wenn ich gefragt würde, was ich vorziehen würde: den Terror derer, die etwas nicht wissen wollen, oder den Terror derer, die etwas besser wissen wollen, dann gäbe ich den ersteren unbedenklich und in jedem Falle den Vorzug. (*GW* 18:27)

The position is 'suspicion of anyone who is too positive about his ideas; it is still the (as Brecht himself calls it [*GW* 20:46]) nihilism of his earliest plays, which have a background of social problems but take no position. They tend, on the contrary, to praise the morality of survival of the individual, i.e., pragmatic amorality. In 1919 Brecht had written that he was against "teachers," people who enjoy knowing better, including "the petty revolutionaries, those that abolish the Kaiser and introduce communism, and conservatives who fight them. . . . The absolute pacifist and the absolute militarist, they are the same fools" ("die kleinen Revolutionäre, diejenigen, die den Kaiser abschaffen und den Kommunismus einführen, und Konservativen, die sie bekämpfen. . . . Der absolute Pazifist und der absolute Militarist, das sind die gleichen Narren") (*GW* 20:7). Six years later this relativistic position had not changed. But it was getting more untenable. He was being forced into absurdities, ironies where he himself probably did not know what he really meant, cynical laughter with a touch of desperation. In the fragment on Shaw he even proceeds to say, "It is progress that makes me throw up" ("Es ist der Fortschritt, der mich so ankotzt") (*GW* 18:27), and to praise conservatism—positions that hardly sit well with almost everything else he had written.

In criticizing Shaw, and in comments written on *A Man's a Man* at this time and other political statements, Brecht seems to be trying to imitate Shaw's own technique: the statement of outrageous positions in a tone that leaves the reader guessing whether the intent is ironic or earnest. What is one to make, for instance, of this sentence written around 1926? "The trouble with great men (for they *are* an evil) consists in the fact that there are too few of them. There ought to be a mass of them, let's say: a proletariat" ("Das Übel der großen Männer (denn sie *sind* ein Übel) besteht darin, daß es zu wenige gibt. Es müßte eine Masse davon geben, sagen wir: ein Proletariat") (*GW* 20:16). The other earliest notes collected in the volume *Writings on Politics and Society* are similarly so saturated in irony that it is impossible to conclude any political direction from them. Brecht was being careful, overcareful, not committing himself to any position, playing the invincible role of skeptic and cynic.

The year 1926 is the crucial one in Brecht's development. It marks the greatest change not only in his attitude to America but also in his politics and his dramatic theory. In all three of these fields, he became *conscious*: former instincts and inchoate contradictory attitudes began to crystallize, come under sharp intellectual scrutiny, and resolve themselves into a set of well-defined and interrelated ideas that would remain with him for the rest of his life. The confusion in his thinking had to be resolved. It was being pushed partly by his inability to finish writing any of his dramatic projects, and partly by his reading about America (which in 1926 continued to challenge his "nihilist" stance). As we have seen, he was steering toward a crippling dilemma in his philosophy: on the one hand a glorification of progress and the machine age, on the other a foreboding of annihilation and feeling of futility, arising from his cynicism. At the same time his fascination with cities and America reached a peak, and expanded into the area of economics. We will finish our examination of Brecht's reading about America by looking specifically at the books he read in the year 1926, to get some idea where the intensified interest in economics came from. Then in Part B we will look at the crisis to which this interest took him in the unfinished plays of 1926, and then at the effects of this crisis on his picture of America, his politics, and his dramatic theory.

Harris, "My Life and Loves"

We cannot know in what order Brecht read the books listed below, but he read them all in 1926, or very shortly before. We will begin arbitrarily with Frank Harris's *My Life and Loves*, printed in Berlin in 1926 under the title *Mein Leben* (*My Life*). Brecht wrote a short review (*GW* 18:48–49) praising the book for its "documentary value," a term he was to use often. The review claims that Harris is a great liar, but that his book is very useful because it shows us the system of values of a type of man; in other words, the picture Harris gives of himself is Harris's conception of the ideal of the age. He supposes himself the self-made man, the young European boy who runs away to America and becomes a success. A success at everything—intellectual abilities, women, and money are all his in unbelievable quantities.

The book contains interesting documentary material on America too; it is the very embodiment of the American dream come true.

68

Harris makes good first as a young boy in New York shining shoes, constructing bridges, and fornicating; then as a hotel boy in Chicago; then as a cattle rustler; then as a friend of famous people; finally as an intellectual (that is, he could memorize phenomenally, which he believed made him an intellectual). He sympathizes with the Marxism of the professor who "discovers" him, but his political philosophy consists of asserting rather stridently that socialism and individualism can somehow be combined.

Harris criticizes America's Puritan morals, lack of (sexual) liberty, and low cultural level, describes the horror of a lynching during the Chicago fire, and protests vigorously against the torture of conscientious objectors in World War I; but he also speaks of America with extreme affection, feeling it really is the land of opportunity (as most people who manage to make their fortune there feel). He has clearly racist prejudices, especially in relation to the Negro women he "loves" (uses), and his ideas on preventing pregnancy are terrifying. He is a strange and conceited specimen.

When in the early 1880s he met Marx, he was impressed by Marx's "deep human pity and sympathy . . . the heart better than the head—and wiser."[25] *Capital* (volume two) was also a great book—"No one who ignores it should be listened to on social questions"[26]—but Marx himself, Harris says from a fully self-confident equal level, in conversations shut himself off from "hearing anything against his pet theory, one-sided though it was."[27]

Harris went to Berlin in 1918 to publish the autobiography because he could not find anyone to do it in the prudish United States. While there he met George Grosz. Harris's descriptions of America probably interested Brecht; but they fall into the pattern to which he was by then quite accustomed, and he would hardly have taken them as gospel. They can not be classified as ideas; they are simply the reproduction of stereotypes and prejudices: "It is a genuine document, although it is the best that an enormous liar could produce" ("Es ist ein wirkliches Dokument, obwohl es das Beste ist, was ein ungeheurer Lügner zustande bringen konnte") (*GW* 18:48).

Mendelsohn, "America: An Architect's Picture Book"

Another kind of document that Brecht used as source material was photographs of America. He mentions skyscrapers often, and it is easy to see why: he actually collected postcard pictures of the largest buildings in Chicago, to have a visual symbol of what the huge growth looked like. Not only did this visual aid help him steep himself in the right atmosphere; it also found its way into his work as concrete detail, almost in the style of *Neue Sachlichkeit*. These postcards (from 1925) can be found among the materials for *Joe Fleischhacker* along with many newspaper clippings about wheat and the stock market.

There are many other instances of Brecht's use of photographic sources. In a note about the growth of cities, for instance, he mentions explicitly a photograph that loosed a train of thought:

> I saw a photograph of the entrance to Broadway in New York (the gate of this cement gorge, over which "Danger!" is written) and tried hard to figure out what people will be able to say about the distractions of these cities when their time is up.

> Ich habe eine Photographie vom Eingang des Broadway in New York gesehen (das Tor dieser Zementschlucht, über dem "Danger!" steht) und mir Mühe gegeben, herauszubringen, was man, wenn ihre Zeit um ist, über die Circenses dieser Städte wird sagen können. (*GW* 15:76)

He answers that it will not be the events one thinks of "while looking at such imposing photos" ("bei der Betrachtung solch imposanter Fotos") that will last, but the things that were fun: Chaplin's films, jazz.

What could be the "imposing photo" that inspired this strange and grotesque vision of an entrance to Broadway like the entrance to hell? We can answer this question definitively: it is a picture in Erich Mendelsohn's photographic essay *Amerika: Bilderbuch eines Architekten* (*America: An Architect's Picture Book*).[28]

A full-page photograph on page 30 of this large-format book shows a close-up of the previous photograph of one end of Broadway. In the back is a tall sunlit building with thirty-three floors and regular rows of closely set windows; Mendelsohn comments on the technical achievement but the inhumanity of squeezing an average of 5,000 to 15,000 people into one building. The foreground buildings are in the shadow, dark and forbidding, and seem to march into a long line of their type. People and cars are heading into the dark narrow street; it is easy to imagine them being swallowed by an ominous fate once they are inside. A fourteen-story building on the right side is under construction; there is a cement or wooden bridge built out in front of it covering the sidewalk, to protect pedestrians walking beneath the construction. In the close-up the tunnel for pedestrians looks as though it filled the whole street—like a more practical, American version of the gate to a European city—and above the passageway is a large sign (referring to the construction, not the road ahead) reading: DANGER.

Either Brecht misinterpreted the picture, or he had an excellent eye for ironic detail. In either case, his use of this picture is revealing: it shows in miniature how he adapted information about America to his own use, how something he considered a characteristic detail could be the stimulus for a whole train of thought. This is why we see him using the same concrete details again and again: they have very specific symbolic meaning for him.

A glance through the book by Mendelsohn is enlightening; it must have made a strong impression on Brecht. Divided into sections on "The Typically American," "The Heightened Civilization," "The World Center—The Money Center," "The Gigantic," "The Grotesque" ("Das typisch Amerikanische," "Die gesteigerte Zivilisation," "Das Weltzentrum—das Gelzentrum," "Das Gigantische," "Das Groteske"), it contains visual examples of much that Brecht associated with America. He read it in 1926, the year it was printed, and declared it one of the best books of the year, praising its "outstanding photos, all of which one could really hang separately on the wall, and which give the (certainly misleading) impression that the big cities are habitable" ("ausgezeichnete Photos, die man eigentlich fast alle einzeln an die Wand heften kann und die den [bestimmt trügerischen] Anschein erwecken, als seien die großen Städte bewohnbar") (GW 18:51–52). The camera has an eye for the essential design and manages to catch a gesture, as Brecht might call it, in each building. Studying the pictures in the book today, an American can reconstruct some of the effect this country must have had on Europeans in the twenties.

Mendelsohn's book contains not only pictures but also short, large-print, pithy, almost expressionist comments on each of them. Some of these leave an almost visual imprint on the mind, as strong as that of the pictures. The introduction sounds familiar to the reader of those works by Brecht that equate America with a new age, cruel but grand:

> Altered, heightened dimensions of life energy, of spatial relations and of traffic. . . .
> Driven upwards by unforeseen accumulation of money, pumped up

in an unprecedented short time from immigrants' port to business center
of the world. A conglomeration of fairy-tale wealth and armies of the
needy. . . .

For what is forbidden, what allowed, where dimension allows itself
every liberty and knows no respect for the traditional scale of
comprehension. . . .

America is today still so deep in the period of exploitation, the
primitive function of daily necessity, that it has no time for thoughts
about itself, about the purpose of its living lifelessness. . . .

Seeing America today is therefore being thrilled with perspectives.
Here we recognize for the first time the whole monstrousness of negative
civilization, but at the same time in this chaos we see the first reference
points of a new age. . . . Whirlwinds are only harbingers. . . .

This land gives everything: the worst refuse from Europe,
civilization's abortions, but also hopes of a new world.

Veränderte, gesteigerte Dimensionen der Lebensenergie, der Raum-
verhältnisse und des Verkehrs. . . .

Hochgetrieben von unvorhergesehener Geldhäufung, aufgepumpt in
beispiellos kurzer Zeit vom Einwandererhafen zum Geschäftszentrum
der Welt. Ein Konglomerat von Märchenhaftem Reichtum und Not-
armeen. . . .

Denn was ist verboten, was erlaubt, wo die Dimension sich selbst jede
Freiheit genehmigt und vor überkommener Begriffsweite keinen Re-
spekt kennt. . . .

Amerika steckt heute noch so tief in der Periode der Ausbeutung, der
primitiven Funktion des täglichen Bedürfnisses, daß es für Gedanken
über sich selbst, über den Sinn seiner lebendigen Leblosigkeit keine Zeit
hat. . . .

Amerika heute zu sehen, ist deshalb ein perspektivischer Rausch. Erst
hier erkennen wir die ganze Ungeheuerlichkeit der verneinenden
Zivilisation, aber gleichzeitig in diesem Schwimmbrei schon die ersten
Fixpunkte einer neuen Zeit. . . . Wirbelwinde sind nur Vorbo-
ten. . . .

Dieses Land gibt alles: Schlechteste Ablagerungen Europas, Zivili-
sations-Ausgeburten, aber auch Hoffnungen einer neuen Welt. (Pp. vi-
ix)

There is the same simultaneity of two visions of America here as in
Brecht: it is a terrible place, but what a potential! For Mendelsohn,
America is an organic, energy-driven chaos that has yet to be
understood and controlled; a picture of 43d Street in New York
bears the caption, "Impossible to imagine the spirit that will
someday organize it" ("Unmöglich, den Geist sich vorzustellen, der
das einmal ordnen soll") (p. 55). The language Mendelsohn uses to

try to describe the visions is full of crackling and roaring sounds, images of speed and force and noise: New York's skyline is to him "Fast entrance, turns, curves, space cataract, space battle, infinite triumphal delirium" ("Schnelle Einfahrt, Wendungen, Kurven, Raumkatarakt, Raumschlacht, unendlicher Seigesrausch") (p. 21). A picture of the el in Chicago is accompanied by a description of the noise it makes right in the middle of the city: "The European goes blind from the noise, but the American has adjusted his nerves and hears nothing any more" ("Der Europäer wird blind vor Lärm, aber der Amerikaner hat seine Nerven angepaßt und hört nichts mehr") (p. 16). Americans have, through adaptation to inhuman conditions, really become a new race of tough and practical people. These are the people that we see in *Dan Drew* and *Joe Fleischhacker* (Brecht's main projects of that year), single-mindedly pursuing their absolutely worldly goals.

Mendelsohn has pictures of Wall Street too: "Stock exchange, the bourse, and Equitable Trust. On the far side of Broadway, Trinity Church—money and God" ("Stock exchange, die Börse, und Equitable Trust. Jenseits des Broadway Trinity-Church—Geld und Gott") (p. 23). This juxtaposition is not infrequently used by Brecht. But for all his talk of capitalism, there is a tone of admiration discernible in Mendelsohn's text beyond which Brecht had already gone. Mendelsohn's attitude is: America is brutal, but it is so marvelous. Brecht's is: America may be marvelous, but it is so brutal. In Brecht's recommendation of the book there is also a certain tone of superiority looking down at Mendelsohn's naïveté.

Perhaps Mendelsohn's most striking picture, which he repeats from various angles, is the one of a complex of massive grain elevators and silos made of concrete. This, too, is Chicago, and the accompanying text describes the special trains and ships that bring grain to the central city from Canada, Illinois, Wisconsin, Michigan, and Indiana: all the midwestern states provide the city. Chicago is the collection point for the country's agriculture, just as in *The Pit* food crises radiate outward from Chicago to the world. The functional beauty of the silos (not an American invention but uniquely imposing in these pictures) represents what is best in America: matter-of-factness, getting down to business on a gigantic scale. This was another visual help to Brecht, who was working on a play about the grain market in Chicago.

Mendelsohn's principal message on city architecture is the lesson of the silo picture: honesty about function is beautiful. He complains that useless decoration (baroque frills, Roman columns) on the American skyscrapers reveals the fear in America's people that they have no culture. Their great achievements come when they dare to look into the technical future with confidence: "technical beauty, the new romanticism" ("technische Schönheit, die neue Romantik") (p. 74). The imagination is most stimulated by powerful expressions of purpose. America is most attractive when it admits its brutality rather than copying European decadence. There are two possible paths for architectural development:

> Either one swears by the eternal validity of historical forms or one refuses to be intimidated by history's judgment and tries to find, out of purposes and materials, the suitable formal expression for our time.

> Entweder, man schwört auf die Immergültigkeit der historischen Formen, oder, man lehnt den Angstblick auf die Historie ab und versucht, aus Zweck und Material den unserer Zeit entsprechenden Formausdruck zu finden. (P. 63)

This is remarkably similar to what Brecht believed and practiced in his drama and theater. Expressionism (he calls it sarcastically "Oh-humanity dramatics" ("Oh-Mensch-Dramatik" [*GW* 17:945]) and glorification of the individual soul were in Brecht's opinion no longer contemporary, nor was naturalism, which was too defeatist. The dramatist of the new age must embrace the technical achievements and understand their implications, use every possible new technique on the stage, make his drama relevant to the innovations that the audience knows in its everyday world. The new drama must break down the bourgeois idea of art as decoration and preservation of what is old, and replace the old conception with a new one of an art that is relevant to the present and the future.

Thus the occasional similarity between Brecht's technique and *Neue Sachlichkeit*, a style that Europeans claim originated in America (but more likely it originated in their own admiration of America's supposed *Sachlichkeit*—matter-of-factness).[29] That style, which was a pendulum reaction of postwar German artists against expressionism, tried to make poetry out of the objects of everyday contemporary life; technology played an especially large role precisely because it had previously been scorned as unpoetic. Brecht

74

never seemed to fall into the temptation of writing exclusively about inanimate objects,[30] but rather with his effortless eclectic genius adopted the most useful quality of *Neue Sachlichkeit* and sprinkled it generously through his writing, as in his brilliant use of concrete detail and his determination as a director that actors have respect for the technique of how things are done. Concretization was from the beginning terribly important to Brecht, but not an end in itself. Its function is well illustrated by Bernhard Reich's reminiscence of Brecht's direction of *Edward II* in 1924:

> When for a certain epoch the sentence "It is Thursday" was spoken, he nodded at me, proud of far-reaching concretization of time. Seeking concretization, he later came to his concept of the historic and poetic—a day becomes a particular day by means of the important event, rich in consequences, that occurs on it.

> Als bei einer Epoche der Satz *"Es ist Donnerstag"* gesprochen wurde, nickte er mir zu, stolz auf weitgehende Konkretisierung der Zeit. Die Konkretisierung erstrebend, kam er später zu seinem Begriff des Historischen und Poetischen—ein Tag wird zu einem bestimmten Tag durch das wichtige und folgenreiche Ereignis, das an ihm geschieht.[31]

So, similarly, the many skyscrapers, radio antennas (radio was the exciting new way to communicate with the New World), Virginia cigars, and bottles of whisky that appear in Brecht's drama and poetry during the period of about 1926 are not fetishes but concrete signs of the new age he is talking about; they are both its cause and its manifestation. Brecht's plays are about human beings. But these concrete technological details anchor the human beings in reality (i.e., a particular stage of social development); they make people's problems very real, not imagined (romantic). The technique of concretization is a cornerstone of Brecht's style: again and again he uses a single concrete detail to incorporate the whole idea or setting he wants to express.

It is this same courage to be thoroughly modern—the refusal to look back—that Mendelsohn praises in the best American architecture. He insists that the only honest approach to building is the attempt to find formal expression in the purposes and materials of our time. Both Brecht and Mendelsohn were strongly influenced by the rapid progress and optimism of America in the twenties, and so they embraced progress, determined always to look forward. Brecht was almost obsessed with newness, and he identified with the pioneer spirit. However, he was also able to understand the settler spirit (as described by Tarbell), as well as the economic duress that industrialization and urbanization created for the less competitive and the lower classes. The dream of Tahiti and of the Old Country or the savannah in *Jungle* is an early expression of this understanding; in *Joe Fleischhacker* the ruin and degradation of a family that moves from the savannah to Chicago is still more explicit.

Anderson, "Poor White"

One source of this increased understanding was Sherwood Anderson's *Poor White*, which Brecht also read in 1926. From this novel he learned about the anguish of Americans who look back at the simple, country days with nostalgia. This is not a position Brecht himself could ever take, but the dream of the free and simple past before urbanization and industrialization haunts many of his characters in the American plays.

Elisabeth Hauptmann notes on 8 June 1926:

> About Easter Brecht had discovered a new lending library. *Poor White* by Sherwood Anderson made a strong impression on him; he wrote the poem "Coals for Mike" after it.

> Um Ostern herum hatte Brecht eine neue Leihbibliothek entdeckt. "Der arme Weiße" von Sherwood Anderson macht einen großen Eindruck auf ihn; er schreibt danach das Gedicht *Kohlen für Mike*.[32]

(For a discussion of that poem, see below, p. 93.)

Among the drafts for *Fleischhacker* is another hint that *Poor White* made a strong impression on Brecht: he has copied out a description of how cattle are transported from the Far West to Chicago, the "giant city of the prairie" ("Reisenstadt der Prärie"), and brought to the slaughterhouses. At the end of the passage he writes the source: "POOR WHITE by ANDERSON" ("DER ARME WEISSE von ANDERSON") (BBA 524, 60). It is not clear how Brecht intended to use the quotation.

Also mentioned in the *Fleischhacker* notes is Jack London. His name follows what is presumably a quotation from one of his works: "the heart of this man, to whom the seasons are just specks and whose dreams end barbarically," ("das herz dieses mannes, dem die jahreszeiten flecken sind und dessen träume barbarisch enden") (BBA 524, 48). Undoubtedly London's novels helped form Brecht's concept of adventure and tough, heroic men in America. That

London was a socialist probably had less effect; as we have seen, Sinclair's and Piscator's early socialist arguments fell on rather deaf ears.

But the influence of *Poor White* is clear. Anderson makes explicit what Brecht had already suspected about the stage of history characterized by men moving to the cities. That theme was the historical background to earlier books Brecht read, but here the causes and effects of industrialization and urbanization are the central topic of the whole book. *Poor White* is probably the source that really solidified Brecht's concentration on "Human Migration to the Big Cities," the rubric under which he intended his studies around 1926 to appear.

The plot of *Poor White* is summed up in a short passage where Anderson describes the quiet towns of farmers and craftsmen, and then writes about the sense of something new coming:

> A sense of quiet growth awoke in sleeping minds. It was time for art and beauty to awake in the land.
> Instead, the giant, industry, awoke.[33]

The book begins as the story of Hugh McVey, a poor white from Missouri who is trapped in the contradiction between the southern laziness he inherits from his father and the ambitiousness of his foster-mother. To please her and to overcome his fear of his own passive nature, he constantly pushes himself, but remaining shy and lonely he centers his attention on mechanical things. When he moves north and east to Bidwell, Ohio, he becomes an inventor. The town itself now becomes the subject of the story: how it develops into an industrial city, the ambition of some of its citizens to push into the future, the tragedy of men who try to hang on to the past, and occasional diatribes by the author against the similar transformation of the whole country. Eventually Hugh becomes aware that his inventions are hurting people. He is thoughtful about this dilemma, but there is obviously nothing he can do, just as there is no way to hold up the whole industrial revolution. There are strikes against mechanization and there are a few speeches by socialists, but the majority of men have been infected with the cruel fever of progress. Anderson utterly condemns blind progress, showing only its bad effects; but his book is a sad and resigned polemic, not one offering a fighting solution. He sees no way to slow down history.

Brecht's attitude was very different, but this book was a

77

contribution to some of the criticism that runs through his urban works. Anderson's social criticism is a sad cry of despair at the tremendous loss of beauty and sensitivity; the whole book is subdued and plaintive, the author's position defeated from the beginning. There is no attempt to see what can be made of the new age, how to transform the new forces of production (for that is what he is portraying) into means to a more human life for all rather than a more lucrative life for some. In short, Anderson only looks back with a sigh, not forward with determination. Brecht never allows a backward glance: dreams of escape to exotic and primitive landscapes or of return to the old family homestead are never more than dreams. He sharpens the contradictions in the present reality of his plays to the point that they cannot be accepted with a resigned sigh: they cry for resolution. Progress is glorified as bringer of the grand new age, but misery and desire to escape are likewise emphasized.

There is a poem spoken by the boy Calvin Mitchell from the electric chair, in *Joe Fleischhacker* (see below, pp. 91–92), that is a translation from the negative to the positive of Anderson's bitterness in the following sentence:

> In making way for the newer, broader brotherhood into which men are some day to emerge, in extending the invisible roofs of the towns and cities to cover the world, men cut and crushed their way through the bodies of men.[34]

The boy in the electric chair in San Francisco uses the same images but in fanatical praise. And at the same time the misery accompanying the great transformation is made far more acute and desperate than in Anderson's book. Brecht shows not ugly architecture but people dying. Anderson shows the far-reaching effects of the industrial revolution on people's souls; Brecht shows the effects on their way existence.

Yet, of course, *Poor White* is a very important book for its "documentary value." Perhaps Brecht's interest in it will encourage more Americans to take Anderson more seriously, for he captures the fear and excitement of the age of growth that left small people feeling lost, almost as well as Thomas Wolfe. *Poor White* reproduces the feeling of a great change; it shows how the mood of an age penetrated into the lives of all the people living in that age:

Overnight, towns grew into cities. A madness took hold of the minds of the people. Villages . . . became small cities within a few weeks.[35]

A vast energy seemed to come out of the breast of earth and infect the people. Thousands of the most energetic men of the Middle States wore themselves out in forming companies, and when the companies failed, immediately forming others . . . . It was a time of hideous architecture, a time when thought and learning paused. Without music, without poetry, without beauty in their lives and impulses, a whole people, full of the native energy and strength of lives lived in a new land, rushed pell-mell into a new age.[36]

Myers, "History of the Great American Fortunes"

It may have been the many descriptions in *Poor White* of the new ruling class—the Rockefellers, Morgan, Frick, Gould, Carnegie, and Vanderbilt,[37] who became powerful purely through financial speculation—that prompted Brecht in the same year to read Gustavus Myers's brilliant historical study *History of the Great American Fortunes*.[38] This amazing book, 700 pages long, was available in translation in Germany from 1916. It was written just after the turn of the century, at the same time as the early muckracking works of Sinclair and Lincoln Steffens, but it is not a fictionalized account of a microcosm of social injustice, nor is it a biography; it is a vast study of the growth of wealth in the United States from colonial times to the twentieth century, an extraordinarily carefully researched and documented work. It is perhaps the first significant example of what is today called "power structure research," that is, research on the connections between financial interests and government policy, with the aim of exposing class bias. The book is simply an exposition of facts, written to be sure in polemical style, but there is never any doubt that the occasional comment is justified by the documentation. And furthermore, Myers's information, interpretation, and style of presentation are so fascinating that this long book on economics reads, as Brecht says, like a mystery story. And Brecht loved mystery stories.

That is another clue to Brecht's interest in economics: it is well known that he was a fanatic reader of mysteries (*Kriminalromane*). This was confirmed by his wife, who said that he read masses of them throughout his life, and by some of his own comments on literature.[39] The intellectual exercise involved in finding the key facts to solve a murder mystery is similar to the investigation of the underlying economic causes of readily visible phenomena. Sinclair, Jensen, Paquet, Anderson, all wrote descriptions of the social types and relations of this new age, but Brecht with his mystery-story attitude wanted to know what forces really lay behind the developments that those authors usually presented as pure phenomena. This is not to say that Brecht's interest in murder mysteries was the cause of his interest in economics but that they both sprang from the same analytic mind.

Brecht writes in 1926 "For lovers of criminalistic reading, *Myers' History of the Great American Fortunes* is a feast" ("Für Liebhaber kriminalistischer Lektüre ist *Myers* 'Geschichte der großen amerikanischen Vermögen' ein Fressen")—and not just because the money magnates were criminals. He continues: "It's well known that matters having to do with money are taboo in polite society and its literature. I assume it's because there is so much spirit in them (in the money matters)" ("Bekanntlich sind Angelegenheiten, die mit Geld zusammenhängen, in der guten Gesellschaft und ihrer Literatur verpönt. Ich nehme an, weil so viel Geist drin steckt [in den Geldangelegenheiten]") (*GW* 18:52). The implication is that literature should concern itself with financial affairs, and Brecht's literature will. The interest in economics was also partly the climax of his concentration on unliterary sources, many of which originated in Americanism.[40] Originally the cult of sport, cigar-smoking, and workers' clothing was an act of rebellion against the literary establishment; now the continued rebellion against the irrelevance of literature led to first a faddish, then a serious, interest in the economic base of society. And once Brecht had read Myers, there could be no turning back from the knowledge gained there: on the one hand, cold facts and analysis about the financial giants whom Anderson just mentions as shadowy background figures, and on the other, a perspective that makes sense out of history. It might well have been after reading Myers that Brecht noted down, "The American histories alone yield a minimum of eight plays" ("Die amerikanischen Historien allein ergeben im Minimum acht Stücke") (*GW* 15:70).

It would be impossible to summarize Myers's book or to quote enough from it to make evident the influence it had on Brecht. There is a detailed account of each of the capitalists Brecht writes about in *Dan Drew*—Vanderbilt, Drew, Fisk, Gould—as well as more than one hundred pages on J. P. Morgan, model for Mauler in *St. Joan*. The stock market swindles of the Erie Railroad crew receive about twenty pages. It is not possible to know to what extent Myers influenced Brecht's fragment *Dan Drew*, which is otherwise an adaptation of just one book. But there is one detail not mentioned in the source, which is probably taken from Myers: the name of Fisk's mistress, Josie Mansfield. Myers reports that Fisk bribed a judge to hold court in Josie Mansfield's apartment.[41] This must have caught Brecht's attention: he gives "josy mansfield" a lament to speak on the lot of a poor girl who comes to New York to make money, becomes a prostitute, and grows old there (BBA 194, 59).

There are two principal lessons that Brecht will have learned (at least in part) from Myers. First is the approach to the study of social relations which says that understanding history requires understanding the mechanism of finance. The other is an absolutely consistent class perspective, made far more explicit in Myers's book than in any of the fictional works Brecht had been reading about America. The American "Revolution" and the Constitution are presented as vehicles of class rule for the propertied, and the law and the courts as well as governors and administrators, with very few exceptions, are either simply bought by the magnates or serve the ruling class out of conviction or their own class interest. And as in *St. Joan of the Stockyards*, religion too is a means of keeping the poor from revolting.

Myers's intention is not to lash out at individual criminals or to express or create shock at frauds; in his preface he differentiates himself not only from the admirers of wealth but also from the sensationalist muckrakers. He himself wishes to show that

> while it is true that the methods employed by these very rich men have been, and are, fraudulent, it is also true that they are but the more conspicuous types of a whole class which, in varying degrees, has used precisely the same methods.[42]

He complains of the sensationalists:

> They give no explanation of the fundamental laws and movements of the present system, which have resulted in these vast fortunes; nor is there the least glimmering of a scientific interpretation of a succession of states and tendencies from which these men of great wealth have emerged. With an entire absence of comprehension, they portray our multimillionaires as a phenomenal group whose sudden rise to their

sinister and overshadowing position is a matter of wonder and surprise. They do not seem to realise for a moment—what is clear to every real student of economics—that the great fortunes are the natural, logical outcome of a system based upon factors the inevitable result of which is the utter despoilment of the many for the benefit of a few.[43]

The reason for quoting this introductory passage at length is that Brecht in *Dan Drew* did not really follow its warning. (He started work on *Drew* before reading Myers; conceivably Myers's argument convinced him to stop.) Brecht too presents the great finance kings as "a matter of wonder and surprise"; though he undoubtedly took to writing about the stock market in an attempt to expose class rule, what he produced on paper is still rather awed by the grandeur of it all. And there is no sign whatsoever of the effect the Drews and Vanderbilts have on the lower classes; the only characters in *Dan Drew* are the members of the Erie ring, plus one woman. One of Myers's virtues is that from time to time he interjects into his narrative of the great fortunes an analysis of working class conditions at the same point in history, showing, for instance, that most laws were passed to protect the rich from the poor and describing concretely the living conditions of the workers. That Brecht does nothing of the kind in *Dan Drew* is a sign that he based it almost exclusively on the pseudo-autobiography of Drew.

His simplification of financial politics in *Dan Drew* is some justification of the criticism by Martin Esslin:

> The writings of Lincoln Steffens and other muckraking American authors, Upton Sinclair's *Jungle* and accounts of the destruction of coffee and wheat to raise prices contributed to the somewhat crude idea he had formed of the great buccaneers of capitalism like Dan Drew and Commodore Vanderbilt.[44]

We know that Brecht had read enough other materials to have a pretty sophisticated idea of how these men worked; it was not Brecht's idea but his presentation that was crude, and he probably realized that himself. But the crudeness that Brecht would have found wrong is rather a different kind from what is meant by Esslin, much of whose book attempts to show that Brecht was a sentimentalist rather than a communist. Esslin thinks Brecht is selling capitalism short, whereas Brecht would criticize himself with obscuring its bad effects by sensationalizing it.

But more important for us is the long-range effect Brecht's

attempt at adapting the story of Daniel Drew had on his conception of America. Bouck White's book is one in a series of works Brecht read at this time that all together produced a very convincing case that America is both ruled and ruined by the men who control its wealth. *The Pit*, the story of the corruption of Chicago's *nouveau riche* wheat dealers, who will let the world starve for the fun of the speculation game; *The Book of Dan Drew*, the minute study of the workings of one speculator's mind and of his techniques in the market and their effects; *Poor White*, a wistful look back at what is crushed and forgotten when the cities grow up; and finally the *History of the Great American Fortunes*, which put into a class context all the stories of individual exploitation and presented them as the rule and not the exception: all these books about America made it impossible to accept the old myth of greatness and democracy any more. After reading them, Brecht could only use the myth to show how it has perverted human values, as in *Mahagonny*. If people like Dan Drew and Curtis Jadwin are typical of the American system, as Myers claims, then this system must be changed. That is the lesson of *St. Joan of the Stockyards*.

B. POEMS AND FRAGMENTS

Brecht's Creative Crisis

But Brecht did not arrive at these conclusions merely through reading. Brecht was a writer, and it was when he reached a crisis in his writing, when he was unable to go any further on the projects that he had started, that he was forced to think through his attitudes and find exact answers to questions raised by the plays he was trying to write. Obviously, reading a book and accepting what it says passively is very different from trying to write a play whose aim is to make as clear as possible the message of that book: to write he really had to understand. But more than that, writing was his occupation, his only means of being productive. If he was unable to write, he could not do anything; and if something was preventing him from writing, he could not circumvent it and do something else; he had to solve the problem.

The only significant work Brecht finished during this period (1923 26) was *A Man's a Man*, which he had started working on, under the title *Galgei*, as early as 1920 21.[45] It was essentially completed, according to Ihering, in 1924.[46] The next two years saw many revisions, but they were minor, formal changes. He finished *A Man's a Man* in a period of ideological uncertainty, and he remained for some time thereafter confused about its meaning. There are many different drafts of prefaces to the play,[47] and they all take different positions. (See below, pp. 172–74.)

Few of Brecht's poems were written in these years either; until 1922 and starting again about 1929, he was prolific in poetry. About five or six stories were published during 1923–25, then a flurry of them in 1926, then nothing till the thirties. Everything else seems to have remained unfinished. Nothing came of most of the plays Elizabeth Hauptmann noted Brecht was working on in 1926. She lists *Inflation (Whores); Charles the Bold, Parody of Americanism; Robinsonisms in the City; Joe Meatcutter in Chicago (Wheat); Dan Drew (The Erie Railroad)—(Inflation [Mentscher]; Karl der Kühne, Parodie auf den Amerikanismus; Robinsonade in der Stadt; Joe Fleischhacker in Chicago [Weizen]; Dan Drew [Die Erie-Bahn])*[48]— and there were more projects around that time, plans and sketches that hardly anyone knows about. They *all* remained fragments. *Dan Drew* and *Joe Fleischhacker* are the only ones of these that were worked out in any detail; of the rest, some are only four or five pages of notes in the Archive, and of others there is no trace at all. In all there are about twenty ideas and sketches for plays preserved in the Archive from the approximate period 1924–26, and about as many again from 1927 to 1929.[49] (As we will see, 1924–26 was an involuntary and 1927–29 a voluntary dry period.)

Brecht wrote a note at the end of July 1925[50] that shows how disoriented he was:

> I vacillate a lot about pledging myself to literature. Till now I have done everything with the left hand. I wrote when something occurred to me or when I got too bored.

> Ich schwanke sehr, mich der Literatur zu verschreiben. Bisher habe ich alles mit der linken Hand gemacht. Ich schrieb, wenn mir etwas einfiel oder wenn die Langeweile zu stark wurde.

He lists the reasons for writing all his works: *Baal* as satire of a popular (expressionist) play, *Drums* to make money, ballads for evenings in Augsburg, sonnets out of boredom, and so on. "Were I to decide to try to make it with literature, I would have to turn a game into work, and excesses into a vice" ("Würde ich mich entscheiden, es mit der Literatur zu versuchen, so müßte ich aus dem Spiel Arbeit machen, aus den Exzessen ein Laster") (*GW* 15:69). Again, there is a mixture of truth and irony here; *Drums* certainly had more artistic purpose than just making money, and the testimony of Brecht's contemporaries as well as his own obvious delight at playing with language leave no doubt that writing was enjoyable for him. What he is expressing here goes deeper; he is asking whether he wants to think of himself above all as a writer; whether literature is important enough so he could devote his life to it. The feeling of uselessness, of dilettantism that he reveals here was the almost inevitable result of the amoral position he carefully cultivated and maintained from 1918 to 1926. With this position he was bound to ask sooner or later, Sure, writing is fun, but what is it *for*?

The problem was not a lack of ideas or material; he has plenty to write about for forty plays, he says. As he goes on to talk about what his subject matter will be, his tone changes from the discouragement of the cynic to the enthusiasm of the creative scientist fiddling with his formulas again. He is eager to make studies on all the important topics of the day—but he does not really know what to say about them:

As for material, I have enough. . . . For a heroic landscape I have the city, for a point of view relativity, for a situation the human migration to the big cities at the beginning of the third millenium, for content the appetites (too big or too little), for training of the audience the social battle of the giants. (The American histories alone yield a minimum of eight plays, the World War just as many. . . .)

Was den Stoff betrifft, so habe ich genug. . . . Als heroische Landschaft habe ich die Stadt, als Gesichtspunkt die Relativität, als Situation den Einzug der Menschheit in die großen Städte zu Beginn des dritten Jahrtausends, als Inhalt die Appetite (zu groß oder zu klein), als Training des Publikums die sozialen Riesenkämpfe. (Die amerikanischen Historien allein ergeben im Minimum acht Stücke, der Weltkrieg ebensoviel. . . .) (*GW* 15:70)

By this time he was quite certain that the important content for literature was not individual emotions and the struggle to remain an individual but the giant social struggles. The themes he mentions are nearly all related to the city-Americanism-progress complex. Those themes had formed the background for *Jungle*, but by some time in

1924 (which is when Brecht read *The Pit*) they gained paramount importance.

Brecht's Poetry

The change in emphasis is particularly evident in Brecht's poems. To understand the change we will look very briefly at his earlier poems, then examine the America and city poems of 1925–26 more closely.

The poems are a more accurate record than the plays of what was occupying Brecht at any particular moment, partly because they are often much easier to date (he usually wrote and rewrote the plays over a period of years), and partly because he expressed himself more immediately in them ("My poetry has a more private character"—"Meine Lyrik hat mehr privaten Charakter"[51] [1926]). On this second point, though, we should be careful: many poems, especially the early ones, are in the mode of the dramatic monologue, spoken not by Brecht but by typical *Erscheinungen* or manifestations of the age. But precisely this technique shows us what *subjects* Brecht thought were currently important, though it may not show us what he thought about them.

Brecht's very earliest poems, published under the name Bertold Eugen, are mostly embarrassingly patriotic war poetry.[52] When he begins publishing under his own name in 1916, his poems tend to be expressionistic or love poems with vague settings or none at all, though his talent for satire and lightly mocking nonsense about his friends is also evident from the start. War is a frequent topic; but although we know Brecht was a pacifist, there is no ideological position on war in the poems. They are mainly monologues showing how miserable it was: "Song of the Red Army Soldier" is an example. These early poems are by no means the normal sentimental and sophomoric attempts of youthful poets riding on the coattails of current popular expressionism; they are written in Brecht's terse and very individual style almost from the beginning. What Feuchtwanger says about the language of Brecht's first three plays applies also to his poems of that time: "Brecht's German is the voice of the time, with its enormous matter-of-factness and sensuousness, its wild, fanatic precision" ("Brechts Deutsch ist die Stimme der Zeit, von einer enormen Sachlichkeit und Sinnenfälligkeit, von einer wilden, fanatischen Präzision").[53] The matter-of-factness is even stronger in the poems than in the early plays; their self-control is emphasized by their strict strophic forms.

About 1920, the year his mother died, death became a morbid fascination for Brecht, together with the Baudelairean aesthetic of finding beauty in decay—except that in Brecht's case the opposite happens: he finds decay in beauty. The well-known examples of this vision, "Remembering Marie A." and "On the Drowned Girl," are both from 1920.

"Song of the Railroad Gang of Fort Donald," 1916, is Brecht's earliest published reference to America. It is also the beginning of a long fascination with heroism and natural catastrophes; Fort Donald in Ohio is the frontier, Lake Erie as dangerous and exotic as the Pacific Ocean. The idea of Fort Donald later becomes Alaska in *Mahagonny*—but *Mahagonny* is a satire. Is this? It is hard to believe that even at the age of eighteen Brecht could have written it with a completely straight face, and future use of similar themes reinforces the notion that his attitude toward the heroes of Fort Donald was at least partially ironic.

In 1921, at the time Tahiti became a motif in *Jungle*, Brecht wrote a poem called "Tahiti," a tongue-in-cheek nonsense poem about the same kind of adventurous spirit as that of the Fort Donald men, but ending in seasickness, drinking schnaps, and having a child by a seagull. The entire first verse is later adopted into *Mahagonny*, with Tahiti becoming Alaska; several of the *Mahagonny* songs were written in the early twenties and published in *Home Devotions*, Brecht's first collection of poems. The context into which he later put them in *Mahagonny* makes it clear that he himself did not accept the myth; rather, they are examples of the thoughts of human types in the new age.

During this early period there are few poems on political subjects; only one ("Song of the Red Army Soldier") is a reflection of the 1918 revolution, and several are on war and death. The character types and the moods of the times are represented but not the events.

Certainly the most significant early poem, not only because it is brilliantly written but also because it sums up the mood of the earliest works and simultaneously contains in embryo the themes that will follow, is "Of Poor B.B." (1922). No one but Brecht could have written this poem with its paradoxical mixture of painful honesty and self-protective irony, of bitterness and hopelessness

87

expressed with a sardonic smile and a determination not to be discouraged, of guilt and fear and loneliness immediately negated by cynicism. Many of the motifs of *Jungle* reappear in this key autobiographical statement—cold, people as animals, the move from country to city, survival, the good life, and especially nonchalance as a life style: Garga must not be affected by his family's tragedy, B.B. must not let his cigar go out in the earthquakes to come. That is, of course, the attempt at an amoral position: do not try to get me involved.

As important in the poem as "B.B." is the city. It represents a new age, an age of no sentimentality. We know that we are only forerunners, Brecht says, but we do not delude ourselves into thinking that what comes after us will be particularly wonderful. We are not trying to build anything new, we are only trying to get the most we can out of this hard new age. The cities we have built are more stupendous than anything man has yet accomplished—but they will not last. In the long run nature will win. Brecht quotes this poem later in talking about what postwar dramatists saw as their task:

> The important thing was to demonstrate the rationality of reality. . . . This drama . . . saw a great age and great personages and so prepared documents of them. And yet it saw everything in flux ("So we have built the long houses of the island Manhattan . . .").

> Es galt, die Vernünftigkeit des Wirklichen nachzuweisen. . . . Diese Dramatik . . . sah eine große Zeit und große Gestalten und fertigte also Dokumente davon an. Dabei sah sie doch alles im Fluß ("So haben wir gebaut die langen Gehäuse des Eilands Manhattan . . ."). (*GW* 15:218)

The city is heroic partly for the very reason that it cannot last: the mad tempo, the high buildings and thin antennas that are thought to be indestructible, the alienation from any sense of purpose or human contact, all are symbols of both strength and frailty. But: "In the asphalt city I am at home. . . . and content in the end" ("In der Asphaltstadt bin ich daheim. . . . und zufrieden am End") (*GW* 8:261).

This poem is only a presentiment of how very at home Brecht was to be in the asphalt city in the next years. The poems from 1925–26 are almost all about the city. It was not just a fascination; it was an obsession. For at the same time that Brecht felt at home in the city, he also felt oppressed by it. Many of the poems about the city are really about wanting to get away from the city. This is the escape motif that is so strong in *Jungle* and *Mahagonny* too. Human beings move into these cities and build breathtaking structures, and then keep building them until there is no psychic room for human beings any more and fear grips them and they want escape. But they cannot go back to the prairie or the Old Country; that is only regression. They must move forward; they must progress to some new goal that Brecht could not yet articulate. Brecht was not aware what direction his thought would take, but the contradictions in his writing implied that something *had* to change, a new age had to be founded because the age of asphalt and mammoth industry had become unbearable. Brecht did not see any future; he only saw the attraction and the repulsion of the city and the urge to get out, the urge to step out of history—which is impossible. At the end he foresaw only destruction and disaster, the constantly threatening hurricanes and earthquakes waiting for vengeance on man. And faced with eventual disaster, he found the only response an aggressive existential resignation.

These city poems begin (if the chronology in the *Werke* is correct) with "Bidi's Opinion of the Great Cities" (1925). We already know Bidi (Brecht's nickname) from "Tahiti"; now he expresses himself on some of the themes in "Of Poor B.B.": the wind will eat up the cities, unknown forces are slowly wiping out the Big Dipper, the big city, and the moon. The next poem, "Of the Crushing Weight of the Cities," is a fantastic vision of the speed with which skyscrapers are built:

> So short was the time
> That between morning and evening
> There was no noon
> And on old familiar ground
> Stood mountains of concrete.
>
> So kurz war die Zeit
> Daß zwischen Morgen und Abend
> Kein Mittag war
> Und schon standen auf altem, gewöhnetem Boden
> Gebirge Beton.
>
> (*GW* 8:130)

Then come poems on the speed of progress: society has advanced so fast that horses and old cars are already forgotten. Then there is "Come With Me to Georgia"

> Look at this town and see: it is old . . .
> Come with me to Georgia
> There we'll build a brand new town
> And when the town is too full of stone
> Then we just won't stay.

> Sieh diese Stadt und sieh: sie ist alt . . .
> Komm mit mir nach Georgia
> Dort bauen wir halt eine neue Stadt
> Und wenn diese Stadt zu viele Steine hat
> Dann bleiben wir nicht mehr da.

(GW 8:135)

(Two more stanzas substitute "women" and "ideas" for "city.") Dissatisfaction is setting in, not just fear of speed and catastrophe at the end but also the urge to flee—and flee again.

There is a "Mahagonny Song" here too (the other three were written several years before). Mahagonny is not just a city. It is the utopia of the philistine petty bourgeois or *Spießbürger*, as Arnolt Bronnen tells us;[54] in Brecht's symbology it is the nightmare of what the cities can become for people who have no purpose but keeping themselves occupied and spending their money, in short, *people who live exactly as he recommends, but without irony*, without having recognized the futility of it all. They are: the petty bourgeoisie.

About 1926 Brecht wrote a series of poems that he later collected under the name "From a Reader for City Dwellers." Most of them are very depressing dramatic monologues on how to survive in the city,[55] and at the same time they are portraits of the human waste and degradation in the cities. They are not funny.

There are many more poems on cities from this period, but their main themes are in the poems listed above. The two in which Brecht expresses most strongly both the cruel heroism of the cities' new age and the terrible impatience, leading to ruin, that the dream of progress produces are both from *Joe Fleischhacker*. It is important to know that the first, "On the Human Migration to the Big Cities at the Beginning of the Third Millenium," is spoken from the electric chair by the son of the poor Mitchell family, a man with the pioneer spirit whom Brecht characterizes thus in the play: "a beaming hard person goes like a knife through frisco eats his share of meat ruins

90

his share of women and lands hard on the electric chair" ("ein strahlender harter mensch geht wie ein messer durch frisko ißt seinen teil fleisch ruiniert sein teil frauen und landet schlag hart auf dem elektrischen stuhl") (BBA 524, 14). For Calvin Mitchell individual lives are not important at all; important is the new age, the feeling of pride at having had even a glance at this progress that is so much larger than man and yet man-made. He is the embodiment of an enthusiasm so ruthless that it becomes a kind of idealism, a way of achieving meaning beyond one's own life. Brecht in his mood of futility must still have felt some perverse attraction to this brutal heroism.

This is the poem spoken by Calvin Mitchell, quoted in its entirety because the theme is central to Brecht's thought and because many formulations found here are repeated in later plays:

Many say the age is old
But I have always known it is a new age
I tell you: not by themselves
Have houses grown for twenty years like mountains from ore
Many move each year to the cities as if they expected something
And on the laughing continents
The word is getting around that the great dreaded ocean
Is a little water.

I will die today, but I am convinced
The big cities now await the third millenium
It begins, it cannot be stopped, already today
It only requires one citizen, and a single man
Or woman is enough.

Of course many will die in the upheavals
But what is it for one person to be crushed by a table
If the cities are consolidating:
This new age may only last four years
It is the highest that will be given to humanity
On all continents one sees people who are foreign
The unhappy ones are no longer tolerated, for
To be human is a great affair.
Life will be considered too short.

Viele sagen, die Zeit sei alt
Aber ich habe immer gewußt, es sei eine neue Zeit
Ich sage euch: nicht von selber
Wachsen seit zwanzig Jahren Häuser wie Gebirge aus Erz
Viele ziehen mit jedem Jahr in die Städte, als erwarteten sie etwas
Und auf den lachenden Kontinenten

Spricht es sich herum, das große gefürchtete Meer
Sei ein kleines Wasser.

Ich sterbe heut, aber ich habe die Überzeugung
Die großen Städte erwarten jetzt das dritte Jahrtausend
Es fängt an, es ist nicht aufzuhalten, heute schon
Braucht es nur einen Bürger, und ein einziger Mann
Oder Frau reicht aus.
Freilich sterben viele bei den Umwälzungen
Aber was ist es, wenn einer von einem Tisch erdrückt wird
Wenn die Städte sich zusammenschließen:
Diese neue Zeit dauert vielleicht nur vier Jahre
Sie ist die höchste, die der Menschheit geschenkt wird
Auf allen Kontinenten sieht man Menschen, die fremd sind
Die Unglücklichen sind nicht mehr geduldet, denn
Menschsein ist eine große Sache.
Das Leben wird für zu kurz gelten.

(*GW* 8:143–44)

But not everyone who lives in the new age is able to be satisfied by merely being alive (for a while) in that heady time. The whole Mitchel family has moved from place to place in America, like the speaker of "Come with Me to Georgia," looking for more and more riches but finding less and less; finally they end up in Chicago starving, fighting each other with knives, and in the end freezing to death. They sing the song of modern dissatisfaction, "Song of a Family from the Savannah." It is the other side of the first song.

And once we had money and prospects
Work for the week and Saturday evening free
And no place was good enough for us.

Und wir hatten einst Geld und Aussichten
Arbeit die Woche und frei am Samstag abend
Und an allen Orten war es uns zu schlecht.

(*GW* 8:145)

These two poems, then, express Brecht's main interests in early 1926: the migration of humanity to the cities, the grandeur of a new age but also its cruelty, and a sense of futility and impending disaster. Added to this list was a newfound fascination with the stock market (and commodity market), which is expressed in the play fragments of 1924–26 but not in the poems. The city had now become the overriding image that collects all these themes into one complex, and as we have seen from Elisabeth Hauptmann's list of plans for 1926, the city was still identified completely with America.

Another American poem Brecht wrote in 1926 is very different, though. "Coals for Mike," the poem based on a passage in *Poor White* by Anderson, exists totally outside the world of the harsh cities. This poem is an interesting example of Brecht's technique of adaptation: in the context of the novel the paragraph on Widow McCoy, whose husband's old friends throw her coal from the passing train, is insignificant;[56] it is a tiny little vignette, one of those distracting details that critics would say destroys the unity of the novel. But for Brecht it was a found poem that he hardly changed at all; he moved the words around a little and wrote it from his own point of view as the discoverer of the little story, ending it with:

> This poem is dedicated to the friends
> Of the brakeman Mike McCoy
> (Died of too weak a lung
> On the coal trains of Ohio)
> For comradeship.

> Dieses Gedicht ist gewidmet den Kameraden
> Des Bremsers Mike McCoy
> (Gestorben wegen zu schwacher Lunge
> Auf den Kohlenzügen Ohios)
> Für Kameradschaft.

> > (*GW* 9:670)

It is the comradeship or friendliness that made the short passage jump out at Brecht the reader; later he might have called it proletarian solidarity. Friendliness is an important theme for Brecht, which we will not have an opportunity to discuss, since the plays about America are mostly about hard people. But if we think ahead to Gruscha and Shen Te and "The Legend of the Origin of the Book Dao De Jing,"[57] we realize that friendliness is one of the really positive values throughout Brecht's work, of course in an understated manner, without sentimentality. It is the necessary human antidote to the poison of the cities and alienation. It is also an aspect of Brecht's own personality that is mentioned strikingly often in reminiscences by people who knew him, which may come as a surprise to those who know only the severity of his plays.[58]

Oddly, Brecht chose not to publish this poem with others from that period that we have looked at; he saved it for the *Svendborg Poems*, most of which were written in the thirties. There it is in the

section called "Chronicles," which compares interestingly with the
section of the same name in the *Home Devotions*. In the *Home
Devotions* all the "Chronicles" are adventure stories, filled with the
decay of exotic landscapes—Brecht's early twenties attitude:

> One should browse through the third lesson (Chronicles) in times of raw
> natural forces. In times of raw natural forces (cloudbursts, snowstorms,
> bankruptcies, etc.) one should turn to the adventures of bold men and
> women on foreign continents.

> Die dritte Lektion (Chroniken) durchblättere man in den Zeiten der
> rohen Naturgewalten. In den Zeiten der rohen Naturgewalten
> (Regengüsse, Schneefälle, Bankrotte usw.) halte man sich an die
> Abenteuer kühner Männer und Frauen in fremden Erdteilen.[59]

The "Chronicles" of the *Svendborg Poems* are also about bold men
and women in foreign parts of the earth, but the tone is utterly
different: calm, certain of the worth of human beings and what they
are accomplishing, extremely simple in language, and unpreten-
tiously proud. "Dao De Jing" is here, and the well-known
"Questions of a Reading Worker," and "Appropriation of the Great
Metro by the Moscow Workers on April 27, 1935." These are, in
short, poems about the creation of a new person and new society, a
person and society of which Brecht wholly approves, without his
earlier irony. This was what he needed to pull him out of the
sarcastic and nihilistic hole he had dug by 1926. "Coals for Mike" is
proof that he already saw signs of a way out, but he did not know
what to name them. Another sign was his reaction to a notice he read
about a demonstration by unemployed and starving miners in
Budapest. He made a poem about it, around the same time as "Coals
for Mike," and he felt that it too did not belong in *Home Devotions*
with its poems about the city as jungle; he would like to save it for a
different collection, "that deals with the new person" ("die sich mit
dem neuen Menschen befaßt").[60]

But at that time Brecht probably could not have defined what he
meant by the new person. He had always been sympathetic with the
poor, and was beginning to see the necessity of their fighting for their
rights; and at the same time he was writing about economic
machinations of the rich, so with hindsight it is clear in which
direction his thoughts had to move. But it was not perfectly clear to
him at the time. As far as we can tell, the fragments of 1924–26 are

94

studies in the fascination of ruthless progress and big finance, but not clear indictments of them. The two later plays that absorb all this material, *Mahagonny* and *St. Joan of the Stockyards*, are very different in tone from the earlier fragments. But Brecht was not yet ready to write *Mahagonny* or *St. Joan*; as we work through the play fragments set in America, we will see that he was himself still partly caught up in the thrill of Calvin Mitchell's "new age."

We will look first at the two quasi-biblical fragments about building the cities, which relate to *Mahagonny*, and then at the two about big finance, which are later transformed into *St. Joan*.

"Man from Manhattan"

In 1924 Brecht worked on an opera about another kind of "new man," a representative of an earlier contradictory age. (Later he might have analyzed the new man of the poems mentioned above as the beginnings of socialist man in a capitalist society, and the new man of these play fragments as the beginnings of capitalist, progress-minded, urban man in a feudal or frontier society.) In fact, from *Drums in the Night* on he had portrayed historical periods of great change and confrontation, and the human types who cause, and are affected by, the changes; that is a large part of his fascination with the urbanization theme. This opera fragment, which exists in two versions called *Man from Manhattan* and *Sodom and Gomorrah*, is explicitly about the human misery caused by the "fever" of progress. The "man" of the title is tempted by the rich growth of the cities as Curtis Jadwin (about whom Brecht read in the same year) is tempted by the wheat market. The opera has a simple theme as Brecht summarizes it:

> The man is gripped by the fever of construction of the conquest of america and of the founding of cities so much that he can't think of the suffering of one single honest man.

> den mann erfaßt das fieber des aufbaus der eroberung amerikas und der gründung der städte so sehr daß er nicht an die leiden eines einzelnen ehrlichen mannes denken kann. (BBA 214, 76)

(In the *Sodom and Gomorrah* version it is a woman, with her *story* about the growth of America, that distracts the man.)

The situation is based on Schiller's ballad "Die Bürgschaft" ("The Guarantee") about which Brecht later wrote a satirical sonnet implying that morality is not as simple today as in Schiller's time

(*GW* 9:611)). But Brecht has asked changed the ending. In Schiller's version the man who has another to substitute for him returns. Brecht asks: What happens if the person who was supposed to die fails to return? What sort of diversion could hold him up and make him forget his bond? What kind of punishment would he eventually suffer, if any?

The story is: a man steals a horse in the prairie in Ohio. When he is caught, he must be executed, but he begs for time to go visit his father. In *Man from Manhattan* the father is dying in "Frisko," whereas in *Sodom and Gomorrah* he owes several railroad cars full of wheat to a "hard man." The thief can only be let free if another man acts as his security. This the owner of the horse, John Brown, the man from Manhattan, promises to do; although he does not know the thief, he trusts him as a matter of faith. The chorus warns him:

> John Brown do not do it.
> Do you know him then?
> The law must be fulfilled . . .

> Tu es nicht John Brown.
> Kennst du ihn denn?
> Das Gesetz muß erfüllt werden . . .

But John Brown answers:

> For he said it and I
> believe what he said
> For on this earth
> Where a man can't keep his word
> There is no place for John Brown . . .

> Denn er sagt es und ich
> glaube, was er sagt
> Denn auf dieser Erde
> Wo ein Mann nicht sein Wort hält
> Ist kein Platz für John Brown . . .

(BBA 214, 70)

The thief agrees to return before the moon changes once, and he runs off. He meets a friend who tells him his father has died; but he misses his ship (!) to return to Ohio because the friend's sister (Anne Smith) has stayed to keep him company, and told him "to cheer him

up the only story she knows namely the story of america   but in
the telling three months go by" ("um ihn zu erheitern die einzige
geschichte die sie weiß nämlich die geschichte amerikas   darüber
vergehen aber drei monate") (BBA 454, 96). He has fully forgotten
John Brown, and gives evasive answers when people come and ask
him about a man in Manhattan and a man in Ohio. The third time he
even denies his substitute. The substitute, John Brown, is put to
death.

In a notebook Brecht jotted down these lines for the man to say:

i've been seized by the fever
of city building and of oil
my thoughts were prairies and the trains to illinois
i forgot over the wheat from dakota
my father and mother and a man in manhattan

mich hat erfaßt das fieber
des städtebaus und des öls
meine gedanken waren prärien und die züge nach illinois
ich vergaß über den weizen von dakota
meinen vater und die mutter und einen mann in manhattan
(BBA 461, 58)

Three pages later in the bound notebook he noted plans for "mortimer fleischhacker" and a "mahagonny-opera" on a page dated July
1924. The similarity in theme of the three planned projects is clear
from the few lines spoken (presumably) by the thief in *Man from
Manhattan*.

Both the themes and the details of the opera are closely related to
Brecht's other American studies of 1924–26, and also to the previous
play *In the Jungle*. It is clearly part of the planned series on the
human migration to the big cities. The man (in the *Manhattan*
version) goes to "Frisko" and is seduced by it, like the son in
Fleischhacker; the son's song, "On the Human Migration to the Big
Cities at the Beginning of the Third Millenium," could just as well
have been included in *Man from Manhattan*. The electric chair
(man's own retribution) appears in both *Fleischhacker* and *Sodom
and Gomorrah*, as well as in *Mahagonny*. The poem "Song of a Man
in San Francisco" (1927?) is also remarkably similar in theme as well
as setting. Trapped by the fascinating growth of the city, the speaker

97

of that poem denies his wife in the East, just as the man from Manhattan forgets the good man who offered himself as a bond for him. That poems ends:

> Ten years go by quickly when houses are being built.
> I've been here ten years and want
> More. On paper
> I have a wife in the East
> Over the faraway land a roof
> But here
> There's something happening and fun and
> The city's still growing.

> Zehn Jahre vergehen rasch, wenn Häuser gebaut werden.
> Ich bin zehn Jahre da und habe Lust
> Nach mehr. Auf dem Papier
> Habe ich eine Frau im Osten
> Über dem fernen Boden ein Dach
> Aber hier
> Ist etwas los und Spaß, und
> Die Stadt wächst noch.

(GW 8:306)

Also, possible influence of *The Pit* is evident in the mention of wheat and in the plot, which involves the ruination of one good man by another.

By far the most important part of *Man from Manhattan* is the brilliant long poem "anne smith tells the story of the conquest of america." Both the cruelty and the fascination of America's development find clearer and deeper expression here than anywhere else in Brecht's work, for instance in the final lines:

> the states that were there however had the names:
> arkansas   connecticut   ohio
> new york   . new jersey and massachusetts
> and today still
> there are oil and men and it is said
> it is the greatest race on earth
> that lives now and they all
> build houses and say
> mine is longer and are there when there is oil
> ride in iron trains to the ends of the world
> grow wheat and sell it across the sea
> and die no longer unknown but are

98

an eternal race in the earth's
greatest age

es hießen aber die staaten die es gab:
arkansas   connecticut   ohio
new jork   new jersey und massachusetts
und heute noch
gibt es öl und männer und es heißt
es ist das größte geschlecht der erde
das jetzt lebt und alle
bauen häuser und sagen
meines ist länger und sind dabei wenn es öl gibt
fahren in eisernen zügen an die enden der Welt
bauen den waizen und verkaufen ihn überm meer
und sterben nicht mehr unbekannt sondern sind
eine ewige rasse in des erdballs
größter zeit

Anne Smith's poem also has a long section on the genocide
against the Indians, which Brecht had already mentioned with anger
in *Jungle*. She begins with the idyllic scene: grazing lands from
Atlantic to Pacific, nothing but red men, bears, and buffalo. But:

one day a man with white skin came
he roared and spewed out chunks of iron
when he was hungry and he was
always hungry

eines tages kam ein mann mit weißer haut
der krachte und spie eisenklötze
wenn er hunger hatte und er hatte
immer hunger

Three hundred years long the red man died; but the white man split
open the earth and brought forth oil, and the rivers produced gold

. . . and all around
the wooden huts grew out of rotting grass and
out of the wooden huts grew mountains of stone   they were
called cities   into them went
the white people and said on the earth
a new age had broken out that is called: the iron . . .
and with music and shrieking the white people sat
in the eternal prairies of stone . . .

99

        . . . . und ringsum
wuchsen aus faulendem gras die hölzernen hütten und
aus den hütten von holz gebirge aus stein die waren
städte geheißen   drin ging
das weiße volk und sagte auf dem erdball
sei angebrochen eine neue zeit die gennant wird: die
eiserne . . .
und mit musik und geschrei saß das weiße volk
in den ewigen prärien aus stein . . .

(BBA 214, 75)

Here we have the picture of the heroic city of the new age built on destruction of all that is natural. That is the setting of the play.

The plot outline of *Sodom and Gomorrah* concludes four years later with the thief still living on his farm with wife and child; "he smokes and instructs his son in the primer   honesty   courage but there are strange signs in the land" ("er raucht und gibt dem sohn unterricht in der fibel   ehrlichkeit   mut aber es gibt merkwürdige anzeichen im land"): the wheat does not grow and the woods are yellow in April. But the man fails to notice the signs, and so God must send a rain of fire "like over the corrupt sodom of old" ("wie über das verderbte sodom von alters") (BBA 424, 96). The family perish in the fire, their voices growing weaker as they call to each other, the man remembering his crime, the woman lamenting that she did not know who he was.

Brecht made occasional use of biblical parody and language in many of his plays, especially *The Threepenny Opera*, *St. Joan*, and *Galileo*;[61] but (except for his 1913 one-act drama *The Bible*) it is only in these unpublished fragments that the Bible became the main source for the entire play, and that he consistently imitated its style. An unpublished plot summary of *A Man's a Man*, which is like a writing-class exercise in Bible imitation, was probably also written at this time:

then they all helped together and made a false elephant . . . and so the man sold the elephant that was not his and false besides . . . and so they took him away with them in the same night

da halfen sie alle zusammen und machten einen falschen elefanten . . . also verkaufte der mann den elefanten der nicht sein war und dazu unecht . . . also nahmen sie ihn mit sich fort in derselben nacht
(BBA 348, 68)

100

But Brecht's interest in the Bible was not only stylistic. In these two fragments on Sodom and Gomorrah and the next, on the Flood, he explores the content and significance of the Old Testament. Specifically, his concentration on the Bible coincides with his concentration on destruction by natural catastrophe (and vice versa). This concurrence of preoccupations suggests that his premonition of disaster as the final result of precipituous progress and alienation from nature might be, either actually or symbolically, fear of retribution by an angry god. The biblical (or Judeo-Christian) tradition is the conservative force competing against man's urge for progress; it is the fear that holds us back from accepting the implications of our own breakthrough to a new age. Man can pretend to himself that he is free, but he knows the catastrophe will punish him for this *hybris*. Which means: he is afraid to be free and seeks restraining bonds and rules.

The similarity to the dramatic situation of *The Pit* is striking. Curtis Jadwin, daring to challenge single-handedly all the traders on the wheat market, holding the fortunes of America's farmers and Europe's consumers in his hands, sacrificing his friends, his wife, even his health and reason to become the controller of the country's finances, daring, that is, to ignore advice from traditional traders and to go further than ever man has gone, this hero is finally conquered by the wheat itself: by the forces of nature, which will not stand for such presumption.

Brecht frees himself of this remnant of Old Testament morality, too, by the time he is able to write full plays again. In *Mahagonny* the theme of natural catastrophes as retribution is brilliantly reversed as a typhoon makes a circle around the latter-day Sodom; and in *St. Joan* the analysis has become totally materialist: cold and misfortune are caused by the employers.

"The Flood"

It is in the radio play *The Flood* (with versions called *Decline and Fall of the Giant City Miami* and *Decline and Fall of the Paradise City Miami* [1926]) that we see Brecht work out the theme of natural catastrophe most thoroughly. Accompanying the pages of *Miami* in the Brecht Archive are many newspaper clippings from the *Chicago Daily News*, including one from 22 September 1926 that describes a huge hurricane that killed over a thousand people. With the article

101

there is a map showing the hurricane moving toward the town of Pensacola (Florida). This is obviously the source for the stage directions to the hurricane scene in *Mahagonny*:

> On the screens in the background only a geographical diagram is visible now, an arrow moving slowly toward Mahagonny, showing the path of the hurricane. . . . In Pensacola 11,000 dead. . . . The hurricane has gone around the city of Mahagonny and is continuing on its way.

> Auf den Tafeln des Hintergrundes sieht man nur noch eine geographische Zeichnung mit einem langsam auf Mahagonny zulaufenden Pfeil, der den Weg des Hurrikans anzeigt. . . . In Pensacola 11,000 Tote. . . . Der Hurrikan hat um die Stadt Mahagonny einen Bogen gemacht und setzt seinen Weg fort. (*GW* 2:530–31)

The rest of the source for that strange sequence in *Mahagonny* is likewise to be found among the materials to *Miami*; there are approximately twenty-five more pages of newspaper clippings about hurricanes. Those in German have technical details underlined, probably by Brecht; those in English, which all seem to be from the *Chicago Daily News*, have German translations, presumably prepared for Brecht by Elisabeth Hauptmann. Among the twelve pages of translations, the following can be found (the English is a retranslation):

> A part of Florida was spared by the hurricane. Inhabitants of a strip along the west coast, an elevation of 30 feet, which the storm bypassed [*sic*]. No one guessed the fate that had befallen Florida until the Sunday morning papers were missing and the storm on the east coast was given as the reason.

> THE PALACES OF THE RICH IN A HURRICANE

> THE STORM REACHES THE WEST COAST ["West coast" is strongly underlined by hand, and one of the destroyed cities is named "Hollywood!"]

> Southern Florida's beauty is no more.
>   If anyone imagines that Miami or southern Florida has collapsed because of the catastrophe, he is fooling himself. The spirit and mood in the disaster area are remarkable. No complaints. Sorrow to be sure, but optimism and determination to put the city back in shape quickly.
>   The only help that Miami needs is money and more money for reconstruction.

> Ein Teil Floridas wurde vom Hurrikan verschont. Einwohner eines Streifens an der Westküste, eine Erhöhung von 3 0 Fuß, um die der

102

Sturm herumging. Man ahnte nichts von dem Unglück das Florida betroffen hatte, bis die Zeitungen Sonntag früh ausbliében und man als Grund den Sturm an der Ostküste gab. (BBA 214, 27)

DIE PALÄSTE DER REICHEN IM HURRIKAN (BBA 214, 29)

DER STURM ERREICHT DIE WESTKÜSTE (BBA 214, 30)

Die Schönheit Südfloridas ist dahin.

Wenn sich jemand einbildet, daß Miami oder Südflorida zusammen-gebrochen ist durch das Unglück, so täuscht er sich. Der Geist und die Stimmung in dem Unglücksdistrikt sind bemerkenswert. Kein Klagen. Wohl Trauer, aber Optimismus und Entschlossenheit, die Stadt schnell wieder instand zu setzen.

Die einzige Hilfe, die Miami braucht, ist Geld und wieder Geld, um sich aufzubauen. (BBA 214, 32)

The details of Mahagonny's hurricane are not all that Brecht adopts from *Miami* materials; the miraculous escape of one city, the forced optimism of promoters and the city's need for "money and more money" are all elements of *Mahagonny* that come directly from *Miami* and its sources. It is obvious that *Decline and Fall of the Paradise City Miami* is a preliminary study for what becomes *Rise and Fall of the City of Mahagonny*. But it was definitely originally intended as a separate play, since the early (1927) version of *Mahagonny* contains no mention of hurricanes. The final *Rise and Fall of the City of Mahagonny* (1929) is in fact a fusion of *The Flood/Miami* and the *Mahagonny Song-Play*, with some gold rush mythology and miscellaneous old songs mixed in.

Exactly how Brecht intended to use the hurricane theme in *The Flood/Miami* itself is not clear; the plot synopsis (BBA 214, 23) does not get that far. It begins—in Brecht's opaque ironic style of those years—by stating that it is proof of the energy of the Romans that we still remember the destruction of Pompeii and the other Roman cities; their disaster has horrified men for 2,000 years, and the horror has produced a feeling of solidarity. For completely different reasons, writes Brecht, he is going to try to give some permanence to the memory of the destruction of the City of Paradise, Miami, which happened in "our time." It is scandalous that the San Francisco earthquake has already been forgotten. With that reference Brecht hints that he intends to write about a Miami that is destroyed by natural catastrophe.

The other extant paragraph of this plot summary betrays an

103

excellent knowledge of the real-estate swindles involved in building
the city of Miami; where Brecht got this knowledge we do not know.
He writes that, like Palm Beach, Miami was built, about ten years
before his writing, in an unbelievably short time on Florida's
swamps. A few farsighted people built a huge street through fertile
but unfirm lowlands and started selling the plots on both sides for
high prices. There were no inhabitants yet, but the ground was
gradually drained and divided into cities and streets. In New York
and other big cities, it was announced that the best land and best
people in the world would be in Florida.

The affinity to *Mahagonny* is clear, as well as to the books Brecht
had been reading about the growth of other American cities, and to
his increasing conviction that economic motives underlie history.

The pages of *The Flood*, the other version of the same play, are
written in verse. Brecht concentrates on the cities themselves as
characters in the drama of destruction; here he suddenly portrays
not the beginning of an age but its end. And yet he is writing about
the same time and the same cities, and using the same phrases:

> conversation of the rebuilt cities   they are
> indestructible

> in the years of the flood human types change
> "that is the greatest age humanity has experienced
> (the types get stronger bigger darker   they laugh . . .)

> in the final years epidemics of monstrous inventions
> proliferate   flying people appear   they achieve greater
> fame than people ever have
>   they fall in the water   laughter
> atheism increases

> gespräch der wiedererbauten städte   sie sind
> unzerstörbar
> > (BBA 214, 6)

> in den jahren der flut verändern sich die menschentypen
> "das ist die größte zeit die die menschheit erlebt hat
> (die typen werden stärker größer finsterer   sie lachen . . .)
> > (BBA 214, 17)

> in den letzten jahren verbreiten sich seuchen
> von ungeheuren erfindungen   flugmenschen treten
> auf   sie gelangen zu größerem ruhm als je zuvor

menschen   sie fallen ins wasser   gelächter
der atheismus nimmt zu
(BBA 214, 17)

There are two startling and important new developments here: the
first is a clear expression of the reverse side of the myth of the new
age and fast-growing cities: here the sense of disaster, which lurks in
most of the works that on the surface praise the new age, becomes
explicit and primary. Second, the disaster is identified with the Old
Testament pestilence and God's revenge through natural catastrophe, again specifically with Sodom and Gomorrah.

Ruined is the big city of Gomorrha
Since yesterday the big harbor Yokohama is just water
This morning the paradise city Miami disappeared
And now the powerful Sodom answers no more

Untergegangen ist die Großstadt Gomorrha
Seit gestern ist der große Hafen Jokohama nur mehr Wasser
Heute früh verschwand die Paradiesstadt Miami
Und nicht mehr antwortet jetzt das gewaltige Sodom
(BBA 214, 18)

In this strange anachronistic mixture, Brecht yokes together his own
symbology of American cities and biblical symbology, thereby
altering and commenting on both of them. The Old Testament
conception of sin is concretized into modern contexts ("concretization" in Brecht's terminology means showing the contemporary
parallels),[62] so that we may think of Sodom and Gomorrah as
having been punished for the sins of exploitation and fraud, not just
sins of the flesh. The Brechtian tradition of America—the greatest
age ever, monstrous inventions, greater fame than ever, larger and
stronger human types—receives a connotation of rushing toward
the apocalypse that it has not had before. Technology, the development of a new type of man, confidence are here revealed to be not
entirely positive. We know already, from the human alienation in
Jungle and the nihilistic *carpe diem* theme in the poetry with urban
or American contexts, that Brecht sensed a great deal of evil and
danger in this marvelous new age, but the juxtaposition with the Old
Testament makes the evil and danger explicit.

105

What is more, the floods are heading toward the Old World too:

> In the third month the nameless waters storm
> The mainland of Europe and a great fear spreads

> Im dritten Monat bestürmen die namenlosen Wasser
> Das Festland Europa und eine große Furcht breitet sich aus.
>
> (BBA 214, 18)

Here too the implication is obvious but important to Brecht's symbology: what happens in America is only an early sign of what will eventually happen in Europe as well; Europe is beginning to commit the same sins. America is the vanguard of the new age that will rejuvenate but also destroy the world.

The hurricanes and the Flood, together with the earthquakes that also appear in other parts of Brecht's work—but especially the hurricanes—have almost the function that the cold and snow have in Jensen's *Wheel* and the wheat has in Norris's *Pit*: nature is waiting to reclaim every bit of territory that man has conquered, and the higher the level of technology and subjugation of nature, the harder she will strike. Man's anguish, fear, and guilt that Brecht portrays here come close to the literary tradition of *hybris*. Having dared to challenge the gods of nature and explore further and further into the unknown and unnatural, possessing the insolence to proclaim that he is making a new age, and building boldly into the future without a backward glance at his origins, man lives with the anxiety that he is transgressing some eternal law; modern man feels as if he were sitting on the top of his tallest skyscraper with a thunderstorm approaching, realizing that he has forgotten to build a lightning rod. The cities are growing beyond the comprehension of the human beings who began to build them; some little detail absolutely necessary to survival will have been overlooked, and then lightning will strike. Such a detail could be: the ability to communicate with other human beings (*Jungle*), or the realization that nothing man-made is indestructible ("Of Poor B.B."), or some purpose in life other than making money at anyone's cost (*Dan Drew* and other plays to come).

Later, in *Mahagonny*, the detail that is forgotten in building up the city is that men cannot be restricted and still be happy. When the people of *Mahagonny* discover this "law of human happiness," in the night of terror, the hurricane makes an intentional detour

106

around their city. In *Mahagonny* the fear of punishment for *hybris*, of lurking natural catastrophe, is conquered by yet more *hybris*, by a temendous bluff with which the Mahagonny people plunge into a world completely of their own making; they accept all the consequences of making all their own rules, somewhere in the middle of nowhere, cut off from all tradition. *Mahagonny*, which makes the principal use of the symbol of natural catastrophe, is also the play that overcomes that threat, which has occupied Brecht's imagination since the first American poem, "Song of the Railroad Gang of Fort Donald." But *Mahagonny* goes further. In it, men themselves provide the catastrophe. Existential anxieties about nature's retribution against progress were unfounded; man is free to do whatever he wants and to create any kind of a world he wants; religion is dead, there is no punishment, "anything is allowed." And what man then creates is hell on earth (as in the "Play of God in Mahagonny" ["Spiel von Gott in Mahagonny"]).

"Dan Drew"

The two other American fragments of this period are completely different. Gone are the biblical language and the vast and surreal accounts of divine and natural retribution; instead we have more realist, small-scale studies of manipulation of the stock and commodity markets. Similar is the continuing theme of the building of the cities, and with them monopoly capitalism.

In *Dan Drew*, which Brecht worked on in 1925 just before *The Flood*, we are really dealing not so much with Brecht's ideas as with his adoption and adaptation of Bouck White's ideas. Nearly all the small details of Brecht's fragment are present in White's book, even down to use of the word "spikkilieren" by Drew ("speckilate" in English), the meetings in Delmonico's, and the ending of the work with a newspaper article. We do not know whether Brecht was serious about putting this play on the stage or whether it was more of an exercise for him; but it allows us the opportunity to see unusually precisely what interested him in a source on America and capitalism. Especially important are the impressions of New York and finance that stay with Brecht, not just for *Dan Drew*. White's *Drew* shows the growth of the city of Manhattan from the time when it looked like a Currier and Ives print—when pigs and cattle roamed the streets and the Bowery was a worthless swamp—to the age of the

107

modern metropolis with streetcars, electronics, and mass media. Brecht catches the change in the last scene he wrote, Scene 8:

WALL STREET TOTALLY TRANSFORMED
(the buildings are large and built to last many centuries. it is no longer the work of individuals; now many unknowns are walking around, among them, unrecognized, the old daniel drew)

DREW
see, that is the stock exchange. there from nine to four they do business. before, one knew all that went in and out of there, now one would have to have a giant head. that car belongs to old astor. he was once a simple man.

WALLSTRASSE GÄNZLICH VERÄNDERT
(die gebäude sind groß und für viele jahrhunderte gebaut. es ist nicht mehr das werk einzelner, sondern es gehen viel unbekannte umher, unter ihnen unerkannt der alte daniel drew)

DREW
siehst du das ist die börse. dort macht man von neun uhr bis vier uhr geschäfte. früher kannte man alle die da ein und ausgingen, jetzt müßte man dazu einen riesenkopf haben. dort steht der wagen des alten astor. er war einmal ein einfacher mann.

(BBA 194, 39)

This is parallel to the change in the Midwest shown by *Poor White*, and *The Pit* is of course another contribution to the complex on the growth of cities that Brecht was working on. Because he finally had a source that concentrated on New York instead of Chicago, Brecht abandoned Chicago as setting for one unfinished play, but this brief vacation did not last long. The only other significant use of New York is as the source of the mysterious letters from the Providence of finance in *St. Joan of the Stockyards*. The work on *Dan Drew* probably contributed to that image of New York, though naturally Wall Street is known to everyone without reading whole books on it.

Also reflected later in *St. Joan* is the close relationship between speculator and broker—Mauler and Slift—and their need for secrecy. White's Drew says:

A big operator's business has to be done on the quiet. The relationship between a Wall Street operator and his broker is a close one. In order to manipulate the market, you must keep mum while you are doing it. The broker is the only one besides yourself who knows what you're doing. He is in a position to give you away if he wants to. So I was glad to have a brokerage house that I could be confidential with.[63]

108

The Book of Daniel Drew also explains at length the difference between a bear and a bull in stock market jargon. Brecht uses this terminology often in *Fleischhacker*. In White's book the examples are Drew and Vanderbilt:

> Another difference between the Commodore and me was that he was by make-up a Bullish fellow, whereas most of my life I have been on the Bear side of the market. . . . Even in the darkest hours of the Civil War, he had lots of faith in the future of the country. He seemed to think that in America 'most any kind of stock would go up and be valuable if he only waited long enough.[64]

Brecht adapts this passage almost verbatim. He has Fisk say of Vanderbilt:

> it is a strange man
> he believes in america's future even if he loses everything.
> in the stock market he always says don't sell anything, everything you
>   have will become
> valuable, in america

> es ist ein komischer mann
> er glaubt an amerikas zukunft und wenn er alles verliert.
> er sagt auf der börse immer, nichts verkaufen, alles wird wertvoll was
> ihr habt, in amerika

(BBA 194, 15)

Vanderbilt, according to White, was such an altruist, so convinced his fortune was tied up in his country's fortune, that he gave the government a ship to help end the war. Drew rented ships to the government and was sorry when the war ended. As in Tarbell's book on Gary, we have here the clash of the new and old types of businessman; Drew's type is a dying strain. Bear tactics (preventing the economy from rising) were too upsetting to the economy as a whole, and in the long run unprofitable because unpredictable. It took a thick-skinned man to withstand the hatred that Drew's destructive tactics would bring on him, and in White's book Drew keeps insisting that he doesn't give a damn what people think of him. This too finds an echo in Mauler.

Brecht reproduces in his *Dan Drew* a lecture that Vanderbuilt gives Drew:

> VAND
> you are a strange bird uncle.
> you don't believe in america and you've seen it grow for seventy years

you are still a bear, and only want to gain from destruction.
it's better for you to quit.
the american way is lighter and freer than the way of other countries.
   nothing
holds us down.
a strong fellow can show his strength here and fetch his price.
new york has grown enormous. it can no longer be bought up by three
   men
and we individuals are small, because america grows.

VAND
sie sind ein wunderlicher kauz onkel.
sie glauben nicht an amerika und haben es siebzig jahre wachsen sehen
sie sind immer noch ein bär, und wollen nur bei der zerstörung verdien-
   en.
es ist besser sie ziehen sich zurück.
amerikas art ist leichter und freier wie die art andrer länder. wir sind
nicht beschwert durch irgendetwas.
ein kräftiger kerl kann hier seine kraft zeigen und holt sich seinen preis.
new jork ist ungeheuer groß geworden. nicht mehr so von drei männern
   aufzukaufen
und wir einzelne sind klein, weil amerika so wächst.

(BBA 194, 38)

Vanderbilt rides with America's future and gets rich *with* the country, whereas Drew cannot feel at home in the reconstruction period.
White's Drew complains:

> Somehow or other I have never been able to feel at home in this new age.
> The Country isn't what it used to be when I was in my prime, back in the
> fifties. There's a change in the very religion, to-day.[65]

Brecht's Drew:

> . . . this city grows, but it is godless and i believe it will be
> a hell. the ground is fertile for stone and suffering, that is
> my opinion, truly
>
> . . . diese stadt wächst, aber sie ist gottlos und ich glaube sie wird
> eine hölle. der boden ist fruchtbar für steine und elend, das ist
> meine ansicht, wahrhaftig

(BBA 194, 37)

Drew must be eliminated because his tactics not only make the
railroad unsafe to travel on (Brecht makes much of his turning the
rotten rails around rather than replacing them, and of the many
accidents) but also because in the long run he prevents it becoming

as valuable an enterprise as it might be. He is the acme of the old type of capitalist, investing purely for the sport and the money he can make, not for the growth of the company he directs. White has his Drew present his attitude toward public responsibility always with a pout and an insulted tone; accidents are a bother because people accuse you of murder and make your life uncomfortable. There was a bad accident on the Erie because of rotten rails, "which enemies tried to lay at my door."[66] Brecht combines this egocentric view of the railroad with the statements on the destructive nature of "bear" speculation, and has his Drew say,

> i care more for my wallet than for the railroad that i don't ride on
>
> meine tasche ist mir lieber wie die eisenbahn, auf der ich doch nicht fahre
> (BBA 194, 8)

and

> what is the erie to me, i feel justified in getting
> something out of it for myself, i think we'll turn the tracks around, then
> they'll be new again
>
> was geht mich die erie an, ich fühle mich berechtigt etwas für mich
> herauszuholen, ich denke wir drehen die schienen um, dann sind sie
> wieder neu
> (BBA 194, 22)

Even though the effect on "little people" is not shown, the effect of such maneuvers on the other stock operators and the railroad company was bad enough that they themselves had to get rid of Drew for the sake of stability. This too—the vulnerability of even the rich in capitalism—is recapitulated in *St. Joan* and also in *The Bread Store*. The capitalists themselves must find ways of protecting the interests of their own class. Brecht's *Dan Drew* is a preliminary study of the development later shown in *St. Joan*, from early individualistic and speculative capitalism to cooperative corporate capitalism—which is also the theme of Tarbell's *Life of Gary*. *Dan Drew* does not make the development very explicit. But it is the period of capitalism in which Brecht remained the most interested: the period of free competition, crisis, and early development of monopolies.

It is the period that allowed a rich man to be "self-made," like the "Self-Made Merchant" (*Dollarkönig* in the German version) whose

111

letters Lorimer penned for the *Saturday Evening Post*. The perspective of Lorimer's John Graham is very much like that of White's Dan Drew; both men are vigorous, humorous, self-confident; both books are documents, as Morley puts it in describing Lorimer's book, of "the wheelings and dealings of big business as told from the inside, and presented with no social comment on the justice or injustice of the situation. . . . Lorimer makes of the older Graham a figure who, although he represents the power of the dollar, is nevertheless an appealing, hard-headed, and wonderfully entertaining mentor."[67] White doubtless intended his Dan Drew to be somewhat more distasteful; nevertheless, the tone is remarkably similar.

In *The Book of Daniel Drew*, Drew takes a crybaby attitude to being thrown out of the Erie; he considers it quite unjust that old creditors should still ask for money and investigators should still hold him responsible. Brecht did not get around to writing text for that part but he did leave a plot outline:

```
7.  agreement vand + drew     add fisk + gould      drew must out
8.  gould and fisk ruin dan drew
9.  fisk dies      tweed goes to jail      gould isolated
10. end       drew is wiped out       lear      newspaper notice
```

```
7.  einigung vand + drew      hinzu fisk + gould      drew muß heraus
8.  gould und fisk ruinieren dan drew
9.  fisk stirbt      tweed kommt ins gefängnis      gould vereinsamt
10. schluß       drew wird erledigt       lear      zeitungsnotiz
```

(BBA 194, 67)

It says as much about Brecht's reinterpretation of Shakespeare as about his interpretation of Daniel Drew. He apparently saw Lear as an old Wall Street magnate, who has caused too many disasters through his egotism, and at the end of his life sits about and pouts and plays sick when anyone tries to hang responsibility on him! And Drew as a tragic hero, ruined through not being able to see past his own nose, pitiable perhaps but shaking kingdoms with his moods and ultimately becoming so destructive of order that he must be eliminated. This perspective that allowed Brecht to see very worldly relations in terms of the classics of literature and vice versa was a permanent part of his talent, long after the work on *Dan Drew*; parodies of Shakespeare, Schiller, and Goethe in *St. Joan* and *Arturo Ui* (which are both about economic relations) are only two examples.

Brecht portrays Drew's selfishness and ruthlessness, but it proves impossible for him really to imitate the pouting and self-righteous tone of this extraordinarily powerful man who really is just a child. He also makes no attempt to include the country-style metaphors and proverbs that characterize Drew's speech. The result is that the very quality that makes Bouck White's book fascinating is missing in Brecht's version; Brecht reproduces the mechanics of the stock market but not the naïvely candid self-portrait of Drew. This is probably the principal reason why he gave the project up; the texture of the play he was creating was simply too thin. Since Elisabeth Hauptmann said he worked on *Drew* and *Fleischhacker* simultaneously, he may also have stopped working on *Drew* for the same reason he stopped *Fleischhaker*, namely, because the stock market did not make sense to him. And, as we mentioned before, Myers's criticism of using individualist sensationalism to replace class analysis may possibly have given him pause.

"Joe Fleischhacker"

Brecht put most of his energy in 1926 into *Joe Fleischhacker*, which shows both the machinations of market manipulators and their effect on the little people caught without means in the age of progress. *Fleischhacker* shows a clear conflict between the classes and also combines many themes of the fragments and poems of this period.

Based on the financial manipulations in *The Pit*, it is partly intended as another play in the series on the conflict between the new and the old, with catastrophe as the punishment for too daring acceptance of the new. However, that is a secondary theme in the fragmentary scenes Brecht put down on paper: it is evident in the song on the "Human Migration to the Big Cities," which expresses one character's total involvement in the new age, and in the notes on "NATURE AND BEHAVIOR OF A HURRICANE" (see below, page 121). The Mitchel family, before migrating to Chicago, has been hit by a big wind described in the scene "Hurricane over Texas" ("Orkan über Texas"). This family belongs to the long line of persons Brecht read and wrote about who come from the prairie to the city to make their fortune but end up in ruin instead. Their fate is not very different from that of the Garga family.

It is not clear from the notes Brecht completed what the connection between the Mitchel family and Joe Fleischhacker himself was supposed to be. The Mitchels are apparently robbed and then ruined in the war, but what Fleischhacker had to do with their ruin is impossible to tell. The two plots seem to run parallel in alternate scenes. Here is Brecht's outline of the plot:

1 mitchel family's move to the metropolis chicago
2 at their market j fleischhacker steps forward with a group of bulls who are buying up the grain
3 robbery of the mitchel family on the first day
4 fleischhacker's betrayal aided by rain
5 ruin of the mitchel family in invasion
6 lasting rain and incomprehensible fear confuses fl   he secretly becomes a bull and comes into a corner
    radio   strike
7 death of the mitchel family
8 fleischhacker's great corner
9 calvin mitchel's speech and death
10 the wheat battle
11 end
12
13

1 einzug der familie mitchel in die große stadt chikago
2 an deren markt hervortritt j fleischhacker mit einer gruppe bullen die das getreide aufkaufen
3 beraubung der mitchels am ersten tag
4 fleischhackers verrat durch regen begünstigt
5 zerfall der familie mitchel in invasion
6 andauernder regen und unverständige furcht beirrt fl   er wird heimlich bulle und gerät in einen corner
    radio   streik
7 tod der familie mitchel
8 fleischhackers großer corner
9 calvin mitchels rede und tod
10 die waizenschlacht
11 ende
12
13

(BBA 678, 9)

(Note that in *The Bread Store* there is a "bread battle," doubtless inspired by the "wheat battle" here.)

As in so many cases, Brecht combines two plays he has been working on to make one. In deciding to dramatize *The Pit*, he must have felt that Norris's abstract laments about the ruin of poor farmer families through wheat speculation should be concretized in

114

one example, and he simply interlaced an old play he had abandoned with the *Pit* plot. There is only one page extant from this old play, called "A FAMILY FROM THE SAVANNAH: HISTORY IN ELEVEN SCENES":

a farmer family   father mother son
2 daughters baby with car and furniture
on the road to san francisco

father
because of a bad harvest in the wheat district
caused by floods rain drought
lasting three years after 2 lost
trials against the northsouthern
we started out two weeks ago
in the southern dakota and are coming
six souls with furniture and 500 dollars
after [to?] the big cities of the eastern atlantic
to san francisco to try our luck

eine farmerfamilie   vater mutter sohn
2 töchter baby mit auto und hausrat
auf der straße nach san franzisko

vater
wegen mißernt im waizendistrikt
verursacht durch hochwasser regen dürre
drei jahre durch nach 2 verlorenen
prozessen gegen die nordsüdliche
sind wir vor vierzehn tagen aufgebrochen
im südlichen dakota und kommen
6 seelen hoch mit hausrat und 500 dollars
nach den großen städten des östlichen atlantik
nach san franzisko unser glück zu versuchen

(BBA 524, 92)

This tiny fragment, written on very old paper, is clearly part of the series on migration to the great cities; but Brecht cannot have used *Poor White* as the model for the story of the family, because he read that book about Easter 1926 but started work on *Fleischhacker* in 1924. But it has similarities with *The Octopus* by Norris, the first volume of what would have been a trilogy on wheat, had Norris not died (in 1902) after completing the second volume, *The Pit*. In Germany the two books were published as a single work called *Das Epos des Weizens* (*The Epic of Wheat*); part one (1907) had the title *Der Oktopus: Eine Geschichte aus Kalifornien* (*The Octopus: A*

Story from California, and part two (1912), *Die Getreidebörse: Eine Geschichte aus Chikago* (*The Grain Exchange: A Story from Chicago*). Brecht's only reference to his source is the heading of a page of notes: "FL   From *Wheat*" ("FL   Aus 'Weizen' ") (BBA 524, 117). *Weizen* is the name of the whole trilogy in Germany, and *Weizen* was to be the name of Piscator's planned production of Brecht's play. Furthermore, Helene Weigel remembered *Octopus* as one of the early books Brecht read on America. So the usual assumption that *The Pit* was the only source is apparently wrong; Brecht probably read the first book, *Octopus*, first. However, it is clear that *The Pit* made a far stronger impression on him.

The *Octopus* is set entirely in California, and tells the story of the bitter fight of wheat ranchers against the railroads, which destroyed land and men and women. It is similar to *The Pit* (though more extravagantly written) in that the wheat itself—life, nature—is the real victor; nature's will is done through men, crushing (literally, in one scene) indifferently those who defy it.[68] The book ends on a rapturous note of praise to the wheat and the eternal principle of life, but individual quiet farming families have been destroyed. Several details in the farmer family's history in Brecht's *Family from the Savannah* (later *Joe Fleischhacker*) can be found in *Octopus*. The terrible legal battle that builds the plot of *Octopus* is against the Pacific and Southwestern Railroad, in Brecht the Northsouthern; and in *Octopus*, too, bad harvests are a problem.

Brecht's geography in this early fragment is nonchalant, to say the least; later when he incorporates this scene into *Fleischhacker*, he makes some corrections, but they are not much better. Now the family has left Lake Michigan and is moving with $7,000 cash to the great cities of the eastern continent, beginning with Chicago. It has taken them fourteen days to get from Lake Michigan to Chicago. Brecht of course did not care at all about such inaccuracies; he may have used them purposely to emphasize the mythical—or, better, allegorical—purpose of the American setting. But in the "Song of a Family from the Savannah" (*GW* 8:144–45), he does manage to combine the two routes: there they start in the savannah with wheat, move to San Francisco with a motor shop and jazz, move then to Massachusetts with an oil field (!) and a drill—and then to Chicago with nothing.

116

They are very confident on their way to the city: they come not only to try their luck but (in chorus):

> to place a penny and
> to cut out our piece of meat [flesh]
> and to show them how money is made where we come from
> this chicago had better be on its guard
> that people of our breed don't butcher it like cattle
> before evening comes
> and hang its hide up to dry
> JM
> the big cities they say are dangerous
> but kind to enterprising people
> FAMILY
> we are such people

> einen penny zu setzen und
> unser stück fleisch herauszuschneiden
> und ihnen zu zeigen wie man geld macht bei uns zuhause
> dieses chicago soll auf seiner hut sein
> damit nicht leute unseres schlages es ausnehmen wie ein rind
> vor es abend wird
> und hängen auf zum trocknen seine haut
> JM
> die großen städte heißt es sind gefährlich
> aber günstig unternehmenden leuten
> FAMILIE
> solche leute sind wir

(BBA 524, 2)

This is the very blustering confidence that makes America symbol of the new age for Europeans; it is the sense of success and purpose that builds the great cities. But it is also suspiciously like the optimism with which a European family lands on American shores in *The Jungle*, and for the Mitchel family too the dream is short-lived. Brecht outlines the story of their ruin:

1 francis the son goes ahead to seek quarters
2 he earns
3 the family waiting for him loses everything they have in 5 minutes   the milkman takes up their cause

the milkman is a poor devil who takes nothing from them except what he needs to eat   he takes everything   he guides them for that and sells each piece of advice

117

the son francis a beaming hard person goes like a knife through san francisco eats his share of flesh ruins his share of women and lands hard and fast in the electric chair

one daughter leaves right away   the other incomprehensibly indolent doesn't want to do anything and is sold by her family

the boy leaves the last three who at the end were mowing each other down with knives in the night between saturday and sunday that preceded the end of the november strike by the electric workers   he wanders around through the whole icy night and in the morning he doesn't return to see about them

since they have certainly frozen to death
i can't look at it it must be horrible and
wouldn't help them any more

1 francis der sohn geht voraus quartier zu suchen
2 er verdient
3 die familie auf ihn wartend verliert all das ihre in 5 minuten   der milchmann nimmt sich ihrer an

der milchmann ist ein armer teufel der nichts von ihnen nimmt außer dem was er zum essen braucht   er nimmt sie ganz aus   er führt sie dafür und verkauft jeden ratschlag

der sohn franzis ein strahlender harter mensch geht wie ein messer durch frisko ißt seinen teil fleisch ruiniert sein teil frauen und landet schlag hart auf dem elektrischen stuhl

eine tochter geht gleich weg   die andere von rätselhafter indolenz will nichts tun und wird verkauft von ihrer familie

der knabe verläßt die letzten drei die die letzte zeit mit messern sich gegenseitig niedersichelten in der nacht von samstag auf sonntag die dem ende des novemberstreiks der elektrizitätsarbeiter voranging   er wandert die ganze eisige nacht und kehrt am morgen nicht mehr um nach ihnen zu sehen

da sie ja doch bestimmt erfroren sind
ich kanns nicht sehn sist sicher schrecklich auch
nützt ihnen nicht mehr

(BBA 524, 14)

The son Francis (later Calvin) behaves very like the man in *Man from Manhattan*/*Sodom and Gomorrah* who deserts a friend because he is fascinated by San Francisco, progress, money, and women; here he himself lands in the electric chair, and it is the family he betrayed that is hit by catastrophe. There are other echoes of works we already know: a strike of electricity workers on an icy night in Chicago sounds very much like *The Wheel*; the son deserting the family because he cannot bear to see the terrible state they are in is like *The Jungle* and Brecht's *In the Jungle*. And in the fate of the indolent daughter there is a hint of what is to come in *The Seven Deadly Sins of the Petty Bourgeoisie* (1933), also set in America.

Brecht intends the story of the family to be sentimental, as we see from a very interesting note he made for himself about the *tone* of the play. Here we not only see him follow his suggestion (for *Jungle*) to indicate the locality by simply placing a picture on the wall; we also see him define consciously his own characteristic style. His precise use of words, his mixture of entertainment and matter-of-factness do not come completely effortlessly; he has to plan to write that way and be able to describe it. Note that the description fits the style of *Mahagonny* also:

gray colorless
things
fleischhacker flat as a pebble
in the back a photograph of chicago
all characters submitted to a hard verdict
every word unassailable as a coin
a physical money story in between sentimental family story from dime
    novel
the outline somewhat lumpy not too composed
spreading good spirits
cheap
with a lot in it   flat
bible

grau farblos
sachen
fleischhacker platt wie ein kieselstein
hinten fotografie von chikago
alle figuren hartem urteil empfohlen
jedes wort unangreifbar wie ein geldstück
eine physikalische geldgeschichte dazwischen sentimentale
familiengeschichte aus groschenroman
etwas klotzig der aufriß nicht zu sehr komponiert
gute laune verbreitend
billig
mit viel drin   flach
bibel

                               (BBA 524, 69)

119

From the point of view of the small people who have put all their faith in progress, America, and money and are then ruined, a financial disaster is like a natural catastrophe, subject to the laws of physics. One minute they are climbing upward and full of the optimism of the rich country, and in five minutes they have lost everything. Brecht has them believe that the laws of finance are too complicated for anyone to understand; that they are like natural laws, and subject to occasional unpredictable eruptions. This fatal ignorance, the acceptance of the myth of man's subjugation to inscrutable economic laws, is made poetry and made explicit in *St. Joan*:

> Alas! Eternally impenetrable
> Are the eternal laws
> Of human economy!
> Without warning
> The volcano opens and lays waste the region!

> Wehe! Ewig undurchsichtig
> Sind die ewigen Gesetze
> Der menschlichen Wirtschaft!
> Ohne Warnung
> Öffnet sich der Vulkan und verwüstet die Gegend!
>
> (*GW* 2:735)

The joke in the later play is of course that it is no law of nature but Mauler that has caused the disappearance of all the cattle, and that joke is much of what *St. Joan* is about. The reason *Joe Fleischhacker* was never finished is precisely because Brecht did not understand the functioning of the market well enough to make such a clear statement; he wanted to write a play that explained economic laws and could not do it because they did not make sense to him. In an unpublished foreword to *Fleischhacker*, he writes exclusively about money; as a beginner in the study of economics, he simplifies economic relations to money relations, assuming money as a cause: "money is something very important   this is generally recognized however only a few people admit it," ("das geld ist etwas sehr wichtiges   dies wird allegemein anerkannt jedoch ist es nur wenigen leuten recht"); people are ashamed to say they did anything for the sake of money, he continues, and

that's why everything that occurs around money is almost unknown and in many cases that which is unknown about things because it has to do with money is much more significant than that which is known about them   this causes a false impression to arise

darum sind alle dinge die sich um das geld herum abspielen wenig bekannt und von vielen dingen ist das was über sie unbekannt ist weil es mit geld zusammenhängt viel bezeichnender als das was über sie bekannt ist   dadurch entsteht ein falscher eindruck

(BBA 348, 63)

Although Brecht himself had, to a certain extent, a "false impression," the danger he describes in not understanding money (i.e., economics) certainly applies to the Mitchel family. Because of their naïveté they never know what hit them; it is not only like a volcano (the image from the *St. Joan* passage) but also like a hurricane. This is why among the materials to *Fleischhacker* there are the notes on the

NATURE AND BEHAVIOR OF A HURRICANE:
1) certain signs announce it   but one doesn't know yet how it will move
2) from the beginning, it has a direction one sees it coming toward one
3) to the left and right the houses are still standing

WESEN UND ART EINES HURRIKANS:
1) gewisse anzeichen künden ihn an   jedoch weiß man noch nicht wie er sich bewegen wird
2) vom beginn an hat er eine richtung man sieht ihn auf sich zukommen
3) links und rechts stehen die häuser noch (BBA 524, 126)

Bankruptcy, like a hurricane, seems to select its victims and bear down on them leaving others standing perfectly whole. For the Mitchells it is a complete surprise; speculators can see it coming— they know the signs that the market will move one way or another— but they too may be helpless to escape it.

Brecht uses the word *hurricane* specifically to apply to the catastrophe that destroys the Mitchels, in another memorandum to himself:

peculiarity of money catastrophes
the hurricane that the mitchel family comes into must be as sober and cold as possible . . . it is showing precisely this thin invisible destructive power of money that is so terrible insufficient information

121

ineptitude too little or too much ability to adjust stand in the place of devastating feelings   impossibility of communication . . . the terrible precariousness of the giant cities   that is the battlefield

eigenartigkeit von geldkatastrophen
der hurrikan in den die familie mitchel kommt muß so nüchtern und kalt wie möglich sein . . . es ist gerade diese dünne unsichtbare zerstörende macht des geldes zu zeigen die so furchtbar ist mangelnde information geringe eignung zuwenig oder zuviel anpassungsfähigkeit stehen anstelle von verheerenden gefühlen   unmöglichkeit der verständigung . . . die entsetzliche unsicherheit der riesenstädte   das ist das schlachtfeld (BBA 524, 21)

It is a battlefield he wishes to show, but the war that is fought there is without the emotions of a battle; it is the abstraction *money* that destroys, not human beings, and so there is no visible enemy to fight against. And destruction comes like a hurricane out of the clear blue sky; how can the abstraction money suddenly turn into a destructive force leaving dead, starving, and prostituted victims in its wake? How does the force of a hurricane arise out of still air?

It was to answer this question that Brecht wrote the play: not primarily to show the effect on the Mitchels of belief in the myth of getting rich, but to study the mechanisms of the commodity exchange. Most of the many pages of notes and few pages of finished text are on the subject of the wheat exchange, which Brecht felt was leading him to an understanding of the *primum mobile* of the subjects he had hitherto considered most important: social struggle, building up of industry, war.

But the wheat exchange is not so easy to understand. The financial action in *The Pit* is fascinating drama and made a strong impression on Brecht, but it by no means makes the functioning of the wheat exchange completely clear. It leaves the neophyte with small questions like: what does it mean to sell short? how does one "cover" one's sales? how do bears and bulls operate? *where* is all the wheat the speculators buy?—and with vaguer large questions like: *why* does it work this way? how can men who never even see the wheat control it? And so there are pages of notes to *Fleischhacker* on which Brecht copied down definitions and quotations from Norris's book. On the page with the heading "FL   From *Wheat*" ("FL   Aus 'Weizen' ") we find

Corner—buy up the entire supply
Lambs = small businessmen.
Bears, who tore the bulls down with their teeth.
Scalper = someone who sells below price.
Iowa, Kansas, Illinois, Ohio, Indiana, Nebraska (one single immense wheatfield)

Corner—das ganze Angebot aufkaufen
Lämmer = kleine Geschäftsleute.
Bären, die mit ihren Gebissen die Bullen niederrissen.
Skalper = jemand der unter Preis verkauft
Iowa, Kansas, Illinois, Ohio, Indiana, Nebraska (ein einziges unge-heueres Weizenfeld)

(BBA 524, 117)

which is information taken directly from *The Pit* (probably by Hauptmann: it is typed with capitals, unlike Brecht's usual practice). The following passage is clearly one of the sources:

the Bears strong of grip, tenacious of jaw, capable of pulling down the strongest Bull. . . . the "outsiders," the "public"—the Lambs . . . whom Bear and Bull did not so much as condescend to notice, but who, in their mutual struggle of horn and claw, they crushed to death by the mere rolling of their bodies. (*The Pit*, p. 75)

Another source is Norris's list of the states sending in reports of bad crops expected: Iowa, Kansas, Illinois, Ohio, Indiana, ending with:

But more especially Jadwin watched Nebraska, that state which is one single vast wheat field. How would Nebraska do, Nebraska which alone might feed an entire nation? (P. 183)

In a clarification for himself of part of the plot, Brecht also quotes directly from Norris the phrases in quotation marks:

When the whole bear clique wants to make cover purchases, suddenly there's no more wheat to be had. "Someone owns a gigantic pile of wheat that's not coming to the market, Chicago's visible supply is cornered." J wants to stop this huge increase in wheat farming by reports in the newspapers he has bought. . . . *must* now buy and buy: "the wheat has cornered me." the moment he stops buying the price must go down.

Als die gesamte Bärenklique dann Deckungskäufe machen will ist auf einmal kein Weizen mehr zu haben. "Jemand besitzt einen riesigen haufen weizen der nicht auf den markt kommt, die sichtbare versorgung chicagos ist gecornert". . . . Diese ungeheure zunahme des weizen-baus will J stoppen durch berichte in den von ihm aufgekauften zeitun-

gen. . . . *muß* jetzt kaufen und kaufen: "der weizen hat mich gecornert". im moment wo er nicht mehr kauft muß preis heruntergehen.
(BBA 524, 103)

The sources of the above quotations are in Norris's description of
Curtis Jadwin's corner. The bear clique tries to sell, bringing the
price down, and then buy again, having made a cash profit. But:
"The instant they tried to cover there was no wheat for sale" (p. 312).
The leader of the group, Crookes, muses:

> Somebody has a great big line of wheat that is not on the market at all.
> Somebody has got all the wheat there is. I guess I know his name. I guess
> the visible supply of May wheat in the Chicago market is cornered. (P.
> 313)

Jadwin (whose friends call him "J.," like Brecht's occasional *Jae*
Fleischhacker)[69] has engineered a corner; his problem now is that
with the price so artificially high he has to do something to prevent
farmers from planting unprecedentedly large crops; in fact, it is the
new crop that finally ruins him because he is trapped into having to
buy it all up to maintain his corner. He remarks often to his wife and
his broker that he has not cornered the wheat, it has cornered him.[70]

Brecht spent the most time figuring out how a corner works: in
three different sets of notes he tries to think of all the aspects of such
a deal. So, for instance:

> Difficulties of a corner
> What enemies does F1 make?
> What friends   "   "   " ?
> Where must he get involved?
> Relation to bank, railroad, farm, press . . .
> *Whom does he ruin?*
>
> Schwierigkeiten eines Corners
> Welche Feinde macht sich F1?
> Welche Freunde "   "   " ?
> Wo muß er sich hereinmischen?
> Verhältnis zur Bank, Eisenbahn, Farm, Presse . . .
> *Wen ruiniert er?* (BBA 524, 84)

Another similar list of considerations (also typed and perhaps
compiled by an assistant) is more extensive:

> Bringing about a corner is very difficult. 1. getting warehouses,
> 2. getting the money

124

3. getting the means of transportation
4. paying the rent
5. paying the interest
6. thwarting the intrigues of the railroads
7. bribing the meddling press

Den Corner zustande zu bringen ist sehr schwer. 1. Lagerhäuser zu
  bekommen,
2. das Geld zu bekommen
3. die Transportmittel zu bekommen
4. die Miete zu zahlen
5. die Zinsen zu zahlen
6. die Intriguen der Eisenbahnen zu vereiteln
7. die sich einmischende Presse zu bestechen

(BBA 524, 113)

In *The Pit* Jadwin and his broker discuss similar problems in
securing a corner: paying storage, bribing warehouse people, buying
up newspapers, bargaining with railroads—and of course keeping
the whole thing secret and keeping up to date on every hint of new
developments in supply and demand.[71] (Both Fleischhacker and
Mauler in *St. Joan* bribe and use the newspapers.)

There are also more subtle echoes of *The Pit*, in the characteriza-
tions. Brecht invents two little epithets, presumably for his own
characters, that describe succinctly what happens to Curtis and
Laura Jadwin:

> of a lonely man
>   he ate alone
>   or
>   he slept together and ate alone
> of a woman
>   she has many pasts and no future
>
> von einem einsamen
>   er aß allein
>   oder
>   er schlief zu zweit und aß allein
> von einer frau
>   sie hat viele vergangenheiten und keine
>   zukunft

(BBA 524, 32)

Fleischhacker himself is characterized by the same strange pride
(*hybris?*) that grasps Jadwin when he finds himself in control of the
market:

125

F1. No one knows how much wheat there is in the world. . . . Not considering whether it's possible, I will now, whether it is possible or not, simply do as good a job of buying that wheat as I am a good man.

Fl. Niemand weiß, wieviel Getreide auf der Welt ist. . . . Betrachtend nicht obs möglich ist, will ich jetzt, obs möglich ist oder nicht, einfach so gut einkaufen solches Getreide als ich ein guter Mann bin. (BBA 524, 10)

In the same passage Brecht compares the speculator in wheat to a poker player who never looks at his own cards but only watches the faces of the other players; it is an apt image and shows that Brecht already grasped an essential of speculation in commodities: there is never any contact with the commodity itself; the speculator deals purely in abstractions.

Fleischhacker demonstrates the same boldness when he transfers from being a bull to being a bear, deserting his partner and joining a new clique. Jadwin makes a similar move but without the same style; Fleischhacker's cold-bloodedness is reminiscent of Shlink's firing a trusted old employee for the sake of a new fascination (Shlink's fascination is the struggle against a man, Fleischhacker's is the struggle for money):

> joe
>> because now the frosted-glass face of this chicago
>> is turned toward me jae fleischhacker
>> i obey the wish of monstrous chicago
>> to change at such a height
>> to increase in virtue and
>> to test before i climb higher how
>> healthy i am and so
>> GOES OVER TO MILK
>> today i will chop you my right hand
>> still fairly useful once indispensible
>> you dirty hand from murky times off
> shaw
>> 's more than we expected jae
> brown
>> 's good
> table
>> 's dangerously good
>
> joe
>> weil jetzt das milchglasige gesicht dieses chikago
>> auf mich jae fleischhacker gerichtet ist
>> gehorch ich dem wunsch des ungeheuren chikago

126

anders zu werden auf solcher höh
an tugend zuzunehmen und
mich zu prüfen eh ich weiter steig wie
gesund ich bin und drum
GEHT AUF MILK ZU
hacke ich jetzt dich meine rechte hand
heute noch nützlich einst ganz unentbehrlich
schmutzige hand aus trüber zeit heut ab
shaw
   sist mehr als wir erwarten jae
brown
   sist gut
table
   sist gefährlich gut

                             (BBA 524, 5)

In this, the first scene in the Fleischhacker plot (scene two of the play), Chicago again plays the role of a living character; Fleischhacker imagines it is the city itself that gives him his strength and challenges him to push his profits further and further. The city of Chicago (like other cities and like America) is organized on the principle of a social-Darwinist struggle for money; that is the very essence of its existence, and Joe is simply fulfilling its laws. He is to become the executor of the city's will. He speaks of an obligation to the city to be virtuous and to prove himself in the same terms as an obligation to God.

Another version of the same scene is set surprisingly not in the *Weizenbörse*—Board of Trade—but in an office near the Chicago stockyards. Here, instead of obeying the wish of Chicago, Joe says he will shake off "the stockyards' brutal blow from behind" ("des schlachthofs rohen nackenschlag") (BBA 524, 42). There is no mention of wheat, and the names of the other characters are unfamiliar. The stockyard scene is titled "scene i," which could mean Brecht wrote it before deciding to combine the Fleischhacker story with the Mitchel family story. Or it could be a *later* adaptation of the Fleischhacker theme to the meat industry, the embryo of *St. Joan of the Stockyards*. Fleischhacker's name suggests, however, that Brecht's original conception of the play might have dealt with meat, not wheat (perhaps based on the Lorimer book), but every reference we know of says it was to be a play about the Chicago wheat market; often it is called *Weizen*. So it is impossible to tell when the thought occurred to Brecht to write a play about the capitalist relations of the meat industry; but it is clear that *St. Joan* became the home of the theme of commodity speculation that never was completed in *Joe Fleischhacker*.

The actual financial speculations and mechanisms are very similar in the two plays. That is evident from a page in the *Fleischhacker* materials (BBA 524, 24) on which Brecht figures out the arithmetic of Joe's transactions. Most but not all of that scenario is from *The Pit*; the rain, for instance, is not. For all his rhapsody over the forces of nature, Norris mentions very little about the factors that control the supply of wheat (which is the principal information causing fluctuations in market price; speculators slavishly follow statistics on expected crop size).

But Norris was not Brecht's only source of information. He had contemporary history as inspiration and teacher too. In 1925 one of history's most infamous wheat corners was engineered by the Barnes pool in Chicago. In that year the wheat exchange was twice as old as when Norris wrote about it (it was founded in Chicago in 1877), but its methods had not changed at all. During the two months the Barnes group controlled the market, daily wheat sales in Chicago sometimes reached $380 million, or several times the daily volume of sales on the New York Stock Exchange.[72] The Chicago wheat exchange is in fact even in normal times the largest exchange in the world, both in price variation and in sales volume. Considering that it is also an artificial and unnecessary injection of speculation into the normal mechanism of production and consumption (wheat prices are determined by the gambling of persons with no practical connection whatever to wheat) and that this speculation directly affects farmers and consumers through the whole world, it is easy to see why Brecht chose wheat as the vehicle for his study of the inmost workings of finance and capitalism.

The worldwide consequences of activities in the Chicago Board of Trade were particularly evident during the Barnes corner; American and European newspapers were full of the news of the deal, which was reported with the suspense of a national sports match. There are pages and pages of clippings with the materials to *Fleischhacker*. They date from 1925 to 1929; most of them however are from 1926–27. This is an important indication of the period in which Brecht worked on *Fleischhacker* and related subjects. Brecht intended *Fleischhacker* to be set closer to Norris's time—the title of one page of text is "THE GREAT WHEAT CRISIS IN THE CHICAGO BOARD OF TRADE IN THE YEAR 1908" ("DIE GROSSE WAIZENKRISE AN DER CHIKAGOER WAIZEN-BÖRSE IM JAHRE 1908") (BBA 524, 44)—but he was dissatisfied with the information in *The Pit* and went on an extensive search for deeper explanations from contemporary sources. (The turn of the century was also the original setting for *St. Joan*.)

One of the earliest clippings, with underlining by Brecht or an assistant, is from the *Neues Wiener Journal* (*New Viennese Journal*) of 10 March 1925. Brecht studied it carefully, and incorporated it. This article identifies the Barnes group as cause of the boom in wheat, describes the very complex maneuvering of the group and its crash because of the tactics of the bears, who forced Barnes to bring out all his supply of wheat. When all this wheat was dumped on the market, a panic and lowering of prices resulted at once. To try to keep the price up, the bull group spread reports that Russia had bought approximately 300,000 tons of wheat from American sources, and that because of drought India would have a 30 percent smaller crop than expected. Brecht adapted this article about rumors right away, when he was still calling Joe Fleischhacker "Jae":

> Jae says to the 4 bulls: you must buy wheat. There were 4 good years, this year will be a bad one. You know there is a drought through the whole world. Grain will be very scarce. You must buy grain, and it will reach a high price.

> Jae sagt zu den 4 Bullen: ihr müßt Getreide kaufen. Es waren 4 gute Jahre, dieses Jahr wird ein schlechtes sein. Ihr wißt, es ist eine Dürre in der ganzen Welt. Das Getreide wird sehr rar sein. Ihr müßt Getreide kaufen, und es wird einen hohen Preis erzielen. (BBA 678, 10)

These are the four bulls whom Fleischhacker betrays, having already betrayed his partner to join them. Brecht sketches the second betrayal on the same page, and then goes on to the overabundant rain; perhaps that was a factor in 1925.

Brecht also intends to have Fleischhacker's corner fail, like those of both the Barnes group and Curtis Jadwin; at the end of the page of reckoning how many bushels Joe buys to make his corner, Brecht adds the next step in the plot: that Joe has not included everything in his plans, and unexpected wheat is suddenly thrown on the market. This is a simplification of the situation both in *The Pit* and in 1925, when it was the plotting of a whole group of bears that broke the big bull. Perhaps an unexpected supply of wheat was the real cause of the break in 1908. It is of course in the background in *The Pit*: nature's forces cannot be held back; wheat will grow, and "the pit" senses this seismically and takes courage to fight the bull.

But Brecht then jilts his sources and saves Fleischhacker by introducing rumors of war. The market recovers, and Joe's wheat is a gold mine. Brecht does this probably in order to make a comedy (for Joe) out of the play, preventing sympathy for the speculator, as well as to exploit the irony that war is healthy for the economy. Brecht found hints about the effect of war and war rumors on the market in White's *Dan Drew* as well as in *The Pit*.

There are many more clippings and other contemporary sources among the materials to *Fleischhacker*. A summary of the entire year of 1925 is given in a yearly report of the National City Bank, and in a four-page article from a Berlin paper. A few clippings are about finance or the stock market in general, such as one from 4 March 1926 with the large headline "A Billion Dollars Speculated Away!" ("Eine Milliarde Dollars verspekuliert!") describing excitement in the New York Stock Exchange: "Scenes of madness . . . Before closing the stock exchange was literally like a madhouse . . . Clothes were torn" ("Wahnsinnsszenen . . . Vor dem Schluß glich die Börse buchstäblich einem Tollhause . . . Kleider wurden zerrissen").[73] But almost all of the many newspaper articles are about the narrower subject of the wheat market, in both Chicago and Europe.

And still that was not precise enough for Brecht; he demanded better and better information. There are pages of notes to *Fleischhacker* preserved that consist of nothing but numbers— attempts at figuring out the exact arithmetic of the exchange.

Elisabeth Hauptmann remembered that Brecht read articles by Richard Lewinsohn, alias Morus, in preparation for *Fleischhacker*. Lewinsohn was an excellent columnist on economic matters and a specialist on the stock exchange for the *Vossische Zeitung*, Berlin; under the name Morus he wrote articles for *Die Weltbühne*, a magazine of the left.

Brecht (and Hauptmann) even traveled from Berlin to Vienna to ask a broker there questions about how the wheat market works.

130

Perhaps the very short memorandum on "benefits of the grain exchange" ("nützen der getreidebörse") stems from this interview:

assumption of the risk   the world's grain is divided up   the fixed
price covers real grain   the price stands between harvests

übernahme des risikos   das weltgetreide wird eingeteilt   der
fixierte preis erfaßt wirklich getreide   der preis steht zwischen den
ernten (BBA 524, 21)

But these few "benefits" of the grain exchange are not necessary, and to Brecht they hardly seemed enough to justify the arbitrariness with which absolutely unproductive capitalists, interjected without real function as middlemen between the producers and wholesale buyers of most raw materials and staples, could control the lives and deaths of millions of people throughout the world.

Brecht had read many times already that this was what capitalism was about; he had read Sinclair and Lorimer and Myers and White and Norris and Jensen on American society, and he had admired Piscator's proletarian theater and had lived through the October Revolution and the Munich soviet, and he himself had rebelled from the beginning against hypocritical bourgeois values. But through none of this had he felt a need to analyze and judge the political and economic system that he lived under and that ruled the country he considered the wave of the future; he wrote plays and poems and theater criticism that assumed a critical attitude toward society, but they were reflections of that society, "documents," not analysis and far less prescriptions for change.

About 1924, feeling that the urge to make money is a more basic social force than the theater usually admits, he elected to begin writing plays on economic motives; these he set in America because there people were, bless them, honest: it was the one place where everyone admitted his real motives, and so the simplification necessary to make a dramatic point was credible against that background. America was also the country where the transformation from a rural, tribal, or feudal sort of society to an urban and technological society was evident on an accelerated and grand scale; it was the perfect setting for the study of sociological changes in the transition to a new age, a transition that was also taking place in Europe, though more slowly. *Joe Fleischhacker* started out to be another in the series of studies of the migration to the cities. *In the Jungle* was the first; it examined the struggle for survival and its result, loneliness. And *Fleischhacker* was to study the struggle for survival and its cause, the economics of the city.

But the study dragged on and on. More and more materials were collected for it, but apparently the more Brecht read and asked, the less it all made sense. He pieced together a plot, worked out the very mathematics of the trading, but could not understand the logic of the system. The more he read, the less possible it was for him to write the play, nor could he finish any other projects he had been working on—which were all on similar themes—as long as he could not make clear the rationale behind the market.

Looking back about ten years later, Brecht wrote a poem on the subject of trying to understand the wheat exchange; the poem shows that the experience was a crisis in all aspects of his life.

When I years ago while studying how Chicago's wheat exchange works
Suddenly understood how they controlled the world's grain there
And yet didn't understand it and lowered the book
I knew right away: you have
Come upon a bad business.

There was no feeling of bitterness in me, and the injustice
Didn't frighten me then, only the thought
They can't do that, the way they're doing it! filled me completely.
These men, I saw, lived from the harm
That they caused, not from their usefulness.
This was a situation, I saw, that could be maintained
Only through crime, because it was bad for the majority.
And thus must each
Triumph of reason, invention or discovery
Lead only to yet greater misery.

These and similar thoughts came to me in that moment
Far from anger or grief as I lowered the book
With the description of the wheat market and Chicago's Board of Trade.
Much work and unrest
Awaited me.

Als ich vor Jahren bei dem Studium der Vorgänge auf der Weizenbörse Chikagos
Plötzlich begriff, wie sie dort das Getreide der Welt verwalteten
Und es zugleich auch nicht begriff und das Buch senkte

132

Wußte ich gleich: du bist
In eine böse Sache geraten.

Kein Gefühl der Erbitterung war in mir, und nicht das Unrecht
Schreckte mich da, nur der Gedanke
So geht das nicht, wie die's machen! erfüllte mich gänzlich.
Diese, sah ich, lebten vom Schaden
Den sie zufügten, anstatt vom Nutzen.
Dies war ein Zustand, sah ich, der nur durch Verbrechen
Aufrecht zu halten war, weil zu schlecht für die meisten.
So muß auch jede
Leistung der Vernunft, Erfindung oder Entdeckung
Nur zu noch größerem Elend führen.
Solches und Ähnliches dacht ich in diesem Augenblick
Fern von Zorn oder Jammer, als ich das Buch senkte
Mit der Beschreibung des Weizenmarkts und der Börse Chikagos.
Viel Mühe und Unrast
Erwarteten mich.

(GW 9:567–68)

The crisis reached its climax. Brecht stopped writing. It was no
use until he understood. After the premiere of *A Man's a Man* (25
September 1926) he asked for advice on which works to read about
political economy, socialism, and Marxism, and bought them; he
took a vacation and wrote in a letter: "I'm stuck eight shoes deep in
Capital. I've got to know that now exactly" ("Ich stecke acht Schuh
tief im 'Kapital'. Ich muß das jetzt genau wissen").[74]

Chapter Three

Brecht's Political Development

Just as it was impossible for Brecht to continue writing without
learning to understand economics, so it would be impossible for us
to continue analyzing what he wrote about America after he studied
economics without a brief look at what he learned. For his reading
of *Capital* and other works on political economy, beginning in 1926,
caused the most significant turning point in his entire life. Until now
we have seen him as a harsh critic of bourgeois social relations, but
more an angry young man than a reformer. His private stance is
cynical, and his literary stance is amoral aestheticism; his attitude
toward America is that it is both grand and cruel, and that it
represents man's highest level of progress so far.

All these positions change in the next few years, as a result of the
change in his politics. His politics change because he reads Marx;
and he reads Marx because of his interest in America. But when he
applies the theories he learns from Marx back to America, after
committing himself to the importance of moral principles in art, he
finds his conception of that advanced country has changed drastically, so that it no longer seems so advanced. In fact, he comes to call
the American (and German) system "the old"; he has discovered the
system that is to supersede it. Socialism becomes "the new," always a
positive term for Brecht.

Not only Brecht's commitments and his attitudes toward America
undergo change; he also experiments in new "didactic" forms and
develops the epic theater as a vehicle for his new politics. The change
in style is also impossible to understand without a prior examination
of exactly what it was he learned when he gave up writing *Joe
Fleischhacker* and read political economy for two years.

It is always risky, of course, to divide a writer's life into periods and claim that a certain biographical event represents a real hiatus or conversion. The GDR poet Johannes R. Becher's description of Brecht's conversion to Marxism is surely too simple in its absolute differentiation between before and after:

> Brecht's turn to us happened like this. . . . The crisis began. Labor got cheaper. Bread got more expensive. Brecht undertook to write a play with wheat as the hero. The explanations of the political economists were deceitful and helpless. Brecht was demanding and persistent. Wheat led him to Marx, Marx to Lenin. The play never came about. But a new Brecht came about, one who left the middle ground and joined the ranks of the communist cultural workers.

> Brechts Wendung zu uns vollzog sich so. . . . Die Krise begann. Die Arbeit wurde billiger. Das Brot wurde teurer. Brecht nahm sich vor, ein Stück zu schreiben, dessen Held der Weizen war. Die Erklärungen der Nationalökonomen waren verlogen und hilflos. Brecht war anspruchs-voll und beharrlich. Der Weizen führte ihn zu Marx, Marx zu Lenin. Das Stück kam nicht zustande. Aber ein neuer Brecht kam zustande, der das Zwischenterrain verließ und sich in die Reihen der kommunisti-schen Kunstarbeiter stellte.[1]

Especially in Brecht's case such isolation of single events as turning points would seem foolhardy, because of his habit of working on plays for years, using and reusing the same materials through what might seem to be different periods.

On the other hand, Brecht himself felt what happened to him when trying to write *Fleischhacker* was his road to Damascus. This is evident from the poem "When I years ago . . . " just quoted, as well as from his recurrent, almost obsessive use in the following years of wheat and the wheat market as examples of both economic injustice and the proper material for the new theater.

In 1926–27 he wrote in a short poem,

> Why do I eat bread that costs too much?
> Isn't the price of grain in Illinois too high? . . .
> Is it wrong for me to eat?

> Warum esse ich Brot, das zu teuer ist?
> Ist nicht das Getreide zu teuer in Illinois? . . .
> Ist es falsch, daß ich esse?

> > (*GW* 8:293)

In 1928, he complained in an essay on the new drama, "The battles over wheat and so forth can't be found on our stages" ("Die Kämpfe

135

um den Weizen und so weiter sind nicht auf unseren Bühnen zu finden") (*GW* 15:174).

February 1929, notes on "epic" theater: "a play set, for instance, in the wheat exchange cannot be done in the grand form, the dramatic form" ("ein Stück, das etwa auf der Weizenbörse spielt, kann in der großen Form, der dramatischen, nicht gemacht werden") (*GW* 15:186)—because the drama must prevent identification with a world that is wrong.

December 1929, a review of Samuel Butler: "He conceives 'happy' in that double meaning it has when 'happy [lucky] ventures' (such as on the wheat market) are spoken of"; ("Er faßt 'glücklich' in jener Doppelbedeutung, die es hat, wenn von 'glücklichen Unternehmungen' (etwa auf dem Weizenmarkt) gesprochen wird") (*GW* 18:74).

In 1931, Brecht coined the term "dialectical drama," and wrote that it was first developed when playwrights began recognizing the polemical message in the material itself "(already in preliminary studies to plays like *Wheat!*)"; ("[schon in Vorstudien zu Stücken wie 'Der Weizen'!]") (*GW* 15:225).

In 1930–31 he wrote a series of poems for children called *The Three Soldiers*: three "soldiers" return from the war and cause as many deaths among the civilian population as the war did. The soldiers are Hunger, Accident, and Cough, and they cannot understand why the people do not defend themselves against them. (When they are put to death in revolutionary Moscow, they are finally happy.) The ninth poem in the series (*GW* 8:352–54) is based on the Americans' dumping of wheat into the ocean to keep the price up during the depression (which is essentially what Mauler does with cattle, in the face of starvation).

Finally, in 1935–36 Brecht wrote an article on the theater of the twenties; when looking for an example of the necessity of the epic style, he again chose his play about wheat rather than plays actually finished and performed: "No one should expect that processes in the wheat market in Chicago . . . are less complicated than processes in the atom"; ("Niemand kann erwarten, daß die Vorgänge auf dem Weizenmarkt in Chicago . . . weniger kompliziert sind als die Vorgänge im Atom") (*GW* 15:238).

It would perhaps not be so impressive that Brecht mentioned wheat often as a symbol had he not also written very directly and—unusually for him—with no trace of irony about the meaning of the

Fleischhacker experience for him. Elisabeth Hauptmann notes in July 1926 that it was the most important learning experience for Brecht up to that time:

> The most important change during the work occurred while we were looking over materials for *Joe Fleischhacker*. This play was supposed to . . . show capitalism on the rise. For the play we collected technical literature, I myself interviewed a series of specialists, even at the Breslau and Vienna stock exchanges, and in the end Brecht started reading political economy. He maintained the practices with money were very opaque, now he had to see how it was with the theories about money.

> Die wichtigste Umstellung während der Arbeit geschah bei der Überprufung des Materials für *Joe Fleischhacker*. Dieses Stück sollte . . . den aufsteigenden Kapitalismus zeigen. Für dieses Stück sammelten wir Fachliteratur, ich selber fragte eine Reihe von Spezialisten aus, auch auf den Börsen in Breslau und Wien, und am Schluß fing Brecht an, Nationalökonomie zu lesen. Er behauptete, die Praktiken mit Geld seien sehr undurchsichtig, er müsse jetzt sehen, wie es mit den Theorien über Geld stehe.[2]

Brecht himself was not less emphatic. In 1926, presumably just after he had given up trying to write *Fleischhacker*, he wrote a poem putting his failure, if it can be called that, in historical perspective:

> Recently I wanted to tell
> You, with malice aforethought
> The story of a wheat dealer in the city
> Chicago. In the middle of the recitation
> My voice left me quickly
> Because I had
> Suddenly recognized: what hard work
> It would be, to tell
> This story to those who are not yet born
> But who will be born and will live
> In completely different kinds of times
> And, the lucky ones! will be unable
> By then to understand what a wheat dealer is
> Of the sort that we have here.

> Neulich wollte ich euch
> Erzählen mit Arglist
> Die Geschichte eines Weizenhändlers in der Stadt
> Chikago. Mitten im Vortrag
> Verließ mich meine Stimme in Eile
> Denn ich hatte
> Plötzlich erkannt: welche Mühe

137

Es mich kosten würde, diese Geschichte
Jenen zu erzählen, die noch nicht geboren sind
Die aber geboren werden und in
Ganz anderen Zeitläuften leben werden
Und, die Glücklichen! gar nicht mehr
Verstehen können, was ein Weizenhändler ist
Von der Art, wie sie bei uns sind.

He imagines himself explaining and explaining seven years long, and none of his unborn audience understanding, till he finally realizes that what he is describing *cannot be understood*:

Then I recognized that I
Was relating something that
A person cannot understand.

Da erkannte ich, daß ich
Etwas erzählte, was
Ein Mensch nicht verstehen kann.

(*GW* 8:150)

His listeners ask him why he could not see through such an obviously false system, and when he tries to explain they simply give up on him, "With the casual regret / Of happy people"; ("Mit dem lässigen Bedauern / Glücklicher Leute") (*GW* 8:151).

It is this imagined discussion that leads him to the conclusion with which he begins the poem, that language is nowadays incomprehensible because it is spoken by a decadent generation (it is "the language of a people in decline," ["die Sprache von Untergehenden"]), who have nothing to say to the new generation. And with the first person plural he includes himself, now, in the new generation ("So we can no longer understand them," ["Daß wir sie nicht mehr verstehen"]): he has learned something since trying to write the play. It is no longer necessary for him to understand the contemporary wheat traders—from their own point of view. What he will do is try to see the present with the eyes of the future, to portray evil conditions as historically caused, and therefore temporary and changeable ("but the point is to change it"). The historical perspective, exemplified by this poem, is the perspective of epic theater.

Ten years later Brecht wrote the poem "When I years ago . . . ," quoted at the end of the last chapter. He already had been in exile three years, and his subjects were primarily fascism and exile; but the memory of the study of wheat in Chicago was still vivid in his mind. The 1936 poem makes a statement surprisingly similar to that of the 1926 poem. Here too the playwright learns that the wheat market is incomprehensible because irrational. But here he recognizes that early experience as the beginning of a new period in his life. He was not angry, he says, but he knew that he had stumbled on an evil thing and that he was not going to be able to continue living an unconcerned life now that he knew what had to be done. "Much work and unrest / Awaited me" ("Viel Mühe und Unrast / Erwarteten mich").

Apparently also written during his emigration (possibly as an introduction to a poetry reading in Russia) is an autobiographical sketch in prose describing his early apolitical attitude. He had been the barracks delegate to a soldiers' soviet in 1918, he says, but upon taking up writing he could not seem to get beyond nihilistic criticism of bourgeois society. Not even the powerful influence that Eisenstein and Piscator had on him made him study Marxism, perhaps because he was so scientifically oriented. This is the attitude we have called "amoral," the attitude Brecht later condemned in his play *Galileo*. In the sketch Brecht presents that attitude as a problem in his early life that had to be overcome.

> Then a kind of occupational accident helped me along. For a certain play I needed Chicago's wheat exchange as background. I thought I would be able to acquire the necessary information quickly by making a few inquiries of specialists and practitioners. It happened otherwise. No one, neither well-known writers on economics nor business people—I traveled from Berlin to Vienna after a broker who had worked all his life at the Chicago exchange—no one could explain the processes of the wheat exchange to me adequately. I won the impression that these processes were simply inexplicable, i.e., not to be grasped by reason, i.e., unreasonable. The way the world's wheat was distributed was simply incomprehensible. From every point of view except that of a handful of speculators this grain market was one big swamp.

> Dann half mir eine Art Betriebsunfall weiter. Für ein bestimmtes Theaterstück brauchte ich als Hintergrund die Weizenbörse Chicagos. Ich dachte, durch einige Umfragen bei Spezialisten und Praktikern mir rasch die nötigen Kenntnisse verschaffen zu können. Die Sache kam anders. Niemand, weder einige bekannte Wirtschaftsschriftsteller noch Geschäftsleute—einem Makler, der an der Chicagoer Börse sein Leben lang gearbeitet hatte, reiste ich von Berlin nach Wien nach—, niemand konnte mir die Vorgänge an der Weizenbörse hinreichend erklären. Ich

gewann den Eindruck, daß diese Vorgänge schlechthin unerklärlich, das heißt von der Vernunft nicht erfaßbar, und das heißt wieder einfach unvernünftig waren. Die Art, wie das Getreide der Welt verteilt wurde, war schlechthin unbegreiflich. Von jedem Standpunkt aus außer demjenigen einer Handvoll Spekulanten war dieser Getreidemarkt ein einziger Sumpf. (*GW* 20:46)

The term *Betriebsunfall*, or occupational accident, is important. As we have said, Brecht was unimpressed by all the arguments he had heard on socialism and the necessity of engaging oneself in the fight against capitalism; and he heard many such arguments, particularly in the literature he read about America. *It was not until his own productivity was endangered* that he found himself forced to look into the matter.

Important also is his insistence on logic. He wanted to be able to present certain mechanisms in their essence, in simple, logical form that would make sense to an audience; he was from beginning to end an advocate of clear thinking. He came to trust his belief that what is not logical is wrong—both factually and morally wrong. I got the impression, he says, that these processes were inexplicable, that is, impossible for the reason to grasp, that is: unreasonable.

He concludes:

The intended drama was not written; instead I began to read Marx, and then, only then, I read Marx. Only then did my own scattered practical experiences and impressions really come alive.

Das geplante Drama wurde nicht geschrieben, statt dessen begann ich Marx zu lesen, und da, jetzt erst, las ich Marx. Jetzt erst wurden meine eigenen zerstreuten praktischen Erfahrungen und Eindrücke richtig lebendig. (*GW* 20:76)

Looking back, Brecht seems to consider it was quite amazing that it took him so long to turn to Marx. He must have had strong resistance to Marx beforehand, because once he finally did start reading *Capital*, all his own experiences fell into place; it became possible for the first time to fit them into a rational system, to make them "come alive."

What exactly did the acquaintance with Marx's theories mean for Brecht? What it did not mean was joining the Communist Party (KPD); on the contrary, he was rather skeptical of organized Marxists for a while. (Some critics would claim: forever. They ignore the very close teamwork between Brecht and the East

140

German regime, and read only Brecht's critical comments, failing to grasp that these are written in the spirit of socialist self-criticism, or, as Brecht himself says in an article on the subject, "When I drive, being myself at the wheel I criticize the course of my car by steering" ["Wenn ich Auto fahre, selbst am Steuer, kritisiere ich den Lauf meines Wagens, indem ich steure"]).[3]

Marxism meant for Brecht first of all understanding the nature of conflict. He became aware not only that he wrote his plays to provoke reaction but also that the bourgeoisie had been the false target for provocation. This realization is clear in a note on *Baal* from 1926. When he wrote *Baal*, he says, he thought he would be shocking the bourgeoisie. But that class was so decadent that it only criticized the *form* of the play (i.e., it did not feel touched by the issues, if it even understood them). Now he sees that the real opponent to the figure of Baal is the proletarian (*GW* 15:64). In other words, Brecht now felt that the purpose of the play had been to provoke a specific argument from a working-class audience, namely that Baal's reaction to bourgeois society is an inadequate one.

In a similar light Brecht was able (much later) to reinterpret *Drums in the Night*: he says he had no conception when he wrote it of the importance of the 1918 revolution (in which he himself took part!); but he instinctively realized that Kragler was not seriously involved in the revolution (*GW* 17:945–46), that he was the typical social democrat who quits as soon as he has what he wants, and that it was important for the working class to learn to recognize this type of false revolutionary (*GW* 17:967). In Brecht's later interpretation, *In the Jungle* came close to showing class struggle without his being aware of it, and *A Man's a Man* was a parable on the individual and the collective (Brecht gives various different interpretations to the value of the collective). In 1927 he rewrote *In the Jungle* for the book edition, leaving out most of the personal and psychological allusions; they no longer seemed to him valid subjects for drama.

All these reinterpretations became possible because Brecht became aware of class struggle. Marx and Engels claim that the history of all hitherto existing society is the history of struggle between classes, and Brecht, who had always considered his plays pieces of concrete history, endeavored to see his past work in that scheme. Further, he realized the necessity of an audience that would have absolute criteria for judging the *usefulness* (the word becomes very important in Brecht's aesthetics) of the content of any play. This is the exact opposite of Brecht's earlier amoral position: now there is a truth, there is the possibility of being right or wrong, and characters on the stage are there to provoke the audience into thinking about whether the life-attitude shown is right, i.e., useful for the achievement of their goal. Only the workers have—have to have—the knowledge that these criteria are absolute: for them it is a matter of life and death, for the intelligentsia it is intellectual stimulation. "The real opponent I can only expect to find in the working class. Without my sensing *that* opposition I couldn't have created the type [Baal]" ("Den wirklichen Gegner kann ich mir nur im Proletariat erhoffen. Ohne *diese* von mir gefühlte Gegnerschaft hätte dieser Typ von mir nicht gestaltet werden können") (*GW* 15:64).

On the same manuscript page as the comment (1926) on *Baal*, Brecht wrote (possibly later):

> I must confess, it wasn't until I read Lenin's *State and Revolution* and then Marx's *Capital* that I realized where I stood philosophically. I don't mean to say that I reacted *against* these books, that would seem highly incorrect to me. I just think I felt at home here, in *these* oppositions.

> Ich muß gestehen, daß ich erst, als ich Lenins "Staat und Revolution" und danach Marx' "Kapital" gelesen hatte, begriff, wo ich, philosophisch, stand. Ich will nicht sagen, daß ich *gegen* diese Bücher reagierte, dies schiene mir höchst unrichtig. Ich glaube nur, daß ich hier, in *diesen* Gegensätzen, mich zu Hause fühlte. (*GW* 15:2*)

That he emphasizes not having really reacted *against* Marx and Lenin indicates he was not yet ready to subscribe fully to their ideas either. But he now knew, and knew for good, exactly what the important topics were to explore, where the productive contradictions lay. It is a truism that drama is based on conflict, but his new insight was that only some conflicts are meaningful to show (productive, or causing change). They are class conflicts, the struggle between supporters of an old society and the forces that must produce a new one.

Brecht mentions here that he read Lenin's *State and Revolution* before *Capital*. It was available in German from 1918, but probably he read it immediately before *Capital*, as an introduction to Marxism. It is a good one, particularly on the revolutionary role of the proletariat and on the transition to socialism. Marx's and

Engels's writings on those subjects are systematized and commented upon by Lenin in lucid style. However, there is little explanation of the exact economic workings of capitalism, and this is what Brecht needed to answer his questions on the Chicago wheat market. Lenin undoubtedly whetted Brecht's curiosity considerably and was also most probably the source of his new interest in the working class. But Brecht knew, or soon saw, that for a real understanding of capitalism there was no shortcut: *Capital* had to be studied.

Elisabeth Hauptmann told me that Brecht broadened his knowledge of Marxism systematically, and that he questioned and tested his new knowledge again and again. Many of his acquaintances remember incessant discussions on socialism, revolution, and political economy. He visited the Marxist School for Workers (MASCH) in Berlin, and attended lectures by the sociologist Fritz Sternberg and by the Marxist philosopher Karl Korsch. Although Brecht soon outgrew Sternberg and criticized Korsch, his correspondence with Sternberg is very interesting; and he and Korsch discussed and learned from each other—mainly by letter—until Brecht's death. Brecht of course spent years studying Marxism; some of his reactions are recorded in notes he wrote (printed as "Marxist Studies" in the *Writings on Politics and Society*); but the more detailed record of his thought will be in his letters, which are not yet available to the public.

The two years immediately after 1926 were dedicated to a particularly intense study of Marxist political economy; we can tell this by the books Brecht read. *Capital* is a year's study in itself, but Hauptmann remembered him also reading Lenin's *Left-Wing Communism: An Infantile Disorder* and Plekhanov's *Role of the Individual in History*, as well as material on Lassalle and the International. We can see influence from these books in his work of the late twenties: he treats the problem of anarchistic tendencies in revolutionary movements in *The Measure Taken*, and the relation of individual and mass was perhaps his principal subject in the *Lehrstücke* on *Einverständnis* (acquiescence), and in essays on the role of the artist.

We also find in Brecht's library Marxist books that were published in 1925 and 1926, such as Bukharin's *Der Imperialismus und die Akkumulation des Kapitals (Imperialism and the Accumulation of Capital)*[4] and Jakob Walcher's *Ford oder Marx: Die*

143

praktische Lösung der sozialen Frage (*Ford or Marx: The Practical Solution to the Social Question*).[5]

Finally, Brecht lists books on Marxism as some of the best books of the year in answer to the surveys by *Das Tagebuch* in 1926 and 1928 (*GW* 18:51-52, 65-66). In 1926 he recommends Henri Guilbeaux's biography *Wladimir Iljitsch Lenin: Ein treues Bild seines Wesens* (*Vladimir Ilyich Lenin: A Faithful Portrait of His Nature*)[6] (more evidence that Lenin, whom he calls a "phenomenon," was important to him in that year), and the pictures in *Geist und Gesicht des Bolschewismus: Darstellung und Kritik des kulturellen Lebens in Sowjet-Rußland* (*Spirit and Face of Bolshevism: Description and Critique of Cultural Life in Soviet Russia*).[7] In 1928 he recommends a biography, *Marx, Leben und Werk* (*Marx: Life and Work*), by Otto Rühle,[8] a book of whose style he does not entirely approve but that presents a great doctrine clearly, which (he says) is more important.

Of course, these books that we know he read on Marxism are only a fraction of what the indefatigable reader Brecht must have studied; and the many conversations with economists and sociologists also had a strong effect. It is hopeless at this point to try to identify all the sources of his political education. It is also unnecessary for our purposes. We know that the writings of Marx himself, notably *Capital*, represented to Brecht the new beginning.

We have stated that the first new perspective Brecht gained from reading Marx was the universal historical principle of class struggle. The second was learning to see his own plays as documentary material, or data for a Marxist interpretation:

> When I read *Capital* by Marx I understood my plays. . . . Of course I didn't discover that I had unconsciously written a pile of Marxist plays. But this Marx was the only viewer for my plays that I had ever seen. For a man with his interests must be interested by precisely these plays. Not because of their intelligence, but because of his. It was material for his observation.

> Als ich "Das Kapital" von Marx las, verstand ich meine Stücke. . . .Ich entdeckte natürlich nicht, daß ich einen Haufen marxistischer Stücke geschrieben hatte, ohne eine Ahnung zu haben. Aber dieser Marx war der einzige Zuschauer für meine Stücke, den ich je gesehen hatte. Denn einen Mann mit solchen Interessen mußten gerade diese Stücke interessieren. Nicht wegen ihrer Intelligenz, sondern wegen der seinigen. Es war Anschauungsmaterial für ihn. (*GW* 15:129)

144

Here Brecht claims no superiority for his own plays over those of any other dramatist who portrays reality—naturalists, for example. But he has discovered that there are significant and nonsignificant *interpretations* of the portrayals of reality. In the future he will be trying to solicit the right kind of interpretation, for it is important not only that he and Marx understand his plays but also that the audience learn to think like Marx.

For the next few years the idea of drama as document, data, or material occupied him. We have seen that in 1926 he praised Frank Harris's book for its documentary value and suggested that should be the purpose of literature altogether; the word "document" was his high praise for Chaplin (*GW* 18:138), and he also praised the classics (in conscious contradiction to some Communists) for their material value (*GW* 15:175), meaning literally the value of the materials that go into the work. No one should find it wrong that the Vandals used Roman wood-carvings for firewood, he says (*GW* 15:105); i.e., no one should find it wrong that a Marxist audience sees class struggle as the *useful* subject in a play intended to be about a metaphysical struggle).

A similar analogy provided the title of Brecht's later dialogues on dramatic theory: *Buying Brass*. A philosopher comes into the theater and wants to use it ruthlessly for his own purposes, which are not those of the theater people. It is, the philosopher says, as though he were to go into a music store and ask to buy a trumpet because he needs brass. The theater should be a true reflection of events among men (reality, like brass, is the material), and allow the taking of a position by the audience (*GW* 16:500). This aesthetic of course still allows the writer to produce amoral plays. But Brecht did not say it was his intention to write plays himself that were mainly useful as brass, for their sociological raw material; he used the term in interpreting his early plays and defending the usefulness of the classics. Shakespeare for instance: "He is absolute material" ("Er ist absoluter Stoff") (*GW* 15:119).

Plays written before the development of the "new theater" (theater put in the service of the working class) were to be used, Brecht decided after reading Marx, for their documentary value: the message (*Tendenz*) of the author was to be ignored, and the situation portrayed by him was to be interpreted by the audience. For himself, as an adherent of the new theater, Brecht had more ambitious plans:

not only the presentation of situations to an audience but the education or creation of a new kind of audience. That also is a principal perspective of epic theater.

In short, upon giving up trying to write *Fleischhacker* and reading Marx instead, Brecht made a complete about-face from his previous position. He now wanted to put theater in the service of a political movement. In order to understand accurately the extent of the change, let us look more closely at Brecht's early political stance, which we have until now simply characterized as "amoral."

It was not Brecht's *political* position that made an about-face but rather his ideas on the uses of theater. His politics had always been to the left of center (except for patriotic essays he wrote as a sixteen-year-old schoolboy), that is, he was always anti-bourgeois. Long before he had any theoretical knowledge of the historical role of the bourgeoisie, he was cursing it with furious energy. But when we look closer, this rebellion unmasks itself as a rebellion against the older generation, not against the capitalist class. In the important notes on dialectical drama, written in 1931, Brecht looks back on his and his friends' early work and calls it idealist and capitalist. Although the pettiness of bourgeois thought was condemned in it, he confesses, the grandeur and ruthlessness of the bourgeoisie's accomplishments was praised; the rebellion was "merely a generation question," ("lediglich eine Generationsfrage") (*GW* 15:218). Many other remarks by Brecht, with which we are already familiar,[9] also emphasize his early political naïveté. He felt that he was revolutionary purely by virtue of being young, and that the function of the new generation was to create chaos, knock down the old order, and refuse to "understand" the old generation or be understood by it (*GW* 18:36–37). That was still Brecht's attitude in early 1926; in that year he wrote a great deal against the older generation.

It was this notion that all older people are reactionary and all younger people revolutionary (or at least destructive to the old order) that prepared for his disappointment at the poetry of 400 young poets in the contest he judged at the end of 1926: "What use is it to strike several generations of harmful older people dead or, what is better, to wish them dead, if the younger generation is nothing but harmless?" ("Was nützt es, mehrere Generationen schädlicher älterer Leute totzuschlagen oder, was besser ist, totzuwünschen, wenn die jüngere Generation nichts ist als harmlos?" (*GW* 18:56). Brecht

146

chose instead of the entries a poem on the subject of sport; he was still faddishly interested in whatever nonliterary fields would provoke the literary bourgeoisie. But we see in his comments on the poetry contest signs of his new attitude as well: he writes that poetry must have *Gebrauchswert* (use value, a Marxist term) and documentary value, and that the literature of the declining bourgeoisie is by all means an expression of class struggle, namely, of reaction.

Also in 1926 he wrote that the fight between the generations would be a fight for the means of production, i.e., the presses, the theaters, etc. (*GW* 18:39). At the same time he began using the term *bourgeoisie* in a more precise sense and to oppose it, not just to himself and his rebellious young artist friends, but to *working class*. And soon the furious railing at the older generation died out of his diction, and he judged everyone as being on the side of one *class* or another. Questions about what role the artist or intellectual could play in the working-class struggle replaced the assumption that he and the entire younger generation of writers were automatically playing a revolutionary role.

Brecht felt from his earliest days as a playwright that he was on the side of rebellion, but he did not know exactly where the barricades were. The inability to finish a play because of his ignorance and the subsequent study of Marx put new content in his rebellion and taught him always to ask whether an emotional act really served the necessary revolution, whether every particular act or play was *useful*. This is the autobiographical reason for the severity of the decision in *The Measure Taken* (1929–30).[10]

Almost incidental to this rebellion of the young writer against the stuffy bourgeoisie, expressed in his articles and reviews, is the background in Brecht's early plays. It was to these plays that he referred when he wrote toward the end of his life that although his political consciousness was shamefully poor, nevertheless he had sensed social discrepancies without recognizing their origins, and reproduced social conflict in his works (*GW* 19:397); and that he knew almost nothing precise about the Russian Revolution but had a presentiment of the fighting spirit of the working class in *Drums* (*GW* 17:945–46); and that he came close to writing about the real struggle—the class struggle—in *Jungle*, without knowing it (*GW* 17:949).

This could be an opportunistic reinterpretation of his early plays;

a case can be made that since they in fact supported no particular doctrine, but were rather (as he himself says) true pictures of the times and therefore material for observation, any position could be read into them, and that Brecht when he lived under a Marxist regime decided to read a Marxist position into them. So claim Western critics of the school that creates and believes the legend of Brecht as the opportunistic anticommunist who denied his beliefs and cooperated with the East German regime because it gave him a sumptuous theater. So, for instance, Martin Esslin, the father of this school: "He did not, as he later tried to make it appear, and as the official legend now fostered in the Communist world proclaims, support the Russian Revolution from the moment he heard of it."[11] Of course not, nor did he ever claim to have; nor can there be any pretense that he did, since his references to the subject such as "On Looking through My First Plays" (*GW* 17:945–52) are as available in East Germany as in the West. Every time Brecht wrote about his early political attitudes, he was painfully honest about how naïve and even reactionary they were. Once when he describes his experience in the Bavarian soldiers' soviet, he admits frankly that he was not enthusiastic, found his position as delegate too much work, and was unable to think politically. He ends by saying he does not particularly like to think about it (*GW* 20:25). In the comments in the early plays, too, Brecht's tone is confessional.

The point is, he was an embryonic socialist in spite of himself. The image he had of himself was that he was blasé and interested only in pastimes with which to while away time while waiting for catastrophe ("Of Poor B.B."); it was good form to rail against the theater-bourgeoisie and tradition but bad form to become seriously engaged in fighting *for* anything. Thus the sympathetic presentation of Kragler in *Drums*: he shocks Anna's petty-bourgeois family, but he avoids dedication to the revolution. Baal, Kragler, Eduard, Garga are all characterized primarily as persons who maintain their individuality and self-interest come what may. Galy Gay, in the original conception, is a negative parable: he is what happens to people who have no sense of self.

But this is only the principal character in each play. Their stories are told against, and in interaction with, a background of complex social reality. It is in this portrayal of the milieu that Brecht's political observations are expressed. And although he does not say something must be done about the conditions shown, he does definitely sympathize with the poor and oppressed and recognize that something is very wrong with the system that produces their misery. The mercilessness of the social system and the dehumanization of its objects are quite clear. This is not simply the result of realistic portrayal of the age; Brecht's early plays are slightly more "Marxist" (in the sense of "leftist") than he himself says in his comment on Marx as their best interpreter. There were reasons why he chose those particular backgrounds where he could just as well (were he not Brecht) have demonstrated the necessity of defense of the fatherland or other proto-fascist lessons. But it was not until the decision to write a play on the wheat market that he found a theme where the message was implicit in the material itself (*GW* 15:225). When there was a social message in the earlier plays, it was the result of conscious additions, selection, and emphasis.

For instance, *Baal* is not a paean to individualism but a satire on it; it was written as a criticism of an expressionist play. Baal lives an intense life and has no regrets, but he destroys all human life he comes in contact with. Baal, close to nature as he is, is himself the natural catastrophe that threatens civilization; he is pure id without any superego or civilizing drive; he is perhaps poetic and exciting and is certainly preferable to bourgeois vicarious living, but he is above all destructive. The reaction the play should produce is that Baal is no answer because he produces nothing; he only destroys and then himself decays. But if Baal is destructive, it is in response to a destructive society. "Baal's art of living shares the fate of all other arts in capitalism: it is attacked. He is antisocial, but in an antisocial society" ("Die Lebenskunst Baals teilt das Geschick aller anderen Künste im Kapitalismus: sie wird befehdet. Er ist asozial, aber in einer asozialen Gesellschaft") (*GW* 17:947). Any attempt to fit into society would be equally wrong. Either he must be destroyed or he must destroy. Baal demonstrates through badness and selfishness what characters in many of Brecht's plays demonstrate through goodness and unselfishness: a world in which it is impossible to be good must be changed; a world in which one must be bad should lead to the same conclusion. But the particular nature of this world is scarcely analyzed.

In *Drums in the Night* the social context is obvious: the necessity for revolution, the reaction of the bourgeois Balicke family, the

149

return of a soldier from war who finds no thanks at home. The oppressed workers fight for their rightful share in society, the bourgeois ex-soldier fights for his rightful woman; both have been exploited by the Balickes, factory-owners who play nationalistic songs and religious hymns on the record player and make money on the war. Only the rebellious workers feel sympathy for the unwanted soldier returned from war. He seems in fact to join them just because they are human to him; and when the woman he wants provides him with this human warmth, he leaves them again. Here is Brecht's simultaneous recognition that the world should be changed and his refusal to involve himself in that fight. The plot supports private life; the context and primary impact of the play support revolution. Kragler has a bad conscience at the end; he screams at the audience that it is all only illusion: "It's ordinary theater. Those are boards and a paper moon" ("Es ist gewöhnliches Theater. Es sind Bretter und ein Papiermond" (*GW* 1:123). This is romantic irony used by the character to rationalize his failure. But he cannot help what he does; love is the stronger need for him. And it is right, Brecht implies here, to do that which is true to your own character. But why the bad conscience? How did Brecht himself feel about not having taken his role in the soldiers' soviet seriously?

Fritz Sternberg, the sociologist whom Brecht met in early 1927 and later dubbed his "first teacher," remembers Brecht's approximate words in their first discussion. They were spoken after Brecht began to read Marx, but they refer to a process that began as soon as he finished *Drums*:

> I once wrote a drama *Drums in the Night*, and although the First World War and the Bavarian revolution made up the background, the relation of a man to a certain woman was the focus of attention. . . . Since I wrote that drama, the relation of a man to a woman can do longer provide me with a vision that would be strong enough for writing a whole drama.

> Ich habe einmal ein Drama "Trommeln in der Nacht" geschrieben, und obwohl der erste Weltkrieg und die bayerische Revolution den Hintergrund bildeten, stand doch in diesem Drama die Beziehung eines Mannes zu einer bestimmten Frau im Mittelpunkt. . . . Seitdem ich dieses Drama geschrieben habe, ist es mir nicht mehr möglich, aus der Beziehung eines Mannes zu einer Frau eine Vision zu gewinnen, die stark genug wäre, ein ganzes Drama zu schreiben.[12]

150

"It is ordinary theater": Kragler's bad conscience is Brecht's own. The very act of writing the ending of *Drums in the Night* made Brecht realize Kragler's decision was wrong: too traditional to be "new" theater, and morally wrong.

His next play was radically different. Not only did he avoid love between man and woman for a long time to come, but he wrote with *Jungle* a play that was dramatically and philosophically completely new. Simultaneously he began his study of the great cities and the "new age."

In the Jungle contains the beginnings of Brecht's social consciousness. The Garga family is destroyed not only because of George's private affair with Shlink; their fate is representative of the fate of all who come from the "flat land" to the city without money. They can barely exist; they are trapped, dependent on George's meager earnings. He dreams of Tahiti because all that he can do is dream. His girl friend Jane is equally trapped; she can never stop sewing clothes. A bottle of schnaps is a holiday for her, and prostitution is the only escape besides death. Shlink, member of the exploiting class, has to divest himself of his property in order to be able to fight with Garga at all; otherwise their relationship would be the conventional one between ruler and ruled or exploiter and exploited.

Ironically, in *their* fight, whoever is at any moment physically better off is losing, because he has fought to gain material advantage, not psychological. This underscores the fact that, for all the social background in the play, theirs is not a social but a metaphysical struggle; it is again, as in *Drums*, a case of individual interest that destroys the collective in the background. The social struggle in this play is the struggle of the Garga family to stay alive. Like the family in Sinclair's *The Jungle*, they just barely make it until disaster strikes; in their case, the disaster is that the breadwinner cannot stand it any more and feels he has to be free.[13] But had that not happened, some other emergency would have destroyed the family.

Ernst Schumacher points out, in his meticulously Marxist interpretation of Brecht, that *In the Jungle* shows not only the material but also the spiritual effect of capitalism. The theme of the play is *Vereinzelung* (the process of people becoming isolated from each other), and the creation of the desire for community:[14] these are

151

the effects of capitalism not only on the workers but also on the bourgeoisie. It is Shlink who is lonely. Having built up his business for ten years, he finds that all he has gained is meaningless. Capitalism also causes hatred of the family, says Schumacher, and turns people into commodities—Shlink wants to buy Garga's opinion. But Schumacher is not clear on what Brecht consciously intended and what was unconscious. He says on the one hand that Brecht reproduced the conditions of capitalism only unconsciously,[15] but on the other hand he claims Brecht intended by the use of irony to develop the idea of an abstract behavior *ad absurdum* so as to show that there can be no real conflict without concrete relations to class conflict.[16]

Marxist criticism can take any work of literature and describe the class relations presented in it; this should not be confused with the author's own consciousness. Brecht was more accurate than Schumacher is for him when he wrote that his early plays were not Marxist, but reading Marx told him how to interpret them (*GW* 15:129). Brecht was a little too modest; as we see from this examination of the contexts of his early plays, his political position where he had one was unequivocally on the left. But Schumacher goes too far, failing to differentiate between the primary and secondary levels. The play is *about* a struggle that has nothing to do with social relations, but this struggle occurs against a *background* of capitalist oppression. Brecht's political message is contained almost exclusively in the background story of the Garga family.

It is perhaps a weakness of the play (which leads to confusions in interpretation) that Brecht requires two completely different sets of reference for the two plots; this weakness is eliminated in *Fleischhacker*, where the events on one level are the direct cause of the events on the other. There both plots are in the economic sphere, whereas the metaphysical struggle in *Jungle* is in a completely different category from the economic ruin of the family, despite some cause and effect relationship. This is another example of Brecht's split-level consciousness in those years: the attempt to separate private affairs from social. It is still the problem of *Drums in the Night*.

The Life of Edward the Second of England is less uniquely Brecht's: it is both an adaptation of Marlowe and a joint project with Lion Feuchtwanger (who, however, contributed much the smaller part).[17] But it is constructed on the same dialectic as the other early plays: private versus public interest. Because of Edward's passion for Gaveston, the people of the kingdom suffer. In the other play Brecht and Feuchtwanger wrote together (*Calcutta, May 4th*), a private passion in a ruler leads to suffering for the people—but the passion is for road-building, hardly a sexual passion. The situation is the imperialist occupation of India, which may have given Brecht the idea of putting *A Man's a Man* in the same setting.

In all Brecht's own plays so far, there has been a social system needing change, and people living in it seeking a private escape through the natural passions. These persons who escape into a private life do some harm to others, but they are not the root cause of suffering. Themselves victims, they accept a personal escape rather than a permanent solution through collective action. That description makes the plays sound highly political, but their emphasis is always on the private actions and desires of the principal characters. Despite Brecht's new style, he still considered the valid subject matter of the drama to be individual love, hate, loneliness, communication, personal freedom, faith in self—in short, all the private passions that literature has traditionally built on.

But meanwhile a new approach was welling up in Brecht, which became public when he finished *A Man's a Man* in 1926. The pattern of focus on private passions changed radically. Here Brecht confronted the problem of individual versus collective explicitly. Galy Gay is the man whose sense of identity is so weak that he "lets his private fish swim away"; his desire to belong to the collective becomes so strong that he denies his wife and eventually his own name and identity—which by then really does not exist any more. He neither asks questions nor cares what the truth is when he can find a material advantage for himself; he is the man who cannot say no. He is precisely the opposite of the principal characters in Brecht's previous plays. They all escape out of the social relations pictured, but he submerges himself in them, or rather he takes himself out of one set of conditions and subjugates himself completely to another set. But at no time does he strive for freedom or a private life, and he has no passions.

Did Brecht recognize that it was wrong to seek a private existence and decide to write a play on the process of socialization? Certainly not. Such an interpretation misses the tone of the play. The fact is, every time Galy Gay thinks he is being particularly clever and fooling the soldiers, it is they who are manipulating him, taking shameless advantage of his simple-mindedness. The only exception is the final scene, where Galy Gay has turned into a fanatical war machine.

Because of the parable character of the play, it cannot be definitely classified as right or left; like the foreground plot in *Jungle*, it simply shows a process. Brecht is doing just what he says he is doing: proving that a man can be rebuilt, that one can do anything one wants with a man (*GW* 1:336).

A few concrete details point toward an exposé of conditions under capitalism: after all, it is an imperialist army that Galy Gay is seduced into. Schumacher may be right when he writes that the scene where the elephant is sold demonstrates the fate of workers who hope to escape their oppression by becoming small businessmen.[18] However, capitalism is hardly the central theme of the play.

If there was one specific political target for the criticism implied in *A Man's a Man*, it was probably the totalitarianism of the developing Nazis. Different early friends of Brecht have different memories of his consciousness of fascism around the time of Hitler's *Bierkellerputsch*: Arnolt Bronnen remembers that Brecht was made very uncomfortable by the "Brown Shirts" in Munich in 1923, that the word "Mahagonny" first occurred to him when he observed the wooden color and behavior of the masses of middle-class fascists. " 'When Mahagonny comes, I'm going,' Brecht said as good-by" (" 'Wenn Mahagonny kommt, geh' ich', sagte Brecht zum Abschied").[19] Bernhard Reich, on the other hand, writes of the putsch:

> Arnolt Bronnen claims that Brecht was already concerned about "National Socialism" then. I can't remember any statements by Brecht to that effect. The day after the rout of the Hitler nonsense he rehearsed especially intensely, to compensate for time lost the day before.

> Arnolt Bronnen gibt an, daß sich Brecht damals schon über den "Nationalsozialismus" besorgte Gedanken gemacht habe. Ich kann mich an diesbezügliche Äußerungen des jungen Brecht nicht erinnern. Den nächsten Tag nach dem Kehraus der Hitlerei probierte er besonders intensiv, um den Zeitverlust vom Vortag zu kompensieren.[20]

Fascist tendencies were growing during the time Brecht worked on *A Man's a Man*, but it is not a play about fascism. It is a play about the relation between individual and collective. Apparently Brecht noticed that all his plays had at least on the surface supported individualism, and decided to try the experiment of writing a play that did exactly the opposite: proved there was no such thing as an individual.

But this play is as amoral as the others. The novelty is more formal than ideological: rather than building two parallel plots, one of which is political and one personal, Brecht produced here a single integrated story with many possible applications to political reality.

How he happened to turn from that parable to writing (or trying to write) on economic themes cannot be seen from looking at the plays. There is hardly any connection between *A Man's a Man* and the proliferation of attempts from 1924 to 1926 to write on American financial relations. The answer is sooner to be found in Brecht's sources on America that we have already examined, but even they do not explain why he began to be so *interested* in economics. The interest seems to have developed with his plan of writing a series about the migration to the big cities, which automatically involves the development of technology and capitalist industry; that this theme must involve study of economic exploitation is clear from the subplot in *Jungle*. We can only assume that Brecht's analytical mind, plus the reading of certain key books like *The Pit*, led him down a more and more specialized path because he had to understand how the cities worked in order to write about the lives of people living in them.

This brief study of the political content of Brecht's earliest plays should make clear that when his interest in economics brought him to Marxism, he by no means changed his political direction. From the beginning he had sympathy for the poor; he portrayed exploitation and alienation and the transformation of human beings into commodities; he reacted instinctively against bourgeois values; he was a pacifist and anti-nationalist; and he was a materialist and anti-idealist.

Why, then, did he consider his initiation into systematic Marxism to be an epochal new beginning? What did Marxism do for him?

Marxism *ended Brecht's political naïveté.* Through long and careful study of the Marxist analysis of social development, Brecht

155

was able to develop a sophisticated philosophy that comprehended all social phenomena. Sternberg tells the story of Brecht's treatment about 1930 of young writers who came to him for advice on their plays: he pointed to a shelf with five copies each of *The Communist Manifesto*, Engels's *Socialism: Utopian and Scientific*, and other Marxist texts, and asked if the young writer had read them. When the answer was no, and it always was, Brecht gave him a copy of each pamphlet and told him to read them. If he still felt his play stood up, then he could return for a second visit.[21] Brecht was fully aware of what had caused the transition from naïveté to analysis in himself.[22]

Marxism *taught Brecht the names for concepts he already had.* It fit Brecht's intuitive sympathies and isolated political tendencies, which he had expressed in his early plays, into a system with clear cause-and-effect relationships and with a precise terminology. He could now consciously develop a philosophy and find definitive answers to questions he had always left unanswered. That meant that instead of merely reproducing observed phenomena in his writing he could show the *causes* of the phenomena. It was a thrilling experience for him at last to find a set of ideas and explanations that he could consider objectively right. As he read Marx, he recognized his own barely conceptualized ideas, but he found them not only supported but also fitted into a world analysis.

His excitement at learning names for his own recognitions expressed itself in a proliferation of the use of Marxist terminology in the next years. We have already seen that *bourgeoisie* and *working class* acquired precise meanings and received frequent use. *Commodity, means of production, dialectic, class struggle,* and many other Marxist terms became common in Brecht's writing. He also kept a notebook in which he wrote studies of topics suggested to him by Marx.[23] These studies are attempts to apply to his surroundings and to the theater the insights and language he learned from reading Marx. They are unrelated to each other and often cryptic, since we cannot know which particular passage in his reading prompted them; but they are interesting because they demonstrate Brecht's feeling of intellectual excitement at discovering this new language, and his desire to try it out on all possible different subjects.

Marxism *showed Brecht what to fight against.* His plays now began to deal with capitalism itself, not just its results. He dropped his pose of rebellion and began thinking seriously about strategy. This included thinking about the role of the theater in a political revolution, not just a revolution of the theater. And so he began to write political plays that emphasized his new recognition: who the real enemy is, how it happens that some people starve and others get rich. This was the direction in which *Dan Drew* and *Joe Fleischhacker* were already moving; *Capital* made it a one-way road.

Marxism *showed Brecht what to fight for.* Implicit throughout *Capital* and explicit in other Marxist writings is that wherever capitalism is irrational, socialism is the rational alternative. It was the irrationality of capitalism—the Chicago wheat market was incomprehensible because unjust—that drove Brecht to Marx; and it is clear that if he could not only find the inconsistencies explained but also find a cure, he would be interested. He accepted socialism, once he understood it, because to his highly rational mind it made sense.

This view of socialism as *simple* because so logical is stylistically expressed in the simplicity of form Brecht chose for his agitprop plays: the *Lehrstücke* (ca. 1929–30) and *The Mother* (1931). Werner Hecht makes a revealing comment on this point with regard to *The Mother:*

> Ever since the premiere bourgeois critics have constantly found fault with the "primitive form" of the play (which Brecht chose, after all, with much art, as can be seen from the many textual variations). What in fact angers them is that they are being "enlightened" in the theater over a few basic questions of communism.

> Bürgerliche Kritiker bemängeln ohne Unterlaß seit der Uraufführung die "primitive Form" des Stückes (die Brecht mit viel Kunst, durch die vielen Textvarianten verfolgbar, schließlich gewählt hat). In Wahrheit sind sie darüber verärgert, daß sie im Theater über einige Grundfragen des Kommunismus "aufgeklärt" werden.[24]

The point is, what appeared to be primitive form was consciously chosen to show exactly what the critics did not want to see: the logical simplicity of communism. Brecht expresses that idea in primer-book style in the song "In Praise of Communism," which he wrote for *The Mother:*

> It makes sense, you can understand it. It is easy.
> You are not an exploiter and so you can grasp it.

157

It is good for you, find out more about it.
The stupid call it stupid, and the dirty call it dirty.
It is against dirt and against stupidity. . . .
It is not chaos
But order
It is the simple thing
That's hard to do.

Er ist vernünftig, jeder versteht ihn. Er ist leicht.
Du bist doch kein Ausbeuter, du kannst ihn begreifen.
Er ist gut für dich, erkundige dich nach ihm.
Die Dummköpfe nennen ihn dumm, und die Schmutzigen nennen ihn
    schmutzig.
Er ist gegen den Schmutz und gegen die Dummheit. . . .
Er ist nicht das Chaos
Sondern die Ordnung
Er ist das Einfache
Das schwer zu machen ist

(GW 2:852)

Brecht knew shortly after he started reading Marx that the socialist revolution must come; he wrote in 1926:

> In my opinion it's certain that socialism, revolutionary socialism, will change the face of our land in our lifetime. Our life will be filled with struggles of exactly that kind.

> Nach meiner Ansicht ist es sicher, daß der Sozialismus, und zwar der revolutionäre, das Gesicht unseres Landes noch zu unseren Lebzeiten verändern wird. Unser Leben wird mit Kämpfen gerade dieser Art ausgefüllt sein. (GW 15:66–67)

This recognition, prompted by the sheer logical and moral force of Marx's argument, jerked Brecht for the first time, and forever, out of his early amoral stance. He now knew what he had to fight for. *Knowing* was "the simple thing" ("das Einfache"); but who would make the revolution and how, and what should his own role be?

Marxism *showed Brecht who would fight.* The poor did not have to remain passive victims, as they had been when he showed "sympathy" for them. In 1920 he had called Gerhart Hauptmann's *Rose Bernd* "a revolutionary play" (*GW* 15:24) because it showed the suffering of a poor farm girl. In 1928 he wrote:

> The fate of Rosa Bernd, the weavers and so on can no longer be perceived as tragic and so can no longer be alleged to be tragic in an age that can already reduce these catastrophes simply to a deficiency of

158

civilization, for the elimination of which the age has already worked out perfectly practical suggestions.

> Das Schicksal der Rose Bernd, der Weber und so weiter kann nicht mehr als tragisch empfunden und also auch nicht als tragisch vorgegeben werden in einer Zeit, welche diese Katastrophen schon auf einen bloßen Mangel der Zivilisation zurückführt, den zu beheben sie schon höchst praktische Vorschläge ausgearbeitet hat. (*GW* 15:173)

It is not tragedy when the poor simply accept their lot and do not fight back; it is pure folly. Furthermore, Brecht wrote about 1930, naturalist drama is a crime because it presents contemporary conditions as "natural," i.e., permanent, and human beings as pieces of nature, unable to change conditions (*GW* 15:207).

Evoking pity is only a tactic to prevent change. Reading Marx taught Brecht to think of the poor not as objects of pity who are always with us but as a class of fighters, the force for change in the contemporary world. There was no room in Brecht's revolutionary Marxism for charitable help for the poor. Persons who attempt it in his plays meet with the bitterest failure: either mere ineffectiveness, or a downright counterrevolutionary effect (e.g., *The Measure Taken, St. Joan, The Good Person of Sichuan.*) From the time he began reading Marx, Brecht no longer wore his worker's cap just as a protest against literary high society; he was consciously on the side of the working class, because they were the group in whose own interest it was to make the revolution, and who therefore would be the fighters. The rejuvenating effect he had previously sought in New World culture he now sought from the working class, the revolutionary force. Not that the two are by any means mutually exclusive—most of Brecht's early nonliterary influences had been from American popular or lower-class culture—but solidarity with, inspiration from, and respect for the working class is different from a mere escape from stuffy bourgeois art. For instance, Brecht credited the working class with the development of dialectical thinking (*GW* 20:76), which shows his respect, since he himself became a master at dialectics (see every page of *Refugee Conversations!*).

Finally, Brecht learned from Marxism to *take his own writing seriously*. This eventually led him out of the creative crisis he was in, but only after long study and much self-questioning on the role of the artist. Having learned that revolution was necessary and that it

159

would be made by the working class, Brecht, like every intellectual who becomes a Marxist, was confronted with the question whether persons of middle-class origin could contribute anything to the revolution. Brecht certainly did not identify himself with the bourgeoisie!—in fact, he thought of himself as a class traitor. In the 1938 poem "Driven Out for Good Reason," he wrote:

> When I was grown and looked around my world
> I found I didn't like the people of my class
> Nor giving orders nor being served
> And I abandoned my class and hung around
> With ordinary [lesser]people.

> Als ich erwachsen war und um mich sah
> Gefielen mir die Leute meiner Klasse nicht
> Nicht das Befehlen und nicht das Bedientwerden
> Und ich verließ meine Klasse und gesellte mich
> Zu den geringeren Leuten.

(GW 9:721)

But being alienated from one's own class is not positive reason enough for being dependable help when another class fights to take power. In *Drums in the Night*, Brecht had already written a play showing that anyone who joins the revolutionary working class without needing a revolution for himself is not reliable. This is also a theme of *St. Joan*. Brecht wrote about this problem often, particularly when he first started reading Marx. Always strict and unsentimental in his thinking, he accepted from the start Marx's contention that revolutions are made by classes, in their own self-interest, not primarily by individuals. In 1926 he wrote, "Real revolutions are not engendered (as in bourgeois histories) by feelings, but by interests" ("Die wirklichen Revolutionen werden nicht (wie in der bourgeoisen Geschichtsschreibung) durch Gefühle, sondern durch Interessen erzeugt"). It was necessary for intellectuals, then, to find their own reasons for needing a revolution:

> If the intellectuals want to participate in the class struggle, they must intellectually conceive their sociological constitution as unified and caused by material conditions. Their opinion, heard frequently these days, that it is necessary to submerge themselves in the proletariat, is counterrevolutionary. . . .
> The proletariat's interest in the class struggle is clear and unambiguous, the intellectuals' interest, which is historically verifiable, is harder to explain. The only explanation is that the intellectuals can

160

expect the development of their (intellectual) activity only through a revolution. That determines their role in a revolution: It is an intellectual role.

Wollen die Intellektuellen sich am Klassenkampf beteiligen, so ist es nötig, daß sie ihre soziologische Konstitution als eine einheitliche und durch materielle Bedingungen bestimmte intellektuell erfassen. Ihre häufig zutage getretene Ansicht, es sei nötig, im Proletariat unterzutauchen, ist konterrevolutionär. . . .
    Das Interesse des Proletariats am Klassenkampf ist klar und eindeutig, das Interesse von Intellektuellen, das ja historisch feststeht, ist schwerer zu erklären. Die einzige Erklärung ist, daß die Intellektuellen nur durch die Revolution sich eine Entfaltung ihrer (intellektuellen) Tätigkeit erhoffen können. Ihre Rolle in der Revolution ist dadurch bestimmt: Es ist eine intellektuelle Rolle. (*GW* 20:53)

Sternberg writes that about 1930, at the time of the depression and Hitler's rise to power, Brecht believed the job of a writer was to analyze and to make suggestions on what reason each particular subgroup in the middle class would have for needing a revolution; to denote this motive, together they invented the word *Umwälzungsgrund* (reason for revolution) and shortened it to *Ug*.[25] As a partial answer to the question of the intellectual's *Ug* (pronounced "oog"), Brecht came back to his old theme of freedom (*GW* 20:56)—but not the kind of freedom Garga had sought, not simply an individual escape, but rather a freedom that would be permanent and universal because based on a change in the economic and social system. In *Refugee Conversations* (1940–41), the worker tells the intellectual that intellectuals are exploited: "They have to rent out their head to the employer as we do our hands" ("Sie müssen ihren Kopf ausvermieten an die Unternehmer wie wir unsere Hände") (*GW* 14:1482).

To make his revolutionary role as a dramatist clear, Brecht used class terminology in referring to the theater: the owners and producers are the capitalists, those who write plays are the workers (*GW* 15:136, 171): they own no means of production and have nothing to sell but their labor, and have no voice in how their own plays are to be produced and how they are to be used, i.e., to what ideological purpose before what audience. It is not in the realm of possibility that the bourgeois interests that own the theaters would change them, just as Rockefeller cannot transform Standard Oil into a socialized enterprise. Therefore, the demand for a new theater

161

is the demand for a new social system (*GW* 15:172), and dramatists are revolutionaries when they regard themselves as a cultural proletariat and use the fighting methods of the working class.

And how can the working class use intellectuals? "To shoot holes in bourgeois ideology . . . For study of the forces that 'move the world' . . . To develop pure theory farther" ("Um die bürgerliche Ideologie zu durchlöchern . . . Zum Studium der Kräfte, die 'die Welt bewegen' . . . Um die reine Theorie weiterzuentwickeln") (*GW* 20:54). These answers are not as simple as they sound, of course. Brecht, like most Marxist intellectuals, spent a good part of his life thinking about the role of intellectuals and the middle class in general in a revolution to be made by the workers.

The artist is a special case in the intelligentsia. Brecht thought about and discussed the role of art and especially theater right to the end of his life, including a good deal of argument with East German cultural policies. But it is important to note that from the beginning of his Marxist study, the question was always *how* he as an artist and intellectual could take part in the revolution, not whether he wanted to.

From then on, Brecht considered himself both a communist and an artist, and he remained convinced that theater could be useful in a revolution and in a socialist country. He saw no need to sacrifice his belief in art for communism or his belief in communism for art. This pushed him to extraordinary new forms in drama, theater, and poetry, because he was always interested in the *usefulness* of his work, without ever neglecting its quality. Thinking of new forms, he juxtaposed the world of crass business and the world of poetry and asked, "Can we speak about money in the form of the iamb?" ("Können wir in der Form des Jambus über Geld sprechen?") (*GW* 15:197). His answer was to use the most heroic classical forms precisely to talk about money, but in a satiric style. In *St. Joan* and *Ui* the Shakespeare, Goethe, and Schiller parodies are intended not to make the classics look ridiculous but to show how once progressive forms become an ideological cover for reaction and to show the importance of economic laws, which Brecht considers equivalent to the older conceptions of providence and fate. Although he felt the classics were reactionary when used by today's bourgeoisie, Brecht decided they could be put to revolutionary uses if seen through new (workers') eyes. The city and the stock market were the new battlefields.

But in every case—reactionary or progressive—art was engaged on one side or another. Never was it to be seen as neutral; naturalism for instance, because of its defeatism, tended to prevent revolution. And worse:

> The working class has the terrifying position that art is harmful, because it distracts the masses from the struggle. But it hasn't distracted the bourgeoisie from its struggle, not for one minute.

> Das Proletariat steht auf dem schreckeneinflößenden Standpunkt, Kunst sei schädlich, da sie die Massen vom Kampf ablenke. Aber sie hat die Bourgeoisie von deren Kampf auch nicht abgelenkt, keine Minute. (*GW* 15:65)

The bourgeoisie knew how to use art as a weapon in class struggle; the working class must learn how to do the same. It would be a mistake simply to want to get rid of art, as recommended by some people on the left; here Brecht was adamant. He always believed both that art could be useful and that it was a valid pursuit for itself as well. Brecht openly criticized leftists who polemicized against art, and he defended the necessity that art develop as collective expression, rather than being ordered by individuals to express something in particular. Art had its own needs and laws of development. It would serve the class that produced it because it was collective in nature, but it could not be forced; then it would no longer be art (*GW* 15:66).

We have then in Brecht a communist who cared equally for the integrity of his art and for the use to which it could be put in his political cause. Disagreements between him and the Communist Party (KPD) or its GDR descendant the Socialist Unity Party (SED) were intensely interesting discussions on the use of art for political education. Brecht refused to compromise either on his belief in communism or his belief in art, which makes his comments on the subject important and unusual reading.

The interaction between art and politics—specifically between theater and education to communism—became the central theme of his thought for the thirty years he lived after reading Marx. In the first period of this preoccupation, he wrote in order to teach persons living under capitalism about the machinery of capitalism and methods of revolutionary discipline. In the second period, he wrote works against fascism, and political parables. And in the third, he wrote and directed plays to contribute to the development of a

163

communist consciousness in a socialist country. In all these phases (which are influenced by historical circumstances), Brecht believed the particular function that theater could have in the revolution was to *teach*. It could teach negatively—the nature of capitalism (and its distortion, fascism)—and positively—revolutionary tactics, the nature of socialist and communist man, and the dialectic between individual and collective. The word *teacher* became for Brecht the highest praise, and the process of learning became the most fascinating human activity.

After his *Schaffenskrise* (creative crisis) in the second half of the twenties, Brecht never again hesitated to define himself primarily as a writer; but at the same time, he was never again "just" a writer. In short, he had found a purpose outside his work that made it imperative that he continue. This is what reading Marx in 1926 did for him; this is why he considered that year and that experience the turning point in his life.

As Marxism brought a purpose to Brecht's drama, that purpose brought it a new form. Or, more exactly: he had already started writing about new subjects, and "just grasping the new subject matter requires a new dramatic and theatrical form" ("schon die Erfassung der neuen Stoffgebiete kostet eine neue dramatische und theatralische Form") (*GW* 15:197), but he did not begin writing dramatic theory until it became clear to him what he wanted to accomplish with his drama. His theories of drama and theater, which he wrote prolifically after reading Marx, were (like his adoption of Marxism itself) largely a process of putting names to instincts and practices already evident in his work. The difference is that in this field he created his own terminology. That is one of Brecht's contributions to revolutionary theory.

Audiences and critics had always sensed that there was something strange and new about Brecht's writing. But until 1926 the newness had been largely a rebellion against the sterility of the old theater. After 1926 Marxism helped him coordinate the new formal possibilities he had found more or less by accident before; he combined them into an aesthetic system that was a consistent result of the philosophical system he was adopting. That is: his dramatic theory became the logical and *necessary* means to promote the socialist revolution through theater. His "epic theater," as he first called it, was not an arbitrary invention; he could show logically why it was necessary for political purposes. It was also not a private idiosyncracy of Brecht's; it was convincing to others working in revolutionary dramatics. Günter Weisenborn, who worked with Brecht on production of *The Mother*, wrote:

> In the course of long conversations I had with Brecht about Germany, I recognized that his theory of epic theater is almost indispensable for certain specific purposes. . . . I soon concluded that, at least when the theme of the play is political behavior, the epic form of theater is the best.

> Im Verlauf langer Unterhaltungen über Deutschland, die ich mit Brecht führte, erkannte ich, daß seine Theorie vom epischen Theater für ganz bestimmte Zwecke kaum zu entbehren ist. . . . Es ergab sich für mich bald, daß die epische Form des Theaters zumindest dann die beste ist, wenn das Thema des Stückes politisches Verhalten ist.[26]

Brecht formulated the theory of epic theater in detail for the first time in the well-known notes to *Mahagonny*, where he contrasted lists of attributes of the "dramatic" form and the "epic" form, for instance:

doing	telling a story
suggestion	argument
the unchangeable person	the changeable and changing person
one scene for the other	each scene for itself
thinking determines existence	social existence determines thinking
emotion	reason
handelnd	erzählend
Suggestion	Argument
Der unveränderliche Mensch	Der veränderliche und verändernde Mensch
Eine Szene für die andere	Jede Szene für sich
Das Denken bestimmt das Sein	Das gesellschaftliche Sein bestimmt das Denken
Gefühl	Ratio[27]

These are elements of Marxist theory, but they are also stylistic techniques Brecht had used before. Piscator called his own theater epic; Brecht in fact says that naturalist drama was the first epic drama, because it was an attempt to bring Zola's novels to the stage

165

(*GW* 15:214). And he also suggests his own first play, *Baal*, as an example of early epic form (*GW* 15:133). But it is clear that *Baal* was by no means what Brecht meant when he began, after reading Marx, to write a whole theory of epic theater.

Happy with Brecht's late plays but unhappy with his theories, some Western critics like to say that he was a greater dramatist than theorist and that the late plays contradict the schematic theory of epic theater. Of course they do, if the notes to *Mahagonny* are taken as definitive; even when he wrote them, he said they were not definitive, and later he revised his theory considerably. About 1930–31 he practically stopped using the term "epic" theater, which is unfortunately the term that posterity has clung to, and started calling what he was writing and writing about "dialectical" theater. Its meaning becomes clearest when we compare the *Lehrstücke* to *A Man's a Man*: in the latter (earlier) play there is no conflict, Galy Gay is simply manipulated. In the *Lehrstücke* there are both conflict and the need to find an answer: *The Measure Taken*, for instance, presents what seems to be an insoluble dilemma; it can only be resolved with reference to the *context*, namely, the necessary strategy for revolution. The play is not self-contained; solution of the problem presented in it requires thought about reality. (The correct answer may even change depending on historical conditions when the play is performed.) In *The Mother* there is a standard theme of psychological theater: estrangement of the son from the mother. It is transcended with reference to "the third thing," which is the context of the play: their common fight for revolution. Again: in *The Yea-Sayer* and *The Nay-Sayer*, the dilemmas presented cannot be solved simply from the dramatic premises of the plays. The audience must think of the values beyond the plays; it is forced to bring external criteria for judgment. Dialectical theater then is the putting of a certain conflict within a historical context.

This began, Brecht later claims, when economics were brought into drama. The economic basis of life is the context into which conventional conflicts are placed; the purpose of theater is to show the relationship, thereby providing new insights about the conventional conflicts. Theater should descend as deep as it can into the base or substructure (*GW* 15:132–33); if it remains a creature only of the superstructure, it will continue to be pure entertainment, or "culinary." These convictions were developing in Brecht before he started reading Marx, rather as a result of his interest in America,

which led him independently to a concentration on economic
themes in drama. Thus it is that America led Brecht not only to
Marx but simultaneously, or even a little earlier, to epic theater.
Elisabeth Hauptmann makes this fact clear in her description of
Brecht's work on *Joe Fleischhacker*. We have already quoted the
part of her journal entry from 26 July, 1926, in which she tells how
Brecht was determined to see if he could understand theories about
money (see above, p. 137). The entry continues:

> Before he made the at least for him very important discoveries in this
> direction, he already knew that the hitherto existing (grand) dramatic
> form was not suitable for demonstrating such modern processes as the
> distribution of the world's wheat or the biographies of people of our
> time or for that matter any act that has consequences. "These things," B.
> said, "are not dramatic in our sense, and when one 'poeticizes' them they
> are no longer true, and drama isn't that kind of thing any more anyway,
> and when one sees that today's world no longer belongs in the drama,
> then the drama just doesn't belong in the world." In the course of these
> studies Brecht established his theory of "epic drama."

> Bevor er noch in dieser Richtung zumindest für ihn sehr wichtige
> Entdeckungen machte, wußte er aber, daß die bisherige (große) Form
> des Dramas für die Darstallung solcher modernen Prozesse, wie etwa
> die Verteilung des Weltweizens sowie auch für Lebensläufe der Men-
> schen unserer Zeit und überhaupt für alle Handlungen mit Folgen nicht
> geeignet war. "Diese Dinge", sagte B., "sind nicht dramatisch in unse-
> rem Sinn, und wenn man sie 'umdichtet', dann sind sie nicht mehr wahr,
> und das Drama ist überhaupt keine solche Sache mehr, und wenn man
> sieht, daß unsere heutige Welt nicht mehr ins Drama paßt dann paßt
> das Drama eben nicht mehr in die Welt." Im Verlaufe dieser Studien
> stellte Brecht seine Theorie des "epischen Dramas" auf.[28]

It was the conviction that new subjects must be shown that led to
the theory of epic theater; but Brecht later chose to call his own
version dialectical theater; and he restricted the term *epic* to
production and acting: "epic style of presentation" ("epischer
Darstellungsstil"). This was probably to differentiate his own
theories from the many early productions (e.g., Piscator) that he had
named "epic." So when he writes that "dialectical theater"
developed with the addition of economics to naturalism (*GW*
15:216), he is probably referring to everything he wrote from about
1926, and simply renaming it.

Probably the principal stylistic means of "dialectical" theater was
Verfremdung, or dramatic alienation, i.e., making the familiar
strange. Brecht did not use the term, however, until the later thirties

167

(Ewen says 1936, in connection with the Danish production of *The Roundheads and the Peakheads*).[29] But Brecht had used the *technique* almost from the start. He writes in 1954 that he had not been aware of the possibilities of dramatic alienation when he wrote *Drums in the Night* (*GW* 17:946), but his explanation of why he chose the American milieu for the next play, *In the Jungle* (see above, p. 15), is an example of an alienation effect.

In fact, not only was America Brecht's first experiment with setting as alienation effect; that remained a principal use of the American setting throughout. In *Arturo Ui* (1941) the American background is there to make the characters' actions appear as social phenomena or "types," produced by a certain set of social or economic relations. Were the plays set in Germany, the audience would react to the characters as exceptional individuals (*GW* 17:971–72).

Brecht used this technique, then, as early as 1921. But he did not have a programmatic purpose for it, and so did not formulate a name and a theory for it, until he felt he was sure of the relation between social structure and individual behavior. Then he was able to say that a play set in the wheat exchange cannot and must not have "dramatic" form, which encourages empathy, because it is wrong for the audience to believe it possible to understand or identify with the world as it is (*GW* 15:186).

In 1939 Brecht was able to define dramatic alienation and provide a full explanation of its *purpose*. Definition:

> To "alienate" an event or a character means in the first instance simply to take the obvious, familiar, evident from the event or character and to produce astonishment and curiosity over it.

> Einen Vorgang oder einen Charakter verfremden heißt zunächst einfach, dem Vorgang oder dem Charakter das Selbstverständliche, Bekannte, Einleuchtende zu nehmen und über ihn Staunen und Neugierde zu erzeugen. (*GW* 15:301).

Purpose: presenting behavior as a social phenomenon that has specific causes, and therefore is *not* a universal principle. It must occur to the audience that in another society the character might have acted differently. To "alienate" means, then, to historicize. And the value of historicization is that the audience does not consider characters on the stage unchangeable and helplessly ruled by fate; rather, it sees that people are a certain way because conditions are a certain way, and vice versa. Both character and the conditions could be different. Brecht gives a primer-book example of the technique of historicization when he writes about his experience in trying to finish *Joe Fleischhacker*, in the poem "This Babylonian Confusion" (see above, pp. 137–38): from the point of view of later, liberated generations, the behavior of the wheat speculators and of the people who allow themselves to be exploited is strange and incomprehensible.

At the same time as he started talking about *Verfremdung*, Brecht also developed his dramatic theory further and began calling his plays not just "dialectical" but "non-Aristotelian" drama. A definition of the new term is simple: it is theater that does not produce empathy (and therefore, also, not pity or fear or catharsis). But the theory that is subsumed under this concept is a new step, a complication and sophistication of the earlier theories, now covering not only non-culinary opera and *Lehrstücke* but also Brecht's great late plays.

The prevention of empathy or identification was also an element of Brecht's art from the beginning; he wrote in 1922 that he hoped in *Baal* and *Jungle* to have avoided the mistake of most art: "its attempt to carry away" ("ihre Bemühung, mitzureißen") (*GW* 15:62) (i.e., to affect the audience's emotions). But he was unable to say why his way was any better; it was only different. The audience should remain in "splendid isolation," he continued—using the English words—because interest in the *Gleichnis* (parable) is a higher kind of interest. Why is it higher? Brecht could not say until he knew what he wanted to make images or parables *of*. As Hans Mayer points out, this kind of intellectual theater was still art for art's sake: it was producing a particular kind of pleasure; i.e., thinking; it was not yet teaching a historical context.[30] (That is similar to the criticism Brecht later made of his character Galileo.)

In summary; there are stylistic elements of epic/dialectical/non-Aristotelian theater and of dramatic alienation in almost all Brecht's work. But Brecht himself did not know what the purpose of these techniques was until he developed a philosophy that demanded of him that he use drama not just to interpret the world but to change it. This happened directly as a result of his interest in America; in fact, he began to discover some of the principles of Marxism and of epic theater even before reading Marx, while working on a play on America.

When we say Brecht gained all this political and artistic perspective by reading Marx, we do not mean that he immediately overcame his creative crisis; on the contrary, he continued to produce very little in 1927 and 1928. But it was no longer paralysis; it was deliberate. He was learning how to walk before he could run. He remained convinced that he should write plays explaining economic mechanisms, but he had to understand economics thoroughly before he could write the plays. Sternberg notes:

> When we were talking about the necessity of reason, I once told him he might hate me later on. As long as he tried to form a picture of today's society through use of reason, he would not be able to write. And this period could last a long time. Brecht admitted this. And in fact, in the first two years that we knew each other he wrote very little. But at the same time Brecht said he would struggle against the feelings of hatred for me, since he would know where they came from. Understanding reality was, he said, a life-and-work necessity for him.

> Als wir über die Notwendigkeit der Ratio sprachen, sagte ich ihm einmal, er werde mich vielleicht später hassen. Solange er versuche, sich über die Ratio ein Bild der heutigen Gesellschaft zu machen, werde er nicht schreiben können. Und diese Periode könne lange Zeit dauern. Brecht gab dies zu. Tatsächlich hat er in den ersten zwei Jahren, in denen wir uns kannten, nur sehr wenig geschrieben. Aber Brecht meinte gleichzeitig, er werde die Haßgefühle gegen mich bekämpfen, da er ja wisse, woher sie kämen. Für ihn sei die Erfassung der Wirklichkeit eine Lebens-und Schaffensnotwendigkeit.[31]

If, as Sternberg feels, Brecht did later come to dislike him, it was because their political differences made it impossible for them to talk (Sternberg found Brecht too Stalinist) and not because Brecht resented having been seduced away from his writing for two years. His study of the roots of social relations was, as he said, absolutely necessary for him—and for his work.

It was a study that he carried out intensely for the first two to two-and-a-half years; Käthe Rülicke-Weiler writes that "Brecht devoted more than two years—from 1926 to 1928—primarily to the study of Marxism and gave up writing plays." ("Brecht verwandte mehr als zwei Jahre—von 1926 bis 1928—in erster Linie aufs Studium des Marxismus und verzichtete aufs Schreiben von Stücken.")[32] During that time he wrote musicals, which were transitional pieces without the agitprop purposes of the plays that he began writing in 1929. Only after two years of intense study did he feel qualified to write the kind of play that *Fleischhacker* had set out to be: a play requiring a knowledge of Marxism. The development of Brecht's thought in those two years and the later refinements of it are subjects for another study. Such a study would be crucial to an understanding of Brecht, and more: a contribution to the theory of learning and influence. Reinhold Grimm says that Brecht's study of Marx was comparable in intensity and effect to Schiller's study of Kant[33]—and it has hardly been investigated at all.

Brecht seems at first to have mistrusted organized socialism and concentrated his study and writing on the criticism of capitalism. The Communist Party does not appear in his imaginative work until *St. Joan*, and in his essays and notes he is critical of the Party and of socialists. This fact should invalidate the psychological interpretation of some critics who wish to "excuse" Brecht's belief in communism by saying he needed a stern discipline. Brustein, for instance, writes: "His attraction to Communism, therefore, can also be ascribed to the fact that it offers a system of regimentation, a form of rational control over his frightening individualism and terrifying subjectivity"; and "Brecht responded as eagerly to the Communist discipline as to the Communist dogma; there is something almost religious about his attachment to his new creed."[34]

The fact is that Brecht's early interest in Marxism was not primarily characterized by a desire to submit to discipline. It was clearly born of the desire to *understand*: as Brecht himself makes perfectly clear, it was a rational, not a psychological motivation. What he wanted to understand was capitalism, and his work continued for a while to be an exposure of capitalism. It was the emphasis on rationality that eventually made Brecht see the need for positive action and therefore discipline, and he wrote several plays showing how discipline (= strategic action) must be learned. But there is no evidence that he welcomed discipline *per se*, or for psychological reasons. It was the goal (he had never had a goal before), communism, that he welcomed, because it was rational and just. Discipline was the necessary and often unpleasant means to achieve the goal.

Dedication to revolution came to him fast but dedication to a party or organization much more slowly. In fact, he never joined the

171

KPD or the SED (many dedicated communists do not), but by 1930 he approved in the main of their direction.[35] Thus he was able to say honestly to the literal-minded House Unamerican Activities Committee that he had never been a Communist, though of course in fact he was every inch a communist, and people who knew him in America say (with exasperation) that he was indefatigable in proselytizing.

In one of the first studies he wrote after he began reading Marx, Brecht described the Party in unflattering terms: "a rather small-minded, but strong and sly petty bureaucracy" ("eine geistig ziemlich niedrige, aber kräftige und schlaue Kleinbürokratie") (*GW* 20:49) that would be swept away without sentimentality after the revolution because it would turn out to have material interests different from those of the working class. One has to respect the Party, Brecht wrote, because it held a mass of a million people together in the opposition—but it clearly did not appeal to his sense of what the revolution should look like. In short, Brecht held at that time what might forty years later be called a "new left" position.

His objection to a boring bureaucracy is echoed in a projected foreword to *A Man's a Man* from 1926[36] that was never published. Here he criticizes socialists for not being seriously enough involved in struggle: their arguments are so weak that one can only conclude they do not know what they want, which must mean they are not suffering as much as they claim. "i am curious what socialism is . . . it is absolutely vague and fuzzy" ("ich bin neugierig was sozialismus ist . . . er ist absolut vage und verschwommen"). He continues: one must really control oneself to avoid exploding in anger on hearing what nonsense an otherwise useful man speaks. When he has heard socialists in debate, he has usually chosen their side, "but their babble was dreadful" ("aber ihr geschwätz war entsetzlich"). They react emotionally but are ashamed of emotions. They claim they cannot express themselves because the bourgeoisie will not allow the working class to learn how to think, but Brecht finds that an insipid argument: to express oneself one only needs strong feelings. He has never heard, for instance, of a polar explorer who starved because he could not say in Eskimo that he was hungry or because he was too hungry to talk. Brecht "allows himself to conclude" from the fact that the worker cannot express himself that his emotions are too weak. "but that is a monstrous accusation" ("das ist aber ein ungeheurer vorwurf") (BBA 348, 31).

Brecht knew that the poor suffered; this we have seen sufficiently in his early plays. What he most likely meant in this very strange outburst is: the working class would know well enough what it wanted and be able to say so in plain language, if only the socialists would stop confusing things with their gibberish. Brecht continues:

> having arrived here i will allow all possible objections except the one that socialism is something clear i mean as clear as a struggle requires.

> hier angelangt lasse ich alle möglichen einwände zu nur nicht den daß sozialismus etwas klares und zwar etwas so klares ist wie es zu einem kampf nötig ist. (BBA 348, 32)

As in other writings of this time, he was *for* the struggle, but found the means of the organized group too far from the direct emotional idea of revolution, too unclear and tied up in subtle tactical considerations. Probably there was some validity in his criticism, but probably he also suffered from the romanticism of the revolutionary neophyte who wants quick direct action and no politicking. (It is also possible that Brecht meant to contrast socialism to the more revolutionary communism; in light of what he says about the Party, however, it is more likely that he meant to contrast both forms of organized Marxism to revolution.)

The foreword seems to have little to do with *A Man's a Man*. The connection is simply that that is a play about a man who does not think clearly, which is the danger the socialists are imposing on the working class. But Brecht wrote another foreword to *A Man's a Man*, in 1927. It is on first sight also strange; it tries to maintain that Galy Gay becomes stronger when he gives up his own personality; that by becoming part of the mass he can only win, that in fact he is a predecessor of the "new type of person" who is the goal of our future. To be sure, Brecht ends by saying to the audience, "But perhaps you'll come to another opinion. Against which I would be the last person to object" ("Aber vielleicht gelangen Sie zu einer anderen Ansicht. Wogegen ich am wenigsten etwas einzuwenden habe") (*GW* 17:978). That could mean Brecht had exactly the opposite opinion from what he wrote and only wanted to provoke thought.

Brecht's critics on the right will claim he was making fanatic application of the communist contempt for individuality, the same fanaticism that he reveals in the *Lehrstücke* on acquiescence, and that he is blind here to the nature of the collective Galy Gay joins.

173

But Brecht does not say that this particular collective is good, only that the process of learning to be part of a collective is a necessary step toward a socialized society that will contain the "new person." Let us remember Marxist theory: the increasing collectivization of industrial capitalist society creates a new consciousness in the working class, who eventually find it necessary to destroy anachronistic private ownership of their factories in order that society be structured in the way that technology and consciousness now make possible. Galy Gay is already the collective man; when his sort get together the revolution will come. Brecht stretched *A Man's a Man* there a little to give himself a concrete example from his own works of the theories he was reading; 1927 is the year in which he revised *In the Jungle*, leaving out much of the private touches. It is also the year in which he wrote *The Flight of the Lindberghs*, later *Flight over the Ocean*, praising man's oneness with technology and the possibilities of technological progress to liberate rather than enslave. In all these cases Brecht worked with the new theories he was learning, testing them with his own experiences and studies. His sometimes farfetched reinterpretations are comments on his thoughts on Marxism at the time: neither of the forewords quoted has much to do with *A Man's a Man*. He used his own plays, as he felt Marx himself would, as *Anschauungsmaterial* (material for observation), sociological data.

In 1930 he also attempted the last rewriting of *Baal*, left in fragment form as *Bad Baal the Antisocial Man*. Here Baal was to be made to look like a useless romantic aesthete, and the workers whom he meets have the more serious business of avoiding starvation to worry about. This fragment was apparently part of the cycle of works in which Brecht tried to illustrate Marxist theories: *The Bread Store, Fatzer, Nothing Will Come of Nothing*, and *Bad Baal the Antisocial Man* were all written about 1929–30, and they all remained fragments. This new emphasis is also clear from the changes Brecht made at the same time in *The Threepenny Opera* for the filmscript, which was to be called *The Lump on the Head:* the beggar hordes Peachum unleashes threaten to destroy the whole status quo, Macheath and his gang expropriate a bank, and their clothing is suddenly transformed into business dress as they step from a stolen car to the bank steps.[37]

Brecht's "conversion" to Marxism did not occur quite as suddenly

174

as Saul's to Christianity then after all. As Lenin explains it, there are three revolutions in thought contained in Marxism: the development of the *philosophy* of dialectical materialism to apply to human society, the development in *political economy* of a "scientific" explanation of capitalism based on the theory of surplus value, and the development of *socialism* from a utopian appeal to intellectuals to a program for class struggle.[38] Brecht began his study with the critique of capitalism, and the first works he wrote after starting to read Marx reflect his first reading. His interest in dialectics developed slowly but steadily and eventually informed every aspect of his style and even his nomenclature; materialism was easier to grasp and is expressed baldly in the famous anti-idealist line "First comes eating, then comes morality" in the *Threepenny Opera* of 1928. About socialism and the methods of struggle necessary to achieve it, Brecht seems to have learned more slowly. We do not know exactly which Marxist works Brecht read after *Capital*, but we can state with certainty that after 1926 the next big change in his thought, at least as far as it is expressed in his writings, came in 1929, when he began to write not only against capitalism but also for communism, and began to approve the methods of the Communist Party.

Sternberg dates Brecht's "conversion" to communism from May Day 1929. He describes the workers' demonstration, which had been forbidden. The workers held it anyway, while he and Brecht watched from a window. The police broke up the demonstration, and to the observers' horror twenty were shot.

> When Brecht heard the shots and saw that people were hit, his face turned whiter than I had ever seen him in my life. I believe it was not least this experience that led him more and more strongly to the communists.

> Als Brecht die Schüsse hörte und sah, daß Menschen getroffen wurden, wurde er so weiß im Gesicht, wie ich ihn nie zuvor in meinem Leben gesehen hatte. Ich glaube, es war nicht zuletzt dieses Erlebnis, was ihn dann immer stärker zu den Kommunisten trieb.[39]

Not the least important thing, but surely a single experience was also not the only, or even principal, cause for Brecht's "conversion." To understand Brecht's development from critic of capitalism (a position he came to through his interest in America) to fighter for communism, it is necessary to turn again to his studies of the American system.

175

Chapter Four

1927–1929
Studying Marx:
"Mahagonny" and the
Learning Plays

"Mahagonny Song Play," and "The Rise
and Fall of the City of Mahagonny"

The first dramatic work that Brecht finished after starting to read
Marx was again set in America. This time, however, it was a frankly
mythical America, a geographical impossibility composed of
various American dreams Brecht had collected in his more naïve
days. *Mahagonny*, a *Songspiel* (Song Play) and Brecht's first of
many ventures into musical theater, simply provided a framework
for the five "Mahagonny" poems from the early twenties that Brecht
had included in the *Home Devotions*, plus one new poem, "But This
Entire Mahagonny," which gave the earlier poems a bitter and
ironic twist. Originally, Brecht had probably not intended that those
early poems on the decadent pleasures should be a criticism of
capitalism: they were portraits of contemporary attitudes, with
some heroism and some desperation. It is the context he provides in
the *Songspiel* that turns the old songs into bitter criticism of
American capitalism. This is, of course, another example of Brecht's
discovery, upon reading Marx, that his early writings were good
data for a study of human relations under capitalism; he was now in
a position to make a Marxist analysis of his own very accurate but
untheoretical observations. He called the expanded version a
"description of customs and morals" ("Sittenschilderung") (*GW*
2:1*).

   Mahagonny does not have the programmatic intent that informs
Brecht's works beginning in 1929; it is more like an explanation, in

parable form, of the origins of the different kinds of alienation capitalism produces: alienation from the enjoyment of labor and from the enjoyment of the fruits of labor, alienation between man and woman, alienation between old friends. All are caused by the interpolation of money between people and their desires. But there is absolutely no suggestion what to do about the problem. Paul Ackermann dies recognizing he has pursued a false happiness, and Mahagonny falls ever deeper into chaos, but no way out is suggested. The Director's Script of 1927 calls it a "Dance of Death" ("Totentanz").[1] The piece is, in short, anti-capitalist in implication, but it (like *The Threepenny Opera*) could easily have been written by a bourgeois reformer. There is nothing in any work Brecht wrote before 1929 that would necessarily have to come from the pen of a communist.

Nevertheless, the premieres of both the *Mahagonny Songspiel* (Baden-Baden, 1927) and *Rise and Fall of the City of Mahagonny* (Leipzig 1930) caused scandals; Lotte Lenya thinks the theater scandal in Leipzig was the worst in history.[2] The bourgeoisie, who expected to see classical opera in its opera house, was certainly convinced that it was seeing communist propaganda, as is evident from the reviews. A Professor Ernst Müller, for instance, protested in the *Allgemeine Musikzeitung* against the presumption

of making an opera stage of the rank of the Leipzig one, where today *Fidelio*, tomorrow *Tristan*, and Good Friday probably *Parsifal* appears, into a playground for criminals, whores, pimps, a gathering place for communist demonstrations.

eine Opernbühne vom Range der Leipziger, auf der heute "Fidelio", morgen "Tristan", am Karfreitag wahrscheinlich "Parsifal" erscheint, zum Tummelplatz von Verbrechern, Dirnen, Zuhältern, zum Sammelort von kommunistischen Demonstrationszügen zu machen.[3]

For the production three days later in Kassel, Brecht and Weill toned the opera down slightly, in particular the allegedly "communist" demonstration at the end. Weill wrote,

We now have a version which the Pope himself could no longer take exception to. It is made clear that the final demonstrations are in no wise "Communistic"—it is simply that Mahagonny, like Sodom and Gomorrah, falls on account of the crimes, the licentiousness and the general confusion of its inhabitants.[4]

177

Brecht was still more interested in shocking the bourgeoisie than in building working-class consciousness. For *Mahagonny* is, in the final analysis, a picture of petty-bourgeois life unveiled, written for the bourgeoisie in order to confront it with its own hypocrisy; it is a play designed to catch the conscience of the king. This is why it is so appealing. It has wonderful, sophisticated satire, compared to the stark direct statements of positive lessons written later for workers. Its music, as Brecht later feared, comes almost too close to being "culinary": it traps the audience by appealing to our own sentimental taste and then slaps us with the satire. No members of the consumption-oriented society can fail to see ourselves in *Mahagonny*, even leftists: even those who reject the commercial ideology will still be seduced into self-recognition by the music.

This was not just Weill's addition to Brecht's text; it is impossible to differentiate sharply between Brecht as author of the text and Weill as author of the music. The two worked very closely together on both; Weill says that he and Brecht worked together almost a year on the text of the opera,[5] and Brecht had composed melodies to some of the songs already.[6] Weill's versions of the "Alabama Song" and "Benares Song" are almost exactly like Brecht's, and the others bear some resemblance. Furthermore they agreed completely in all their writings on the task of music in the theater, Brecht explaining what Weill was doing as naturally as if he had done it himself, which to a certain extent (both actually and through advice) he had.

It also would be a mistake to make a very sharp distinction between the two versions of *Mahagonny*, the *Songspiel* and the full-length opera. According to Weill's notes in the 1930 program, he composed music for the five Mahagonny songs in the *Home Devotions* as a stylistic study for the opera that he and Brecht had already begun.[7] He wrote the music during the month of May 1927, and his archivist, David Drew, reports that Weill announced to his publishers at the beginning of May that "a subject for a large-scale tragic opera is already worked out."[8] In fact, Brecht had planned a "*mahagonny-oper*" as early as July 1924, as we know from a dated notebook (BBA 461, 61); and Elisabeth Hauptmann claims that when the poems called "Mahagonny Songs" were first written about 1920 and 1921, Brecht intended them to be part of a play.[9] Lotte Lenya remembers that Brecht and Weill started work on the full-length opera immediately after returning to Berlin from the premiere of the *Songspiel.*[10] The two were really one continuous work, not an original and a later revision.

Work on *Mahagonny* was briefly interrupted three times for other musicals Brecht and Weill wrote together. In the middle of 1928, they took a short break (Lenya says it was a few months,[11] Drew that it was a few *weeks!*[12]) to fulfill a contract they had from the director Aufricht in Berlin. He wanted an adaptation of John Gay's *Beggar's Opera. The Threepenny Opera*, written as an aside during the work on *Mahagonny*, was performed on the last day of August 1928. It became such a success that Brecht, Weill, and the company of actors decided (according to Elisabeth Hauptmann) to put together another play quickly, to be able to keep together the group that had so much enjoyed producing *The Threepenny Opera*. Hauptmann wrote *Happy End*, but Weill wrote the music and Brecht suggested the story and may have written the song texts. Then there came another contract from the Baden-Baden Music Festival for Brecht and Weill; this time they wrote a new kind of work, a didactic radio play. *The Flight of the Lindberghs* (renamed *Flight over the Ocean* when Brecht learned of Lindbergh's support for Hitler; Brecht said, significantly, that Lindbergh "got lost in the swamp of our cities" ["verlor sich im Sumpf unserer Städte"] [*GW* 2:3*]) became the formal model for the communist *Lehrstücke* Brecht wrote in 1929-30. Both *Flight of the Lindberghs* and *Happy End* were performed in the summer of 1929.

But throughout 1927-29 *Mahagonny* was Brecht's principal project. Drew says that during the late summer and early autumn of 1927, Weill and Brecht worked on it together almost daily; yet the score was not finished until April 1929, two years after it was begun.[13] It represents the most complete dramatic expression of Brecht's thought and attitudes in the years between his discovery of Marx and his conscious commitment to communism. (Klaus Schuhmann, in writing about Brecht's poetry to 1933, also considers the years 1926-29 a "transitional period."[14] But he investigates reasons for Brecht's ideological development mainly in contemporary German events: Nazism, the Weimar Republic, working-class struggles. It is the contention of this study that Brecht's entire political development to 1931—his attitude toward capitalism hardly changed after that—can be read from his works on America, and that America may have been at least as strong an influence as

179

Germany in causing this development.) And yet *Mahagonny* was not a very strenuous or serious work: it is an easy criticism of capitalist society; it is, as Brecht himself continually insisted, "fun" ("ein Spaß"). Since the other two and one-half plays he wrote in this period also cost a minimum of exertion, it is apparent that his serious study was occurring apart from his playwriting or even taking precedence over it; at any rate, he had not yet broken out of his creative "crisis." He could still say of the music-dramas written in 1927–29 that he wrote them "with his left hand." In fact, his most enthusiastic critic, Ihering, wrote in 1931, "I have always regarded *The Threepenny Opera* as a secondary work, meant for giving entertainment theater a different substance, a different form" ("Ich habe 'Die Dreigroschenoper' immer als ein Nebenwerk betrachtet, geeignet, der Unterhaltungsdramatik eine andere Substanz, eine andere Form zu geben").[15] This does not mean that the musicals are not excellent works, but only that they did not force Brecht into much new thinking. Although *Mahagonny* took several years to complete, the work on it was not very intense. A great deal of *Mahagonny*, in fact, is composed of elements from earlier works that Brecht reshuffled and quoted.

Of course, it was not out of laziness that Brecht adapted and reused material. On the contrary, he regarded all his plays as unfinished and revised them again and again. In keeping with his attitude that his own works and those of other authors were partly documentary material, he adopted from them whatever he found useful to make a point about society.

The American plays in particular borrow from each other because they are all part of the complex about mankind's migration to the cities: this theme is particularly apparent in *Mahagonny*, with its lumberjacks from Alaska and women from Havana, Oklahoma, or Alabama. In the 1930 and 1931 versions, the lumberjacks all had unmistakably German names, in accordance with the immigrant tradition of Sinclair's *Jungle*, *The Wheel*, *Flags*, and Brecht's *In the Jungle*. They are double immigrants: first to the New World, then from the most primitive and hard life in Jack London's Alaska to the most civilized (decadent) and soft life in the prototype of The City. Brecht and Weill recommended the substitution of German names for their original American names when the work was performed in

Germany, to avoid an overemphasis on Americanism, as Weill explains in a letter to the publishers:

> The use of American names for *Mahagonny* runs the risk of establishing a wholly false idea of Americanism, Wildwest, or such like. I am very glad that, together with Brecht, I have now found a very convenient solution . . . and I ask you to include the following notice in the piano score and libretto: "In view of the fact that those amusements of man which can be had for money are always and everywhere exactly the same, and because the Amusement-Town of Mahagonny is thus international in the widest sense, the names of the leading characters can be changed into customary forms at any given time."[16]

The technique of using foreign settings to make the familiar strange always created the problem of striking the best balance. Apparently Brecht and Weill feared the German audience was happy not to recognize itself at all, when the exotic setting provided sufficient excuse. Brecht's disclaimer after the production of *In the Jungle* (see above, p. 15) represents a similar retreat from the danger of letting the audience become too fascinated by the setting. *Mahagonny* is not *about* America; it is about capitalism. It is *set in* (mythical) America so that capitalist relations can be generalized and abstracted. But it is meant to affect how Germans view Germany.

However, Brecht's problem with the audience's reactions does not influence our study of his own attitudes toward America. Changing the names does not change the gold rush, Florida, and the mythology of the lawless West on which Mahagonny is obviously based.

Leokadja Begbick is lifted from *A Man's a Man*, but most other details are adapted from poems or unfinished plays about America. Since many of the projected plays about America and the cities were not finished, it was an especially happy solution to insert their component parts into *Mahagonny* and *St. Joan of the Stockyards*.

The most obvious secondhand elements are, of course, the songs. It would be interesting to know how much the final *Mahagonny* has in common with the plans for a Mahagonny play in 1920–21 and a Mahagonny opera in 1924; it would give us more precise information on the development of Brecht's anti-capitalism. But we can judge some from the songs themselves.

The original five "Mahagonny Songs" were first published in Brecht's *Home Devotions*. The principal edition of that collection was the one Brecht revised in 1927. Weill may well have come upon him just as he was working on the new edition; Weill says he was fascinated by the idea of writing an opera about "Mahagonny," a "paradise city" ("Paradiesstadt") the very first time he met Brecht in the spring of 1927.[17]

In the "directions for use of the poems" in the *Home Devotions*, Brecht wrote that the section "Mahagonny Songs" was "the right thing for hours of luxury, consciousness of the flesh, and arrogance. (So, it comes under consideration for a very few readers.)" ("das Richtige für die Stunden des Reichtums, das Bewußtsein des Fleisches, und die Anmaßung. [Sie kommt also nur für sehr wenige Leser in Betracht.]) (*GW* 8:170). In this ironic instruction is contained some of the idea of Mahagonny as the type of the capitalist city. "Mahagonny" is (as Bronnen reported about the invention of the word in 1923) a petty-bourgeois utopia; of greater importance by 1927 is its dependence on wealth—which is only available to a few readers. It is no longer a dream for all of a place to escape to; now it is Brecht's portrait of the voluptuous life actually led by the rich and arrogant few, and it is aimed at them. Schumacher's criticism, that the opera is illogical because the persons inventing and carrying out the capitalist ethic are workers,[18] is irrelevant. They have become rich men through their work, and now they want to reap the rewards of wealth. Insofar as *Mahagonny* is addressed to the working class at all, it says: years of sacrifice in order to make money are completely pointless, because the paradise the money can bring is hell; it is more alienated than the work itself.

This is the meaning of the repeated desire to return to Alaska: there the four men worked hard and lived like human beings together. Brecht was not for the abolition of work; rather, work should become an immediate pleasure rather than a painful means of making money with which to buy pleasure. Pleasure bought with money is no pleasure because the money takes precedence. Alaska, even though it is also primitive and is simply substituted for Tahiti in the poem "Tahiti," does not play the same role here as Tahiti in *Jungle*. Alaska is where the men came from, like the flatland for the Garga family. Mahagonny is where they want to go. Mahagonny is the realization of the earlier Tahiti dream: the escape, the natural paradise. Here Brecht carries to its conclusion what would have happened if Garga and characters in early poems had actually gone to Tahiti, where a week is seven days without work (*GW* 2:502) and where they hoped to be cured of "syphilization" ("zi-zi-zi-zi-zivilis") (*GW* 2:507). The result is an increase in all the evils of civilization because the paradises are run purely on a profit basis.

The "zivilis" pun comes from the "Mahagonny Song No. 1" in the *Home Devotions*. Here already there is an indication of what Mahagonny will become: the men expect to buy a laugh from the mouth of the moon with the paper money they have under their shirts—but then again, they don't think much of that lovely green moon with its great dumb mouth. They want to escape civilization and buy the corporeal and decadent pleasures—horseflesh and woman-flesh, whisky-table and poker-table—but they also have a cynical attitude; they do not really expect to enjoy it.

The second "Mahagonny Song" pushes the money theme further. Mahagonny is expensive; everyone who stays there is skinned and is paid dollars for his skin; he loses every time but it is worth it—at first. By the last refrain the men win every time but it is not worth it: "but they get nothing out of it" ("doch sie haben nichts davon"). In the opera the song is divided so the first two verses are sung by the men at the beginning of the "Drinking" ("Saufen") scene, but the last verse is sung at the end of the scene. Paul, who bought the drinks, has discovered he cannot pay; he has tried in his drunkenness to sail back to Alaska on a bar-table, and has ended in deep disappointment on finding he is still in Mahagonny.

The third Mahagonny song in the *Home Devotions* is the song of God in Mahagonny. God is helpless to punish the men for their crimes; he can no longer frighten them with the threats of hell because they know they are already there. This is the first hint of the theme of natural catastrophe and divine retribution, which is central to the opera: when men dare to flout all moral traditions, no natural punishment like the flood or hurricanes can reach them. When Paul Ackermann discovers in the face of imminent destruction that everything is allowed, the destruction ostentatiously avoids Mahagonny, leaving men to destroy each other. The song of God in Mahagonny has the same function. Paul forgets himself briefly in his terror of the electric chair and tries to use God (justice external to men) as a last salvation; the Mahagonny people laugh cynically, show him a charade about how meaningless the concept of God is for a people who make their own laws, and electrocute Paul.

In all these songs there has been no indication that Mahagonny must necessarily be in America. Dollars are an international currency. In fact, even in the opera itself, it is only by inference that one concludes America is the model for Mahagonny: what other land has a gold rush, hurricanes, poker, whisky, and an electric chair? But exotic names of places in Burma (Mandelay) and India (Benares) are used indiscriminately; the city is set up under a rubber tree; Jenny comes from both Havana and Oklahoma; and to sail to Alaska, Paul has to cross the equator. Rather than saying *Mahagonny* is set in America, we should say Brecht purposely made it a mythical land, but with some very American characteristics. He said, together with Weill and Neher, in the Director's Script for 1930: "The name 'Mahagonny' just designates the concept of a city. It was chosen for its sound (phonetics). The geographic location of the city is irrelevant" ("Der Name 'Mahagonny' bezeichnet lediglich den Begriff einer Stadt. Er ist aus klanglichen [phonetischen] Gründen gewählt worden. Die geographische Lage der Stadt spielt keine Rolle.").[19] Thus, it is wrong to think of geographical confusion as an oversight: it is intended to underline the mythical character of the city, so the audience realizes Mahagonny is an allegory for contemporary life. This is double alienation: not only a foreign country but a mythical version of it.

The last two Mahagonny songs in the *Home Devotions* were written in 1925.[20] They are both in English, strengthening the American feeling, but one is about Alabama and one about Benares. And they are both about dependence on the trappings of civilization: if we don't find the next whisky-bar, pretty girl (boy, in the opera) and little dollar, I tell you we must die; and there is no whisky, no bar, no telephone in this town. Worst of all, Benares (the escape) is said to have perished in an earthquake. Oh, where shall we go! Here, too, much of the meaning of *Mahagonny* is anticipated: the sense of desperation, the need to escape, and the worst fate, having no more escape.

For the full opera Brecht chose one more early *Home Devotions* poem, "Against Temptation." Paul sings it in the terrible hour of the hurricane, immediately upon discovering that nothing is forbidden. The song states the reason: there is no return; life is short so enjoy it in large gulps; fear cannot touch you, because you die like all animals and nothing comes afterward. This is unmitigated nihilism, not just criticism of capitalism but criticism of the human condition. However, it is primarily an anti-religious statement: there is no afterlife, therefore no divine punishment. This atheism, which was certainly also Brecht's, leads to the recognition that men make their own laws, as in *Mahagonny*, but it does not have to mean chaos and the law of the jungle and money. It could also be a source of hope: freed of superstition, people could build a rational and just society. But in 1922, when the poem was first published, Brecht did not yet see that implication, nor does Paul Ackermann in *Mahagonny*. The poem comes from Brecht's period of bravado, of forging an existence in the face of meaninglessness. The speakers of all these early poems are tragic heroes just as the gold-rush America *Mahagonny* is set in was the cruel and lawless land that requires its people to be heroes, a land therefore to be admired. (That judgment was of course later reversed by Brecht in *Galileo:* "Unhappy the land that needs heroes" ["Unglücklich das Land, das Helden nötig hat"] [*GW* 3: 1329]).

The heroism of fighting against natural enemies becomes more sophisticated with the help of technology in *Flight over the Ocean* (1928-29). There it is qualitatively different because it is a collective endeavor. In *Mahagonny* it is still brute strength and individual escape. But Mahagonny is the civilized, overcivilized, world, and such individual escape into meaning through battling nature is no longer possible there, as it was in Alaska. So another poem of the early twenties used in *Mahagonny*, "Tahiti," instead of being gently satirical becomes a sad anachronism. " 'Stormy the Night' is excellent when you lose your courage," (" 'Stürmisch die Nacht' ist vorzüglich, wenn man den Mut verliert"), says Heinrich, playing at sailing to Alaska on the bar-table top (*GW* 2:544)—but in Mahagonny, where the "sailors" after all land, courage does not help. What Paul needs is money. The same song title, which is a line in "Tahiti," was quoted by George Garga in his outburst against "the many upright and hardworking people": "may the Flood come over them with 'Stormy the Night and the Waves Roll High' " ("die vielen braven und fleißigen Leute": "die Sintflut soll kommen über sie mit 'Stürmisch die Nacht und die See geht hoch' ").[21] In *Mahagonny* the one verse is in quotation marks; presumably the song was popular in the early twenties.[22] Brecht used it in *Jungle* in connection with the Flood, which is one more hint that *Mahagonny* is partly about the outdatedness of divine retribution: since natural catastrophes can do no harm in Mahagonny, there is nothing to be gained through bravery against nature. All other relations have given way to the social relations based on money.

The "Mahagonny Song No. 4" was also written in the early twenties,[23] but for some reason Brecht never included it in the *Home Devotions*. It is spoken by a mother encouraging her son to be—here again—brave, this time in boxing; but when he has made his mark, to leave and come to Mahagonny. But only the chorus is used in *Mahagonny:* when you sit with the people from Mahagonny, you too will smoke, smoke will rise from your yellow skins. Sky like parchment, golden tobacco; when San Francisco burns down, everything in it that you call good will fit in a sack. This is another *carpe diem* poem, with the premonition of destruction of the cities.

In none of these early poems is there any indication that Brecht found the concept of a leisure city for the rich very appealing, and yet the activities there are largely what Brecht himself enjoyed: smoking Virginia cigars, boxing. But Brecht always recommended these as good medicine for the bourgeois theater, not as the complete content of life. In 1935 he wrote, "The theme of the opera *Mahagonny* is the culinary attitude itself" ("Das Thema der Oper 'Mahagonny' ist der Kulinarismus selbst") (*GW* 15:476): the citizens of Mahagonny are ruined by their passivity, their desire always to be entertained.

The four-line poem "On Cities" spreads the feeling of purposelessness from Mahagonny to cities in general. With the tense changed to the present it frames the "Mahagonny Song No. 4" in the opera:

> Beneath our cities are gutters
> In them is nothing and over them is smoke.
> We're still inside. We have enjoyed nothing.
> We're vanishing fast and slowly they're vanishing too.

> Unter unsern Städten sind Gossen
> In ihnen ist nichts und über ihnen ist Rauch.
> Wir sind noch drin. Wir haben nichts genossen.
> Wir vergehen rasch und langsam vergehen sie auch.
>
> (*GW* 2:505)

186

This could have been written for any of the planned works on cities; in *Mahagonny* it has the function of showing what the immigrants to Mahagonny want to escape from: noise, smoke, discord. "So let's go to Mahagonny!" ("Drum auf nach Mahagonny!") But what happens in Mahagonny? The more modern persons (of whom Brecht would have been one) find they cannot stand the quiet and harmony. No one can ever be happy there, something is missing. And so Paul discovers the law of human happiness: do whatever you want to make yourself happy. The poem "Blasphemy," from "Poems Belonging with the Reader for City-Dwellers,"[24] incorporates the laissez faire philosophy in the moral sphere: if you want money, take it; if you want a house, live in it; if you want to think a thought, think it:

> In the interest of order
> For the sake of the state
> For the future of humanity
> For your own well-being
> You may!

> Im Interesse der Ordnung
> Zum Besten des Staates
> Für die Zukunft der Menschheit
> Zu deinem eigenen Wohlbefinden
> Darfst du!

(GW 2:528–29)

But the result of this anarchy based on money is that Mahagonny becomes worse than the cities the men have left. For it is only possible to enjoy this society, where each person buys his own happiness, by giving up all sentiment toward other people; one is forced to be selfish. Garga mastered the technique in *Jungle* and survived the fight against Shlink; Jenny and Heinrich master it in *Mahagonny* and they too survive. But all have had to dehumanize themselves; like Baal, they have to be "bad" to survive in a bad world. And Jenny's and Heinrich's best friend is executed. Jenny justifies not paying Paul's debt for him by singing back at him the very song *he* had made up to proclaim the new order of egoism:

> You lie in the bed that you make for yourself
> No one will come tuck you in
> And if someone kicks then it's me
> And if someone gets kicked then it's you!

Denn wie man sich bettet, so liegt man
Es deckt einen keiner da zu
Und wenn einer tritt, dann bin ich es
Und wird einer getreten, bist's du!

(GW 2:530)

Paul's mistake was allowing his sense of human sympathy free rein, and this is the downfall of every "good" character in all Brecht's plays set in capitalist society.

Two songs in Mahagonny were adapted from English-language recordings of the day, according to Werner Otto.[25] They are the strange "I think I'd like to eat my hat up . . . ", which Paul sings to express his utter boredom in the too-quiet Mahagonny, and "Can bring him vinegar . . . ," sung over Paul's corpse in the finale. The text of neither song is very significant in itself, but as with this whole collection the context turns it into a symptom of the age. If the songs were known to the audience to be American, that would of course increase their significance too, as symptoms of the most extreme stage known today of the disease the opera diagnoses.

One more song can be traced to a source: "Fast, boys, hey! / Start to Sing the Song of Mandelay" (sung by the men waiting in line for their turn in the brothel) is part of the "Song of Mandelay" in *Happy End*. These songs, all expressing the desperate search for entertainment in a world without meaning, are really interchangeable, and Brecht did interchange them ruthlessly, as the Berliner Ensemble still does today.

Brecht inserted into nearly all his plays songs he had already written that do not have directly to do with the plot or characters but make a comment on the same topic from another perspective. Thus it makes no difference that the songs often describe events in faraway exotic places where no one in the play has ever been; they are sung by the actors as songs, not as dialogue set to music. The proper response to them is to ask: what does that song describe that is similar to the subject of the play? The opera *Mahagonny* uses songs the same way as the plays, as commentary on a particular type of attitude or behavior.

The use of music was an important part of Brecht's earliest "epic" theater theories. He wrote in 1935 that the new kind of music necessary for epic theater was invented by Weill when he wrote the music to the *Mahagonny Songspiel*; he had previously written

188

rather complex serious music, but bravely broke with tradition when faced with composing "more or less banal song texts." The new music had to serve epic theater, and

> epic theater is primarily interested in people's behavior with each other, *when it is historically significant (typical).* It works out scenes in which people behave so that the social laws under which they live become visible.

> Das epische Theater ist hauptsächlich interessiert an dem Verhalten der Menschen zueinander, *wo es socialhistorisch bedeutend (typisch) ist.* Es arbeitet Szenen heraus, in denen Menschen sich so verhalten, daß die sozialen Gesetze, unter denen sie stehen, sichtbar werden.

In order to show typical behavior, the music had to contain typical emotions and yet be simultaneously ironic, so that the audience would maintain a critical position. Weill's music accomplished this double task remarkably. It helped to unmask bourgeois ideology

> precisely by behaving purely emotionally and not throwing out any of the usual attractions . . . It became as it were the muckraker, provocateur, and denouncer.

> gerade indem sie sich rein gefühlsmäßig gebärdete und auf keinen der üblichen Reize verzichtete . . . Sie wurde sozusagen zur Schmutz-aufwirblerin, Provokatorin und Denunziantin. (*GW* 15:474)

Sentimentality *was* allowed—but in order to underline the banality of the words and of the character. At the same time the audience had to be prevented from becoming involved in sentiment. Therefore, all illusion was removed from the staging of the music (the characters broke out of their roles to sing, the message of the song was projected on a screen, the orchestra was visible on the stage), and the cool, self-mocking jazz forms were used.

This style of theater music Brecht named *gestisch*, because the audience is aware that it is being *shown* something just as when an actor makes a gesture with his body. "Practically speaking gestic music is music that allows the actor to present certain basic 'gests' " ("Praktisch gesprochen ist gestische Musik eine Musik, die dem Schauspieler ermöglicht, gewisse Grundgesten vorzuführen"). (Brecht's neologism *Gestus*—the basic gesture of a passage, character, or scene—meant almost the same thing as the English theater term "subtext." "Gestic music" was music capable of making a comment on the action or the text.) And here we return to the

189

importance of the American tradition, from which Weill learned jazz and Brecht learned so much of the popular culture he championed: "So-called cheap music, especially in cabaret and operetta, has been a kind of gestic music for some time already" ("Die sogenannte billige Musik ist besonders in Kabarett und Operette schon seit geraumer Zeit eine Art gestische Musik") (*GW* 15:476). For Germans, American jazz was an extremely important step toward matter-of-factness and self-irony. Brecht was consciously determined to separate again the elements Wagner had brought together as *Gesamtkunstwerk* ("total art work"): text, music, visual media, and acting (*GW* 17:1010–11). The more independent they were of each other, the more conscious the audience would be of their use to show something, to make a point.

Mahagonny, it is clear, is more important for the development of Brecht's ideas on form than on ideology. That is, in fact, the significance of all the works in this interim period: the happy accident of Brecht's meeting with Weill provided the chance for him to experiment with, and perfect, the idea of epic theater that had come to him while working on *Joe Fleischhacker*. He wrote as late as 1935 that the production of *The Threepenny Opera* in 1928 was the most successful demonstration of epic theater (*GW* 15:473). He did not feel that *Mahagonny* was an adequate piece of revolutionary theater, though it did have a "society-changing" function, namely, putting the "culinary attitude" up for discussion. "It still sits splendidly on the old branch, so to speak, but at least it saws away at it (absentmindedly or from a bad conscience) a little bit" ("Sozusagen sitzt es noch prächtig auf dem alten Ast, aber es sägt ihn wenigstens schon (zerstreut oder aus schlechtem Gewissen) ein wenig an") (*GW* 17:1016), he wrote of *Mahagonny*.

But such an innovation in form could not really lead to a change in society because opera itself could not help being "culinary" to a certain extent. His comment on *Mahagonny* continues: "*Real* innovations attack the base" ("*Wirkliche* Neuerungen griefen die Basis an"). Brecht felt that the opera *Mahagonny* had pointed the way to its own destruction as a genre by revealing the commodity nature of pleasure and pleasure-seekers. In short, opera could not destroy capitalism without first destroying itself. But that is only the *tendency* of the epic opera thought out to its logical conclusion. Actually, of course, the theaters were and are capable of putting on any number of self-destructive shows and the audience capable of simply consuming them. Recognition of the futility of trying to change society through the commercial theater led Brecht after writing *Mahagonny* to seek radically different audiences: workers and high-school students and even grade-school students. *Mahagonny* can only be seen as an experiment in what opera could be; Brecht himself never had much faith in its political effect.

It was a great advantage to Brecht to be able to work with these light experiments in form while doing his heavy study of Marxism. But gradually the implications of Marxism became clear for him; Sternberg says: "There was probably no sentence of Marx's that moved him more strongly than the one that the philosophers till now had only interpreted the world in various ways but the important thing was to change it" ("Es gab wohl keinen Marxschen Satz, der ihn stärker berührte als der, daß die Philosophen bisher die Welt nur verschieden interpretiert hätten, daß es aber gelte, sie zu verändern").[26] Brecht found it necessary to leave the entertaining opera behind and work on "*real* innovations" that "attack the base." In 1938 he stated his new approach to the opera:

> The opera *Mahagonny* was written 1928–29. In the next works attempts were undertaken to emphasize the instructive more and more, at the cost of the culinary. That is, to develop an instructional object out of a means of enjoyment and to rebuild certain institutions from places of amusement to publicity organs.

> Die Oper "Mahagonny" wurde 1928/29 geschrieben. In den anschließenden Arbeiten wurden Versuche unternommen, das Lehrhafte auf Kosten des Kulinarischen immer stärker zu betonen. Also aus dem Genußmittel den Lehrgegenstand zu entwickeln und gewisse Institute aus Vergnügungsstätten in Publikationsorgane umzubauen. (*GW* 17:1016)

Brecht became formally very strict with himself; strongly influenced by Waley's translations of Japanese Noh plays (translated into German for him by Hauptmann), he began writing the *Lehrstücke*, starting with *Flight over the Ocean* (1928–29). Kurt Weill worked on music for this new experiment, too, and on the *Lehrstück The Yea-Sayer*, but he then separated from Brecht until they wrote their last work together in 1933. That work, *The Seven Deadly Sins of the Petty Bourgeoisie*, is a ballet, with an ideology similar to that in *Mahagonny* and a setting in several of the United States. *Flight over the Ocean*, like the epic musicals, shows the stirrings of a need for a new form but does not yet fully incorporate the political philosophy Brecht was accumulating. (See below, pp. 204 ff.) It is pure praise of technology, and America is presented not as capitalist but merely as the very confident other side of the ocean. It is a play on a very limited subject; *Mahagonny* is much richer.

Yet *Mahagonny* too is incomplete in its exposition of capitalism. It is a truly uncomfortable satire of the commercial society, where all pleasures and people become commodities, to be bought and sold; regardless of what other laws or values there may be, paying up is the highest law and money the highest value. The beautiful sad poem about the cranes suggests that even love is an illusory value; Jenny's behavior when Paul runs out of money proves it. When Paul bets all he has on his friend's boxing, there is hope that there may be room for human gestures; but the entire courtroom of spectators lives by the rules and insists that there is no escape, Paul must die for allowing spontaneity and sympathy to overcome his sense of business. Sitting in the electric chair, Paul recognizes that his ruin was sealed when he first entered the city of Mahagonny to buy happiness with money. This recognition sums up the message of the opera:

> Now I'm sitting here and have had nothing. I was the one who said: Everyone must cut out a piece of meat, with every knife. But the flesh was rotten! The happiness that I bought was not happiness, and freedom for money was not freedom. I ate and was not satisfied, I drank and grew thirsty.

> Jetzt sitze ich hier und habe doch nichts gehabt. Ich war es, der sagte: Jeder muß sich ein Stück Fleisch herausschneiden, mit jedem Messer. Da war das Fleisch faul! Die Freude, die ich kaufte, war keine Freude, und die Freiheit für Geld war keine Freiheit. Ich aß und wurde nicht satt, ich trank und wurde durstig. (GW 2:560–61)

The echo of Job in these lines is consistent with parody of Bible and hymnal throughout *Mahagonny*, especially during the hurricane. But the use of the Bible in connection with natural catastrophe and life in the capitalist cities is more than just parody; it is a recapitulation of the theme of the American fragments from 1924–26: *The Man from Manhattan, The Flood, Joe Fleischhacker*. Paul Ackermann is the first completion of a long list of characters who set out to conquer the world ("cut out their piece of meat," which is also the Mitchel family's expression in *Fleischhacker*), who then become trapped by the city and are finally destroyed. The dramatic situation—delivering a last speech from the electric chair—is, of course, the same as Calvin Mitchel's. But the speech is very different. *Mahagonny* is the play where the fear of divine or natural retribution is conquered and men are left to destroy themselves alone:

> We don't need any hurricane
> We don't need a typhoon
> For the worst that it can do to us
> We will do to each other soon.
> The hurricane is bad
> Worse yet is the typhoon
> But the worst of all is man.

> Wir Brauchen keinen Hurrikan
> Wir brauchen keinen Taifun
> Denn was er an Schrecken tun kann
> Das können wir selber tun.
> Schlimm ist der Hurrikan
> Schlimmer ist der Taifun
> Doch am schlimmsten ist der Mensch.
> (*GW* 2:526)

This song from the night of horror in Mahagonny is reminiscent of the lines in *Man from Manhattan*,

> the world
> is very bad
> but the worst is
> the human race

> die welt
> ist ganz schlecht
> aber das schlechteste ist
> die menschheit
> (BBA 214, 72)

There man's evil was punished by God (i.e., nature); in *Mahagonny* man's evil is its own punishment. But this song fragment does not contain the total message of the opera. *Mahagonny* is not a condemnation of man's evil nature; on the contrary, several characters show signs that they would like to be kind. It is the system of buying and selling in Mahagonny that makes men cruel to each other.

The hurricane itself, of course, also comes from *Miami* and *Fleischhacker*. *Miami* is, in fact, almost completely taken up into *Mahagonny*. Both cities are called "paradise city." Both plays tell the story of the rapid growth and destruction of a resort city that is basically parasitical, making money by advertising in the metropoles. Mahagonny seems sometimes to be in Florida; the neighboring city destroyed by the hurricane, for instance, is Pensacola. Clearly the city of Miami and the play Brecht had started served as partial models.

But one of the clippings Brecht saved with the materials to *Miami* is titled (Hauptmann's translation) "THE STORM REACHES THE WEST COAST" ("DER STURM ERREICHT DIE WESTKÜSTE"), and "West coast" ("Westküste") is strongly underlined (BBA 214,30). In the same article one of the destroyed cities is named Hollywood. It is possible that Brecht was honestly confused here and thought the hurricane went all the way to the West Coast of the country rather than just Florida's west coast. That would partly explain why the city of Mahagonny seems to be simultaneously in Florida and in or near California. Brecht simply combined the public-relations stunt that built Miami Beach with the gold rush, which he probably knew from Jack London and from the German translation of stories by Bret Harte, which he had in his library under the title *Kalifornische Erzählungen* (*California Tales*). They are in fact similar phenomena. The gold rush is an excellent subject for Brecht's purposes: a whole land is gripped by the fever, willing to risk everything in order to get money from rivers. It is the perfect combination of the pioneer spirit with the mercenary.

Leokadja Begbick and company are not, however, ordinary gold diggers; they are criminals as well, fleeing from the law. On the way to the "gold coast," their car breaks down in the desert, and they decide to build a city right there in the middle of nowhere, which will catch people on the way to and from the coast like a net, and coax their gold from them by selling all pleasures. This entire description has an uncanny and prophetic similarity to modern-day Las Vegas, on the road to California, with its well-known underworld connections and its reputation for allowing everything, provided it is paid for. A city that lives not so much from the productive work of its inhabitants as from tourist trade, its role in the economy of the country is to provide an outlet for persons, often working-class, who

194

have made their money elsewhere, where they can enjoy getting rid of huge amounts of surplus. "They lost out every time. / But they got something out of it" ("Sie verloren in jedem Falle / Doch sie hatten was davon"). If one thinks of Las Vegas, the pleasure city, the lessons of *Mahagonny* become clear; love, entertainment, excitement are all unreal (vicarious, decadent) when their real purpose is to make money. The city of Miami Beach is, of course, also a good example of this dead end in capitalism; as a city for rich vacationers and pensioners, it too can provide everything for money except authenticity.

Certainly these cities are two of the most unfortunate manifestations of the American spirit. Brecht was himself a fervid admirer of boxing and jazz and Chaplin and much of American literature. So we must answer several questions that are often raised about *Mahagonny*: does it express what Brecht really thought of America? And: even though it claims to condemn American society, does it not really betray a love of anarchy and bravado? And (this one asked both from the left and from the right, which really makes it two questions), does it present an adequate picture of capitalism?

First: *Mahagonny* is a portrait not of America but of the alienation produced by commercial society, a theme straight out of *Capital*. Brecht came to study the topic because of his interest in the American myth, incorporated in its cruellest form in the great American cities. The use to which he put America in his plays never claimed to represent the whole truth about the country. In *Mahagonny* the picture of the capitalist system is deliberately incomplete. The play makes no pretense of showing the production process or the exploitation of the working class (unlike *St. Joan*). It shows only that even if one does manage to get rich in capitalist society, there is no real pleasure to be had because the means, money, becomes the end: bought pleasure in Mahagonny is no pleasure, bought freedom is no freedom; eating does not satisfy, and drinking leaves one thirsty. In Mahagonny Brecht concocted a mythical city, a chronological and geographical impossibility, with features inspired by certain American cities, historical events, literature, music, and sport, but also inspired by the theory of capitalism. As Brecht began to study capitalism, especially since interest in America had first led him to the study, it was inevitable that America should become the dramatic model. In his essays as

195

well, he always used Standard Oil and Rockefeller as examples of capitalist institutions[27] rather than Krupp and Stinnes. (Since he read other works by these authors, he may have read Ida Tarbell's *The History of the Standard Oil Company* or Upton Sinclair's *Oil!*) Also, as he learned more and more about the theory of capitalism, particular works on the nature of America had less influence on his portrayal of that country; he was interested in dramatic expression of a theory, and his symbols became more fixed.

So the question of whether the theory adequately describes America is irrelevant; Brecht cared more whether America adequately illustrated the theory, and there can be no doubt that it did, and proudly. The United States was and is the self-proclaimed model of free-enterprise capitalism; Brecht did not invent that.

But perhaps he was secretly still attracted to it. Many critics believe he was, pointing out that after all *Mahagonny* is *ein Spaß* (fun). That is, in fact, Brecht's own criticism of his opera's inadequacy. But not because his subconscious love of capitalist anarchy and tough individualism could not be suppressed by Marxist dogma; rather, because the very nature of opera is "culinary." A reading of the text alone, with the strict attempt to forget the music, makes clear that Brecht's conception really is a mercilessly bitter satire, much more drastic than *The Threepenny Opera*. It is Weill's music that seduces an audience into enjoying the show and then (instead of thinking about its own suspect reaction) drawing the false conclusion that Brecht really would have liked to live in Mahagonny himself. Yes, Brecht was very fond of boxing. And of lumberjacks from Alaska or railroad builders at Fort Donald. And of jazz. And undoubtedly of eating, drinking, and making love. The point of *Mahagonny* is the *perversion* of all these activities and people: they have become compulsive, the search for stimulation and pleasure becomes more and more frantic, and nothing satisfies.

And what about *In the Jungle*—"The chaos is used up. It was the best time" ("Das Chaos ist aufgebraucht. Es war die beste Zeit")? For Brecht that chaos was ended with *Jungle* itself, and by the time he wrote *Mahagonny*, he was insisting on rational order in society. It was the irrationality, the swamp (jungle) character of the Chicago wheat market, that had shocked him into studying capitalism. Showing America as anarchistic was nothing new: Chicago in

Jungle and *Fleischhacker* was also an incomprehensible jungle for the people from the flatland, it also required "THE STRUGGLE OF ALL AGAINST ALL" ("DEN KAMPF ALLER GEGEN ALLE"). New was the concentration on the capitalist system (or aspects of it) and the clear ideological condemnation.

But if *Mahagonny* is supposed to lay bare the mechanism of a system, surely it is unfair to select just one aspect of that system and judge the whole system by its worst manifestations—say the voices from the right. But most admirers of the United States would not agree that Miami, Las Vegas, and unlimited opportunity for the moneyed are the worst aspects of the country—on the contrary. That criticism is perhaps applicable to *St. Joan*, but *Mahagonny* intends to demonstrate that precisely the fulfillment of the American dream, the best capitalism has to offer, is humanly unsatisfying. Not that Brecht did not also find much in American culture that is satisfying, but most of that is not the cream of capitalism but rather the beginnings of a revolt against capitalism. Long before he started using the word *capitalism*, Brecht differentiated sharply between conservative and progressive culture. When he opted for popular mass culture instead of bourgeois individual "high" art, Brecht was instinctively operating on the Marxist principle that capitalism creates the conditions for its own destruction by creating collective man and collective culture. Thus Brecht was able to continue approving wholeheartedly of some American cultural achievements even while learning more and more to condemn the American political and economic system.

But then the voices on the left become loud: if he wanted to teach what is wrong with the system, he should have shown how it really works, including the ownership of means of production and the exploitation of labor to create surplus value, rather than choosing such an artificial milieu with no production at all; *Mahagonny* could lead to the false conclusion that abolition of money would solve everything. Basically this criticism says that *Mahagonny* is not a very serious work, and of course that is true. It does not intend to be. It intends to be a subversive work, with catchy tunes and a lot of fun but a devastating moral. It is not a complete and complex investigation of the mechanisms of capitalist exploitation; it is more a tying-together of threads Brecht had left dangling before he read Marx than it is an illustration of the new concepts. Brecht knew, of

197

course, that *Mahagonny* was not an adequate explanation of how capitalism works—the cause of the "crisis," for instance, is hardly economically grounded at all—and *St. Joan* and *The Bread Store* are attempts at accomplishing that more difficult task. If we say, nevertheless, that *Mahagonny* is an exposition of the *system* of capitalism, we mean not that the entire system is explained but that Brecht is showing logical conclusions of a theory: his characters act as representatives of certain social types or classes; their motivation is to be sought in the pressures their economic and social position puts on them and not in any individual, psychological drives.[28]

The question of whether Brecht thought America was really like Mahagonny is a useless question. The point is, *Mahagonny* shows the *tendencies* of the system that rules America; in that sense, even were there no American city remotely like Mahagonny, the play would be an accurate though incomplete picture of the inner logic of all American cities.

"Happy End"

The other two dramatic attempts Brecht worked on in 1928 that are set in America (*Happy End* and *Flight over the Ocean*) make far less claim to be an accurate portrayal of the capitalist system than *Mahagonny*. The first, *Happy End*, is not primarily Brecht's work. But a study of it is necessary for an understanding of Brecht's development because it is an important source of themes in later works. *Happy End* is the story of Hallelujah-Lilian, who is kicked out of the Salvation Army for adopting the ways of the underworld character she tries to convert, but who ultimately brings about a Gilbert-and-Sullivanesque happy ending with religious, criminal, and law-enforcement characters all turning out to be each others' long-lost lovers. It is concretely set in Chicago, yet it is more unreal than *Mahagonny* precisely because it does not attempt to disclose anything about the nature of society. Its ideology does not go much further than making a connection between the criminal underground and the local government, while taking a swipe at the Salvation Army in the process too. In *The Threepenny Opera* the connection criminals-police-religion was clearly established and given an irrefutable logic; *Happy End* simply accepts the social structure demonstrated by The *Threepenny Opera* and relates the amusing story of certain individual fates. *Mahagonny* and *The*

Threepenny Opera established the dialectical necessity of corruption in a bad system; in *Happy End* it is gratuitous.

There is a certain amount of controversy about *Happy End's* authorship; but recently the situation has become fairly clear. Herta Ramthun, of the Brecht Archive, said[29] that Brecht suggested the plot, but Hauptmann wrote the text, with corrections and, above all, songs by Brecht; Emil Burri also helped with the text. (A letter from Brecht to Elisabeth Hauptmann in the Archive contains part of the plot.[30]) Frau Hauptmann herself said modestly[31] that it was a collective endeavor, but she probably felt constrained to maintain that impression both out of loyalty and for copyright reasons. In a note in the Archive, on the other hand, she says the contents of *Happy End* follow a little story that she had in an old issue of an American magazine. Brecht, she says, advised her to adapt the story because it contained all the elements of a kind of folk literature that is the basis for film and magazines. He also promised her a few songs for the piece. Furthermore, Hauptmann continues, the story contained a "not uninteresting portion of the concept America" (BBA 348, 18). Unclear is only the question of the source in the American magazine, supposedly a story by a certain Dorothy Lane. No one (including me) has ever been able to find this story,[32] so it is generally assumed to have been invented, and Dorothy Lane is assumed to be nothing more than a pseudonym for Elisabeth Hauptmann. Also the plot contains references to a suspiciously large number of pet interests of Brecht and his collaborators. However, none of this proves that there never was an obscure short story in some uncatalogued popular magazine.

What is probably the first version of *Happy End* is preserved in the Archive under the title *Salvation Army Play* (BBA 1357). On its first page is written "Hauptmann," and it is typed with majuscules, and not on Brecht's typewriter. But none of the technical evidence would be necessary to show that it is not by Brecht; there is no trace of his characteristic and always recognizable style. His aphoristic compactness, his dialectical absurdities and logical forked-sticks, his "gestic" syntax, above all his sardonic humor are all missing, replaced by a style without describable characteristics, that is, a lack of style. The general direction of the plot is the same as in the final typescript of *Happy End*;[33] but many details are different, and there is only one short song ("Go forth into battle . . . "). The most obvious assumption is that this is the version Hauptmann prepared, and that Brecht then added some songs and made suggestions for plot and dialogue changes. (The final version, however, also has few signs of Brechtian style, except for the songs.)

Interesting in the *Salvation Army Play* version is the complete adoption of Brecht's short story "Four Men and a Poker Game or Too Much Luck Is Bad Luck," published in 1926. In the *Salvation Army Play* one of the bank robbers keeps winning at a poker game against his will; he notices that the others are beginning to act strange, but he cannot stop winning no matter how hard he tries. He leaves his money lying on the table, but they remind him of it; finally he tries to leave, but they follow him and shoot him. The barmaid, Saidie, runs back in and cries, "Too much luck is bad luck!" ("Zuviel Glück ist kein Glück!"). Such unimaginative adoption of the exact plot of a previous work would be unusual for Brecht, and in the final version of *Happy End*, there is no hint of it; the "Governor" is shot for having pocketed part of the booty. The close imitation is probably explained by Hauptmann's admiration for Brecht's story. In April 1926 she noted:

> I am charmed by the beginning of B's short story: "Too Much Luck Is Bad Luck." The first sentence reads: "We sat in wicker chairs at Havana and forgot the world." I find that splendid, and I can remember it. After a beginning like that anything that can happen between heaven and earth can happen in the story. (Quotability!)

> Ich bin entzückt von dem Anfang der Kurzgeschichte von B.: *Zuviel Glück ist kein Glück.* Der erste Satz lautet: "Wir saßen in Korbstühlen auf Havanna und vergaßen die Welt." Das finde ich herrlich, und das kann ich mir auch merken. Nach einem solchen Anfang kann in einer Geschichte alles passieren, was zwischen Erde und Himmel passieren kann. (Zitierbarkeit!)[34]

Also printed in the year 1926 was the edition of Shaw's *Major Barbara*[35] in Brecht's library, which has many similarities to *St. Joan of the Stockyards* and probably also provided an inspiration for the unconventional Hallelujah-Lilian.

Sinclair's *Jungle* may also have influenced the *Salvation Army Play*. Not only does the severed finger of one of the gangsters lie around in the guesthouse because no one wants to carry it away (which reminds one of the fingers severed in the meat machines in *The Jungle*); there is also reference to the dead pigs in Packingtown

(BBA 1357, 5), and to the worst cold spell and worst unemployment ever in Chicago.

In both versions there is mention of the First National Bank and of Standard Oil, but not in a context to give them any meaning. Similarly, in the *Happy End* version one criminal asks another whether he has read the newest detective story (*Kriminalroman*) yet; and the criminals discuss boxing and consider themselves to be sportsmen, and they read the *Chicago Tribune*. But these details are just mentioned in passing; they are not alone enough to make the play an example of the "concept of America."

This concept is contained more in the attitudes of the gangsters than in any of the details: they admire each other for cold-blooded revenge and unsentimental ruthlessness; they consider criminal acts against the society legitimate, and the fun of the play comes from the toughness of the characters. However, *Happy End*'s Americanization of the *Threepenny Opera* milieu eliminates most of the latter play's humor; the gangsters are impressive only because of their brutality and not because of the incongruous high sense of style and propriety of a British Macheath.

Brecht used the gangster world of Chicago later in *Arturo Ui*, where it is not so harmless. More important, however, for Brecht's future work is the introduction here of the Salvation Army. He had briefly mentioned it in *Jungle*, but without social implications. In *Happy End* the Salvation Army is still politically insignificant, but that play marks the beginning of a fascination with the "Army of God," so that within a year it symbolized all Brecht's ideas of the role of religion in capitalism. During the depression he visited the soup kitchens and prayer haunts of the "Army" in Berlin; he made it central in both *The Bread Store* and *St. Joan*, and in exile in Sweden he was still collecting materials on the Salvation Army and writing a fragment on it.[36] The Salvation Army is a superficially proletarian sort of institution that was the perfect vehicle for Brecht to demonstrate his ideas about the role of religion in capitalism precisely because it (in William Booth's own words) "goes for the center and goes for the worst," i.e., the most depressed sector of the working class. The aggressive, military religiosity of the "Army," its drumbanging method of advertisement, is simple-minded speeches and very secular sorts of symbolism and nomenclature make it an organization that clearly tries to speak to the uneducated; these qualities

would appeal to Brecht's preference for crudity over bourgeois
subtlety. But at the same time, he was always clear that the real
purpose of the "Army" was to dampen the struggle, to "co-opt" the
people it addressed, and that it was simply a tool, probably a
conscious tool, of the capitalist class. He did some research of his
own on the Army's funding;[37] we see the results of this research
portrayed in *St. Joan.*

Bernhard Reich, who helped direct *Happy End*, claims influence
on the transformation of Hauptmann's Salvation Army play into
the more subtle critique of religion and capitalism of *St. Joan*:

> In my opinion, we have in *Happy End* an attempt with an unsuitable
> subject. What do the efforts of the Salvation Army lieutenant, the pure
> maiden Holidey who would like to convert the head of a clan of rascals,
> show in the end? Suppose the gangster improves—neither success nor
> failure is relevant. But if Holidey wanted to persuade a capitalist to
> abandon his unchristian behavior, the girl's failure could illuminate
> some important relations. Brecht said he'd like to think about that. He
> thought about it: *St. Joan of the Stockyards* carries the *Happy End*
> project further.

> Ich meinte, im "Happy End" haben wir einen Versuch am untauglichen
> Objekt. Was zeigen schon die Bemühungen des Leutnants der Heilsar-
> mee, der reinen Jungfrau Holidey, die den Häuptling eines Gaunerclans
> bekehren möchte? Gesetzt, der Gangster bessert sich—weder Erfolg
> noch Mißerfolg sind relevant. Wenn aber die Holidey einen Kapitalisten
> überzeugen möchte, von seinem unchristlichen Handeln abzulassen,
> könnten durch einen Mißerfolg des Mädchens manche wichtigen Ver-
> hältnisse erhellt werden. Brecht meinte, er wolle darüber nachdenken.
> Er dachte nach: "Die heilige Johanna der Schlachthöfe" führt den
> "Happy-End"-Entwurf weiter.[38]

It is true, nothing is really changed when the gangsters join the
Salvation Army. They had not even been able to do much harm in
their latest bank robberies, because the days of the small skilled
worker were gone; only stocks were in the safes, and the big
businesses—the real criminals—were too much competition: "What
is a skeleton key compared with common stock, what is breaking
into a bank compared with founding a bank" ("Was ist ein Dietrich
gegen eine Aktie, was ist ein Einbruch in eine Bank gegen die
Gründung einer Bank").[39] This is the moral that informs revised
versions of the *Threepenny Opera*, and it is the only political
statement in *Happy End*. But it has nothing to do with the Salvation

Army; the gangsters could just as well have become circus performers for all the significance their joining the "Army" has.

Nevertheless, Brecht took a good many details from *Happy End* when he wrote *St. Joan*. The cast of "Army" characters is similar. The song "Take care, pay heed! . . . " is used in *Happy End, The Bread Store*, and *St. Joan*. The style of Lilian's speeches is similar to Joan's; they both use simple and very secular but clever similes. (This image in *Happy End*, for instance, appears again in *St. Joan* [*GW* 2:675]: "You are cowards . . . to tread across God's threshold into His light, for there it would be revealed that you do not have a stand-up collar on, but at best a rubber collar" ["Ihr seid Feiglinge . . . über Gottes Schwelle in sein Licht zu treten, denn dort würde es sich zeigen, daß ihr keine Stehkragen umhabt, sondern bestenfalls einen Gummikragen"]).[40] Joan is altogether very similar to Lilian; she is as irreverent and fresh to the great capitalist Mauler as Lilian to the great criminal Bill, and they are both thrown out of the "Army" for behavior unbecoming to a Salvation Army lass. But every time Brecht adapts a detail of the *Happy End* plot into *St. Joan*, he uses it to make a point. Lilian learns nothing, Joan learns everything.

The use of the Salvation Army in *Happy End* is not ideological—nor is the use of any of the other American elements. Hauptmann's remark that it contains "not uninteresting" elements of the concept of America is revealing: these elements are in fact only treated as "interesting." Fascination with technique—be it the technique of robbing a bank, the technique of boxing, or the technique of converting souls—remains an end in itself. The play appeals to the European attitude that America is full of quaint characters and lifestyles; therefore it is entertaining in its own right.

Hauptmann seems to have learned the *Neue Sachlichkeit* technique of paying loving attention to the details of how things work. But of course this is unfair to her; Brecht had a hand in *Happy End* too, including its direction on stage, and made no attempt to give it any significance. It is one more indication that he was not primarily interested in his writing but in his study during those years. *Mahagonny* was a pastiche of old songs and fragments; *The Threepenny Opera* was written at record speed on commission; *Happy End* was an intellectually lazy "culinary" pastime. And even the Americanism was no advance over the somewhat faddish attitude Brecht had toward America before 1926; in fact, ideologically the play, were it by Brecht, would belong to the period of the song of the Fort Donald railroad men.

"Flight over the Ocean" and the Learning Plays

This uncritical interest in America ran parallel in time to Brecht's criticism of capitalism as exemplified by America. But the two are not necessarily contradictory, nor does their concurrence mean that Brecht was torn between love and hatred, emotional attraction and ideological rejection, or any other kind of confusion. On the contrary, he was very conscious of what he thought, and his attitudes on a great variety of scattered subjects were perfectly consistent with Marxism, even before he began studying Marx.

It is Marxist theory that the possibility of communist consciousness and communist social organization grows out of the conditions that capitalism creates. Brecht had instinctively admired just the aspects of Americanism that Marxism considers progressive developments in capitalism. Mass culture was one of these. He started affecting sport, jazz, popular songs, Chaplin, and the like as a reaction against bourgeois individualism and sentimentalism; later he became aware that they were manifestations of working-class culture. He admired technology very early, from a *Neue Sachlichkeit* point of view, which is also a rebellion against sentimentalism and idealism. Nowhere does Brecht suggest that machines oppress or dehumanize man; they may de-individualize him, but that is a necessary step (Brecht learned) to a greater humanity.

America was, of course, the most industrialized country, and from the beginning Brecht's model for technological progress, which is one of capitalism's positive achievements and simultaneously (in orthodox Marxist theory) a basis for communism. The series on migration to the big cities, always associated with America, treated one aspect of industrialization: the collectivization and new forms of struggle forced on men by progress. *Flight over the Ocean* (1928–29), the dramatization for radio of Lindbergh's flight across the Atlantic, treats another aspect: technology itself, and man's conquering of nature through the use of technology.[41]

Written during the time of work on *Mahagonny*, this first *Lehrstück* also overcomes the fear of natural catastrophe, although from a different point of view. In both plays man alone is capable of doing anything; there is no other force or divinity that will avenge itself upon him or help him. Both these plays are important breakthroughs against the old notion of *hybris*, preparing the way for the recognition that man can also change his society and his own nature.

In *Mahagonny* human beings do not achieve anything after their discovery that they are omnipotent; the society they create, rooted in the laws of profit, destroys them. In *Flight over the Ocean* the discovery of atheism is hopeful. A Promethean view of man's positive possibilities informs the tone: "When I fly I am / A real atheist" ("Wenn ich fliege, bin ich / Ein wirklicher Atheist") (*GW* 2:576). Atheist is a positive word for Brecht. It means: one who fights against the superstition that man cannot control his fate. The important section called "Ideology" ("Ideologie") in *Flight over the Ocean* states unequivocally that the advance of science makes God unnecessary. *Learning* was becoming important to Brecht: here he writes that there are two classes of man, not exploiter and exploited, but exploiter and ignorant. There can only be exploitation because there is ignorance; when the working class learns about its conditions, it eliminates them. And it eliminates the power of nature over man and with it belief in gods:

> Therefore take part
> In the struggle against the primitive
> In the liquidation of the hereafter and
> The banishment of every god, where
> Ever he surfaces

> Darum beteiligt euch
> An der Bekämpfung des Primitiven
> An der Liquidierung des Jenseits und
> Der Verscheuchung jedweden Gottes, wo
> Immer er auftaucht.
>
> (*GW* 2:576–77)

Brecht did not believe that the working class would become more revolutionary as it became poorer, but rather as it became more conscious and as the means to create a better life were invented. He believed progress was revolutionary:

But it is a battle against the primitive
And an effort for the improvement of the planet
Comparable to dialectical economics
Which will change the world from the ground up.

Aber es ist eine Schlacht gegen das Primitive
Und eine Anstrengung zur Verbesserung des Planeten
Gleich der dialektischen Ökonomie
Welche die Welt verändern wird von Grund auf.

(*GW* 2:575)

Flight over the Ocean is, then, a further development of the atheism theme in *Mahagonny*; but whereas in the opera it led only to chaos, in the *Lehrstück* it combines with science and progress and it is revolutionary.

From this perspective Brecht's America is truly positive. Nothing is mentioned about Rockefeller and Ford, only the workers in San Diego who built the *Spirit of St. Louis* and with whom the fliers feel solidarity. America is full of confidence about the flight; the primitive Scottish fisherman are skeptical ("Why look there, where it / Can never be?" ["Wozu da schauen, wo es / Doch niemals sein kann?"] [*GW* 2:583] is an argument repeated by Galileo's opponents.) And America proves to be right in *Flight over the Ocean*. Because it is the land that most believes in progress, America is the most revolutionary land, although it is also the most capitalist land.

The very poem that Calvin Mitchell spoke from the electric chair in *Joe Fleischhacker* is quoted by the fliers. But now it is a justified vision of true progress; there it was a fiendish vision of the human sacrifice necessary to build the great inhuman cities. The first verse is worth repeating, to show the remarkable adaptability of Brecht's jigsaw-puzzle pieces that he fit into different contexts. The dialectical change in meaning that this one verse can have is as startling as the change in his whole picture of America. The words, or concrete details, are constant; but the historical context, and therefore the evaluation, changes. (See also the discussion of "Vanished Glory of the Giant City New York," below, pp. 226 ff.)

Many say the age is old
But I have always known it is a new age
I tell you: not by themselves
Have houses grown for twenty years like mountains from ore
Many move each year to the cities as if they expected something
And on the laughing continents

The word is getting around that the great dreaded ocean
Is a little water.

Viele sagen, die Zeit sei alt
Aber ich habe immer gewußt, es ist eine neue Zeit.
Ich sage euch, nicht von selber
Wachsen seit 20 Jahren Häuser wie Gebirge aus Erz
Viele ziehen mit jedem Jahr in die Städte, als erwarteten sie etwas
Und auf den lachenden Kontinenten
Spricht es sich herum: das große gefürchtete Meer
Sei ein kleines Wasser.

But then instead of continuing, "I will die today, but I am convinced / The big cities now await the third millenium" ("Ich sterbe heut, aber ich habe die Überzeugung / Die großen Städte erwarten jetzt das dritte Jahrtausend"), the *Flight over the Ocean* version substitutes:

I'm flying now as the very first over the Atlantic
But I am convinced: tomorrow
You will already laugh at my flight.

Ich fliege jetzt schon als erster über den Atlantik
Aber ich habe die Überzeugung: schon morgen
Werdet ihr lachen über meinen Flug.

(*GW* 2:575)

The fliers' feat is only one in a long, optimistic process of conquering the primitive. At the beginning, the song continues, we and our technology are primitive; let us fight nature until we ourselves become "natural." The play ends with praise of the courage to do what has never been done before. It calls the epoch of man's flight across the ocean the time "when humanity / Began to recognize itself" ("wo die Menschheit / Anfing sich zu erkennen"), but the poem that ends the play is also a dedication to "the not-yet-achieved" ("das noch nicht Erreichte").[42] The whole play expresses an unadulterated optimism that is unique in the early Brecht (except for the more sober but moving optimism of *The Mother*). Here is the best chance to understand what could be attractive about America.

But *Flight over the Ocean* cannot be interpreted independently. Just as it is a dialectical *Aufhebung* (synthesis: a combination of elimination, preservation, and carrying to a higher level) of *Fleischhacker* and *Mahagonny*, so is *The Baden Play for Learning Acquiescence* (1929) a dialectical opponent to *Flight over the*

Ocean. It begins with exactly the chorus that ended *Flight over the Ocean*, but now that it is the introduction to a play, this chorus asks: what *is* "the not-yet-achieved" ("das noch nicht Erreichte")? Unfortunately, the end of the play is confused, so it is not clear exactly what Brecht wanted the next step to be; he recognized this weakness himself and wrote, "The play proved at the end to be unfinished: there is too much weight given to dying in relation to its small use value" ("Das Lehrstück erwies sich beim Abschluß als unfertig: dem Sterben ist im Vergleich zu seinem doch wohl nur geringen Gebrauchswert zuviel Gewicht beigemessen") (*GW* 2:3*).

Nevertheless, it is clear at the beginning what the fliers have not accomplished: they have not helped create a society where men help each other; they have invented a wonderful machine that conquers nature, but they have had no effect on social relations. The leader of the "learned chorus" relates similar achievements—discovery of America and growth of cities there, invention of the steam engine, scientific and philosophic research—but after each achievement mentioned the chorus responds, "It didn't make bread any cheaper" ("Das Brot wurde dadurch nicht billiger"). The third time the chorus adds:

> Rather
> Poverty has increased in our cities
> And for a long time now no one has known
> What a human being is.

> Sondern
> Die Armut hat zugenommen in unseren Städten
> Und es weiß seit langer Zeit
> Niemand mehr, was ein Mensch ist.
>
> (*GW* 2:592–93)

Here Brecht returns to the theme of the growth of the cities and their inhumanity, the theme of 1924–26. The fliers relate of themselves: "We were caught up in the fever / Of city-building and oil" ("Uns hatte erfaßt das Fieber / Des Städtebaus und des Öls") (*GW* 591). We know these lines already from *Man from Manhattan*. Now five years later Brecht is using exactly the same image, but it is not the suffering of a single man that the fliers forget; their moral failure plays on a much larger stage. As machines and speed became ends in themselves,

> We forgot in the battles
> Our names and our face
> And in the swifter takeoff
> We forgot our takeoff's goal.
>
> Wir vergaßen über den Kämpfen
> Unsere Namen und unser Gesicht
> Und über dem geschwinderen Aufbruch
> Vergaßen wir unseres Aufbruchs Ziel.
>
> (*GW* 2:591)

The dialectical relation between *Flight over the Ocean* and *The Baden Learning Play* is clear from this criticism of the fliers by the learned chorus:

> For example: while you flew, crept
> Something similar to you on the ground
> Not like a human!
>
> Zum Beispiel: während ihr flogt, kroch
> Ein Euch Ähnliches am Boden
> Nicht wie ein Mensch!
>
> (*GW* 2:593)

Flight over the Ocean, like *Mahagonny*, is an incomplete picture of American, or industrial, society: it shows only the promise of progress. *The Baden Learning Play* raises doubts again; it is a play that only asks questions.

These three plays together show more clearly than Brecht's notes in "Marxist Studies" how he developed his political understanding. *Mahagonny* shows his interest in the theory of alienation caused by money; *Flight over the Ocean* shows his hope for the revolutionary potential of technical progress; and the *Baden Learning Play* shows him checking, doubling back, and putting progress in its social context.

The Baden Learning Play and *Flight over the Ocean* (and of course *Mahagonny*) also show clearly the two sides of Brecht's attitude toward America: simultaneous admiration of technical progress and hatred of social injustice and poverty. Both these elements coexisted in his understanding of America at least from the time he wrote *Jungle*; but it is Marxism that brought them together. They are contradictions, but it is not inconsistent for one person to hold both positions because they are contradictions that are actually

209

present in capitalist society. As Brecht recognized in the plays about cities, industrialization and urbanization can produce terrible suffering; in *Mahagonny* he wrote about the spiritual poverty they can produce; in *Flight over the Ocean* he turned around and praised the conditions they could create, namely, "atheism" or the courage to progress. But in the *Baden Learning Play*, he insists that those conditions are only preconditions.

The antiphonal dialogue between the fliers and the chorus can be read—in places—as an argument between America and Europe. The lead singer says:

> One of us has come over the ocean and
> Discovered a new continent.
> But many after him
> Have built great cities there with
> Much work and cleverness.
>
> Einer von uns ist über das Meer gefahren und
> Hat einen neuen Kontinent entdeckt.
> Viele aber nach ihm
> Haben aufgebaut dort große Städte mit
> Vieler Mühe und Klugheit.

(GW 2:592)

And the fliers present the ideology of that America, with its unlimited confidence but no direction. The pilot, who is now called Charles Nungesser, is the most "American": "I flew for nothing and no one. / I flew for flying" ("Ich bin für nichts und niemand geflogen. / Ich bin für das Fliegen geflogen") (*GW* 2:606—moral neutrality again). But the contrast between America and Europe is not consistent. If Brecht wrote the play to answer the question "What should have been our reaction had Lindbergh's flight failed?" then he had to have the Europeans simultaneously lower and higher on the scale of progress than the fliers, the Americans. This is the reason for the division into a "learned chorus" and a crowd: the crowd learns together with the fliers from the learned chorus or new man, whose geographical position is unclear. The learned chorus thinks a step beyond the Americans, who know how to progress technically but not socially. It represents those who think beyond the achieved to the not yet achieved; it is the coming generation of whom the fliers in *Flight over the Ocean* say, "tomorrow / You will already laugh at my flight" ("Schon morgen / Werdet ihr lachen über meinen Flug").

We have then, in the transition period of 1927–29, two different conceptions of America, which are in Marxist theory perfectly consistent: in *Mahagonny* and *Happy End*, America is the land of justified criminal rebellion against a capitalist society; chaos, anarchy, and lawlessness are romanticized to be sure, but it is shown that they actually produce alienation. The mood is of a frantic kind of consumption-oriented decadence. In *Flight over the Ocean* and *The Baden Learning Play*, America is the land of technological progress, where workers cooperating together can achieve a positive atheism and produce machines that conquer the old gods of nature. There is no question that this was a progressive development in Brecht's eyes, as well as in Marx's.

Something of this same dialectical irony—that advanced capitalism and industrialization are both good and bad—is expressed also in the poem "Song of the Machines" (1927?), written for a planned "*Ruhrrevue*" that was never realized. Here too there is radio contact with America (Brecht seems to have been impressed by radio partly because it brought America closer); but there is question as to what language to use. The answer is that the language should be the singing of machines, "Which are understood here and in America / And everywhere in the world" ("Die man versteht hier und in Amerika / Und überall in der Welt"). The comment on the machines' song follows:

> That is the wild howling of our daily work
> We curse it and we're fond of it
> For it is the voice of our cities
> It is the song we like to hear sung
> It is the language that everyone knows
> And soon it will be the world's mother tongue.

> Das ist das wilde Geheul unserer täglichen Arbeit
> Wir verfluchen es und wir haben es gern
> Denn es ist die Stimme unserer Städte
> Es ist das Lied, das uns gefällt
> Es ist die Sprache, die alle verstehen
> Und bald ist es die Muttersprache der Welt.
>
> (*GW* 8:297–98)

The "Crane Songs," also written for the *Ruhrrevue*, say expressly that the machines and their operators, the workers, both belong to the working class and will fight together to achieve a new social order. Brecht portrays the machine in the hands of the capitalist as an instrument of oppression for the worker; in the worker's own hands, it can be an instrument of liberation.

In Brecht's writing from now on, all technical advances as well as all ideological products are to be judged according to whom they serve. Particularly important is the invention of the radio, because it belongs to both categories: it is a technological advance and an instrument of ideological expression. But of course it belongs to the bourgeoisie. Brecht was excited by the possibilities radio offered and disgusted by the uses to which it was actually put. This is why he wrote *Flight over the Ocean* for radio. For a while he must have cherished the idea of revolutionizing this marvelous new invention as he intended to revolutionize theater, but he found the ruling class had even better control of the radio than of the theater. During Brecht's period of study of Marxism, images of cities filled with antennas are frequent; even in Hauptmann's *Salvation Army Play*, Lilian compares reception of God with reception of radio waves.

The radio was the first new instrument of mass communication since printing was invented, and Brecht sensed what importance it could have. From 1927 to 1932 he wrote several essays collected together as "Radio Theory." In comments on *Flight over the Ocean* (1930), he writes that it is important not to provide the radio with material but to change it, through a kind of revolt by the listeners (*GW* 18:125–26). By 1932 this seemed hopeless to him; the radio was invented too soon. If it is to have any function at all, he writes, it must be transformed from a means of distribution to a means of communication; it must receive from the listener as well as broadcast to him (*GW* 18:129—the pedagogical technique he uses in *Flight over the Ocean*).

Brecht's argument here is almost exactly like Upton Sinclair's in *Oil!*, available in German from Malik Publishers from 1927. Brecht writes, "The radio [has] *one* side, where it should have two. It is a pure distribution apparatus, it merely allots" ("der Rundfunk [hat] *eine* Seite, wo er zwei haben müßte. Er ist ein reiner Distributionsapparat, er teilt lediglich zu") (*GW* 18:129); and he talks about the lack of interest that the state has in experimenting with democratic radio. Sinclair writes, "The radio is a one-sided institution; you can listen, but you cannot answer back. In that lies its enormous usefulness to the capitalist system. . . . It is a basis upon which to build the greatest slave empire in history."[43]

212

Already in 1927 Brecht admired the invention of radio but wondered what it was for. His images in the article "Radio—An Antediluvian Invention?" are significant here: he says that the first he heard of the radio was from ironic newspaper articles about a regular "radio hurricane" that was devastating America; nevertheless, it seemed to be a really modern matter. This is the symbology of *The Flood*, *Miami*, and *Mahagonny*: man's extension of his own nature (*hybris*) is threatened by natural catastrophe; here the invention itself is the catastrophe. Of course, Brecht himself did not think the radio would destroy America; on the contrary, it seemed to be a great step forward. Only when he found out how idiotic the programming was did he get the terrible feeling that, far from being modern, the radio was "an unimaginably old piece of equipment that was lost to memory in its time through the Flood" ("eine unausdenkbar alte Einrichtung, die seinerzeit durch die Sintflut in Vergessenheit geraten war") (*GW* 18:119).

An invention is usefully new or progressive only when it forces social change and improvemnt; the radio seems, however, to be equivalent to the "flying people" ("Flugmenschen") who appear in the years of the Flood in *The Flood*: "in the final years epidemics of monstrous inventions proliferate   flying people appear . . . they fall in the water   laughter" ("in den letzten jahren verbreiten sich seuchen von ungeheuren erfindungen   flugmenschen treten auf . . . sie fallen ins wasser   gelächter") (BBA 214, 17). The Flood wipes out the results of a bad experiment; it is the symbolic expression of Brecht's temptation to be attracted to nihilism. It is undialectical. But Brecht knew that it is not possible to wipe the whole thing out and start fresh, that the forces for change could develop only within existing society. Thus *The Flood* itself and *Flight over the Ocean* are written for the radio not to destroy the monstrous invention but to utilize and transform it. Brecht concluded that radio was only as modern as its application to progressive ends.

Brecht began a poem about his experience in writing *Flight over the Ocean* that suggests new pedagogical uses for the radio; although written in 1930, it is very similar to the 1936 poem about the *Joe Fleischhacker* experience, "When I years ago."

It is hardly a poem really; rather, it is an attempt to discipline his thoughts by writing in lines, so as to understand the failure of his

213

plan for transforming radio. The plan, he says, had taken into account the exact nature of available technology, the growth of needs and demands of the people, the increasing concentration of means of production, and the necessity of educating many more people in the use of technology; therefore, it aimed at simple schooling in the spirit of mechanics (*GW* 8:329). The plan was very reasonable, but it was a failure because, no matter how many compelling reasons there were for fulfilling it, one reason was always missing. The fragment breaks off before he says what that reason was. From his other writings, though, it is clear that his reason was something to do with the fact that radio was controlled by the ruling class and his plan held no advantage for them.

This was apparently another important learning experience for Brecht: he learned that rationality is not enough to get a suggestion adopted unless it appeals to self-interest. After *Mahagonny* he stopped addressing his protest and suggestions to the bourgeoisie and turned to youth and workers as a new audience.

It is a measure of the strength of his political engagement that he was able to forfeit a big name in the bourgeois theater just after his success with *The Threepenny Opera*. Writing smaller-scale plays to be performed by workers and students in their own territory instead of in conventional theaters was a big step toward political effectiveness but a big step away from fame; it is a hard move for a playwright to make.

Style

It was not only the move away from professional productions that was difficult. At the same time that he turned to new audiences, Brecht changed his style radically. Tendencies that had been hinted at in *A Man's a Man* became paramount: the rich, metaphorical language of the early dramas was unsentimentally disposed of, and only the starkest simplicity remained. This new ascetic style is the bane of translators; in translation it sounds not ingeniously simple but ingenuously simple-minded. It is the kind of simplicity that takes much longer to write than does complexity: "the simple thing that's hard to do" ("das Einfache, das schwer zu machen ist") (*GW* 9:463— like communism itself in Brecht's poem). It was not easy for Brecht to write in such a style; it meant a sacrifice of a part of his creativity, of precisely the language for which Ihering had so admired him in the early twenties. No longer did Brecht's characters speak in images of life and decay straight from the gut; they began to speak a highly stylized, compact, rational and yet colloquial language, in which every word contained a thought and a gesture. Brecht observed that the rational form of the *Lehrstück* actually produced a stronger emotional effect than the less controlled forms (*GW* 15:242—that is, the *Lehrstück* produced emotions leading to action, not to catharsis); but for the author it was certainly not easy to chisel and chisel away at all the rich outer texture until only the simplest, most comprehensible and comprehensive piece of pure material was left. The complexity of the *Lehrstücke* lies entirely in the dialectical confrontation of two opposed ideas and the necessity of choosing—not choosing arbitrarily but finding the right choice. All other complexity is eliminated so that the dialectic in the material itself can become completely visible.

Brecht described the sacrifice that this new controlled style involved, in a 1938 note comparing the *Svendborg Poems* to the *Home Devotions*:

The *Home Devotions*, my first lyric publication, carries without doubt the stamp of the decadence of the bourgeois class. Fullness of the senses includes confusion of the senses. Discrimination in expression includes elements of decline. Wealth of motives includes the factor of aimlessness. Vigorous language is sloppy, etc. etc. In contrast to this purpose the later *Svendborg Poems* stand for a retreat as much as an advance. From the bourgeois standpoint an astounding impoverishment has taken place. Isn't everything more one-sided, less "organic," cooler, more "conscious" (in the derogatory sense)? My comrades-in-arms will not, I hope, just let that pass. They will call the *Home Devotions* more decadent than the *Svendborg Poems*. But it seems to me important that they recognize what the advance, insofar as it can be established, has cost. Capitalism has forced us into the struggle. It has laid waste our environment. I don't walk "just strolling along in the woods" but among police. There is still fullness, the fullness of struggles. There is discrimination, that of problems. No question about it: literature is not flourishing.

Die "Hauspostille", meine erste lyrische Publikation, trägt zweifellos den Stempel der Dekadenz der bürgerlichen Klasse. Die Fülle der Empfindungen enthält die Verwirrung der Empfindungen. Die Differenziertheit des Ausdrucks enthält Zerfallselemente. Der Reichtum der Motive enthält das Moment der Ziellosigkeit. Die kraftvolle Sprache ist salopp, usw. usw. Diesem Zweck gegenüber bedeuten die späteren "Svendborger Gedichte" ebensogut einen Abstieg wie einen Aufstieg.

215

Vom bürgerlichen Standpunkt aus ist eine erstaunliche Verarmung eingetreten. Ist nicht auch alles einseitiger, weniger "organisch", kühler, "bewußter" (in dem verpönten Sinn)? Meine Mitkämpfer werden das, hoffe ich, nicht einfach gelten lassen. Sie werden die "Hauspostille" dekadenter nennen als die "Svendborger Gedichte". Aber mir scheint es wichtig, daß sie erkennen, was der Aufstieg, sofern er zu konstatieren ist, gekostet hat. Der Kapitalismus hat uns zum Kampf gezwungen. Er hat unsere Umgebung verwüstet. Ich gehe nicht mehr "im Walde so für mich hin", sondern unter Polizisten. Da ist noch Fülle, die Fülle der Kämpfe. Da ist Differenziertheit, die der Probleme. Es ist keine Frage: die Literatur blüht nicht.[44]

Here it is quite clear that the simplicity of his language was difficult and almost sad for Brecht; he forced himself to it for political reasons. This was finally real political commitment. In 1926 a crisis in his creative work drove him to the study of politics; by 1929 the process came full circle, and his political commitment forced a change in his creative work. He had to put his work at the service of something larger than immanent aesthetic principles; in this historical period writing for him could never be limited to self-expression.

In the comment on the *Svendborg Poems*, Brecht said he felt it was important that his comrades understand what is lost by commitment to political literature. It is indeed important, for it shows that his commitment was not born of a need for discipline and that he was not at heart ruthless or Stalinist. The regret he expresses in recalling his old style that he has had to reject shows that the choice in *The Measure Taken* was an agony, not a pleasure. Brecht was a humanist revolutionary. He would have liked to have been soft, but he felt compelled by the times he lived in to be hard. That is the theme of many wistful statements during the period when he used his art to fight Nazism.

The poem "Bad Time for Poetry," for example, ends with the lines:

> In my song a rhyme
> Would almost seem like arrogance to me
> Inside me contend
> Enthusiasm over the blossoming apple tree
> And horror over the house-painter's speeches.
> But only the second
> Forces me to my writing desk.
>
> In meinem Lied ein Reim
> Käme mir fast vor wie Übermut.

216

In mir streiten sich
Die Begeisterung über den blühenden Apfelbaum
Und das Entsetzen über die Reden des Anstreichers.
Aber nur das zweite
Drängt mich zum Schreibtisch.

(GW 9:744)

(The house-painter is, of course, Hitler.)

There are many references in the poems of the thirties to the curse of having been born in "dark times," in the "time of disorder"; the best-known is in the justifiably famous poem "To Those Born After," which as the last poem in the *Svendborg Poems* makes a key autobiographical statement analogous to "Of Poor B.B." in the *Home Devotions*. The historical period in which he lives, Brecht writes in "To Those Born After," forces his generation to fight evil by themselves becoming hard and unfriendly; as in "This Babylonian Confusion" he speaks to a future generation who may not understand how difficult it was to live in an age when a conversation about trees was almost a crime.

> Truly, I live in dark times!
> . . . .
> What kind of times are these, when
> A conversation about trees is almost a crime
> Because it includes silence about so many abominations!
> . . . .
> I came into the cities at the time of disorder
> When hunger ruled there.
> I came among people at the time of rebellion
> And I was outraged with them.
> . . . .
> Streets led to the swamp in my time.
> Language betrayed me to the butcher.
> I could do little. But the rulers
> Sat more securely without me, that I hoped.
> . . . .
> You who will emerge out of the flood
> In which we perished
> Think
> When you speak of our weaknesses
> Also of the dark time
> Which you escaped.
> . . . .
> Besides we do know:
> Even hatred of baseness

Distorts the features.
Even anger over injustice
Makes the voice hoarse. Alas, we
Who wanted to prepare the ground for friendliness
Could not ourselves be friendly.

Wirklich, ich lebe in finsteren Zeiten!
. . . .
Was sind das für Zeiten, wo
Ein Gespräch über Bäume fast ein Verbrechen ist
Weil es ein Schweigen über so viele Untaten einschließt!
. . . .
In die Städte kam ich zur Zeit der Unordnung
Als da Hunger herrschte.
Unter die Menschen kam ich zu der Zeit des Aufruhrs
Und ich empörte mich mit ihnen.
. . . .
Die Straßen führten in den Sumpf zu meiner Zeit.
Die Sprache verriet mich dem Schlächter.
Ich vermochte nur wenig. Aber die Herrschenden
Saßen ohne mich sicherer, das hoffte ich.
. . . .
Ihr, die ihr auftauchen werdet aus der Flut
In der wir untergegangen sind
Gedenkt
Wenn ihr von unseren Schwächen sprecht
Auch der finsteren Zeit
Der ihr entronnen seid.
. . . .
Dabei wissen wir doch:
Auch der Haß gegen die Niedrigkeit
Verzerrt die Züge.
Auch der Zorn über das Unrecht
Macht die Stimme heiser. Ach, wir
Die wir den Boden bereiten wollten für Freundlichkeit
Konnten selber nicht freundlich sein.

(GW 9:723–25)

It is a truly authentic revolutionary speaking those lines, one who keeps his commitment alive by questioning and by remembering what the revolution is to be made *for*, not just against.

A few years earlier Brecht had written an entire poem about the political necessity of limiting his style and subject matter, which is simultaneously a limiting of one's own fulfillment and experience:

Exclusively because of the increasing disorder

218

In our cities of the class struggle
Some of us have decided in these years
No longer to speak of harbor cities, snow on the roofs, women
Smell of ripe apples in the cellar, sensations of the flesh
All that makes a person rounded and human
But to speak more of the disorder
Thus to become one-sided, arid, caught in the affairs
Of politics and the dry, "unworthy" vocabulary
Of dialectical economics
So that this terrible compacted concurrence
Of snowfalls (they aren't only cold, we know that)
Exploitation, tempted flesh and class justice
Won't engender in us approval
Of such a many-sided world, pleasure in
The contradictions of such a bloody life
You understand.

Ausschließlich wegen der zunehmenden Unordnung
In unseren Städten des Klassenkampfs
Haben etliche von uns in diesen Jahren beschlossen
Nicht mehr zu reden von Hafenstädten, Schnee auf den Dächern,
    Frauen
Geruch reifer Äpfel im Keller, Empfindungen des Fleisches
All dem, was den Menschen rund macht und menschlich
Sondern zu reden nur mehr von der Unordnung
Also einseitig zu werden, dürr, verstrickt in die Geschäfte
Der Politik und das trockene "unwürdige" Vokabular
Der dialektischen Ökonomie
Damit nicht dieses furchtbare gedrängte Zusammensein
Von Schneefällen (sie sind nicht nur kalt, wir wissen's)
Ausbeutung, verlocktem Fleisch und Klassenjustiz eine Billigung
So vielseitiger Welt in uns erzeuge, Lust an
Den Widersprüchen solch blutigen Lebens
Ihr versteht.

$(GW\ 9:519)$

That Brecht began writing poems about nature after moving to
East Berlin is often taken as a sign that he was not really dedicated to
communism. But we can see from this poem that he considered
private life and nature to be human and proper subjects for poetry,
and it was only the inhumanity and unnaturalness of the age that
forced him and others to write not about what makes man human
but about the prevailing disorder. As he writes in Me-Ti, it will be
possible to write poetry about the sound of falling raindrops when
there are no more homeless people who get the raindrops between

219

their neck and collar (*GW* 12:509). (Compare the poem "Landscape of Exile" [*GW* 10:830–31]). For him socialism was the human system, and when he went to live in East Germany, he allowed himself finally to write about private subjects; he was able at last to become "rounded," not "one-sided." Perhaps in those last years he even allowed himself to close his eyes to some of the less socialist practices of his government while he wrote about nature and private subjects in the *Buckow Elegies*. That is a question for some other book.

The laments quoted above stem from the period when he was using his writing to fight fascism. But the language in the last poem is directed against all capitalism, not just fascism. And the painful decision to give up richness of style for ideological clarity dates from Brecht's "conversion" to socialism, not from the beginning of the National Socialist regime and his exile. This decision became evident in 1929: after finishing *Mahagonny*, Brecht's dramatic work was devoted exclusively to *Lehrstücke* and other variations on didactic plays.

Between 1926 and 1929 he had been studying socialism and the critique of capitalism diligently, but he had not really committed himself in his artistic work. Now suddenly came full engagement. Every word he wrote, and even the way he wrote it, was to serve the cause by making the nature of the two systems clear, by speaking to the class and generation to whom the future belonged, by being simple and comprehensible and containing nothing irrelevant to the class struggle.

What caused Brecht to break his silence and become totally committed in 1929?

Sources

From the principal plays written in this period, we can see that the entire development from student of Marx to totally engaged artist was very closely related to the development of ideas about America. The three works that took most of Brecht's time from 1925 to 1931 were *Joe Fleischhacker*, *Mahagonny*, and *St. Joan*, all "American" plays. *St. Joan,* begun in 1929, is the most complete expression we have of Brecht's theoretical study of Marxism; it is not only a concretization of many of the theories in *Capital*, it is also (both in form and content) an absolute commitment to whatever means are necessary to make the socialist revolution.

But although the most important plays are about America, looking at the books Brecht read about America is no longer as much help in investigating the influences on his thinking as it was before. His readings served mainly to confirm what he already knew. His factual image of America did not change; he needed no new details to write another play about it. What changed was his evaluation of the image, and the conclusions for action that he drew from his conception of conditions there.

Reading a novel like *The Titan*, by Theodore Dreiser, for instance, hardly had much effect on him; it only repeats the basic themes of the other "Chicago novels": success in the world of high finance, the fascination of the city, the irreversible growth of America into a great industrial power, congruence of financial and political power, and a wistful look back at the now-deserted fields of the rural era. In theme, plot, and style *The Titan* has many similarities to *The Pit*, and it did not provide Brecht with any new material; he listed it as one of the best books he read in 1928 but classified it only as "entertainment literature." ("Unterhaltungsliteratur") (*GW* 18:66).

In 1928 Brecht must also have seen Piscator's production of Upton Sinclair's *Singing Jailbirds*. Frau Hauptmann remembered that Brecht by no means thought all Americans were bad, that he knew about and respected the IWW and Joe Hill, for instance. Sinclair's play is one important source of that knowledge and respect, for it is a play about the Wobblies and the persecution they suffer under the criminal syndicalism law. Although Sinclair makes clear in the postscript that he is personally opposed to the program of the Wobblies, the play portrays them as courageous heroes. It also makes the nature of class justice very clear, both in serious scenes and in one of Sinclair's few really funny scenes, a Wobbly's vision of a trial run against him by the "master-class of the State of California." The play is a strange mixture of sentimental banality and agitprop technique. It is without dialectic or theory, being merely an appeal to the emotions of the workers to stick together and win through martyrdom. Its artistic virtue lies in its constant use of IWW songs sung by choruses of strikers and prisoners; refrains returning again and again make the play both rousing and stylized, like a ballad with a refrain that takes on new meaning with each verse. It is a veritable compendium of labor songs (mostly by Joe Hill, an immigrant), such as "Solidarity Forever," "They Go Wild, Simply Wild Over Me," "Hallelujah, I'm a Bum," "You'll Have Pie in the Sky When You Die," and "The Rebel Girl."

About 1950 Brecht planned a play with the Berliner Ensemble on Joe Hill;[45] perhaps Piscator's production of *Singing Jailbirds* back in 1928 influenced that later plan. But none of the American works he knew in the late twenties had any direct influence on his writing at that time; at most, perhaps, the choruses in the Sinclair play helped give him the idea of using workers' choruses in *The Mother*. Except for *St. Joan*, Brecht's first direct use of an American source after starting to write in the service of communism was not until 1931, when he wrote the poem "Places to Sleep" on the basis of an incident in chapter 45 of Dreiser's *Sister Carrie*.

At least two other plays on American subjects were performed in Berlin in 1929:[46] Erich Mühsam's *Sacco und Vanzetti*—in which the shockingly unjust court processes predominate—and *Reporter*, by Ben Hecht and Charles MacArthur—a light comedy with a background of political corruption, violence, and journalistic sensationalism in Chicago—but again they do not seem to have influenced Brecht. They could only help substantiate the picture he already had of the American system. He already knew of the Sacco-Vanzetti case in 1927 (*GW* 18:53), and he knew of corruption in Chicago at least since reading *The Jungle*.

So, although Brecht continued to read about America during the period between his discovery of Marxian economics and his dedication to communism, no new ideas from his reading are reflected in his work of that period. *Mahagonny* reflects the early influence of Bret Harte and Jack London and the longtime preoccupation with cities and hurricanes; new is the economic doctrine, particularly the understanding of alienation, but not the picture of America. *Happy End* is also a distillation of early stereotypes of America as a land of brutal but charming gangsters and commercial religion. *Flight over the Ocean* focuses only on the positive content of American technical progress; *The Baden Learning Play* presents an antithesis but is not specifically about America. The only two poems Brecht wrote about America in this period (1927–29) also accept the familiar image of America: "Memorial Plaque for 12 World Champions" (1927) praises sports champions and "Song of the Machines" (also 1927) praises technical achievement.

According to James K. Lyon, in 1928 Brecht befriended his first real American, Ferdinand Reyher.[47] Reyher had written a play, *Don't Bet on Fights*, about a self-educated boxer who enters the highest social circles and abandons his own class. The play is likely based on the life story of Gene Tunney. Elisabeth Hauptmann translated it (under the title *Harte Bandagen* [*Hard Bandages*]), and Brecht used all his influence to get it produced in Berlin; it finally opened to great controversy on the last day of 1929. In 1928 Reyher was also working on what he called a "melodramatic and typically American" Frankie-and-Johnny play that was meant to show the history of the American West in microcosm; it later turned into a novel on the history of America as seen through the history of poker! It was never published, but it may well have influenced *Mahagonny*. The discovery of Reyher's influence on Brecht's developing image of America, both in these transitional days and during Brecht's later stay in Los Angeles, is an important corrective to the notion that Brecht became totally anti-American. Reyher was a socialist, not an apologist for capitalism, but he continually strove to show Brecht the concrete little things that he loved about America and its people. He had a vast knowledge and experience of both high and low culture, and through him Brecht gained a more accurate picture of the richness of this country than is usually supposed. In fact, Brecht apparently had either real or fanciful plans to visit the United States about this time. According to Lyon, after Reyher returned to the States, Elisabeth Hauptmann wrote him in August 1929, saying she, Brecht, Weill, and unnamed others planned to come there the following year, and she wrote him again in 1930 expressing the vaguer hope that *The Threepenny Opera* would play there sometime so that they could all come over.

But it is not until *St. Joan of the Stockyards* that an American *literary* influence is directly apparent again. But even there the influence is only from sources Brecht had known for years: *St. Joan* is made up of almost all the plays and fragments he had already written on America and books he had already read. There is no image of America that does not come from sources he knew before

223

he started reading Marx; yet the play is very different from all his previous work. The difference all lies in the meaning given to phenomena that remain the same.

We have already noticed that Brecht's positive commitment to working for socialism did not come until the time when he wrote *St. Joan*. Something happened in 1929–30 besides his reading American literature and reading Marx: both of those were only the preparation.

Chapter Five

1929-1931
The World Economic Crisis
and Brecht's Commitment:
"St. Joan of the Stockyards"

What happened in 1929 was, of course, the world economic crisis. The concentric circles of ruin spreading out from Wall Street throughout the world (just like the image of the wheat exchange's influence in *The Pit*) meant for Europeans the end of the American Dream. It shattered Brecht's world-view particularly because for him America had always been the symbol of strength and life; its system was perhaps unjust; but it was strong; next to decadent Europe America was raw, healthy, and productive.

But Brecht had been studying Marx's analysis of capitalism intensely for three years; the crash must have been an overwhelming confirmation of the implications of the theories and formulas he had been learning so thoroughly. Capitalism *was* doomed!

As for so many Americans, the depression was the most important historic event in shaping Brecht's thoughts. Surprisingly, there are in Brecht's work almost no mentions of Hitler and fascism before 1932; although we know from biographical accounts that he was affected by the increasing terror in Berlin, events in America seem to have been more important to him. Or at least to his writing. We can only know what he thought from what he wrote down, but it is clear that the mythology he pasted together around America served as the set of symbols or the model into which he projected his thoughts about his own society. Thus he would feel events in Berlin deeply but analyze them in terms of the American model. But at the same time his interest in, and knowledge of, America did cause him to follow events there closely, so that he felt immediately touched by the stock market crash, and accorded it more significance in his writings than Hitler's rise.

For at the same time that the crash confirmed Brecht's Marxism, it also destroyed what remnants of illusion he had left about the mythology of virile America. He was still able to use the symbols of that mythology in one of his most brilliant plays, *St. Joan of the Stockyards*, but the myths all turned ironic overnight.

"Vanished Glory of the Giant City New York"

The transformation of the American dream into the American nightmare and the turning upside-down of all the myths are the subjects of the major poem "Vanished Glory of the Giant City New York," a direct response to the stock market crash. We will look at the poem in detail, because Brecht is nowhere more explicit about his attitudes toward America. He is also explicit that this is a turning point in his life, at least as important as the other turning point described in the poem about trying to write *Fleischhacker*.[1]

The first half of "Vanished Glory" is a summing-up of Brecht's own previous positions on America. He speaks not in the first person singular but rather at first completely impersonally, and then in the first person plural. This is his own story, but it is also the story of his generation, and of Europeans in general. The crash on Wall Street has returned them to a feeling of identification with their own countries after a decade of trying to identify with the splendor of the new world:

> Today, when word has gotten around
> That these people are bankrupt
> We see on the other continents (which however are also bankrupt)
> Many things differently, as it seems to us, more clearly.

> Heute, wo es sich herumgesprochen hat
> Daß diese Leute bankrott sind
> Sehen wir auf den anderen Kontinenten (die zwar auch bankrott sind)
> Allerhand anders, wie es uns vorkommt, schärfer.[2]

The two-part structure of the poem demonstrates this new vision: the images of former glory in the first half are repeated in the second half, but all of them are seen from a new perspective:

> What about the skyscrapers?
> We regard them more coolly.
> . . . .
> So high up filled with poverty?

226

Was ist das mit den Hochhäusern?
Wir betrachten sie kühler.

. . . .
So hoch hinauf voller Armut?

The poem contrasts confidence and conspicuous consumption during the decade of economic expansion after the war (which was also Brecht's first decade of dramatic production) with sudden revelation of the unsound structural base. Flamboyant waste turns out to have been overproduction of commodities, which are produced not to fill human needs but to gather profit.

We have already seen the trick of turning all the supposed pleasures and riches into their opposite, in *Mahagonny*. Eating, boxing, loving, drinking, and being free (anarchy) can all be fatal, if they are indulged in to excess—and the entire first half of "Vanished Glory" is about excesses. The excesses climax in the eleventh section, where the poet dissolves in superlatives.

But not only this dialectic comes from earlier works like *Mahagonny*. The images are, in fact, a compilation of the kinds of images and human types that filled Brecht's own plays, poems, and stories until 1929.

The third section talks of the United States as a country that assimilates all races beyond recognition; this recalls the poor French family and Shlink in *Jungle*, and all the literature we know Brecht read about immigrant Americans.

"The voices of their women from the gramophone records" in the fourth section refers to Brecht's early love of American records, with the single weak voice struggling against a whole orchestra (which Hauptmann said reminded them of the individual's struggle against society). The "evening waters of Miami" are here too, echoing *Decline and Fall of the Paradise City*.

In the seventh section Brecht writes, with what appears to be admiration, "Poverty was considered a disgrace there" ("Armut galt dort für schimpflich"). That was certainly the case in *Jungle, Fleischhacker, Threepenny Opera, Mahagonny,* and it reminds us of Brecht's early note about his generation's interest in America, "SHORTLY AFTER THE GREAT WAR" ("KURZ NACH DEM GROSSEN KRIEG"), quoted above, pages 6–7. ("Vanished Glory" begins by asking if anyone remembers New York's fame "In the decade after the Great War" ["In dem Jarzehnt nach dem großen Krieg"]).

227

Americans considered it a sign of pride to be hard and cruel, as Brecht describes it in section 6: they openly, in front of the whole world, got everything they could from their workers and then shot them

> . . . and threw their worn-out bones and
> Used-up muscles on the streets with
> Good-natured laughter.

> . . . und warfen ihre abgebrauchten Knochen und
> Vernutzten Muskeln auf die Straßen mit
> Gutmütigem Lachen.

But, he immediately points out, the Americans reported that same raw determination among striking workers with "sporting recognition" ("sportlicher Anerkennung"); and the longest section in the poem begins by describing boxers in the terms Brecht had used for his friend Samson-Körner. We know the importance sport had had for Brecht. Yet after 1929 he rarely if ever mentioned it. It is Schuhmann's opinion that "Vanished Glory" is in part a rejection of Brecht's earlier admiration for Samson-Körner, and of the whole concept the boxer embodied: the matter-of-fact, physically expressive but unsentimental man.[3] It is true that Brecht rejected the tough sporting type; but the qualities of matter-of-factness and unsentimentality remained important to him, gesture was still very important in acting, and even toughness is sometimes demanded in a situation like that in *The Measure Taken* or *St. Joan*. Brecht did not decide that these qualities were *per se* bad, just as tall buildings and fast cars were not bad: it was their social origins and the uses to which they are put that could make them bad. Boxing had become a trivial pastime and exploiting workers an evil one.

The boxers, of course, also remind us of *Mahagonny*, not just the boxing scene but the whole atmosphere created by men wearing suits "With cotton padding in the shoulders, which made the men so broad / That three of them filled the whole sidewalk" ("Mit den Wattewülsten an den Schultern, welche die Männer so breit machen / Daß drei von ihnen den ganzen Gehsteig beanspruchen"). In the 1931 production of *A Man's a Man*, too, the soldiers wore padded suits, and Peter Lorre suggested the interpolation of a scene where Galy Gay demonstrates how wrestlers deport themselves. Braking his movements and putting his hands in his pockets slowly were mannerisms Brecht had admired in Samson-Körner.

228

Cramming the mouth full of Beechnut chewing gum (also in section 8) may be an allusion to an unpublished song for *Mahagonny* called "The Chewing-Gum Song," which is sung by two men and two women standing by Beechnut posters and chewing in time to the music. It is a song about the hardest, handsomest, meanest, and in fact only man in Mahagonny, whose "whole philosophy was that he chewed gum" ("ganze philosophie war daß er kaugummi kaute") (BBA 460, 60).

In short, the entire imagery and diction of "Vanished Glory" are a kind of recapitulation of Brecht's American phase. We know that America served him as an allegorical model, that Chicago represents Berlin; and in the eighth section the poet confesses that he himself admired and imitated the American mannerisms. There are few *Ach*'s in Brecht's poetry; this poem contains two. "Ah, the voices of their women" ("Ach, diese Stimmen ihrer Frauen") in section 4 is a parody (he is speaking ironically of his past) of stupefied admiration; it is how he *used* to feel. But the tone in section 8 is completely different: first the frenzied exclamation, "What glory! What a century!" ("Welch ein Ruhm! Welch ein Jahrhundert!") and then a new voice, subdued, thoughtful, perhaps after a long pause: "Ah, we too demanded those impressive suits" ("Ach, auch wir verlangten solche breitspurigen Anzüge"). This *Ach* is spoken in the present. It says: don't blame it all on the Americans, we caught the fever too. And: this is a confession. And perhaps also: those *were* golden days when our pleasures were so simple. At the beginning of the poem he suggested America had been "our childhood friend, known to everyone, unmistakable!" ("unser jedermann bekannter, unverwechselbarer Jugendfreund!"), and now he describes the influence of that friend. We are reminded too of the early poem in which Brecht declared:

> And the best thing about America is:
> That we understand it.
>
> Und das Beste an Amerika ist:
> Daß wir es verstehen.
>
> (*GW* 8:286)

But this explicit statement of fascination with America is a description of a time long past. "Vanished Glory of the Giant City New York" eradicates that early statement and many others with its first three lethal lines:

Who still remembers
The glory of the giant city New York
In the decade after the great war?

Wer erinnert sich wohl noch
An den Ruhm der Riesenstadt New York
In dem Jahrzehnt nach dem großen Krieg?

Six years earlier Brecht had written a similar sentence:

Almost every one of us remembers the fall of the Roman cities Hercula-
neum, Pompeii and Stabiae, which took place 2000 years ago.

Beinahe jeder von uns erinnert sich an den Untergang der römischen
Städte Herculanum, Pompeji und Stabää, der vor nunmehr 2000 Jahren
stattgefunden hat.

(BBA 214, 23)

There he stated his intention to write a history of Miami so that after
its destruction it should not be forgotten, and he proceeded to
describe the structure of Miami, making clear where the irrationality lay that would lead to its destruction (symbolized by him at that
time by the Flood). The story of the vanished glory of New York is
very similar. It is interesting that by using the cadences of the
introduction to the Miami story, Brecht can create the impression
that New York existed about 2,000 years ago and is known only
through archaeology. That stylistic device is important because
what Brecht is really saying in this poem is that for him and his
generation the depression divided history into two periods. The
postwar decade of enthusiasm is ancient history; 1929 is the end of
an epoch in Brecht's life. And so there is a tremendous distance, the
images are pulled up out of another eon—although they were
actually still current and believable immediately before the poem
was written.

The perversion of social relations into their opposites is introduced through a mere rumor ("For one day a rumor of strange
collapses ran through the world" ("Denn eines Tages durchlief die
Welt das Gerücht seltsamer Zusammenbrüche"). The myths of
American capitalism depended on confidence for their success. The
moment doubt began to infect people—Americans and Europeans—the system began to fall apart. That is a fairly accurate
representation of stock market psychology, but also of Europeans'
quick loss of admiration for America: suddenly now they could

230

throw off their inferiority complexes. Why, America's superiority had been all bluff! The last lines of the poem are:

> What a discovery:
> That their system of living together showed
> The same lamentable flaw as that of
> More modest people!

> Welch eine Entdeckung:
> Daß ihr System des Gemeinlebens denselben
> Jämmerlichen Fehler aufwies wie das
> Bescheidenerer Leute!

Although the turning point is indicated by nothing more than a rumor, the language used in reaction to the discovery of a new perspective is violent and vituperative. Brecht is not merely disillusioned, he is angry. The second half, a dialectical tour de force, uses exactly the same examples of America's culture as the first half, but it reveals now the hollowness, decadence, and bankruptcy at the core, often quite rudely:

> Records are still sold, admittedly few
> But what are these silly women [goats] telling us, really, who never
> Learned to sing? What
> Is the point of these songs? What have they
> Really been singing to us all these years?

> Noch werden Schallplatten verkauft, freilich wenige
> Doch was erzählen uns diese Ziegen eigentlich, die nicht
> Singen gelernt haben? Was
> Ist der Sinn dieser Gesänge? Was haben sie uns
> Eigentlich vorgesungen all diese Jahre lang?

But—and this is central to an understanding of Brecht's entire concept of America—if we reread the first half after knowing the second half, we begin to wonder just how positive those images at the beginning really were. And we realize that many of them are quite horrible, that they are only made to seem positive by the tone. The tone forces acceptance of the assumption that if America does something that seems cruel, it is because she cannot be bothered by weakness, she has a great destiny to fulfill. "They erected their gigantic edifices with incomparable waste / Of the best human material" ("Ihre riesigen Bauwerke führten sie auf mit unvergleichlicher Verschwendung / Besten Menschenmaterials"). It can be seen as either glorious or inhuman that the Americans wasted

231

human beings. Brecht, we discover, simply reports what he saw the Americans doing. In the second half he reports the same activities but adds a value judgment.

He is shocked not only by the crash but also by his own earlier amoral stance. That is why the economic crisis marks the great hiatus in his life: never again will he be an uncommitted writer. He had been moving in that direction already during the years he was studying Marx, but only after the crash on Wall Street was he able to free himself completely of the earlier admiration for pitiless virility, to put all his energy at the service of the oppressed, and to promote the cause of socialism.

The first half of the poem begins to sound very ambiguous on second reading. "Poverty was considered a disgrace there" ("Armut galt dort für schimpflich"). Does that mean there were no poor, or they were cursed and rejected? "Truly, their whole system of living together was incomparable" ("Wahrlich, ihr ganzes System des Gemeinlebens war unvergleichlich"). Incomparably good or bad, kind or cruel, progressive or irrational? It took the reading of Marx, as Brecht himself said, before he understood his own plays: not that he had written Marxist plays, but that they would serve as excellent data for Marxian analysis because he had recorded exactly what he saw.

The striking structure of this poem is an accurate representation of the form taken by Brecht's own changing attitude toward America. We have been able to say both that this attitude changed and that it did not, because he kept the same images and impressions but changed his assessment of their virtue. He always associated America with opulent waste, contrast of rich and poor, sport, virility, gambling, jazz, skyscrapers, automobiles, toughness and unsentimentality, get-rich-quick schemes and swindles, gangsters, and anarchy. But at first he saw some positive value in these qualities, namely, progress. In the early twenties everything that was new came out of the States. But by 1929 Brecht was convinced that socialism was the system of the future, representing progress, experiment, and newness, so America lost its one justification. We have observed that dialectic in the relation of *Flight over the Ocean* to *The Baden Learning Play*: technical progress is not real progress if it does not help mankind. There had been signs in Brecht's poetry of the previous few years that a new concept of what "the new world"

232

could mean was replacing America: as early as 1926 "Coals for Mike" and "Eight Thousand Poor People Come Up to the City," in 1927, "Ballad of the Steel Helmet" and "Three Hundred Murdered Coolies Report to an International," and in 1929 a very clear statement on a new way of thinking, "The Rug Weavers of Kuyan-Bulak Honor Lenin." America had already begun to lose the excuse of newness, and when the crash happened it became one big ghost town for Brecht.

The fatalistic prophecy of destruction of the cities in "Of Poor B.B." (1922) is fulfilled in "Vanished Glory," complete with the same imagery of useless skyscrapers. But in the earlier poem, Brecht identified himself with the dying culture; now he is observing its death and liberating himself from its influence. The difference between the resigned tone in "Of Poor B.B." and the fighting, angry tone in "Vanished Glory" tells a whole story in itself. In 1922 Brecht could only hope he would not let his cigar go out in the earthquakes to come; in 1930 he knows what he is going to fight *for* and so has a transcendent, not nihilistic, reason to say earthquakes be damned. But there are no natural catastrophes in this poem. After 1929, causation in Brecht's work is secular; it is in fact economic, and traceable to particular men. The Wall Street crash was caused by the irrationality of a system built by men and serving particular men, and by the time of the depression Brecht wanted to use no more literary devices that might obscure that crucial recognition.

The stock market crash inspired other expressions of anger too, but none is quite so bitterly ironic and direct in its portrayal of disillusion as "Vanished Glory of the Giant City New York." In the same year, for instance, Brecht planned a comedy to be called *Barnum*, about "the destruction of New York" (BBA 424, 70). In 1931 he wrote a poem about New York, "Places to Sleep," which describes (and evaluates as reformist) an act of charity: he has heard, Brecht says, that on the corner of Twenty-Sixth Street and Broadway every evening a man stands and finds a night's lodging for the homeless by asking passersby for help. It is winter in the poem— "the snow that was meant for the homeless falls on the street"—and Brecht probably related it to that terrible depression winter in Berlin: in January 1931 there were almost five million unemployed in Germany. But the episode comes from chapter 45 of Dreiser's 1900 novel *Sister Carrie*. (Brecht's "I hear" ["Ich höre"] usually

233

means "I have read.")[4] The poem seems to be the only direct influence the book had on Brecht, but it indicates that he was still reading American social novels in spite of the disenchantment he expressed in "Vanished Glory."

For of course America was still a very important symbol; it now provided the allegorical structure on which to build a thorough analysis of capitalism's cycles. The intention to write a major play exposing the mechanisms of capitalism had by no means left Brecht when he abandoned *Fleischhacker* to read Marx in 1926; on the contrary, his years of study were preparation for that major play on capitalism that he wanted to write.

In fact, Brecht kept coming back to *Fleischhacker* for years. We know from bound and dated notebooks that he wrote twelve pages for it in 1927 and one-page notes in 1928 and 1929.[5] According to Elisabeth Hauptmann, Brecht also intended to complete it while he was in exile in the United States, combining it with *The Bread Store* and calling the new play *The Bread King of Chicago*. She said he never got to it because he had to do writing that would be more immediately profitable.[6]

In fact, Brecht did work with Ferdinand Reyher in 1941 on a screen treatment of *Joe Fleischhacker oder ein Brotkönig lernt backen* (*Joe Fleischhacker, or A Bread King Learns to Bake*), called in English *The King's Bread*. A four-page synopsis is registered with the Screen Writers Guild; there are also a fifteen-page English version (presumably written down by Reyher) and seven pages of notes by Brecht in German.[7] The plot, which Brecht claims to have developed in a couple of hours' conversation with Reyher after telling the latter of the abandoned Joe Fleischhacker play, begins with the same poor farmer family penniless in Chicago; but this time the wife bakes a loaf of bread for the bread king Fleischhacker, who controls all the bakeries in Chicago. In a reversal of the *St. Joan* scene, she is fooled into giving the bread to someone else. But later Fleischhacker tastes it, loves it, and secretly sets her up in business so he can buy her bread. (He eats the bread in her back room with her, incognito, and complains about the rich Fleischhacker.) When he goes on vacation, the family adulterates the bread to be able to stay in business without his support; and when he returns, he is furious to find they have become competitors. He smashes them; but when his own chemists cannot duplicate her recipe for him, he sets the wife up

234

in business again and returns to eating her bread in the back room.[8]

The whimsical story seems not to have the bitterness and cruelty of any of the earlier works it is based on: *Joe Fleischhacker, The Bread Store*, and *St. Joan*. Nevertheless it did not sell. And it is hardly a solution to the old problems Brecht had with the Fleischhacker material in 1926, since it does not deal with the commodity market. Its theme of temporary class reconciliation, based on the greater skill of the worker but the power of the capitalist, sounds almost like an echo of *Mr. Puntila and His Servant Matti*, which Brecht had finished a year earlier. But it is certainly interesting that this material still haunted Brecht fifteen years after he gave it up to read Marx.

Two other film scenarios that Brecht wrote in the United States betray his preoccupation with the Fleischhacker theme then: *All Our Yesterdays*,[9] also written in English with Reyher, is a modernization of *Macbeth* with a butcher named John Machacek as protagonist. It has the subtitle *Lady Macbeth of the Yards*. In Brecht's English Machacek is not a "butcher" but a "steercutter"— clearly derived from "Fleischhacker." And *The Hamlet of the Wheat Exchange*[10] is the beginning of a retelling of the story of Jay Fleischhacker as a "tragedy of hesitation" like *Hamlet*. Most of the few pages of this fragment explain the economics of cornering the Chicago wheat market, emphasizing the "Homeric proportions" of the struggles there.

There is yet another, longer film scenario that betrays Brecht's continuing fascination with the economics of wheat while in America. Written in English (probably not only by Brecht, though the English is rather quaint), *The Goddess of Victory*[11] claims that a close study of the story of Joseph (Genesis 37 ff.) shows it is mainly about the negotiations between Israeli and Egyptian wheat dealers, and that Joseph is able to force higher moral standards by being a better businessman. This lesson is then transplanted to negotiations between American and Italian wheat dealers at the end of World War II, with a clever Italian named Giuseppe escaping a trial for collaboration by trading Italian art to the Americans for wheat to feed hungry Italy. (His American captor is an art lover and partner in a New York wheat firm, "Phare and Potty"—Pharaoh and Potiphar.) Apparently, Brecht had wheat so much on his mind that he could interpret almost anything in its light.

But what happened to *Fleischhacker* in 1929 was that Brecht wrote *St. Joan of the Stockyards* instead. The original version of *St. Joan* was in fact much closer than the published version to *Fleischhacker* and *The Pit*: it was set at about 1900, and had Mauler as an old-style capitalist who really controlled the city of Chicago. He was the master of his own fate, and he, not the "letters from New York," was the ultimate cause of much in the play.

There is no indication of the exact time at which Brecht started writing *St. Joan*; it would be meaningless anyway since it is an adaptation of so much of his early work.[12] The program notes to the Berliner Ensemble production of 1968 imply that he wrote the first version before the stock market crash in October 1929, and then changed the setting to a contemporary one when the crash occurred. It is also possible that he began the early version after the crisis on Wall Street and changed it when the height of the crisis hit Berlin in 1931. (In *Gesammelte Werke* the dates Brecht worked on the play are given as 1929–31 [*GW* 2:4*].)

Commitment

However, it is not necessary to assume that Brecht waited for either of those dates. Economic and political chaos and polarization of right and left were occurring so fast in Germany at the end of the twenties that he was in the process of committing himself to active participation before the shock of the crisis. After the Tenth Party Congress in the Soviet Union in 1925, which presented Lenin's plans for a cultural offensive for the masses, and especially after the Eleventh Party Congress in 1927, many writers were attracted to the idea of art for the workers, and Brecht too wrote a few poems for the Communist satirical journal *Der Knüppel* (*The Nightstick*) starting in 1926.[13] But otherwise he seems to have held rather aloof from active engagement in struggle while he was studying capitalism. We must remember that reading Marx on economics is not at all the same thing as endorsing the Communist Party, let alone working with it. We must also remember, as Klaus-Detlef Müller points out, that

> in the twenties there were extraordinarily divergent tendencies in the interpretation of Marx, and that *the* communism to which Brecht would have turned just did not exist.

> es in den zwanziger Jahren außerordentlich divergierende Tendenzen

236

innerhalb der Marxinterpretation gab, und daß *der* Kommunismus, dem Brecht sich zugewandt hätte, gar nicht existierte.[14]

Brecht started out learning his communism from Fritz Sternberg, who was a left liberal, then from Karl Korsch, with whom he also later disagreed; he had frequent differences about details—almost always matters of cultural policy—with the KPD, the Soviet Union, and later the SED, but that does not mean that he ever failed essentially to support the Party. It is true that he never joined it; that could well have been because he was not willing to be as exemplary and to do as much bureaucratic work as Party membership entails. Käthe Rülicke reports that in conversation he used to call himself a "Bolshevik without a party" ("parteiloser Bolschewik").[15]

Since very few of the notes and fragments Brecht left can be dated, and since his commitment to working-class art and socialism, his return to economic themes, and his newly defined attitude toward America are all crystallized not only simultaneously but also interdependently during the years of the depression, it would be foolish and false to try to pin down particular stages in his thinking to particular months. Brecht was so strongly attracted to dialectical thought partly because his own thought was always in the process of becoming.

What we can say is that certain events confirmed and finalized directions in which Brecht's thought was already tentatively moving, so that we can definitely pinpoint *latter* limits after which he could not return to old attitudes. Although he had already begun some literary activity for workers and students, it was not until the depression that Brecht definitively and consciously became a communist—a "*Bolschewik.*"

It is from the second event that his total commitment to the revolution *as an artist* dates. Already in 1927 he had insisted on judging literature for its use value;[16] but that was still a formal criterion, since it did not stipulate who (what class) should use it. After 1929 literature had to be useful *to the revolution.* As we have observed, that usefulness took several forms during the course of Brecht's life, depending on his historical situation: first, exposure of capitalism and instruction in means of class struggle; second, organization of resistance to Nazism; and third (and most subtle and difficult), the attempt to inculcate values of the new socialist person. But 1929 was the point of no return, after which he could not write

237

apolitical works. As we have seen, Brecht complained often about living in a historical period that forced him to write only on political matters. Having decided to become a conscious agent of history, he had to help remove the need for struggle in society before he could write poetry that was not distorted by struggle: "Capitalism has forced us into the struggle" ("Der Kapitalismus hat uns zum Kampf gezwungen").[17] During the many years of deliberately limiting his style and subject matter, Brecht did not dream that in his own lifetime he would live under a socialist regime in Germany, and may well have expected his literary struggle against capitalism to be permanent. Nevertheless, he recognized that poetry did have valuable functions besides negative propaganda. In 1940 he was ready to accept as valid any literature that could enrich the capacity to experience and to communicate—provided, still, that this would be a socializing, not an isolating, effect.[18] That is the germ of the third phase of Brecht's political aesthetics. For after all, the purpose of overthrowing capitalism was to provide the opportunity for people to develop to their furthest potential, in cooperation rather than in competition with each other.

But in the years of the depression, there was no time for the cultivation of primarily aesthetic sensibility. Germany, very dependent on U.S. financial conditions because of all the short-term loans used to rebuild after the war, suffered a depression far worse than that in the United States. Six million workers, half the work force, were unemployed in 1932. And the misery began in the winter of 1928–29. That winter was a terrible one in Germany, with 2.5 million unemployed. The fascists were gaining popularity frighteningly quickly. It was clear that the country was heading for crisis, and it was time to act, not study. It was then that Brecht started writing his *Lehrstücke*, renouncing the commercial stage.

Sternberg places Brecht's turning to the Party around the spring of 1929, after the May Day demonstration in which Brecht watched the police shoot twenty demonstrators.[19] The importance of that winter and the May Day incident is corroborated by the fact that Brecht began work on *The Bread Store*, a play specifically about unemployment in Berlin, in May 1929. The main theme of *The Bread Store* is the devastating effect of the American depression in Germany, but it is clear from a dated notebook[20] that Brecht did some work on it before the stock market crash of October–November 1929.

Significantly, all Brecht's work on the depression except the more abstract "Vanished Glory" is set in winter; the snow of New York in "Places to Sleep," the snow of Chicago in *St. Joan,* and the cold of Berlin in *The Bread Store,* all threaten to kill the homeless, jobless poor; it is during the winter that it becomes most apparent that the capitalist system does not even provide its workers with the means to stay alive. The cold and desperate winters of the depression in Berlin must have impressed Brecht very deeply—as well as reminding him of the strong emphasis on the cold in all those early books he read about Chicago.

People were freezing and starving to death around him. The strongest capitalist country was collapsing. The historical necessity of socialism was demonstrated conclusively. And Brecht ended his semi-withdrawal. This is clear simply from a look at the dates of his dramatic work. From 1926 to 1928 nothing was finished except a revision of *A Man's a Man* and *The Threepenny Opera,* which was written in a few weeks. In 1929 *Mahagonny, Flight over the Ocean,* and the *Baden Learning Play* were finished (though none of them are strenuous works and the last two are very short); but in 1930–31, Brecht finished *The Measure Taken, St. Joan, The Exception and the Rule, The Mother*—all major revolutionary works. But the number of plays, impressive though it is, is less important than their content and their intended audience. Their content was class struggle, and they were directed at the left, the workers, and sometimes students.

In short, the historical necessity for action in 1929 forced Brecht to step into the arena and start fighting. He fought by teaching the oppressed class how to fight. That is very clearly what his two most militant and party-oriented plays, *The Mother* and *The Measure Taken,* are for and about. But it is also what *The Bread Store* and *St. Joan* are about, though the latter plays are more complex. Those are, not coincidentally, four of his best plays. But even *The Exception and the Rule, The Baden Learning Play,* and *The Roundheads and the Peakheads* are about the tactics of fighting off oppression. All these plays deal with wrong tactics; some present right tactics as well.

Brecht's chief attack was against reformism in all its manifestations. Unemployment and necessity for revolution can be topics for a concerned but uninvolved writer; tactics of revolution can only be the topic of an active fighter. If in fact the young

239

comrade in *The Measure Taken* is in the wrong, then his crime is voluntarism and reformism: although a sincere revolutionary, he learns too late the danger of working only for short-term relief. The coolie in *The Exception and the Rule* does not learn that it is dangerous to treat the class enemy with kindness; but the audience (and the players) learn it.

"The Bread Store"

The strongest lessons about reformism are in the two plays about the depression. *The Bread Store*, showing the effects of New York's crisis on the little people of Germany, also shows the wrong ways of fighting back; that is the educational purpose of the play. Brecht wrote of it: "The play was conceived in the grand style and was supposed above all to make visible a certain attitude during the economic crisis of those years" ("Das Stück war in großem Stil gedacht und sollte vor allem eine gewisse Haltung während der Wirtschaftskrise jener Jahre sichtbar machen").[21] Schumacher lists the *Haltungen*—attitudes and actions—that the play shows to have been wrong: Widow Queck submits to all demands as to inexorable fate; the unemployed fight for a temporary part-time job instead of for state power; solidarity among the victims of exploitation is too fragile (when Widow Queck and her children are evicted, for instance); religious reformism treats only symptoms and thus helps the owners; all are fighting all; it is a senseless fight on an unorganized basis.[22] There is no process of learning; no one in the play recognizes the mistakes and draws conclusions from the recognition.

In *St. Joan*, on the other hand, such a learning process is the main plot movement in the play. That prompted Brecht in 1941 to consider the possibility of encouraging an audience to identify with Joan:

> In a contemporary performance of, say, *St. Joan*, it can be advantageous occasionally to induce empathy with Joan (from today's standpoint), since this figure does go through a process of recognition, so that the empathizing audience can take in the main parts very well from that point of view.

> Bei einer heutigen Aufführung etwa der *Heiligen Johanna der Schlachthöfe* kann es vorteilhaft sein, mitunter eine Einfühlung in die Johanna herbeizuführen (vom heutigen Standpunkt aus), da diese Figur ja einen Erkenntnisprozeß durchmacht, so daß der einfühlende

240

Zuschauer von diesem Punkt aus sehr wohl die Hauptpartien überblicken kann.[23]

That would apply even more strongly to *The Mother*. But it does not apply at all to *The Bread Store*, where getting the point of the play depends on maintaining a critical attitude toward *all* the characters. In fact, *The Bread Store* is one of the best examples of the Brechtian anti-Aristotelian technique. In 1939, considering how to improve *Galileo*, Brecht wrote:

> First the *Fatzer* fragment and the *Bread Store* fragment would have to be studied. These two fragments are the highest standard technically.
>
> Es wäre zuerst das *Fatzer*-Fragment und das *Brotladen*-Fragment zu studieren. Diese beiden Fragmente sind der höchste Standard technisch.[24]

Fatzer and *The Bread Store* are technically of the highest standard because of their consistent use of the techniques of epic theater: since the behavior of all characters in those plays is to be criticized, emotional identification is encouraged with none of them. Furthermore, various techniques are employed to present a "situation with the character of a model," a paradigm rather than a naturalistic slice of life. This is the essence of Brecht's idea of the difference between naturalism and realism. Naturalism portrays visible phenomena (i.e., *appearances*) without explaining them or suggesting how they might be changed; realism uses techniques of abstraction, stylization, nondramatic intrusion, comment, literary parody, and so on, to reveal *reality*: the laws of society that produce the phenomena.

The Bread Store and *St. Joan*, both written during and about the economic crisis, and both showing false ways of dealing with the crisis, are also Brecht's two best examples of writing a plot based on the laws of economic development. They use not only similar themes and some identical passages but also similar techniques. But *The Bread Store* is more limited in scope than *St. Joan*, which covers an extraordinarily large and complex series of interdependent topics. In a sense, although they were written simultaneously, *The Bread Store* prepares the way thematically for *St. Joan*.

St. Joan's development of *The Bread Store*'s themes is evident in four areas of the plot: the use of the Salvation Army, the formal climaxes in economic battles, the belief of some characters that economic laws are incomprehensible, and the kinds of actions taken by the workers.

First: in *The Bread Store*, the Salvation Army helps the rich, not the poor—but its ideological role is not as clear as in *St. Joan*.

Second: there is a "bread battle" ("Brotschlacht") in *The Bread Store*, probably based on the "wheat battle" ("Waizenschlacht") that Brecht had planned for *Fleischhacker* (BBA 678, 9), and there is a "stock market battle" ("Börsenschlacht") in *St. Joan*, based on the dramatic battle in the wheat exchange at the end of *The Pit* (very likely the *Fleischhacker* battle would also have taken place in the wheat exchange). In both *The Bread Store* and *St. Joan*, the battle is portrayed stylistically as the modern version of the battles in classic literature: in *The Bread Store* the Homeric style is parodied to produce a mock epic, reinforcing the point that this particular fight is trivial and not worth dying for; in *St. Joan* the battle is recounted in classic tragic diction by a messenger, as in a Greek tragedy. Like *Fleischhacker*, both these plays are written "in the grand style" ("in großem Stil"); *St. Joan* especially is famous for its parody to the point of blasphemy of the classical traditions. The technique is both further developed and more obvious in *St. Joan* than in *The Bread Store*; the economic function of the battle is also clearer in *St. Joan*.

Third: *St. Joan* provides the answers to the questions about the capitalist system that are raised in *The Bread Store*. In the prologue to *The Bread Store*, the unemployed complain:

> Unfortunately over eating and working
> Stand immovably the laws
> Unknown.

> Leider über Essen und Arbeit
> Stehen unverrückbar Gesetze
> Unbekannte

(GW 7:2913)

The packers in *St. Joan* use the same words:

> Against crises everyone is helpless!
> Immovably over us
> Stand the laws of economics, unknown

> Gegen Krisen kann keiner was!
> Unverrückbar über uns
> Stehen die Gesetze der Wirtschaft, unbekannte

(GW 2:704)

242

and later the small speculators cry:

> Alas! Eternally opaque
> Are the eternal laws
> Of human economics!

> Wehe! Ewig undurchsichtig
> Sind die ewigen Gesetze
> Der menschlichen Wirtschaft!

(*GW* 2:735)

In both plays those laments continue with imagery of natural catastrophe. But we know that by then Brecht realized economic castrophes were made by men, and seemed like hurricanes only to those who had been purposely misled. The play *St. Joan of the Stockyards* shows that economic disaster is not a natural disaster; it shows who is responsible and why, and it shows how those who are responsible maintain the myth that crises are natural, unavoidable, and above all incomprehensible. The ideology imposed on the workers is shown in the repetition of an image: in her first sermon Johanna claims to the workers: "Misfortune comes like rain, that no one maketh but that comes anyway" ("Das Unglück kommt wie der Regen, den niemand machet und der doch kommt") (*GW* 2:674). After Johanna has started seeking individual responsibility, her boss, Snyder, tries to make a deal with the packers (the ruling class in the play) whereby for the price of their rent the "Black Straw Hats" ("schwarze Strohhüte") will combat the "Bolshevik" tendencies among the workers:

> For word has gotten around that misfortune doesn't come about like rain but is made by a few people who get an advantage from it. But we Black Straw Hats want to say to them that misfortune comes like the rain, no one knows from where, and that suffering is their lot and a reward beckons them for it.
> THE THREE PACKING BOSSES
> Why talk of reward?
> SNYDER
> The reward we're speaking of is paid after death. . . . We also want to promise them that the rich will be punished, after they are dead to be precise. . . . And all that for only eight hundred dollars a month!

> Denn es hat sich herumgesprochen, daß das Unglück nicht entsteht wie der Regen, sondern von etlichen gemacht wird, welche ihren Vorteil davon haben. Wir Schwarzen Strohhüte aber wollen ihnen sagen, daß das Unglück wie der Regen kommt, niemand weiß woher, und daß das Leiden ihnen bestimmt ist und ein Lohn dafür winkt.

243

DIE DREI PACKHERREN
Wozu von Lohn reden?
SNYDER
Der Lohn, von dem wir reden, wird nach dem Tode bezahlt. . . . Wir
wollen ihnen auch versprechen, daß die Reichen bestraft werden, und
zwar wenn sie gestorben sind. . . . Und das alles für nur achthundert
Dollar im Monat! (*GW* 2:720)

That is how ideology is made; that is the function of religion in the
service of capitalism; that is why the unemployed in *The Bread Store*
and the packers and small speculators in *St. Joan* are fatalistic: they
are taught to be.

Finally: knowing where responsibility actually lies, the workers in
St. Joan are able to carry out concerted acts against the right target,
as the unemployed in *The Bread Store* are not—or they would be
able to if not for Joan's ignorance, which she too overcomes at the
end.

All four areas in which *St. Joan* is the completion of *The Bread
Store* (the role of religion, the heroic and classic style, the
comprehension of economic laws, and effective action on the basis
of comprehension) are aspects of *ideology*. But *St. Joan* shows that
ideology is produced by economic interest. To explain the ideology,
then, Brecht believed it was necessary to explain the economic
relations. And that is what the play does: it is a dramatization of
Capital.

"St. Joan of the Stockyards"

Here finally Brecht's years of study take clear dramatic form; here
finally he finishes a play incorporating his old interest in the stock
market and the results of his reading on political economy. *St. Joan
of the Stockyards*, the first major play since *A Man's a Man*, is in
every sense the culmination of Brecht's early work. The plays
following *St. Joan* take up new themes and new styles; many are
directed against fascism, and none are as purely socialist as *St. Joan*
and *The Mother* (written in 1931, the year *St. Joan* was finished).
Those two plays represent the zenith of Brecht's early creativity; not
only because they are the last before exile, and not only because of
their literary and ideological excellence, but also because *St. Joan*
gathers up all the motifs Brecht had worked on and left in
fragmentary form since 1924 and fits them into a coherent whole—
while *The Mother* accepts those hard-won insights as given and goes

on to show the next step: how to organize the struggle at which Joan (and the unemployed in *The Bread Store*) failed.

Concerning the quality of *St. Joan*, many of the critics who are not obliged to reject it for being "doctrinaire" consider it one of Brecht's major accomplishments. Theodor Adorno calls it "the central conception of his dialectical theater."[25] Frederic Ewen praises it at length, beginning with: "*St. Joan of the Stockyards* constitutes not only an intrepid *tour de force*, but it is probably one of Brecht's most brilliant and successful dramatic efforts."[26] André Müller describes the play's success at its premiere in Hamburg in 1959:

> Half an hour after the end of the performance the room was still filled with an enthusiastically applauding audience. . . . In recent years there has hardly been a theater event in the Federal Republic that came close to this.

> Noch eine halbe Stunde nach Ende der Vorstellung war der Saal mit begeistert applaudierenden Zuschauern gefüllt. . . . Es hat in den letzten Jahren kaum ein Theaterereignis in der Bundesrepublik gegeben, das diesem gleichkam.[27]

Ernst Bornemann, in his "Epitaph für Bertolt Brecht," calls it "the noblest and most beautifully balanced play that Brecht ever wrote" ("das nobelste und am schönsten ausgewogene Stück, das Brecht je geschrieben hat").[28] And although he still regarded it as a fragment, Brecht himself counted *St. Joan* among his three favorite plays.[29]

There are few plays in the history of drama that are more derivative and eclectic than *St. Joan of the Stockyards*, yet every line is unmistakably Brecht. He has succeeded in this work in exposing the major stylistic and ideological traditions of modern bourgeois Germany, by measuring them against his new Marxist insights. Rülicke-Weiler describes the effect of the clash between form and content (parody) as a technique of *Verfremdung*:

> The verse forms of Shakespeare, Schiller and Goethe come to contradict the content; the inhumanity of a society is exposed through confrontation with a form that was created to express human content. It becomes evident that the vestments of the classic-humanist ideal do not fit the affairs of monopoly capitalism.

> Die Versformen Shakespeares, Schillers und Goethes geraten in Widerspruch zum Inhalt, die Unmenschlichkeit einer Gesellschaft wird enthüllt durch die Konfrontierung mit einer Form, die geschaffen

wurde, menschliche Inhalte auszudrücken. Es wird deutlich, daß den Geschäften des Monopolkapitalismus das Gewand des klassisch-humanistischen Ideals nicht paßt.[30]

Besides the classic poets, she could have mentioned the Bible, which permeates the style of the entire play. It was in 1928 that Brecht was asked what book influenced him most, and answered, "You will laugh: the Bible" ("Sie werden lachen: die Bibel") (*GW* 18:12*).

In 1929 Brecht asked whether a playwright could write about money in iambic forms (*GW* 15:197); in *St. Joan* he gives the answer: yes, but only in parody. In parodying the style of the classics, Brecht by no means meant to ridicule them—he had the strongest respect for them, especially Shakespeare—but rather to demonstrate the Marxist principle that the bourgeoisie was a progressive and creative force when it was the revolutionary class, but that its early ideology and art are hypocrisy when used by today's bourgeoisie to restrain progress and creativity (revolution). Faust's ambivalence was honest a century earlier; but when mouthed by Mauler, Brecht's twentieth-century Faustian man, it is duplicity. In the age of individualism, acts of charity were virtuous; in the age of mass struggle, Brecht's Salvation Army objectively serves the enemies of the individuals it feeds. Even martyrdom is perverted: the true martyrs in Brecht's scheme are not canonized by the ruling class; they are the Saccos, Vanzettis, Luxemburgs and Liebknechts, whose deaths anger and instruct the people. Joan's tragedy is that she is unable to pass on what she learned to anyone who should hear it; her sacrifice is futile because its meaning is perverted by her enemies, and that is possible because she always acts as an individual.

In short, *St. Joan* is a play about how ideology is used to obscure reality. Simultaneously, its effect on the audience is to teach them how to see through the ideology to the reality; as such it is a *Lehrstück par excellence*. The ideology is: Mauler's "humane nature" ("menschliche Natur") and philanthropy, the Salvation Army's promise of reward and punishment in heaven for those who accept the status quo on earth, Joan's individualism and reformism and her disapproval of violence, and of course the pact between the capitalists and the church. The reality is: Mauler's "letters from New York," the need for revolutionary violence and solidarity, and the workings of the capitalist system.

The last theme is brilliantly demonstrated by the very structure of the play. The audience can see that each one of Mauler's apparent concessions to the poor is actually motivated by advice from the inner workings of the system (Wall Street). Each phase of the action is introduced by a letter predicting and advising on the coming stage of capitalist development. The play is divided into five sections representing five stages: (1) the end of prosperity; (2) overproduction; (3) crisis; (4) stagnation; and finally (5) the tendency toward monopoly as a (temporary) solution. Joan merely provides Mauler with the ideological excuses he needs so he will look as though he is not acting only in his own interest. But his every apparent good and spontaneous act is premeditated on the basis of better knowledge of the system. If there is any doubt on that point, a passage in a draft that Brecht did not publish (probably because he thought it unnecessarily obvious) should clear it up:

SLIFT:
helping people mauler you must be ill
MAULER:
don't say that   i have a letter here
from my dear friends in newyork

SLIFT:
leuten helfen mauler du mußt krank sein
MAULER:
sag das nicht   ich hab da einen brief
von meinen lieben freunden aus newjork

(BBA 118, 74)

A detailed and excellent description of the economic plot (i.e., the Marxist analysis of the phases of capitalism), and of the ideological superstructure that Mauler imposes to mislead Joan and that Brecht tears away to teach his audience, is contained in an article by Käthe Rülicke.[31] It would be redundant to repeat her definitive analysis here, except to point out the genius of the play's structure and the audacity of the attempt to dramatize *Capital*.

It is an attempt that necessarily requires simplification, as well as stylization, of reality into what Brecht would call realism (which shows how to change reality) as opposed to naturalism (which portrays reality as inevitable). The simplification and stylization are aided by the use of the American setting. Rülicke-Weiler again:

Dramatic alienation by means of a milieu largely unknown in Germany,

247

in which details could be treated on a large scale or left out, made it easier for Brecht to bring out the economic processes clearly and to make evident the fact that these processes (which, erupting inexplicably and seemingly overnight, determined the events in Germany as well) follow certain laws.

Die Verfremdung durch ein in Deutschland weitgehend unbekanntes Milieu, in dem Details großzügig behandelt oder weggelassen werden konnten, erleichterte es Brecht, die ökonomischen Vorgänge klar herauszuarbeiten und die Gesetzmäßgkeiten der Vorgänge deutlich zu machen, die—scheinbar über Nacht und unerklärbar hereingebrochen —die Ereignisse auch in Deutschland bestimmten.[32]

That is not so very different from Brecht's early rationale for using America as the setting for *In the Jungle* (see above, p. 15).

The theory of *Verfremdung* by means of setting remained remarkably the same, and continued to do so through Brecht's late works, which are set in Sichuan, the Caucasus, ancient Rome, Renaissance Italy, the Thirty Years' War—only once in contemporary Germany and once (*Ui*) in America. The purpose is to be able to concentrate on the paradigmatic aspects (*Modellcharakter*) of the plot and not be distracted by incidental exceptions and variations with which the audience would be familiar in its own country. (Perhaps *Ui* failed to arouse interest in the United States because Americans expected to see themselves mirrored in a play set in America.)

But although the dramaturgical reason for using America stayed the same, the image of America changed. And yet it did not change: it retained all the same outward characteristics. Only the focus was sharpened, so that a formerly illegible background appeared, creating a qualitatively different picture. The new focus, of course, was the result of Brecht's own clearer vision, sharpened by reading *Capital* as well as the books on America that we have discussed, attending classes and provoking countless discussions on Marxism, experiencing and understanding the depression, and committing himself to active struggle on the side of the working class, socialism, and the Communist Party.

Thus, in *St. Joan* Brecht is still using a background that corresponds to the character types in his play, in order that the audience not think them romantic or exceptional; but it is no longer "freedom" ("Freiheit") and "offensiveness" ("Anstößigkeit") that characterize the types and he would not call them "great human types" ("große Menschentypen") without some qualification. There are now moral judgments attached to the characters; in fact, they are no longer interesting as individuals but as the embodiment of moral categories and representatives of specific forces in society. The scheme for the setting of *In the Jungle* no longer fits for *St. Joan* because the latter is not a play about the characters, who are just given a fitting background; to return to the analogy, the background is now in such clear focus that it has become the foreground, and the focus on individual figures is less clear. (Thus Western critics find Mauler too simplified, and Schumacher finds the workers too undifferentiated.)

The background that has become foreground is simultaneously the capitalist system and America. More than any of Brecht's other plays, *St. Joan* is a play *about* America—not just set in America. The setting has none of the mythical qualities and geographical absurdities of *Mahagonny* or *In the Jungle*; it is very concrete and very real, adopted carefully and as accurately as necessary from the many sources Brecht read on the United States, Chicago, and finance. Chicago does still correspond to Berlin, but not as a metaphor or allegory: now Chicago is the *cause* of Berlin. For not only was the capitalist-democratic Weimar Republic a direct product of American postwar investment and influence, the entire capitalist world suffered an economic crisis as a result of the American stock market crash. The German depression was worse than the American because of the German economy's extreme dependence on American capital.

Thus *The Bread Store*, which demonstrates the *effects* of the depression, is set in Berlin,[33] but often mentions New York as the origin of the crisis. In that play Falladah Heep of the Salvation Army asks Washington Myers the *Gretchenfrage* (the question Gretchen puts to Faust), how he feels about God, and he answers:

yes, miss heep, positive, completely positive. but, he naturally has very little influence in new york. it's always said that he has a crowd of rich friends, mr. ford and mr. rockefeller, but unfortunately his friends very often seem to leave him in the lurch.

ja, fräulein heep, positiv, durchaus positiv. nur, et hat natürlich sehr wenig einfluß in new york. man hört immer daß er eine menge reicher freunde hat, herrn ford und herrn rockefeller, aber seine freunde lassen ihn leider anscheinend sehr häufig aufsitzen. (BBA 1353, 24)

The song "Hosanna Rockefeller," written in 1924[34] but included among materials to *The Bread Store*, repeats those names as business partners with God. The chorus is:

> Hosanna Rockefeller
> Hosanna Henry Ford
> Hosanna coal steel and oil
> Hosanna God's word
> Hosanna faith and profit
> Hosanna law and murder.

> Hosianna Rockefeller
> Hosianna Henry Ford
> Hosianna Kohle Stahl und Öl
> Hosianna Gottes Wort
> Hosianna Glaube und Profit
> Hosianna Recht und Mord.

(BBA 1353, 78)

Brecht comments on the plot of *The Bread Store*: "Mrs. Q has bad luck because of New York" ("Frau Q hat Pech wegen New York") and "He [Myers] rebels against New York, the law, and the army" ("Er [Myers] lehnt sich auf gegen New York, das Gesetz, und die Armee").[35] Finally, Herr Flamm, the richest man the unemployed have ever seen, explains to his tenant the baker that he must pay his rent or be evicted, because Flamm is at the mercy of the small banks, which are in the hands of the great banks, which are in crisis because the state is actually thinking of demanding taxes from industry, which has never happened in the memory of mankind,

> because America, to which Europe is in debt up to its neck, is writhing in a horrible crisis, the reasons for which are a complete mystery to the greatest scholars of political economy.

> weil Amerika, dem Europa bis an den Hals verschuldet ist, sich in einer entsetzlichen Krise windet, über deren Gründe sich die größten Gelehrten der Nationalökonomie absolut nicht klarwerden können. (*GW* 7:2923)

Whereas *The Bread Store* leaves everyone wallowing in futile actions or resignation because of ignorance of causes, *St. Joan* exposes those same causes. Since it intends to teach the cause as well as the effect of the crisis, it is set in the country that is itself the cause. Insofar as the mechanisms revealed in the play apply universally to capitalist countries and will be applied by the audience to Germany, and insofar as Brecht uses the American setting as a vehicle for simplification, it is, as usual, a means of *Verfremdung*. But insofar as the background has become foreground so that statements and value judgments are made about America itself, and the relation between America and Germany is one of cause and effect rather than analogy, the American setting is *not* a means of *Verfremdung* but is necessary and natural. Distance in this play is achieved primarily through the style (verse, parody, and unnatural diction and syntax) and the elaborate, "scientific" structure, rather than through the setting.

If America is then in part the subject of *St. Joan*, what is Brecht saying about his subject?

That religion there is hypocritical. That a few men can ruin the lives of millions. That violence is used to keep those men in power. That this situation can be changed if it is understood, but that the ruling class propogates ideologies that prevent understanding. In short, that the United States is capitalist (and how that capitalism works). The two concepts are fused: every detail is both a characterization of America and a characterization of capitalism (at first competitive capitalism, then monopoly capitalism).

Brecht has come a long way since *In the Jungle*. There he intuited that the degradation caused by poverty and the isolation between people were somehow native to America, the land of plenty, but he was not certain that that was bad; it was the cost of progress, the new age required strong men. Now, in *St. Joan*, he knows *why* people fight each other as in a jungle, why they live in poverty in the land of unlimited opportunity; and he knows that it is bad, that it was in fact the cost of progress but that American capitalism itself was only a stage in the progression. *America no longer represents the new age*: it is now the dying culture, and the socialist countries are The New that always fascinated Brecht so much. The classes of people who seemed to him in *Jungle* and *Fleischhacker* to be dying as a sacrifice to the cruel new age become and remain for Brecht the carriers of life and progress into the just new age.

As in "Vanished Glory," the details are the same, but the context and the evaluation are utterly different.

The details about America even come from many of the same sources as Brecht's earlier plays, or they are further developments of those plays (and fragments) themselves. Virtually every source we have examined in the course of this study is reflected in *St. Joan*, and virtually every theme from the earlier works that are set in America (particularly the unfinished ones) is incorporated into this rich play. We will look first at the sources, then at Brecht's adaptation of his own work.

In *St. Joan* we have the fruits of the first work we know Brecht read on America, *The Jungle*. When we examined that novel's influence on *In the Jungle*, we could only determine that the general atmosphere of *The Jungle* must have informed Brecht's emphasis on poverty and his treatment of Chicago, prostitution, and coldness, as well as the concept of the city as Darwinian jungle. The influences on *St. Joan* are much more specific, so much so that we must assume Brecht reread the novel before or while working on *St. Joan*. Nowhere but from Sinclair could Brecht have got his information about the human ingredient in leaf lard; and that accident is explained to the widow in both works with the packers' lie that the man has gone off on a trip. We have here a clear example of Brecht's reaction to, and use of, his reading. The description of that accident caused more sensation than any other passage in the very influential novel. (Sinclair: "I aimed at the public's heart and by accident I hit it in the stomach."[36]) But Brecht, with his command of the technique of dramatic alienation that eludes Sinclair, is able to prevent excessive interest in the gory detail and focus instead on the reaction to which poverty and bribery force the dead worker's widow.

There are other details that Brecht clearly adopted from *The Jungle*. One is the fascinating gravity method of slaughtering hogs, in which the hog's own weight is his undoing. Another is the presence of vast numbers of unemployed, which means that jobs are only available through other workers' misfortune. More general common themes are the evaluation of charity organizations, the strike, the cold, and of course the entire structure of the meat industry.

By now Brecht had also come to agree with Sinclair's conclusion, that socialism is the solution to the horrors of the meat industry. But that conclusion is not very convincing in Sinclair's book, partly because it is an afterthought and partly because the worst horrors described are excesses, which can easily be remedied (and were, partly as a result of Sinclair's book and with the blessing of the government and the larger industries) without altering the structure of the system at all. On his first reading of *The Jungle*, Brecht was moved by the lot of the poor but uninterested in socialism; but in *St. Joan* he is far more revolutionary and more astute in his analysis than Sinclair. In *St. Joan* the need for a socialist revolution is an integral part of the conception of the whole play. It is not a *protest* play, i.e., an appeal to those presently in power; Brecht never wrote protest literature. It is a *revolutionary* play, an appeal to those not in power to take power.

None of the American works Brecht read are revolutionary; Gustavus Myers comes the closest, with his exposé of the immorality of every last link in the system, but his book is only the king of muckraking books: it suggests no alternative and no means of attacking the wrongs he lists, either individually or collectively. George Lorimer, Bouck White, Ida Tarbell, Frank Norris, Theodore Dreiser, all provide fascinating studies of the minds of capitalists and the workings of capitalism, but there are no conclusions even implicit in their studies. Johannes V. Jensen affirms the order of the system over chaos, and Sherwood Anderson mourns what is past more than he envisions a way to a better future. The principal themes of the novels by the last two authors are themes that Brecht no longer takes up in writing *St. Joan*: destructive personal fascination (and homosexuality) and the "Human Migration to the Big Cities." The absence of the second theme is particularly significant because it was the rubric under which he united all his previous American plays, from *Jungle* to *Mahagonny*. But in *St. Joan* there is never a mention of nostalgia for the plains, the savannahs, the countryside, Alaska, Tahiti—there is no comparison of industrial capitalism with feudalism or the early agrarian-frontier ethic. That concern is finished for Brecht. To repeat: newness is represented no longer by capitalism but by socialism; the important conflict is not between the old values and structures and those of the present, but between those of the present and the forces that are struggling to change them in the future.

Thus, ironically, although almost all the American literature Brecht read was social protest, in the play that reflects the sources most he only used them for their inside information on capitalism. He could as well have used the financial journals—and in fact he did. We know about his studies for *Fleischhacker*, including newspaper clippings, and the interview with the Viennese stockbroker. With the

253

materials to *St. Joan* in the Brecht Archive, there is also a floor plan of the Chicago Board of Trade, printed in 1931 (BBA 894, 103–5). The floor areas for the different kinds of grain are indicated, and the accompanying text, underlined by Brecht, explains the techniques of trading, such as hand signals. The scenes of *St. Joan* set in the cattle exchange take account of the buying and selling techniques, at the same time rendering them grotesque with biblical language. In production of course the hand signals can be used, as Brecht undoubtedly intended.[37]

That plan of the Board of Trade also indicates that even in 1931 Brecht still thought of *St. Joan* as an adaptation of the relations of the wheat exchange to the beef trust; we have assumed that the reasons for the change were a rereading of *The Jungle* and the rich possibilities in the symbol of slaughtering meat (for instance, the Black Straw Hats compare today's world to a slaughterhouse).

But although the setting in the stockyards is taken from *The Jungle*, the financial dealings are still basically those described by Norris in *The Pit*, assimilated into *St. Joan* by way of *Fleischhacker*. The most significant difference between Curtis Jadwin's story and Brecht's version in both *Fleischhacker* and *St. Joan* is that Jadwin loses and that is the end of it; he goes off with his wife a happy man, relieved of the burden of wealth, and the reader forgets the market in this conciliatory happy ending. Brecht allows no such escape, and he does not exonerate his capitalists because they are loving husbands. Both Fleischhacker and Mauler rise up to the top again after apparent bankruptcy, Fleischhacker because war breaks out and his wheat becomes a gold mine (BBA 524, 90), Mauler through the conscious use of monopoly capitalism's tactics for pulling out of a crisis: mergers and destruction of the excess product, plus cutbacks in production to raise prices, and cutbacks in wages and employment. In both cases the capitalist system is saved by becoming more brutal. In *The Pit* the future course of the system is not indicated at all; in *Fleischhacker* too there is no indication what will happen after the war. But in *St. Joan* Mauler's solution clearly can only be temporary, because capitalist economics have been shown to be cyclical. The seeds of the next, larger crisis are already apparent in the larger numbers of unemployed and the lower salaries paid to the workers: these two groups are supposed to be the market for the meat that now has a higher price. Brecht is not just registering moral outrage that the workers suffer most from the solution to a crisis; he is also showing that the solution cannot work permanently.

Although Mauler's financial dealings are adopted mainly from *The Pit*, his character has several other sources as well. There are two non-American sources, Faust (Brecht: *St. Joan* "is supposed to show the current stage of development of the Faustian person ["soll die heutige Entwicklungsstufe des faustischen Menschen zeigen"] [*GW* 2:4*]) and Shaw's Underhill in *Major Barbara*. The Faust theme, parodied especially at the end of the play ("Human, there are two souls living / In your breast!" [Mensch, es wohnen dir zwei Seelen / In der Brust!"]) may have occurred to Brecht when he read *Capital*. In volume 1, chapter 24, shortly before his famous "Accumulate, accumulate! That is Moses and the prophets!" Marx uses the Faust theme to describe the capitalist: "Two souls alas do dwell within his breast; / The one is ever parting from the other."[38] He is referring not to an earthly and a heavenly, or selfish and generous, soul, but to the contradiction between consumption (avarice) and accumulation (abstinence). *Major Barbara* was mainly a negative influence on the story of Johanna, since Brecht is protesting Shaw's extremely un-Marxist conclusion that only the rich can help the poor. (I suspect that *St. Joan* also embodies a similar reaction by Brecht against the class reconciliation in Fritz Lang's great 1926 film *Metropolis*: the capitalist, the strike, the saintly woman are all there, but with a very different, naïve message.) Brecht's attitude toward Shaw fluctuated; at the end of the twenties it was ambivalent.[39] From both internal and external evidence, Shaw's Saint Joan seems not to have been a model;[40] Schiller's, on the other hand, was.

But Mauler as capitalist is more directly a conglomerate of the capitalists in all the American books Brecht read. In him we find elements of Dan Drew, the ruthless spectator and swindler, and naïve and hypocritical churchman and philanthropist; of Lorimer's John Graham, the kindly meat-packing king who gives homespun advice to his son Pierrepont; of Tarbell's Gary—the "good" capitalist who cooperated with government and originated mergers—and J. P. Morgan, who contributes Pierpont Mauler's name; of all the great merciless financiers in Myers's compendium; and of Dreiser's Cowperwood, who is essentially the same type as

Norris's Jadwin. Brecht's first version of *St. Joan* is set at the turn of the century, in the period of old-style tycoons described by most of the American books we know Brecht read. Angered by the pieties expressed by so many of these powerful exploiters, Brecht has Joan learn that goodness of character in the class enemy is irrelevant, that it even helps make him more powerful.

We also see the influence of many of Brecht's readings about Chicago in his use of the cold and snow. We have already noted that Chicago's cold is extraordinarily emphasized in books like *The Jungle*, *The Wheel*, and *The Pit*, and that Brecht reflected that emphasis in *Jungle* and in talk of "cold Chicago" ("das kalte Chikago"), meaning Berlin. In *The Bread Store* and *St. Joan* he learns how to make cold and snow socially relevant, not just part of the American "aroma." Brecht himself noted in 1942:

> "Nature" is reflected curiously in my works. . . . In *Drums* and *Jungle* the battlefield is the city. . . . In *St. Joan* [the landscape] is battlefield again (the snowfall is a social phenomenon). *Mother* has no landscape . . . *Courage* renders landscape like *St. Joan*. . . . Human relationships of a direct sort are depicted only in the *Mother*.

> Die "Natur" spiegelt sich merkwürdig in meinen Arbeiten. . . . In "Trommeln" und "Dickicht" ist die Stadt das Schlachtfeld. . . . In "Johanna" ist [die Landschaft] wieder Schlachtfeld (der Schneefall ist eine soziale Erscheinung). "Mutter" hat keine Landscaft . . . die "Courage" gibt Landschaft wie die "Johanna". . . . Menschliche Beziehungen direkter Art sind nur in der "Mutter" wiedergegeben.[41]

This important statement says in effect that all the "landscapes" or settings Brecht has used have been creators of alienation; their role has been to show that capitalist society prevents meaningful relations between men. He probably realized that with hindsight when looking at the earliest plays, but in *St. Joan* (and *The Bread Store*) it is deliberate. There even the weather becomes a social phenomenon. Nature no longer has the symbolic, *deus ex machina* character it had in *Mahagonny*; rather it is a day-to-day danger the workers have to cope with. And responsibility for the weather (i.e., for the suffering it causes) lies with the rich.

Herr Flamm, the richest man in *The Bread Store*, enjoys the winter crispness that is killing the homeless and unemployed:

> At last, a real, lovely winter again! With snow and ice! You actually

never feel fresher than in winter, at noon you bring a real appetite home with you.

Endlich wieder einmal ein richtiger, schöner Winter! Mit Schnee und Eis! Man fühlt sich eigentlich nie frischer als im Winter, man bringt mittags einen richtigen Hunger mit nach Hause. (*GW* 7:2922)

If they could choose whether to be in a heated house or in the fresh air, winter would be something completely different to the unemployed. The winter as they know it is created by the capitalists.

In a discussion of the poem "Places to Sleep," Erck and Gräf explore the snow metaphor and point out that for Brecht the cold of winter is synonymous with the depression:

What determines whether the influence of natural forces on the life of working people is harmful or useful is the social situation. That is why the winter snow is identified with the elementary force of the crisis.

Bestimmend für den schädlichen oder nützlichen Einfluß der Naturgewalten auf das Leben der Werktätigen sind die gesellschaftlichen Zustände. Deshalb wird der Schnee des Winters mit der elementaren Gewalt der Krise identifiziert.[42]

They note that snow is mentioned twenty times in *St. Joan*, and that in this as well as other works by Brecht snow has a meaning completely different from its traditional poetic associations. The key to the significance of snow for Brecht, they say, is in an autobiographical poem from 1935 called "The Playwright's Song":

I see snowfalls appear there
I see earthquakes coming forward there
I see mountains standing there in the way
And I see rivers stepping over their banks.
But the snowfalls have hats on
The earthquakes have money in their breast pocket
The mountains have climbed out of vehicles
And the bursting rivers command over police.
This I expose.

Ich sehe da auftreten Schneefälle
Ich sehe da nach vorn kommen Erdbeben
Ich sehe da Berge stehen mitten im Wege
Und Flüsse sehe ich über die Ufer treten.
Aber die Schneefälle haben Hüte auf
Die Erdbeben haben Geld in der Brusttasche
Die Berge sind aus Fahrzeugen gestiegen

Und die reißenden Flüsse gebieten über Polizisten.
Das enthülle ich.

(*GW* 9:790)

This poem explains the development of Brecht's treatment of natural catastrophe; first it was a symbol of divine punishment, but the depression made him see it as individual responsibility. The snowstorms wearing hats are his own metaphor for what he has learned. (Compare, however, the poem on p. 219; snowstorms are not only cold, we know that.)

What Brecht has learned is also what Joan learns: that whoever says "Misfortune comes like the rain, that no one maketh but that comes anyway" ("Das Unglück kommt wie der Regen, den nienand machet und der doch kommt") is lying; that there are persons who deliberately inflict misfortune; that it is not just "fate." Brecht emphasizes that this is the most elementary lesson the oppressed must learn, so that they know they can change their situation by fighting their enemies. The necessity of naming the enemy is a lesson he repeated often, starting from the time of *St. Joan*. The song "In Praise of the Revolutionary," from *The Mother*, is an example: "And where oppression rules and the talk is of fate / He will name names" ("Und wo Unterdrückung herrscht und von Schicksal die Rede ist / Wird er die Namen nennen") (*GW* 2:859).

In *Refugee Conversations* (1940–41) Ziffel observes how the workers are misled by reading the social-democratic papers:

> They keep hearing that they're ruled by capital, so they overlook the capitalists. They hear conditions are bad, that distracts from bad people.

> Sie hören immerfort, daß sie vom Kapital beherrscht werden, so übersehn sie die Kapitalisten. Sie hören, die Zustände sind schlecht, das lenkt von den schlechten Menschen ab. (*GW* 14:1502)

And by a picture of a Berlin woman standing next to her bombed-out house, Brecht writes in the *War Primer* (published 1955):

> Look no longer, woman: you'll not find them now!
> But providence, woman, shouldn't get the blame!
> The dark powers, woman, that oppress you there
> They have a face and address and a name.

> Such nicht mehr, Frau: du wirst sie nicht mehr finden!
> Doch auch das Schicksal, Frau, beschuldige nicht!

258

Die dunklen Mächte, Frau, die dich da schinden
Sie haben Name, Anschrift und Gesicht.

(*GW* 10:1038)

In *St. Joan* this theme takes the particular form of criticizing capitalism's use of religion to distract from the guilty individuals and guilty class. Because of its focus on the poor, the Salvation Army is an excellent vehicle for that criticism, which is probably why it so fascinated Brecht. The Salvation Army makes a brief appearance in *The Bread Store*, too, where it plays the same role as in *St. Joan*: it aids the rich and confuses the poor. In notes to *The Bread Store* Brecht complains about the uselessness of the Salvation Army's idealism (only in *St. Joan* does he have the "Army" *consciously* collaborate with the capitalists): "Salvation Army: its function: it drags everyone into the swamp with its idealism" ("Heilsarmee: ihre funktion: sie bringt alle in den sumpf mit ihrem idealismus") (BBA 1353, 21). Another note on the same subject shows that the story of Joan was probably originally conceived for *The Bread Store*:

Act 1
Show the uselessness of religion. Not attack on the Salvation Army!
Salvation Army has an interest only in itself, its own advancement, it is
  not interested in people. Wants donors, big earners, not unemployed.
Girl is thrown out because she cares too much about people.

1. Akt
Das Unnütze der Religion zeigen. Nicht Angriff auf Heilsarmee!
Heilsarmee hat nur Interesse an sich selber, daß sie bessert, es ist ihr
  nicht um Leute zu tun. Will Geldgeber, reiche Gewinner, nicht Ar-
  beitslose.
Mädchen fliegt raus, weil es sich zu sehr um Leute kümmert.

(BBA 1353, 2)

Also in notes to *The Bread Store*, Brecht compares schematically the characteristics of the Salvation Army and the Communist party. This list demonstrating the Salvation Army's reformism is especially applicable to *St. Joan*, where the Communists are actually present on stage to show the alternative to reformism.

the c p	the salvation army
at first helps no one	helps the individual
leads the individual to the mass	separates him from the mass

259

considers force a resource	combats force
thinking materially	thinking ideally
succeeds because of the bad situation	in spite of the bad s.
has an interest	is for id. reasons uninterested in changing the s.

die k p	die heilsarmee
hilft zunächst niemand	hilft dem einzelnen
führt den einzelnen zur masse	trennt ihn von der masse
hat als hilfsmittel die gewalt	bekämpft die gewalt
materiell denkend	ideell denkend
hat erfolg durch die schlechte lage	trotz der schlechten l.
ist interessiert	ist aus id. gründen an der änderung der l. uninteressiert

(BBA 1353, 87)

The first two points are also a major concern of the *Lehrstücke*, especially *The Measure Taken*.

The reasons why capitalism needs the ideological figleaf provided by the Salvation Army, and the exact techniques used, are clear only in *St. Joan*. But both *St. Joan* and *The Bread Store* represent a strong qualitative difference from *Happy End*, although *Happy End* is the only source Brecht names for *St. Joan* in his introductory note (*GW* 2:4*). That note indicates only that part of the *story* of Hallelujah-Lilian and the Salvation Army has been adopted; the context and ideology of Brecht's play are completely different from Hauptmann's. When we discussed *Happy End*, we quoted Bernhard Reich's advice to Brecht on how to make the Salvation Army theme more relevant: by allowing the "Army" to convert capitalists instead of petty gangsters. Brecht took this advice by wedding *Happy End* and *Joe Fleischhacker*, two very different plays.

St. Joan is, of course, a great deal more than the marriage of those two plays, especially stylistically, but they provide the primary themes and two of the three interwoven plots: the plot concerning Joan and her relations with the Salvation Army, and the plot concerning Mauler and his machinations on the commodity exchange. The third plot, which is partly new and partly a development of themes from *The Bread Store*, concerns the actions of the workers. They present the real opposition to Mauler, which Joan only thinks she presents, and they replace the equally non-antagonistic Mitchel family in *Fleischhacker*. Like the comparison of Joan with Hallelujah-Lilian, a comparison of the workers in *St. Joan* with the Mitchel family shows how far Brecht had come. The Mitchels are basically like the Gargas in *Jungle*: poor, ambitious, and full of dreams of individual escape, they are trapped by the American urban system and by their very dreams; and they simply go down, without fighting back, except for the sons—George Garga and Calvin Mitchel—who retain the illusion that they have some-how escaped. The overwhelming mood of *In the Jungle* is isolation, and that carries over into *Fleischhacker*. The Mitchel family suc-cumbs because of false consciousness—it does not realize that it belongs to the victims rather than the beneficiaries of capitalism (or Chicago)—and because it is completely isolated, believing it can escape poverty alone, through sheer force of individual, American will.

Something of that isolation or individualism remains in Joan. But the workers in *St. Joan* understand—up to a point—that their strength lies in acting together; they are hardly portrayed as individ-uals. They are, dramatically, real antagonists to Mauler, not just victims.

The story of a speculator who corners the commodity market, then fails, from *Joe Fleischhacker*; the story of a Salvation Army girl who is expelled for taking the job too seriously, from *Happy End*; and the story of an attempted general strike, from Brecht's new experience and conviction—these are the three concurrent plots of the play and their sources. But *St. Joan* also incorporates themes from Brecht's other earlier works. It is the only play he was able to finish on all the economic themes that interested him from 1924, and it represents both his mastery of the theory of capitalism and, apparently, his liberation from the need to write about it. But concerns of the less directly economic plays are also incorporated into *St. Joan*. The possibility of "rebuilding" people is shown by the bribery of Frau Luckerniddle, wife of the man who fell in the vat of lard, as well as in *A Man's a Man*. The problem of reformism, from the *Lehrstücke* and many other works of this period (such as "Places to Sleep"), is a central theme of *St. Joan*. *St. Joan* and *The Mother* are certainly also didactic plays, but Brecht does not call them *Lehrstücke* because their form is completely different, and they are meant to teach the audience, not only the actors.

The conscious adoption of *Lehrstück* themes in *St. Joan* is indicated by the use of some lines in both it and *The Exception and the Rule* (1929–30), such as, "Something like that won't raise itself any higher than the edge of a bowl" ("So was hebt sich nicht höher als bis zu einer Schüssel Rand")[43] and the prologue to the latter play, which uses words of the Black Straw Hats' song:

> In such an age of bloody confusion
> Organized disorder, well planned arbitrariness
> Dehumanized humanity.
>
> In solcher Zeit blutiger Verwirrung
> Verordneter Unordnung, planmäßiger Willkür
> Entmenschter Menschheit.[44]

Also treated in the *Lehrstücke*, and closely related to the problem of reformism, is the problem of individualism. For Joan and for Brecht, that problem arises because they both want to take on the cause of the working class without having been brought up with its oppression or, therefore, its solidarity. With Joan, Brecht shows how middle-class reformers tend to get involved in doubts—most often about the question of violence—and follow the dictates of their (irrational) conscience at precisely the crucial moment when they are being depended upon. But that conscience itself has been formed by their middle-class upbringing. If they really want to work with the working class, they must learn to have more trust in collective decisions than in individual ones. That is what Joan's failure to deliver the letter is about: first, she is afraid there is something about violence in it; second, since she does not have the same background as the workers and does not know what it is like to have nothing to lose, she cannot stand the cold.

These are likely the hesitations that Brecht too had to overcome and against which he struggled. Since *St. Joan of the Stockyards* is a revolutionary play, it is more involved with the author's view of his own life than social criticism, or protest literature, which merely records the faults of society without demanding a course of action from the readers, audience, or author himself. It is the play that represents Brecht's final break with the familiar bourgeois world.

262

That break begins for Joan when she cannot understand why the unemployed workers leave her sermon for a possible job. She tells the Black Straw Hats, "But then I want to know who is to blame for all this" ("Dann will ich aber wissen, wer an all dem schuld ist"). They try to dissuade her, but she is determined to investigate although it jeopardizes her job, and she declares, "I want to know it" ("Ich will's wissen") (*GW* 2:679). The break begins for Brecht when he cannot understand how the wheat exchange works. He sends a letter to Elisabeth Hauptmann announcing that he is reading *Capital* (even though his need to know will jeopardize his writing for three years), and declaring, "I've got to know that now exactly" ("Ich muß das jetzt genau wissen").[45] The break is completed for Joan in her final speech of the play, and symbolically for Brecht in the writing of that speech.

That Brecht did successfully learn to feel at home in the working class is clear from the complete identification with the workers in *The Mother* and subsequent plays. It is partly because he tailored his language to workers that his style achieved its profound simplicity.

Future themes are also prefigured in *St. Joan*. The most important one is the concept of the impossibility of doing good instinctively in an evil society, which finds expression not only in the Salvation Army but also in the dramatic device of the split character. Mauler's two Faustian souls become the two Annas in *The Seven Deadly Sins of the Petty Bourgeoisie* and Shen Te and Shui Ta in *The Good Person of Sichuan*, as well as Puntila and other morally if not physically split characters.

St. Joan is not only the culmination of Brecht's early work but also the kernel of much of his future development. In particular, it expresses the political position that he retained firmly through the rest of his life: he deepened his emphasis on humanism later, but he never wavered in his commitment to communism.

We can see from Brecht's poems that the commitment became all-pervasive. By 1931 the majority were political, a change from his statement of 1926 that his poetry had "a more private character."[46]

His theoretical writings on drama from the thirties are also full of political concepts; or, more correctly, Brecht now fit his dramaturgy into a political and economic framework. This is the time when he started speaking of "dialectical" drama instead of "epic" drama. The

263

important fragment "Dialectical Dramatics," written in 1931, is only one example of the totality of Brecht's Marxism. It is subtitled "Basic Idea: Application of the Dialectic Leads to Revolutionary Marxism" ("Grundgedanke: Anwendung der Dialektik führt zu revolutionärem Marxismus") (*GW* 15:211); and in speaking of the theater, it uses Marxist concepts like "commodity," "means of production," "the viewer as mass," "class character" ("Ware," "Produktionsmittel," "der Zuschauer als Masse," "Klassen-charakter") and, of course, the broader categories of dialectics and economics. In attempting to explain the social role of theater in this essay, Brecht gets so involved in Marxist terminology that he has to explain parenthetically, "an understanding of revolutionary economics is indispensable here" ("ein Verständnis der revolutionären Ökonomie ist hier unerläßlich") (*GW* 15:223).

But the piece written in 1931 is not a brief outburst. Precisely the same terminology fills Brecht's writings on the theater from his last years; his emphasis shifts only from unmasking and destroying capitalism to building socialism.

Postscript

Exile and Return: Brecht and America after 1933

Since Brecht's attitudes toward capitalism remained constant from *St. Joan* (i.e., from the depression) to his death, his attitudes toward America also remained constant, because he was no longer interested in the American myth but only in America as an example of capitalism. Therefore, we will end this study with a very cursory look at aspects of Brecht's later interest in America, without considering his two trips to the United States in 1935–36 and 1941–47. His experiences in this country, their transformation into art, and the influence he left in America are not properly part of a study of the symbolic structure that he created to explain contemporary history and economics in his own country. The poems he wrote in Hollywood about Hollywood are irrelevant to that function of the American myth.

The two dramatic works set in America that Brecht wrote in exile are relevant, but they represent no change. The first one, the ballet *Seven Deadly Sins of the Petty Bourgeoisie* (1933), repeats themes of *St. Joan*, *Mahagonny*, *Poor White*, *In the Jungle*, "Song of a Family from the Savannah," and the whole series on migration to the cities. It portrays the "immorality" of being natural in capitalist society; alienation from self, other men and women, and work; and traveling from city to city in the United States. America is, again, simply the capitalist system.

The last American play, *The Resistible Rise of Arturo Ui* (1941), once more equates Chicago with Berlin. This time the American setting is explicitly an allegory for German events, and Chicago is a caricature of the earlier Chicago myth. The levels of *Verfremdung* in the play make a fascinating study—but the image of America contains little that is new. Al Capone as the specific model is new,

265

but the gangster world still resembles that in Hauptmann's *Happy End*. Perhaps the most significant difference between the use of America for *Verfremdung* in the early plays and in *Ui* is that the declared purpose of *Ui* is to explain Hitler's rise (i.e., a German phenomenon) to the capitalist (American) audience, by putting it in a familiar (i.e., American = capitalist) setting (*GW* 4:3*). Earlier uses of America were intended to make a familiar situation strange for a German audience; *Ui* intends to make a strange situation familiar to an American audience. This device allows *Ui* to make the point that fascism is a kind of capitalism; as in *St. Joan*, the American situation is in a way the *cause* of the German situation. (*Ui* in fact begins with the depression.) Both *St. Joan* and *Ui* also parody Shakespearean verse and the German classics.

Brecht did, of course, still read American literature; occasionally details from it are reflected in his writing. In 1935 he wrote the poem "Dismantling of the Ship Oskawa by the Crew," which, enclosed in quotation marks, is practically a literal translation of a passage in Louis Adamic's *Dynamite: The Story of Class Violence in America* (Brecht collected the relevant pages 386–89 with his many notes and clippings [BBA 1371]). This is one of those poems—like "Coals for Mike" (1926), which is placed just before it in the *Svendborg Poems* and also lifted from an American book—that shows Brecht knew there were friendly and progressive forces among the workers in the United States.

In 1936 Brecht wrote another poem, similar in mood to "Coals for Mike" and "Oskawa," that expresses admiration for the solidarity of the black May Day demonstrator Bill Wood, who helped carry a poster reading "Protect Soviet China!" ("Schützt Sowjetchina!"). The concrete details of "May Day Cantata" suggest that it was inspired by a written account of the 1935 May Day demonstration in New York.

But far from invalidating the judgment that the American capitalist system is inhuman, these anecdotes and individual impressions of America reinforced Brecht's judgment about the system as a whole. Workers perform sabotage on their ship or steal coal for a railroad widow precisely as a defense and an act of rebellion against the inhuman system. Like every good socialist, Brecht did not hate the American people or even America, but only its social and economic system. Discovery of positive working-class

266

individuals could not mitigate his rejection of the system. Americans tend to resent his lack of enthusiasm for the United States. Even socialists seem to feel that he was ungrateful. But Brecht, with his strong grounding in Marxist theory, was clear and consistent in separating the individual from the system, and no amount of friendliness from Americans could make him forget that the United States was the foremost capitalist country of the world and, as such, the enemy. He never wavered in that position, but no one should confuse his ideological consistency with ingratitude to the American people.

Eric Bentley tells the story that when Brecht returned to East Berlin after seven years in the United States, people expected him to tell that he had been miserable there;

> "Oh, no, it isn't like that at all," he'd say, everything is very, very nice— "it's just the Capitalists . . . etc." In short, he didn't let them believe you see lynchings on every street corner.[1]

Brecht's defense of the positive aspects of America derived largely from the only strong friendship he had with a native American, according to James K. Lyon.[2] Not only had Ferdinand Reyher urged Brecht to leave Scandinavia as the Nazis got closer and to come to Hollywood; he also intervened for him with authorities and literary and German-exile friends, helped raise money for the really hard-up Brecht family, promoted Brecht's plays, and translated and adapted *Galileo* and what he called *The Private Life of the Master Race*. He managed Brecht's affairs in the United States after the exile returned home, and sent him American plays for consideration by the Berliner Ensemble. He also collaborated on filmscripts or scenarios with Brecht (notably *All Our Yesterdays* and *The King's Bread*, both set in Chicago). But perhaps most important was the personal view of America that Brecht gained through his friend's eyes. In Brecht's diary entry of 13 February 1942, for instance, we can read of Reyher's attempts to correct Brecht's negative judgments.[3] Reyher taught Brecht about the American labor movement, and Elisabeth Hauptmann told Lyon that in 1946 Brecht intended to write ten forty-minute plays about its historical leaders such as Mother Jones, Mother Bloor, and Eva Pastor. Reyher also took Brecht "prowling" to his favorite haunts in New York, and after his return to Germany Brecht used to write Reyher requesting

267

that the American show visiting German friends the Automat and McManus's pub. Brecht made five cross-country trips by car and rail, seeing and digesting much of the country; one such trip took twelve days.

Lyon's study of Brecht's personal relationship with Reyher makes it clear that Brecht had a lively interest in things American while he was here, and even thought of the United States as the country of the common man. Seliger's study of Brecht's stay here[4] emphasizes his anger, his occasional European prejudice against American culture, and his many observations on exploitation and the impossibility of democracy (which he seems to have seen as reduced to an advertising slogan) coexisting with capitalism.

Both reports agree that Brecht differentiated sharply between the American people and their government or economic system. Clearly, the received impression that Brecht simply hated the United States, insulated himself from direct experience of it, and wrote nothing about it while here, must be revised. However, he also came to feel at first hand, while trying to make a living in Hollywood, the way capitalism can ignore and waste people; he was very bitter about his constant financial predicament and the lack of recognition of his work and abilities. Hollywood represented for him the application of capitalist relations of production to the arts, and he was repeatedly shocked and angered by the necessity of selling and promoting oneself there in order to survive. His poems and scenarios written about America while he was here reflect that conflict between a sympathetic view of working-class Americans and a strong condemnation of American commercialism and exploitation.

During his stay in America, Brecht wrote a few more poems on incidents of friendliness toward him or others by individual Americans: "Everywhere Friends," "The Democratic Judge." But apart from a very few "private" American poems, all the rest are bitter condemnations of America, particularly of Hollywood. "Meditating, so I hear, on Hell . . . ," "Hollywood," "The Fishing Tackle," "The Volunteer Guards," "Again and Again," "Deliver the Goods," "Hollywood Elegies," all are pithy, angry, sometimes brilliant vignettes exposing the capitalist morality of America.

Nor did the anger soften in his last years; although he almost never wrote about America after leaving it, the poem "Song of the Rivers" (1954) criticizes American imperialist control of the Amazon, and the article Brecht wrote in 1950 about his HUAC interrogation ("We Nineteen," *GW* 19:490–93) is extremely bitter against America.

Among unfulfilled plans for the last years were a production in the Berliner Ensemble on Joe Hill[5] and a kind of sequel to *Life of Galileo* to be called *Life of Einstein*. There are many notes for the Einstein play,[6] plus an extensive collection of clippings about Einstein (BBA 2064). Brecht also collected material about Oppenheimer (BBA 2064), whom he knew personally from Hollywood;[7] but he chose Einstein to represent the dilemma of the modern physicist, probably partly because Einstein considered himself a socialist and partly because his very name is a symbol of intelligence. A treatment of Brecht's interest in Einstein, the probable concerns of the play, and a list of sources Brecht read can be found in Schumacher's book on *Galileo* and related plays.[8] Part of the point of the projected play was that in 1955 Brecht still considered the United States as dangerous as Nazi Germany: one of Einstein's tragedies is that he fled Germany only to find "Potsdam in Washington."[9]

In the very last year of his life, 1956, Brecht directed one of the Berliner Ensemble's finest productions, *Trumpets and Drums*, which he adapted from Farquhar's *The Recruiting Officer*. The most significant change from the original is that the English are fighting not a war of equals against the French but a colonial war against the American Revolution. Why did Brecht make this change?

Bernhard Reich describes one of Brecht's many discussions with state officials in the GDR; they were worried that a production of *The Recruiting Officer* would undermine their decision to draft a "people's army":

> But Brecht hoped the Berliner Ensemble version exposed both the predatory nature of the intended war and the profitability of the large recruiting business for the ruling class so clearly that it would be taken unambiguously as directed against the militarization of the revenge-hungry Federal Republic.

> Brecht hoffte aber, daß die Fassung des Berliner Ensembles sowohl den Raubcharakter des beabsichtigten Kriegs als auch den Privatnutzen des großen Werbegeschäfts für die herrschende Klasse so klar aufdeckt, daß

269

sie eindeutig als gegen die Militarisierung der revanchelustigen Bundesrepublik gerichtet aufgenommen würde.[10]

America plays the role in this play of the people who are fighting for liberation, while England is the oppressor, and it is England that represents West Germany. This is very important because it demonstrates the fact that it was not America itself that Brecht condemned but its capitalist and imperialist system. At one time America too had been a revolutionary country.

Although he wrote little about America after *Ui*—the Hollywood poems are the main exception—Brecht collected information on it until he died. There are perhaps fifty books about America in his library (not to mention all the detective stories!), most of them printed in the 1950s. Especially frequent topics are black people in the United States and Alger Hiss. There are also clippings from 1956 on C. Wright Mills's book *The Power Elite*, as well as those from 1954 on Oppenheimer and Einstein. The frequency of clippings from the *New York Times*, the *Christian Science Monitor*, and the *Saturday Review* suggests that he received those publications regularly.[11]

But that is about all there is, and the writings listed are about all he wrote on America; not very much in the fifteen years since *Ui*, not really very much in the twenty-five years since *St. Joan*. America no longer held a disproportionate position in Brecht's reading or writing. Having been reduced from a myth to the prime example of capitalism, America lost most of its fascination for Brecht. He could no longer feel any positive attraction to a myth that he had discovered to be composed partly of lies and partly of bourgeois ideology.

Conclusion

The Old and the New

Brecht stopped writing about America not only because the myth he had created lost its usefulness for him but also because America no longer represented "the new." If there is one single motif that unites all of Brecht's plays, it is his fascination with newness. The word *new* and its derivatives appear with astounding frequency in his critical and theoretical writings. At first he talks mainly about the need for a new theater, new kind of actor, new drama, and new audience, at a time when his rebellion against the old is mainly a rebellion against the older generation, especially in the theater. But although he later infuses the words *new* and *old* with different content, he never changes the values he assigns to the words: the new is always good, the old always bad. About 1928 he wrote a poem with the repeated refrain "Anything new / Is better than anything old" ("Alles Neue / Ist besser als alles Alte") (*GW* 8:314–16); and somewhere he wrote the aphorism "Rather the bad new than the good old" ("Lieber das schlechte Neue als das gute Alte").

As we have seen, for the first decade of Brecht's writing America embodied all that was new, for him as well as most of his friends and his generation. America was the land of technical progress, of confidence in the future, and of the triumph of capitalism over feudalism, or urban life over rural. In it, "the new age had come greater than any previous one" ("die neue zeit war gekommen größer als jede vorhergehende") (BBA 460, 63). As late as 1935 he wrote in a poem (in a more ironic vein) of America: "Whatever is brand new likes to stand in the light there" ("Gern steht das Allerneueste dort im Licht") (*GW* 9:560).

Brecht's changing conception of a "new age" inspired various types of "new people" as protagonists in his plays. He explains why an audience found his first American play, *In the Jungle*, difficult to understand, by pointing to the "new type of person" portrayed there:

> New was a human type who fought a battle without enmity, with heretofore unheard of, that is to say not yet portrayed, methods, as well as his position against the family, marriage, people in general and much more.

> Neu war ein Typus Mensch, der einen Kampf ohne Feindschaft mit bisher unerhörten, das heisst noch nicht gestalteten Methoden führte, und seine Stellung gegen die Familie, zur Ehe, überhaupt zum Menschen und vieles mehr. (*GW* 15:67)

Brecht uses similar terminology in one of his forewords to *A Man's a Man* (1927). More important than all the great new buildings in New York, electricity, and the other achievements of this great age, he says, "*a new human type* is forming now, right now, and the collected interest of the world is focused on his development" ("bildet sich jetzt, eben jetzt, *ein neuer Typus von Mensch* heraus, und das gesamte Interesse der Welt ist auf seine Entwicklung gerichtet"). He continues by giving advice on how to look at Galy Gay:

> it's better if you imagine that you're not hearing an old acquaintance of yours talk, or yourself, as has almost always been the case in the theater till now, but a new kind of type, perhaps in fact an ancestor of this new type of person that I've spoken of.

> da ist es besser, Sie stellen sich vor, Sie hören nicht einen alten Bekannten von Ihnen reden oder sich selber, wie das bisher fast immer der Fall war im Theater, sondern eine neue Art von Typus, vielleicht eben einen Vorfahren dieses neuen Typus Mensch, von dem ich gesprochen habe. (*GW* 17:977)

This formula explains Brecht's dramatic method not only in those two plays but in all his early work. Every play takes a "new type of person," a person who lacks some normal traits or has some traits that will be characteristic of the future, places him in the context of normal contemporary society, and watches the progress of the sociological experiment as the new interacts with the old. With *Baal*, Brecht asks himself, What if I were to show a type "who is absolutely unsocializable and whose method of production is completely unutilizable" ("der absolut unsozialisierbar und dessen Produktionsweise ganz unverwertbar ist") (*GW* 15:140)? The result is destructive to all the people who expect Baal to have a normal conscience.

With *Drums in the Night* Brecht asks himself, What if I showed a type who was totally without idealism, who fought only for what he perceived as his immediate interest, surrounded by people who are committed to a struggle?

> He is the mob. He has—one must admit it—he has no feeling for the tragic, for the pure line, he lacks every sense of duty, he doesn't do what you have to expect of him, he doesn't take the flight into higher realms that is made so easy for him, therein he is perverse.

> Er ist der Mob. Er hat, man muß es gestehen, er hat keinen Sinn für das Tragische, für die reine Linie, er ist ohne jedes Pflichtgefühl, er tut nicht, was man von ihm erwarten muß, er nimmt nicht den Aufschwung ins Höhere, der ihm so leicht gemacht wird, darin ist er pervers. (*GW* 17:957)

(Brecht later decided that although it was the character of Kragler he had viewed as the experiment, it was the real revolutionaries in the play who represented the "new type.")

With *In the Jungle* Brecht asks himself, What if I invented a person who picks a fight to the death with another person for motives that no one else can understand, a person who fights for the sake of fighting and rejects all the traditional rewards?

> Then you mustn't be surprised if in the newer drama certain human types behave differently from your expectations, in certain situations, and also not if your suppositions about the motives of a certain kind of behavior are proved false.

> So dürfen Sie nicht erstaunt sein, wenn in den neueren Dramen gewisse Menschentypen in gewissen Situationen anders handeln, als Sie erwartet haben, und auch nicht, wenn Ihre Mutmaßungen über die Motive einer bestimmten Handlungsweise sich als falsch erweisen. (*GW* 17:970)

With *A Man's a Man* Brecht asks himself, What if I placed into the normal world a person who is exactly the opposite of Baal, "a man who can't say no" ("ein Mann, der nicht nein sagen kann"), who has no sense of identity whatsoever and is totally "socializable"?

This experimental approach to human nature continues in *Fleischhacker* and *Dan Drew*, the stories of two men who are absolutely ruthless; in *Mahagonny*, the story of a man who is not

273

satisfied by the new age; in *St. Joan*, the story of a twentieth-century Faustian man (subjectively "good" but objectively bad) and a woman who insists on finding out the truth; in *The Mother*, the story of an old woman who is capable of learning—and so on.

Through all these early plays, Brecht tries out one kind of "new person" after another, all of them operating on new, unknown sets of values. They are almost dispassionate studies of behavior, experiments with commentary by the lecturer. Or they are like the invention of non-Euclidean geometry or even science fiction: all the normal relations of the world are retained, but one axiom is changed. Suppose parallel lines do not meet? Suppose Galy Gay willingly believes he is not Galy Gay?

It is his excitement about the ability to have a new perspective that causes Brecht to admire Americans for being untainted by the traditional values.

But it can be difficult to distinguish between the beginnings of a new age, with new people in it, and the dying gasps of an old age. Remember Brecht's description, in the fragment *The Flood*, of the rapid biological changes that take place at the time of the Flood, which is the end of an age despite all the innovations:

> that is the greatest age humanity has experienced (the types get stronger bigger darker   they laugh . . .)
> in the final years epidemics of monstrous inventions proliferate   flying people appear   they achieve greater fame than people ever have   they fall in the water   laughter
> atheism increases
>
> das ist die größte zeit die die menschheit erlebt hat (die typen werden stärker größer finsterer   sie lachen . . .)
> in den letzten jahren verbreiten sich seuchen von ungeheuren erfindungen   flugmenschen treten auf   sie gelangen zu größerem ruhm als je zuvor menschen   sie fallen ins wasser   gelächter
> der atheismus nimmt zu (BBA 214, 17)

In the years 1926–29 America, which for Brecht had represented everything new, took on this quixotic character and became the old, as he discovered that many phenomena that had excited him there were really symptoms of decadence. It was as though the Flood had swept across the new continent, destroying what had been the new age and opening the way for a new new age. Brecht uses that precise image in 1953 to sum up his first five plays (including *Edward*):

All five plays together . . . greedy reminiscence of a happier dramatic era, show without regret how the great Flood sweeps over the bourgeois world.

Alle fünf Stücke zusammen . . . gierige Reminiszenz an eine glücklichere dramatische Ära, zeigen ohne Bedauern, wie die große Sintflut über die bürgerliche Welt hereinbricht. (*GW* 17:952)

The new new age was of course socialism, and the Soviet Union became for Brecht the country that symbolized newness, though he was never as rhapsodic about it as he had been about America. Capitalism became "the old." This is clear in a prose poem called "Parade of the Old New" (1938), which makes no sense at all unless one substitutes "capitalism" for "the old" and "socialism" for "the new." It is a vision of fascism, which calls itself national socialism but is really capitalism disguised:

I stood on a hill, there I saw the old coming toward me, but it was the new coming. . . . Round about stood some of those that instilled terror and cried: here comes the new, all this is new, greet the new, be new like us! . . . So the old strode in, disguised as the new, but in its triumphal procession it carried the new with it and it was presented as the old.

Ich stand auf einem Hügel, da sah ich das Alte herankommen, aber es kam des Neue. . . . Ringsum standen solche, die Schrecken einflößten und schrien: Hier kommt das Neue, das ist alles neu, begrüßt das Neue, seid neu wie wir! . . . So schritt das Alte einher, verkleidet als das Neue, aber in seinem Triumphzug führte es das Neue mit sich und es wurde vorgeführt als das Alte. (*GW* 9:729)

A similar use of the abstract words "old" and "new" forms the conceit of a poem from as late as 1950, spoken as advice to the actors of the Berliner Ensemble—"Search for the New and Old":

When you read your roles
Searching, ready to wonder
Look for the new and old, because our age
And our children's age is the age of conflict
Of the new with the old.

Wenn ihr eure Rollen lest
Forschend, bereit zu staunen
Sucht nach dem Neuen und Alten, denn unsere Zeit
Und die Zeit unserer Kinder ist die Zeit der Kämpfe
Des Neuen mit dem Alten.

Here Brecht refers not to the entire social systems of socialism and capitalism but to characters imbued with the values of the two systems. Kattrin is new, Mother Courage is old; and in *The Mother*,

> The cunning of the old woman worker
> Who takes the teacher's knowledge from him
> . . . is new.
> . . . And old
> Is the fear of workers during the war
> To take the leaflets with that knowledge in them.

> Die List der alten Arbeiterin
> Die dem Lehrer sein Wissen abnimmt
> . . . ist neu.
> . . . Und alt
> Ist die Angst der Arbeiter im Krieg
> Die Flugblätter mit dem Wissen zu nehmen.

After all the experimenting with different "new types of people," Brecht settled on the socialist concept of a new person. He had been using the term without knowing where it would lead him. The poem advises the actors to look for qualities of the socialist person and show how these new qualities grew out of the old relations:

> As the people say: when the moon changes
> The young moon holds the old
> A night long in its arms.

> Wie das Volk sagt: zur Zeit des Mondwechsels
> Hält der junge Mond den Alten
> Eine Nacht lang im Arme.

(*GW* 9:793)

Brecht was able to see this same dialectic of the simultaneity of new and old in the earlier phenomenon of Americanism and in his own fascination with America. In 1927 he looks at his previous belief that America was the embodiment of the new age, and sees this belief as a mistake, but a sign of a healthy interest in seeking real change and progress. In speaking of the need for a total change in the theater, he says signs of that change have until now been taken simply for symptoms of disease, which is partially justified since one always sees the decay of the old before the birth of the new; that, however, phenomena such as Americanism appear because of the changes that the truly new influences are bringing about in the diseased body (*GW* 15:131–32). In other words, interest in America was after all a last gasp of "the old," but it was caused by the upheavals accompanying the approach of "the new."

276

For a while it looked to Brecht as though it was America itself that was new, but a theoretical understanding of the way socialism grows out of capitalism, together with wide reading on the effects of American capitalism on the poor, and finally the firsthand experience of the worldwide effects of the depression, all convinced him that the American system was really "the old." Interest in America had been of paramount importance to him because it led him to most of his discoveries about society, but

> What a discovery:
> That their system of living together showed
> The same lamentable flaw as that of
> More modest people!

> Welch eine Entdeckung:
> Daß ihr System des Gemeinlebens denselben
> Jämmerlichen Fehler aufwies wie das
> Bescheidenerer Leute!

(GW 9:483)

Notes

Introduction

1. Richard Ruland, "The American Plays of Bertolt Brecht," *American Quarterly* 15 (1963): 275.
2. Ibid., p. 381.
3. Robert Brustein, *The Theatre of Revolt* (Boston, 1962–64), p. 242.
4. Bryher, quoted in Ulrich Weisstein, "Brecht in America: A Preliminary Survey," *MLN* 78 (1963): 380 n.
5. Heinrich Scheuffelhut, quoted in Werner Frisch and K. W. Obermeier, *Brecht in Augsburg* (Berlin, 1975), p. 51.
6. All references to statements by Elisabeth Hauptmann, Helene Weigel, Herta Ramthun, and Gisela Bahr are from their conversations with me, unless a printed source is given.
7. "Brecht-Abriß," in *Erinnerungen an Brecht*, ed. Hubert Witt (Leipzig, 1966), p. 92.
8. "Erinnerungen an den jungen Brecht," ibid., pp. 40–41.
9. Bertolt-Brecht-Archiv, Mappe 2064 (hereafter abbreviated in the text "BBA," with the page numbers following the folder number).
10. "Gesellenjahre bei Brecht," *Erinnerungen*, p. 248.
11. Bertolt Brecht, *Gesammelte Werke: Werkausgabe Edition Suhrkamp*, 20 vols. (Frankfurt am Main, 1967), 20:10 (hereafter abbreviated in the text "*GW*").
12. BBA 66, 3, quoted in Käthe Rülicke-Weiler, *Die Dramaturgie Brechts* (Berlin, 1968), p. 10.
13. Rülicke-Weiler, *Dramaturgie*, p. 12.
14. Frederic Ewen, *Bertolt Brecht: His Life, His Art, and His Times* (New York, 1967), pp. 113–14.
15. John Willett, *The Theatre of Bertolt Brecht* (London, 1967), pp. 70–71.

Chapter One

1. In the BBA card catalog.
2. Ibid.
3. Bertolt Brecht, *Im Dickicht der Städte: Erstfassung und Materialien*, ed. Gisela Bahr (Frankfurt am Main, 1968), pp. 158–59 (hereafter cited as "Bahr," or simply with page numbers in the text).
4. Excerpts from journals and letter in the BBA card catalog, dated 30 October 1921.
5. Arnolt Bronnen, *Tage mit Bertolt Brecht* (Munich, 1960), p. 86. The letter is probably from the winter of 1922–23.

279

6. Ibid., pp. 47–48. It is possible—if Bronnen is quoting him exactly—that Brecht meant the last sentence or sentences of the first version, which elaborates on the theme: "It was the best time. The chaos is used up, it released me unblessed. Perhaps work will comfort me. It is undoubtedly very late. I feel lonely. *Moti Gui's voice*: East wind!" ("Es war die beste Zeit. Das Chaos ist aufgebraucht, es entließ mich ungesegnet. Vielleicht tröstet mich die Arbeit. Es ist zweifellos sehr spät. Ich fühle mich vereinsamt. Die Stimme Moti Guis: Ostwind!") (Bahr, p. 104).

7. Bahr, p. 161.

8. BBA 348, 64. (Uncorrected version. The revised version is printed in *GW* 17:971–72.)

9. BBA 460, 6; 450, 10, 13, and 18; and 1086, 4.

10. Elisabeth Hauptmann, "Notizen über Brechts Arbeit 1926," in *Erinnerungen*, p. 51.

11. Paul Dessau, "Wie es zum 'Lukullus' kam," in *Erinnerungen*, p. 177.

12. Exceptions: Lorimer, Bouck White (see below, chapter 2).

13. Upton Sinclair, *The Jungle* (1906; rpt. New York, 1960), p. 169.

14. For an enlightening treatment of Brecht's judgment of naturalism, the reader should consult Reinhold Grimm, "Naturalismus und episches Drama," in *Episches Theater*, ed. Reinhold Grimm (Cologne, 1966), pp. 13–35. In some respects (open form, debunking mysticism, bringing science and reality to the stage), naturalism was a precurser of epic theater; but it aimed for total illusion. Brecht credited naturalism with the introduction of realism to the stage, even if it was a fatalistic realism.

15. Today we probably would say that men actually behave far worse toward each other than animals; in criticizing the contemporary social Darwinist justifications of capitalism, Sinclair seems to accept the (Spencerian) social Darwinist misinterpretation of Darwin's theory. Brecht however allows the animal/jungle imagery to be more ambivalent, especially in Shlink, who envies animals their innocence and bodily warmth (Bahr, p. 92).

16. Bahr, p. 158.

17. Ibid., p. 134.

18. For a discussion of some nonliterary influences on Brecht, see Hans Mayer, *Bertolt Brecht und die Tradition* (Pfüllingen, 1961), pp. 30–44.

19. Bahr, p. 145.

20. Hans Otto Münsterer, *Bert Brecht: Erinnerungen aus den Jahren 1917–22* (Zürich, 1963), p. 183.

21. Johannes Vilhelm Jensen, *Das Rad* (Berlin, 1908), pp. 10–11. (My English translations are from the German edition, not the Danish.)

22. Bahr, p. 134.

23. Bernhard Reich, "Erinnerungen an Brecht," Beilage (supplement) to *Theater der Zeit* (Leipzig, 1966), no. 14, p. 12.

24. Cf. Münsterer, p. 50.

25. *GW* 20:337, and 17:1119. Also, in the 1918 and 1919 versions of *Baal*, a young lady with raised eyebrows states that Baal reminds her of Whitman, only more significant. The men in the scene counter with Heine, Verhaeren, Verlaine, and Wedekind (*Baal: Drei Fassungen*, ed. Dieter Schmidt [Frankfurt am Main, 1966], pp. 13 and 84).

26. Jensen, pp. 42–44. (From Whitman's poem, "Starting from Paumanok.")

27. Willett, pp. 91–92.

28. For a discussion of Bret Harte's presumed effect on Brecht, see Klaus Schuhmann, *Der Lyriker Bertolt Brecht 1913–1933* (Berlin, 1964), pp. 39–40.

29. Helfried Seliger gives a lengthy description of that early poem as well as the 1919 plans for an opera to be called *Prärie: Oper nach Hamsun* (BBA 455). An adaptation of Knut Hamsun's story "Zachaeus," the fragment throws interesting light on Brecht's later use of the word *prairie* to mean ruthless competition, and it introduces the themes of wheat, the Midwest, and cold-bloodedness (Seliger, *Das Amerikabild Bertolt Brechts* [Bonn, 1974]).

30. Erwin Piscator, *Das politische Theater* (Berlin, 1929), p. 41.

31. Upton Sinclair, *Prince Hagen: A Phantasy* (Chicago, 1910), pp. 177–78.

32. *GW* 17:949–50. (As pointed out by Michael Morley; see note 37. I am indebted to him for telling me about this discovery.)

33. *GW* 18:10. (*Brecht* mentioned Lorimer; in the edited version in print, Werner Hecht gives us "L.," with a note in the back deciphering Brecht's difficult handwriting as "Lorrimer." Morley makes the correction.)

34. BBA 450, 37–38. (Again, as cited by Morley.)

35. London, 1905 (first published in the United States in 1902).

36. Berlin.

37. "Brecht and the Strange Case of Mr. L.," *GQ* 36 (November 1973): 540–47.

38. Quoted in ibid., p. 543.

39. Bronnen, p. 48 (but see note 6).

40. Herbert Ihering, *Von Reinhardt bis Brecht*, 3 vols. (Berlin, 1961), 2:264. (His name is also often spelled Jhering.)

41. Ibid., 1:274.

42. Ibid., p. 273.

43. Ibid., 2:57–60.

Chapter Two

1. Arbeitskreis Bertolt Brecht, *Nachrichtenbrief* 38 (Cologne, April 1966): 27.

2. Leo Lania, *Welt im Umbruch: Biographie einer Generation* (Frankfurt am Main, 1955), p. 259.

3. Ibid., pp. 259–60.

4. E.g., *GW* 15:237.

5. Piscator, p. 57.

6. However, there is an earlier version, called *Galgei*, from 1918–20. Brecht's "periods" do not have clear boundaries.

7. Lania, p. 264.

8. Ernst Schumacher, "Piscator's Political Theater," in *Brecht: A Collection of Critical Essays*, ed. Peter Demetz (Englewood Cliffs, N.J., 1962), p. 95.

9. Alfons Paquet, *Fahnen: Ein dramatischer Roman* (Munich, 1923), p. 34.

10. Loc. cit.

11. Ibid., p. 72.

12. Ibid., p. 18.

13. Ibid., p. 112.

14. New York, 1925.

15. Reich, p. 10.

16. Tarbell, p. 120.

17. Ibid., p. 121.

18. Ibid., p. 107.

19. Reich, p. 12.

20. Published in very fragmentary form in *GW* 7.

21. Frank Norris, *The Pit* (1903; rpt. Port Washington, 1967), pp. 73–74.

22. 1910; rpt. Larchmont, N.Y., 1965. (Brecht read *Das Buch des Daniel Drew: Leben und Meinungen eines amerikanischen Börsenmannes*, tr. Ewers [Munich, 1922].)

23. George Bernard Shaw, "Die Bibel in Amerika," in *Das Tage-Buch*, Vol. 6, No. 29 (Berlin, 18 July 1925), pp. 1045–50. (The notes in *GW* 18:8* mistakenly give the year as 1926. This mistake suggests that Brecht's piece was probably also written in 1925, not 1926.)

24. Ibid., p. 1045. Retranslation from the German.

25. Frank Harris, *My Life and Loves* (1922–27; rpt. New York, 1963), p. 372.

26. Ibid., p. 371.

27. Ibid., p. 372.

28. Berlin, 1926.

29. For a lucid exposition of *Neue Sachlichkeit*, see John Willett's *Art & Politics in the Weimar Period: The New Sobriety 1917–1933* (New York, 1978).

30. Anyone who supposes that Brecht accepted *Neue Sachlichkeit* uncritically should read his satire on it, "700 Intellectuals Pray to an Oil Tank," *GW* 8:316–17.)

31. Reich, p. 5.

32. *Erinnerungen*, p. 51.

33. Sherwood Anderson, *Poor White*, in *The Portable Sherwood Anderson* (New York, 1949), p. 232.

34. Ibid., p. 172.

35. Ibid., p. 229.

36. Ibid., p. 230.

37. E.g., pp. 170–71.

38. 1910; rpt. New York, 1964.

39. E.g., *GW* 18:28–33, and 19:450–57.

40. Cf. Mayer, pp. 33–40.

41. Myers, p. 414.

42. Ibid., p. 26.

43. Ibid., p. 25.

44. Martin Esslin, *Brecht: The Man and His Work* (Garden City, N.Y., 1960), p. 51. Esslin, Ewen (p. 258), and Ernst Schumacher (*Die dramatischen Versuche Bertolt Brechts 1918–1933* [Berlin, 1955], p. 44) all think Brecht read Steffens. I

have found no confirmation of this in any primary sources (i.e., Brecht's own works and reminiscences by friends), and assume it was only a guess by those critics.

45. *GW* 8:84, and 15:57. Cf. also Münsterer, pp. 166–70.

46. Ihering, 2:60.

47. E.g., *GW* 17:978, 951, and BBA 348 (31–32).

48. *Erinnerungen*, pp. 49, 51.

49. Herta Ramthun, *Bertolt-Brecht-Archiv: Bestandsverzeichnis des literarischen Nachlasses*, Vol. 1 (Berlin, 1969), pp. 295–350.

50. The dating is Dieter Schmidt's information. See Bertolt Brecht, *Baal; Der böse Baal der asoziale: Texte, Varianten und Materialien*, ed. Dieter Schmidt (Frankfurt am Main, 1968), p. 159.

51. Bernard Guillemin, "Was arbeiten Sie? / Gespräch mit Bertolt Brecht," *Erinnerungen*, p. 44.

52. See Schuhmann, pp. 7–25, and Reinhold Grimm, "Brechts Anfänge," in *Aspekte des Expressionismus*, ed. Wolfgang Paulsen (Heidelberg, 1968), pp. 139–40.

53. Lion Feuchtwanger, "Bertolt Brecht," in *Das Tagebuch*, Vol. 3, No. 40 (7 October 1922), p. 1419.

54. Bronnen, pp. 143–44.

55. Walter Benjamin believes these poems describe what it was like to be a political fugitive (such as an illegal Communist). See Benjamin, *Versuche über Brecht* (Frankfurt am Main, 1966), pp. 66–73.

56. Anderson, pp. 317–18.

57. On this poem and Brecht's valuation of friendliness, see Benjamin, pp. 81–83.

58. Cf. "Dreizehn Bühnentechniker erzählen," *Erinnerungen*, pp. 225–39.

59. *GW* 8:169–70. The *Home Devotions* were finished in 1922 (published 1927); the *Svendborg Poems* in 1939.

60. Quoted by Hauptmann in *Erinnerungen*, p. 51.

61. Cf. Thomas O. Brandt, "Brecht und die Bibel," in *PMLA* 79 (1964): 171–76.

62. Cf. comment on *A Man's a Man*, *GW* 17:987.

63. White, p. 206 (p. 187 in the German edition).

64. Ibid., pp. 208–9 (p. 189 in German).

65. Ibid., p. 417 (p. 378 in German).

66. Ibid., pp. 302–3 (p. 275 in German).

67. Morley, p. 546.

68. This scene builds the climax of D. W. Griffiths's early short film based on Norris's books, called "A Corner in Wheat."

69. E.g., BBA 678, 10.

70. E.g., p. 270.

71. See pp. 306, 322.

72. Richard Lewinsohn and Franz Pick, *Sinn und Unsinn der Börse* (Berlin, 1933), p. 159.

73. BBA 524, 62–64; the newspaper is the *8-Uhr Abendblatt*.

74. Quoted by Hauptmann, *Erinnerungen*, p. 52.

Chapter Three

1. Quoted by Sergei Tretjakow in "Bert Brecht," *Erinnerungen*, p. 81.
2. *Erinnerungen*, p. 51.
3. *GW* 19:438. To still any doubts on this subject, see the collection of Brecht's political poems and comments in Arbeitskreis Bertolt Brecht, *Nachrichtenbrief* 36 (February 1966).
4. Berlin, 1926.
5. Berlin, 1925.
6. Berlin, 1923.
7. Vienna, 1926.
8. Hellerau bei Dresden, 1928.
9. E.g., *GW* 12:945, 949, 965, and 975; 19:397; 20:25 and 46.
10. Since I first wrote this, I have come to believe that Brecht does not condemn the young comrade in *The Measure Taken*; rather, the play is a true Lady-or-the-Tiger dilemma in which both the young comrade and the Party are both right and wrong; both compassionate spontaneity and dogmatic gradualism are understood and criticized. See my as yet unpublished paper, "Authoritarianism and Brecht's *Coriolanus*."
11. Esslin, p. 152.
12. Fritz Sternberg, *Der Dichter und die Ratio: Erinnerungen an Bertolt Brecht* (Göttingen, 1963), p. 8.
13. Bahr, pp. 34–35.
14. Schumacher, *Versuche*, p. 70.
15. Ibid., p. 71.
16. Ibid., pp. 66–67.
17. See Volker Canaris, "*Leben Eduards des Zweiten*" als vormarxistisches *Stück Bertolt Brechts* (Bonn, 1973) and Reinhold Grimm, "Brechts Rad der Fortuna," in *GQ* 46 (November 1973): 549–65.
18. Schumacher, *Versuche*, p. 105.
19. Bronnen, p. 144.
20. Reich, p. 5.
21. Sternberg, pp. 30–31.
22. Cf. Brecht's own description of how he came to read Marx, *GW* 20:46.
23. Collected in *GW* 20 as *Marxistische Studien*.
24. *Materialien zu Bertolt Brechts "Die Mutter*," ed. Werner Hecht (Frankfurt am Main, 1969), p. 194.
25. Sternberg, pp. 18–19.
26. Hecht, *Materialien zu "Die Mutter*," p. 178.
27. Bertolt Brecht, *Aufstieg und Fall der Stadt Mahagonny* (Berlin, 1963), pp. 88–89. In slightly different form in *GW* 17:1009–10.
28. *Erinnerungen*, pp. 51–52.
29. Ewen, p. 224. Brecht apparently did not invent the term but translated it

from Russian. This is not the place to go into its history; readers are referred to Stanley Mitchell, "From Shklovsky to Brecht," in *Screen*, Vol. 15, No. 2 (1974), pp. 74–81.

30. Mayer, p. 31.

31. Sternberg, p. 16.

32. Rülicke-Weiler, *Dramaturgie*, p. 16.

33. Reinhold Grimm, *Bertolt Brecht* (Stuttgart, 1961), p. 75.

34. Brustein, pp. 249–50. This interpretation, like others of the Western Brecht-really-belongs-to-us school, depends for its credibility on a lack of knowledge of Brecht's essays, shorter works, and autobiographical notes; it demonstrates the danger of drawing conclusions about an author's biography merely from his major works, a danger that even before publication of the *Gesammelte Werke* could always be avoided by using the facilities of the Brecht Archive.

35. See Sternberg, p. 18.

36. Dating: a first draft of this argument is on the same manuscript page as "Zu 'Baal' " (*GW* 15:64), which the Brecht Archive dates 1926.

37. The three new song additions show the intended change clearly.

38. Lenin, "The Three Sources and Three Component Parts of Marxism."

39. Sternberg, p. 25.

Chapter Four

1. Quoted by Werner Otto in the program booklet to *Aufstieg und Fall der Stadt Mahagonny* in the Deutsche Staatsoper Berlin, GDR, 1964.

2. Staatsoper program.

3. *Allgemeine Musikzeitung* 57 (1930), no. 12, quoted in the Staatsoper program.

4. David Drew, "The History of Mahagonny," in *The Musical Times* 104 (London, 1963): 20.

5. *Leipziger Bühnenblätter*, Nr. 12 (1929–30), quoted in Staatsoper program.

6. They are printed at the end of the *Home Devotions* (but not in the *GW*).

7. *Leipziger Bühnenblätter*, quoted in Staatsoper program.

8. Drew, p. 18.

9. Bertolt Brecht, *Gedichte II* (Frankfurt am Main, 1960), p. 256.

10. Booklet with the recording of *Rise and Fall of the City of Mahagonny* (Columbia No. K3L 243; text written by Lenya in 1957).

11. Loc. cit.

12. Drew, p. 19.

13. Loc. cit.

14. Schuhmann, p. 149.

15. Ihering, 2:334.

16. Drew, p. 19.

17. *Leipziger Bühnenblätter*, quoted in Staatsoper program.

18. Schumacher, *Versuche*, p. 273.

19. *Leipziger Bühnenblätter*, quoted in Staatsoper program.

20. According to Elisabeth Hauptmann in *Gedichte II*, pp. 256–57.

21. Bahr, p. 35.

22. Karl Valentin and Liesl Karlstadt use it in a 1930 skit, where it is titled "Seemanslos." *Das große Karl Valentin Buch*, ed. Michael Schulte (Munich, 1973), pp. 221–22. The English version is a 19th-century ballad by Arthur C. Lamb.

23. *Gedichte II*, p. 256.

24. It is printed with that series in *Gedichte I* (Frankfurt am Main, 1960).

25. Staatsoper program.

26. Sternberg, p. 29.

27. E.g., *GW* 15:172, 269.

28. John Milfull has an interesting perspective on *Mahagonny* in his book *From Baal to Keuner: The "Second Optimism" of Bertolt Brecht* (Bern, 1974). *Mahagonny* is the "dead point" below which Brecht's nihilism could not fall, an uncompromising indictment with no suggestion of any possible solution. Milfull also has a different slant on Brecht's search for a "new type of person."

29. In an interview with me.

30. BBA 209, 68. Reference: Ramthun, p. 401.

31. In an interview with me.

32. I have searched through many bibliographic sources myself.

33. *Happy End: Komödie in 3 Akten von Dorothy Lane, Musik von Kurt Weill*, Felix Bloch Erben, Berlin-Charlottenburg, 1958 (typescript).

34. *Erinnerungen*, p. 50.

35. Fischer, Berlin. For a study of *Major Barbara*'s effect on Brecht, see Karl-Heinz Schoeps, *Bertolt Brecht und Bernard Shaw* (Bonn, 1974).

36. BBA 895, "Schwedische Manuskripte."

37. Thanks for this information to Gisela Bahr. I myself have done some research into the U.S. branch of the Salvation Army, including a visit to its Officers' Training School in Suffern, N.Y.; there I was told that one of the principal sources of funding was the *Reader's Digest*.

38. Reich, p. 14.

39. *Happy End*, p. 59.

40. Ibid., p. 16.

41. Original title *Der Flug der Lindberghs* (*The Flight of the Lindberghs*), changed at Brecht's request when he heard reports of Lindbergh's helping the Nazis. This is also the reason for the new historical model for a pilot, Charles Nungesser.

42. *GW* 2:584–85. This is a significant revision of "das Unerreichbare" ("the unattainable") in the early version, requested by Brecht in a footnote to *Das Badener Lehrstück*. See *GW* 2:3*.

43. Upton Sinclair, *Oil!* (London, 1927), p. 518.

44. Bertolt Brecht, *Über Lyrik* (Frankfurt am Main, 1964), pp. 74–75.

45. BBA 238, 62, and 1080, 26. Reference: Ramthun, p. 395.

46. See Ihering, 2:405–7, 417–19.

47. James K. Lyon, *Bertolt Brecht's American Cicerone* (Bonn, 1978).

Chapter Five

1. "When I Years Ago . . . " quoted in full, pp. 132–33.
2. All quotations from "Vanished Glory of the Giant City New York" are in *GW* 9:475–83.
3. Schuhmann, pp. 236–37.
4. *Die Weltbühne* 1 (1931): 128 ff.; Schumacher, *Versuche*, p. 580 n.
5. BBA 818, 1–12; 823, 46; 827, 26 respectively. Reference: Ramthun, pp. 304, 311.
6. Interview with me.
7. See his two informative articles, "Bertolt Brecht's American Cicerone," in *Brecht Heute* (Frankfurt am Main, 1972), pp. 187–208, and "Bertolt Brecht's Hollywood Years: The Dramatist as Film Writer," in *Oxford German Studies* 6 (1971–72): 145–74.
8. Plot outline from Lyon's summary in "Bertolt Brecht's Hollywood Years," pp. 150–51.
9. Bertolt Brecht, *Texte fur Filme* 2 (Frankfurt am Main, 1969): 438–75. (Also BBA 226).
10. Ibid., pp. 353–55.
11. Ibid., pp. 476–537.
12. The Salvation Army girl theme was also developed in fragments of another play Brecht worked on at the same time as *Happy End*; called *Marie Andersen* or *Gut und Böse* (*Good and Bad*), it was set in Berlin, not the United States. Bertolt Brecht, *Die heilige Johanna der Schlachthöfe: Bühnenfassung, Fragmente, Varianten*, ed. Gisela E. Bahr (Frankfurt am Main, 1971), pp. 211–12.
13. Rülicke-Weiler, *Dramaturgie*, p. 17.
14. *Die Funktion der Geschichte im Werk Bertolt Brechts: Studien zum Verhältnis von Marxismus und Ästhetik* (Tübingen, 1967), pp. 22–23.
15. Rülicke-Weiler, *Dramaturgie*, p. 17.
16. "Short Report on 400 (Four Hundred) Young Poets," *GW* 18:54.
17. *Über Lyrik*, p. 75.
18. "Zu Wordsworths 'She Was a Phantom of Delight,' " *Über Lyrik*, pp. 72–73.
19. Sternberg, pp. 24–25.
20. BBA 363, 52–53 and 55. Reference: Ramthun, p. 332.
21. Quoted in Käthe Rülicke, "Zu Brechts 'Die heilige Johanna der Schlachthöfe,' " in *Theater der Zeit*, Vol. 16, No. 1 (1961), p. 26.
22. Ernst Schumacher, *Drama und Geschichte: Bertolt Brechts "Leben des Galilei" und andere Stücke* (Berlin, 1968), p. 255.
23. BBA 277, 62, quoted in Schumacher, *Galilei*, p. 253.
24. BBA 275, 12, quoted in Schumacher, *Galilei*, p. 247.
25. Adorno, *Noten zur Literatur* 2 (Frankfurt am Main, 1965): 118.
26. Ewen, p. 260.

27. In *Theater der Zeit*, Vol. 14, No. 6 (1959).

28. In *Sinn und Form*, Vol. 9, Nos. 1–3 (1957): *Zweites Sonderheft Bertolt Brecht*, p. 151.

29. Lion Feuchtwanger, "Bertolt Brecht," *Sinn und Form Zweites Sonderheft*, p. 103.

30. Rülicke-Weiler, *Dramaturgie*, p. 145.

31. In *Theater der Zeit* 16:22–39. Shorter versions can be found in her (now Rülicke-Weiler) *Dramaturgie*, pp. 137–46, and in her (Rülicke) "Die heilige Johanna der Schlachthöfe: Notizen zum Bau der Fabel," in *Sinn und Form*, Vol. 11, No. 3 (1959), pp. 429–44. All three treatments are excellent. (The five-part structure described here is her formulation.)

32. Rülicke-Weiler, *Dramaturgie*, p. 137.

33. See *GW* 7:2949.

34. Dated by Herta Ramthun of the Brecht Archive, in an interview with me.

35. *Gedichte II*, p. 247.

36. *The Jungle*, p. 349.

37. In the 1968 Berliner Ensemble version, the scene on the floor of the exchange was the high point of an otherwise fairly uninspired production. The scene was highly stylized and even choreographed, with the groups of growers, buyers, and packers changing their hand signals simultaneously as though in involuntary reaction to some sensed command by the invisible System; the pre-taped choruses were spoken over loudspeakers, and the traders had only to go through the steps of their compulsive dance like marionettes. The printed program showed pictures of the hand signals.

38. Karl Marx, *Capital*, 1 (New York, 1967): 593.

39. In 1928 he spoke of "the great mediocre G.B.S." ("der große mittelmäßige G.B.S.") (*GW* 18:67).

40. See Ewen, p. 261 and n.

41. BBA 279, 21. Printed in Schmidt, *Baal; Der böse Baal*, p. 110.

42. A. Erck and K. Gräf, "Bertolt Brechts Gedicht 'Die Nachtlager': Versuch einer Interpretation," in *Weimarar Beiträge*, No. 2 (1967), p. 244.

43. *GW* 2:807. Cf. 2:677.

44. *GW* 2:793. Cf. 2:671.

45. *Erinnerungen*, p. 52.

46. Ibid., p. 44.

Postscript

1. Quoted in Ruland, pp. 388–89.

2. *Bertolt Brecht's American Cicerone.*

3. Bertolt Brecht, *Arbeitsjournal*, 1 (Frankfurt am Main, 1974): 258–59.

4. Seliger, pp. 219–32.

5. BBA 238, 62; 1080, 26. Reference: Ramthun, p. 395.

6. See Ramthun, pp. 397–98.

7. Schumacher, *Galilei*, p. 321.

8. Ibid., pp. 322–28.

9. Ibid., p. 327.

10. Reich, p. 18.

11. He also had permission beginning in 1952 to subscribe to *Time*, *Life*, and *Newsweek* (information from Gisela Bahr).

Bibliography of Works Consulted

PRIMARY LITERATURE

1. *Brecht Texts*

Brecht, Bertolt. *Gesammelte Werke: Werkausgabe Edition Suhrkamp*. 20 vols. Frankfurt am Main, 1967.

––––––. *Arbeitsjournal*. 2 vols. Frankfurt am Main, 1974.

––––––. *Aufstieg und Fall der Stadt Mahagonny*. Berlin, 1963.

––––––. *Baal; Der böse Baal der asoziale: Texte, Varianten und Materialien*, ed. Dieter Schmidt. Frankfurt am Main, 1968.

––––––. *Baal: Drei Fassungen*, ed. Dieter Schmidt. Frankfurt am Main, 1966.

––––––. *Bertolt Brechts Hauspostille*. Berlin, 1927.

––––––. *Der Jasager und der Neinsager: Vorlagen, Fassungen, Materialien*, ed. Peter Szondi. Frankfurt am Main, 1966.

––––––. *Die heilige Johanna der Schlachthöfe: Bühnenfassung, Fragmente, Varianten*, ed. Gisela E. Bahr. Frankfurt am Main, 1971.

––––––. *Gedichte I* and *II*. Frankfurt am Main, 1960.

––––––. *Im Dickicht der Städte: Erstfassung und Materialien*, ed. Gisela E. Bahr. Frankfurt am Main, 1968.

––––––. *Kriegsfibel*, ed. Ruth Berlau. Berlin, 1955.

––––––. *Poems: 1913–1956*, ed. John Willett and Ralph Manheim. London, 1976.

––––––. *Tagebücher 1920–1922; Autobiographische Aufzeichnungen 1920–1954*. Frankfurt am Main, 1975.

––––––. *Texte für Filme*. 2 vols. Frankfurt am Main, 1969.

––––––. *Über Lyrik*. Frankfurt am Main, 1964.

Feuchtwanger, Lion. *3 angelsächsische Stücke von Lion Feuchtwanger: Die Petroleuminseln; Kalkutta, 4. Mai; Wird Hill amnestiert?* Berlin, 1927. (Edition in Brecht's library: Lion Feuchtwanger. *Two Anglo-Saxon Plays: The Oil Islands; Warren Hastings*. New York, 1928.)

Lane, Dorothy (pseudonym; actually primarily by Elisabeth Hauptmann). *Happy End: Komödie in 3 Akten von Dorothy Lane, Musik von Kurt Weill*. Felix Bloch-Erben ("Unverkäufliches Manuskript"), Berlin-Charlottenburg, 1958.

2. *Reminiscences*

Anders, Günther. *Bert Brecht: Gespräche und Erinnerungen*. Zürich, 1962.

Bronnen, Arnolt. *Tage mit Bertolt Brecht*. Munich, 1960.

Feuchtwanger, Lion. "Bertolt Brecht," *Das Tagebuch* (Berlin), Vol. 3, No. 40 (7 October 1922), pp. 1417–19.

Frisch, Werner, and K. W. Obermeier. *Brecht in Augsburg*. Berlin, 1975.

Hauptmann, Elisabeth. "Mitarbeiter und Mitarbeit bei Brecht," *Theater der Zeit* (Leipzig), Vol. 13, No. 2 (1968), p. 7.

Högel, Max. *Bertolt Brecht: Ein Porträt*. Augsburg, 1962.

Ihering, Herbert. *Von Reinhardt bis Brecht*. 3 vols. Berlin, 1961. (Also spelled Jhering.)

Lania, Leo. *Welt im Umbruch: Biographie einer Generation*. Frankfurt, 1955.

Lenya, Lotte. "Lotte Lenya Remembers Mahagonny," in booklet accompanying Columbia recording K3L 243, *Kurt Weill's Rise and Fall of the City of Mahagonny*.

Münsterer, Hans Otto. *Bert Brecht: Erinnerungen aus den Jahren 1917–22*. Zürich, 1963.

Piscator, Erwin. *Das politische Theater*. Berlin, 1929.

Reich, Bernhard. "Erinnerungen an Brecht," Beilage (supplement) to *Theater der Zeit*, Vol. 21, No. 14 (Leipzig, 1966).

Roth, Wolfgang. "Working with Bertolt Brecht," in *Brecht Heute / Brecht Today* 2, ed. Gisela Bahr et. al. Frankfurt am Main, 1972.

Sternberg, Fritz. *Der Dichter und die Ratio: Erinnerungen an Bertolt Brecht*. Göttingen, 1963.

Witt, Hubert, ed. *Erinnerungen an Brecht*. Leipzig, 1966. (*Brecht As They Knew Him*. New York, 1974.)

3. *Sources Read by Brecht*

Adamic, Louis. *Dynamite: The Story of Class Violence in America*. Rev. ed. New York, 1934.

Anderson, Sherwood. *Poor White*, in *The Portable Sherwood Anderson*, ed. Horace Gregory. New York, 1949. (First German edition: *Der arme Weiße*. Leipzig, 1925.)

Bucharin, N. *Der Imperialismus und die Akkumulation des Kapitals*. Berlin, 1926.

Dreiser, Theodore. "Die Arbeitslosen in New York," *Die Weltbühne* 1 (1931): 128 ff.

———. *Sister Carrie*. New York, 1917.

———. *The Titan*. 1914; rpt. New York, 1959. (First German edition: *Der Titan: Trilogie der Begierde*. Berlin, 1928).

Farquhar, George. *The Recruiting Officer*.

Guilbeaux, Henri. *Wladimir Iljitsch Lenin: Ein treues Bild seines Wesens*. Berlin, 1923.

Hamsun, Knut. *Hunger*. Munich, 1921.

Harris, Frank. *My Life and Loves*. 1922–27; rpt. New York, 1963. (First German edition: *Mein Leben*. Berlin, 1926.)

Harte, Bret. *Kalifornische Erzählungen*. 3 vols. Leipzig, no date.

Jensen, Johannes Vilhelm. *Das Rad*. Berlin, 1908.

Korsch, Karl. *Marxismus und Philosophie*. Frankfurt am Main, 1966.

Lafargue, Paul. *Die Religion des Kapitals*. Vienna, 1930.

Lenin, W. I. *Staat und Revolution: Die Lehre des Marxismus vom Staat und die Aufgaben des Proletariats in der Revolution.* Berlin, 1918.

Lewinsohn, Richard. Economic columns in the *Vossische Zeitung*, Berlin, 1920s.

Lorimer, George Horace. *Letters from a Self-Made Merchant to his Son.* London, 1905. (In German: *Briefe eines Dollar-Königs an seinen Sohn*, tr. O. von Oppen. Berlin, 1905. Also: *Neue Briefe eines Dollar-Königs an seinen Sohn.* Berlin 1905.)

Masters, Edgar Lee. *Spoon River Anthology.* New York, 1918.

Mendelsohn, Erich. *Amerika: Bilderbuch eines Architekten.* Berlin, 1926.

Morus (pseudonym of Richard Lewinsohn). Articles in *Die Weltbühne* in the 1920s.

Myers, Gustavus. *History of the Great American Fortunes.* 1910; rpt. New York, 1964. (First German edition: *Geschichte der großen amerikanischen Vermögen.* Berlin, 1916.)

Norris, Frank. *The Octopus: A Story of California.* 1901; rpt. New York, 1958. (First German edition: *Das Epos des Weizens: 1. Teil: Der Oktopus: Eine Geschichte aus Kalifornien.* Stuttgart, 1907.)

_____. *The Pit* (*Complete Works*, Vol. 9). Port Washington, N.Y., 1967. (First German edition: *Das Epos des Weizens: 2. Teil: Die Getreidebörse: Eine Geschichte aus Chikago.* Stuttgart, 1912.) (Edition in Brecht's library: *The Pit: A Story of Chicago.* Leipzig, 1903.)

Paquet, Alfons. *Fahnen: Ein dramatischer Roman.* Munich, 1923.

Shaw, George Bernard. "Die Bibel in Amerika," *Das Tage-Buch*, Vol. 6, No. 29 (Berlin, 18 July 1925), pp. 1045–50.

_____. *Major Barbara.* (Edition in Brecht's Library: Berlin, 1926.)

Sinclair, Upton. *The Jungle.* 1906; rpt. New York, 1960. (German editions: *Der Sumpf: Roman aus Chicagos Schlachthäusern.* Hannover, 1906, 1922; Berlin, 1923, 1928.)

_____. *Die Maschine.* Berlin, 1921.

_____. *Oil!* London, 1927. (First German edition: *Petroleum.* Berlin, 1927.)

_____. *Prince Hagen: A Phantasy.* Chicago, 1910. (In Brecht's library: *Prinz Hagen: Ein phantastisches Schauspiel.* Berlin, 1921.)

_____. *Singing Jailbirds: A Drama in Four Acts.* Pasadena, 1924.

Tarbell, Ida M. *The Life of Elbert H. Gary: The Story of Steel.* New York, 1925.

Walcher, Jakob. *Ford oder Marx.* Berlin, 1925.

White, Bouck. *The Book of Daniel Drew.* 1910; rpt. Larchmont, N.Y., 1965. (First German edition: *Das Buch des Daniel Drew: Leben und Meinungen eines amerikanischen Börsenmannes*, tr. Ewers. Munich, 1922.)

Whitman, Walt. *Auf der Brooklyn Fähre.* Berlin, 1949.

SECONDARY LITERATURE

Criticism, Biographies, and Miscellaneous

Adorno, Theodor W. *Noten zur Literatur II.* Frankfurt am Main, 1965.

Arbeitskreis Bertolt Brecht, 5 Köln 1, Postfach 26. *Nachrichtenbriefe.* No. 9: Bibliography.

No. 12: Dissertations.

No. 36: Brecht's political poetry, commentary on the GDR and the 17 June 1953 workers' demonstrations.

No. 38: Piscator.

No. 51: Gisela Bahr on *Im Dickicht*.

Arendt, Hannah. "What Is Permitted to Jove." *New Yorker* 42 (5 November 1966): 68–122.

Bathrick, David. *The Dialectic and the Early Brecht*. Stuttgart 1975.

Baxandall, Lee. "The Americanization of Bert Brecht," in *Brecht Heute / Brecht Today* 1, ed. Eric Bentley et. al. Frankfurt am Main, 1971.

———. Introduction to *The Mother*, tr. Baxandall. New York, 1965.

Benjamin, Walter. *Versuche über Brecht*. Frankfurt am Main, 1966.

Berliner Ensemble. Printed programs for their productions of:
Über die großen Städte and *Das kleine Mahagonny*, 1963.
Die heilige Johanna der Schlachthöfe, 1968.
Der aufhaltsame Aufstieg des Arturo Ui, 1961.
Leben des Galilei, 1960.
All printed in Berlin.

———. Pamphlet and text accompanying the recording of *Über die großen Städte* and *Das kleine Mahagonny*. Berlin.

Bondy, François. "*Mahagonny* ou Brecht contre Kipling et Jack London." *Preuves* 191: 78–79.

Brandt, Thomas O. "Bertolt Brecht und sein Amerikabild." *Universitas* 21 (1966): 719–34.

———. "Brecht und die Bibel." *PMLA* 79 (1964): 171–76.

———. *Die Vieldeutigkeit Bertolt Brechts*. Heidelberg, 1968.

Brustein, Robert. *The Theatre of Revolt*. Boston, 1962–64.

Canaris, Volker. "*Leben Eduards des Zweiten von England*" *als vormarxistisches Stück Bertolt Brechts*. Bonn, 1973.

Demetz, Peter. *Brecht: A Collection of Critical Essays*. Englewood Cliffs, N.J., 1962.

Deutsche Staatsoper Berlin. Printed program to their production of *Aufstieg und Fall der Stadt Mahagonny*, ed. Werner Otto. Berlin, 1964.

Dickson, Keith A. "Brecht's Doctrine of Nature," in *Brecht Heute / Brecht Today* 3, ed. Gisela Bahr et al. Frankfurt am Main, 1973.

Dort, Bernard. *Lecture de Brecht*. Paris, 1960.

Drama Review. Special issues on Brecht: Vol. 12, No. 1 (Fall 1967) and No. 2 (Winter 1968); and (then called *Tulane Drama Review*), Vol. 6, No. 1 (September 1961).

Drew, David. "The History of Mahagonny." *Musical Times* 104 (London, 1963): 18–24.

Erck, A., and K. Gräf. "Bertolt Brechts Gedicht 'Die Nachtlager': Versuch einer Interpretation." *Weimarer Beiträge*, No. 2 (1967), pp. 228–45.

Esslin, Martin. *Brecht: The Man and His Work*. Garden City, N.Y., 1960.

———. *Brecht: Das Paradox des politischen Dichters*. Frankfurt am Main, 1962.

Ewen, Frederic. *Bertolt Brecht: His Life, His Art, and His Times*. New York, 1967.

Faßmann, Kurt. *Brecht: Eine Bildbiographie.* Munich, 1958.

Fetscher, Iring. "Bertolt Brecht's America." *Salmagundi.* Nos. 10–11, pp. 246–72.

Frank, Günter. "Zur Rezeption Bertolt Brechts." *Kürbiskern,* No. 4 (1968), pp. 597–606.

Frank, Rudolf, et al. *Das Ärgernis Brecht.* Basel, 1961.

Fuegi, John *The Essential Brecht.* Los Angeles, 1972.

Gersch, Wolfgang. *Film bei Brecht.* Munich, 1975.

Gisselbrecht, Andre. "Bertolt Brecht und die Güte," in *Theater der Zeit.* Leipzig, 1957. Pp. 571–89.

Glauert, Barbara M. *Brechts Amerikabild in drei seiner Dramen.* M. A. thesis, University of Colorado, 1961.

Goldhahn, Johannes. *Das Parabelstück Bertolt Brechts.* Rudolstadt, 1961.

Grimm, Reinhold. *Bertolt Brecht.* Stuttgart, 1963.

–––––––. *Bertolt Brecht: Die Struktur seines Werkes.* Nuremberg, 1962.

–––––––. *Brecht und die Weltliteratur.* Nuremberg, 1961.

–––––––. "Brecht's Anfänge," in *Aspeckte des Expressionismus,* ed. Wolfgang Paulsen. Heidelberg, 1968. Pp. 133–52.

–––––––. "Brecht's Rad der Fortuna." *GQ* 46 (November 1973): 549–65.

–––––––. "Naturalismus und episches Drama," in *Episches Theater,* ed. Reinhold Grimm. Cologne, 1966.

Haas, Willy. *Bert Brecht.* Berlin, 1958.

Hakim, Eleanor. "St. Brecht of the Theatrical Stock Exchange." *Review I (Monthly Review* supplement, 1965), pp. 14–35.

Hecht, Werner, ed. *Brecht-Dialog 1968: Politik auf dem Theater.* Berlin, 1968.

–––––––. *Brechts Weg zum epischen Theater.* Berlin, 1962.

–––––––. *Materialien zu Bertolt Brechts "Die Mutter."* Frankfurt am Main, 1969.

–––––––. *Materialien zu Brechts "Der gute Mensch von Sezuan."* Frankfurt am Main, 1968.

–––––––. *Materialien zu Brechts "Leben des Galilei."* Frankfurt am Main, 1963.

Heller, Paul. "Nihilist into Activist: Two Phases in the Development of Bertolt Brecht." *GR* 28 (1953): 144 ff.

Herrmann, Hans Peter. "Wirklichkeit und Ideologie: Brechts 'Heilige Johanna der Schlachthöfe' als Lehrstück bürgerlicher Praxis im Klassenkampf," in *Brechtdiskussion,* ed. Joachim Dyck et al. Kronberg, 1974. Pp. 52–120.

Hill, Claude. *Bertolt Brecht.* Boston, 1975.

Hoover, Marjorie. "Ihr geht gemeinsam den Weg nach unten: Aufstieg und Fall Amerikas im Werk Bertolt Brechts," in *Amerika in der deutschen Literatur,* ed. S. Bauschinger et al. Stuttgart, 1975.

Kaufmann, Hans. "Der junge Brecht," in his *Krisen und Wandlungen der deutschen Literatur von Wedekind bis Feuchtwanger.* Berlin, 1966. Pp. 366–400.

Kesting, Marianne. *Bertolt Brecht in Selbstzeugnissen und Bilddokumenten.* Reinbek bei Hamburg, 1959.

Killy, Walther. *Über Gedichte des jungen Brecht.* Göttingen, 1967.

Klotz, Volker. *Bertolt Brecht: Versuch über das Werk.* Bad Homburg, 1967.

295

Kohlhase, Norbert. *Dichtung und politische Moral: Eine Gegenüberstellung von Brecht und Camus.* Munich, 1965.

Kussmaul, Paul. *Bert Brecht und das englische Drama der Renaissance.* Bern, 1974.

Lethen, Helmut. *Neue Sachlichkeit 1924–1932: Studien zur Literatur des Weißen Sozialismus.* Stuttgart, 1970.

Lewinsohn, Richard, and Franz Pick. *Sinn und Unsinn der Börse.* Berlin, 1933.

Lißner, Erich. "Es helfen nur Menschen, wo Menschen sind." *Frankfurter Rundschau,* 14 December 1963. (Review of *Die heilige Johanna.)*

Loomis, Emerson R. "A Reinterpretation of Bertolt Brecht: The Moral Choice in *Die sieben Todsünden.*" *University of Kansas City Review,* Autumn 1960.

Lyon, James K. *Bertolt Brecht in America.* Princeton, 1980.

————. *Bertolt Brecht's American Cicerone.* Bonn, 1978.

————. "Bertolt Brecht's American Cicerone," in *Brecht Heute / Brecht Today* 2, ed. Gisela Bahr et. al. Frankfurt am Main, 1972. Pp. 187–208.

————. *Bertolt Brecht and Rudyard Kipling: A Marxist's Imperial Mentor.* The Hague, 1975.

————. "Bertolt Brecht's Hollywood Years: The Dramatist as Film Writer." *Oxford German Studies* 6 (1971–72): 145–74.

————. Über Brecht's Mißerfolg als Hollywood Filmschreiber," in *Literatur in den Massenmedien,* ed. Friedrich Knilly. Munich, 1976.

Mayer, Hans. *Bertolt Brecht und die Tradition.* Pfüllingen, 1961.

Milfull, John. *From Baal to Keuner: The "Second Optimism" of Bertolt Brecht.* Bern, 1974.

Mitchell, Stanley. "From Shklovsky to Brecht: Some Preliminary Remarks towards a History of the Politicization of Russian Formalism." *Screen,* Vol. 15, No. 2 (1974), pp. 74–81.

Morley, Michael. "Brecht and the Strange Case of Mr. L." *GQ* 36 (November 1973): 540–47.

Müller, André. "Der Marxist Bertolt Brecht." *Marxistische Blätter,* Vol. 3, No. 2 (1965), pp. 33–40.

————. "Mit einer Verspätung von 27 Jahren, 'Die heilige Johanna der Schlachthöfe' im Deutschen Schauspielhaus." *Theater der Zeit,* Vol. 14, No. 6 (1959), pp. 58–61.

Müller, Klaus-Detlef. *Die Funktion der Geschichte im Werk Bertolt Brechts: Studien zum Verhältnis von Marxismus und Ästhetik.* Tübingen, 1967.

Muschg, Walter. *Von Trakl zu Brecht: Dichter des Expressionismus.* Munich, 1961.

Niessen, Carl. *Brecht auf der Bühne.* Cologne, 1959.

Petersen, Klaus-Dietrich, ed. *Bertolt Brecht: Leben und Werk.* Dortmund, 1966. (Bibliography, 1957–64.)

Ramthun, Herta. *Bertolt-Brecht-Archiv: Bestandsverzeichnis des literarischen Nachlasses,* Vol. 1. Berlin, 1969.

Rasch, Wolfdietrich. "Bertolt Brechts marxistischer Lehrer." *Merkur: Deutsche Zeitschrift für europäisches Denken* 17 (1963): 988–1003.

Richter, Hans. "Bertolt Brechts Bemerkungen zur Lyrik." *Weimarer Beiträge*, No. 4 (1966), 765–85.

Ruland, Richard. "The American Plays of Bertolt Brecht." *American Quarterly* 15 (1963): 371–89.

Rülicke, Käthe. "Die heilige Johanna der Schlachthöfe: Notizen zum Bau der Fabel." *Sinn und Form* Vol. 2, No. 3 (1959), pp. 429–44.

———. "Zu Brechts 'Die heilige Johanna der Schlachthöfe.' " *Theater der Zeit* (Leipzig), January 1961, pp. 22–39.

Rülicke-Weiler, Käthe. *Die Dramaturgie Brechts: Theater als Mittel der Veränderung.* Berlin, 1968.

Schoeps, Karl-Heinz. *Bertolt Brecht und Bernard Shaw.* Bonn, 1974.

Schuhmann, Klaus. *Der Lyriker Bertolt Brecht 1913–1933.* Berlin, 1964.

Schulte, Karl, ed. *Das große Karl Valentin Buch.* Munich, 1973.

Schumacher, Ernst. *Die dramatischen Versuche Bertolt Brechts 1918–1933.* Berlin, 1955.

———. *Drama und Geschichte: Bertolt Brechts "Leben des Galilei" und andere Stücke.* Berlin, 1968.

Seliger, Helfried W., *Das Amerikabild Bertolt Brechts.* Bonn, 1974.

Seyfarth, Ingrid. "Eine Konzeption für Johanna." *Theater der Zeit* (Leipzig), Vol. 23, No. 16 (1968), pp. 13–17.

Sinn und Form: Sonderheft Bertolt Brecht. Berlin, 1949.

Sinn und Form: Zweites Sonderheft Bertolt Brecht. Berlin, 1957.

Sonnenfeld, Albert. "The Function of Brecht's Eclecticism." *Books Abroad*, Vol. 36, No. 2 (1962), pp. 134–38.

Spalek, John M., and Joseph Strelka. *Deutsche Exilliteratur seit 1933. Band I: Kalifornien.* Bern, 1976.

Steinweg, Reiner. *Das Lehrstück: Brechts Theorie einer politisch-ästhetischen Erziehung.* Stuttgart, 1972.

Suvin, Darko. Program to 1973 production of *St. Joan of the Slaughterhouses* at McGill University.

———, and Michael Bristol. *A Production Notebook to St. Joan of the Stockyards.* Montreal, 1973.

Tank, Kurt Lothar. "Brecht für verrottete Christen?" *Theater Heute*, September 1963, pp. 1–2.

Tatlow, Antony. *The Mask of Evil: Brecht's Response to the Poetry, Theatre, and Thought of China and Japan.* Bern, 1977.

Völker, Klaus. *Bertolt Brecht: Eine Biographie.* Munich, 1976.

———. *Brecht Chronicle.* New York, 1975.

Weideli, Walter. *The Art of Bertolt Brecht*, tr. Daniel Russell. New York, 1963.

Weisbach, Reinhard. "Brecht auf dem Wege zum Verständnis des Proletariats," *Weimarer Beiträge*, No. 5 (1967), pp. 762–95.

Weisert, John J. "Shaw in Central Europe before 1914." *Crosscurrents* 2:273–302.

Weisstein, Ulrich. "Brecht in America: A Preliminary Survey." *MLN* 78 (1963): 373–96.

————. "From the Dramatic Novel to the Epic Theater: A Study in the Contemporary Background of Brecht's Theory and Practice." *GR*, Vol. 38, No. 3 (1963), pp. 257–71.

Wekwerth, Manfred. *Notate: Über die Arbeit des Berliner Ensembles 1956 bis 1966.* Frankfurt am Main, 1967.

————. *Schriften: Arbeit mit Brecht.* Berlin, 1975.

Willett, John. *Art & Politics in the Weimar Period: The New Sobriety 1917–1933.* New York, 1978.

————. *Brecht on Theatre.* New York, 1964.

————. *The Theatre of Bertolt Brecht.* London, 1967.

Wirth, Andrzej. "Der Amerika-Gestus in Brechts Arbeitsjournal," in *Die USA und Deutschland: Wechselseitige Spiegelungen in der Literatur der Gegenwart*, ed. Wolfgang Paulsen. Bern, 1976.

Index

(Note: Works by Brecht are listed under both the German and English titles. Works by other authors are listed under the authors' names, in English only.)

"Abbau des Schiffes Oskawa durch die Mannschaft." *See* "Dismantling of the Ship Oskawa by the Crew"

"Aber dieses ganze Mahagonny. . . . " *See* "But this entire Mahagonny . . . "

"Achttausend arme Leute kommen vor die Stadt." *See* "Eight thousand Poor People Come Up to the City"

Adamic, Louis, *Dynamite: The Story of Class Violence in America*, 266

"Again and Again" (Immer Wieder [in dem Gemetzel]"), 268

"Against Temptation" ("Gegen Verführung"), 184–85

"Alabama Song," 178

Alaska, 36, 37, 87, 182, 185, 196, 253

All Our Yesterdays (Brecht and Reyher), 235, 267

"Als ich vor Jahren. . . . " *See* "When I years ago . . . "

American Revolution, 269–70

Anderson, Sherwood, 253; *Poor White*, 76–79, 83, 93

"An die Nachgeborenen." *See* "To Those Born After"

"Anne Smith Tells the Story of the Conquest of America" ("Anne Smith erzählt die Eroberung Amerikas"), 98–100

"Appropriation of the Great Metro by the Moscow Workers on April 27, 1935" ("Inbesitznahme der großen Metro durch die Moskauer Arbeiterschaft am 27. April 1935"), 94

Aufhaltsame Aufstieg des Arturo Ui, Der. See Resistible Rise of Arturo Ui, The

Aufstieg und Fall der Stadt Mahagonny. See Rise and Fall of the City of Mahagonny, The

Augsburg, 13, 84

"Aus einem Lesebuch für Städtebewohner." *See* "From a Reader for City-Dwellers"

Ausnahme und die Regel, Die. See Exception and the Rule, The

Aus Nichts wird Nichts. See Nothing Will Come of Nothing

"Ausschließlich wegen der zunehmenden Unordnung. . . . " *See* "Exclusively because of the increasing disorder . . . "

Baal, 52, 84, 141, 142, 149, 166, 174, 187, 272–73

Bad Baal the Antisocial Man (Der böse Baal der Asoziale), 174. *See also Baal.*

Baden Play for Learning Acquiescence, The (Das Badener Lehrstück vom Einverständnis), 207–11, 222, 239

"Bad Time for Poetry" ("Schlechte Zeit für Lyrik"), 216–17

"Ballad of the Steel Helmet" ("Ballade vom Stahlhelm"), 233

Balzac, Honoré de, 19

"Bargan Lets it Be" ("Bargan läßt es sein"), 12–13

Barnes group, 128

Barnum, 233

Bavarian *Räterepublik* (Soviet), 148, 150

Becher, Johannes R., 135

"Bei Durchsicht meiner ersten Stücke." *See* "On Looking through My Early Plays"

"Benares Song," 178

Berlin, 9, 13, 14, 22, 49, 225, 233, 238–39, 249. For East Berlin, *see* German Democratic Republic.

Berliner Ensemble, 188, 236, 267, 269, 275

Beule, Die. See Lump on the Head, The

Bible, The, 95, 100–101, 105, 192, 235, 246

Bible, The (*Die Bibel*, play), 100

"Bidi's Opinion of the Great Cities" ("Bidis Ansicht über die großen Städte"), 89

"Blasphemy" ("Blasphemie"), 187

Bloor, Mother, 267

Board of Trade, 60, 128, 254

Böse Baal der Asoziale, Der. See Bad Baal the Antisocial Man

Bread King of Chicago, The (*Der Brotkönig von Chikago*), 234

Bread Store, The (*Der Brotladen*), 111, 114, 174, 198, 201, 234, 238–45, 250, 256–57, 259–61

Bronnen, Arnolt, 13, 44; *Parricide*, 9

Büchner, Georg, *Woyzeck*, 17

Buckow Elegies (*Buckower Elegien*), 220

Bukharin, Nikolai, *Imperialism and the Accumulation of Capital*, 143

Burri, Emil, 199

"But this entire Mahagonny . . ." ("Aber dieses ganze Mahagonny . . ."), 176

Buying Brass (*Der Messingkauf*), 145

Calcutta, May 4th (*Kalkutta, 4. Mai* [Feuchtwanger and Brecht]), 153

"Can bring him vinegar . . ." ("Können ihm Essig holen . . ."), 188

Carnegie, Andrew, 58

Chaplin, Charlie, 9, 70, 145, 195, 204

Charles the Bold, Parody of Americanism (*Karl der Kühne, Parodie auf den Amerikanismus*), 84

"Chewing-Gum Song, The" ("Der Kaugummi-Song"), 229

Chicago, 4, 5, 13–14, 16, 20–29 passim, 40, 41, 47, 54–55, 59, 62, 65, 73, 116, 127, 196–97, 198, 221, 222, 249, 256, 265, 267

Christian Science Monitor, 270

"Coals for Mike" ("Kohlen für Mike"), 76, 93, 94, 233, 266

Cold Chicago (*Das kalte Chicago*), 16

"Come with Me to Georgia ("Komm mit mir nach Georgia"), 90

Communist Party of Germany (KPD), 140, 163, 171–72, 236–37, 248, 259–60

"Crane Songs" ("Kranlieder"), 211–12

Dan Drew, 63, 73, 80, 82, 107–13, 273

Decline of the Giant City Miami (*Untergang der Riesenstadt Miami*). *See Flood, The*

Decline of the Paradise City Miami (*Untergang der Paradiesstadt Miami*). *See Flood, The.*

Decline of the Egoist Johann Fatzer (*Untergang des Egoisten Johann Fatzer*), 58–59, 174, 241

"Deliver the Goods!" ("Liefere die Ware!"), 268

"Democratic Judge, The" ("Der demokratische Richter"), 268

Dessau, Paul, 16

"Dialectical Dramatics" ("[Notizen über] Die dialektische Dramatik"), 264

"Diese babylonische Verwirrung." *See* "This Babylonian Confusion"

"Dismantling of the Ship Oskawa by the Crew" ("Abbau des Schiffes Oskawa durch die Mannschaft"), 266

Dreigroschenoper, Die. See Threepenny Opera, The

"Dreihundert ermordete Kulis berichten an eine Internationale." *See* "Three Hundred Murdered Coolies Report to an International"

Dreiser, Theodore, 253, 255; *Sister Carrie*, 222, 233–34; *The Titan*, 221

Drew, Daniel, 255. *See also Book of Daniel Drew, The*

"Driven Out for Good Reason" ("Verjagt mit gutem Grund"), 160

Drums in the Night (*Trommeln in der Nacht*), 42, 84, 141, 147, 148, 149–51, 160, 256, 273

East Germany. *See* German Democratic Republic

Edward II. See Life of Edward the Second of England

"Eight Thousand Poor People Come Up to the City" ("Achttausend arme Leute kommen vor die Stadt"), 233

Einstein, Albert, 5, 269

"Einzug der Menschheit in die großen Städte." *See* "Human Migration to the Big Cities"

Enemies, The (*Die Feindseligen*), 12

Engels, Friedrich, *Socialism: Utopian and Scientific*, 156. See also Marx, Karl

"Erinnerung an die Marie A." *See* "Remembering Marie A."

Esslin, Martin, 82, 148

Europe (Europeans), 24, 30–31, 41, 61, 62, 65, 71, 72, 73, 89, 106, 117, 225–26, 230–31, 268

"Everywhere Friends" ("Überall Freunde"), 268

Ewers, Hanns Heinz, 63

Exception and the Rule, The (*Die Ausnahme und die Regel*), 239, 262

"Exclusively because of the increasing disorder . . . " ("Ausschließlich wegen der zunehmenden Unordnung . . . "), 218–19

Expressionism, 8, 74

Family from the Savannah, A (*Eine Familie aus der Savannah: Historie in elf Bildern*), 116. See also Joe Fleischhacker

Farquhar, George, *The Recruiting Officer*, 269

Fatzer. See Decline of the Egoist Johann Fatzer.

Feindseligen, Die. See Enemies, The

Feuchtwanger, Lion, 49, 152–53

"Fishing Tackle, The" ("Das Fischgerät"), 268

Fleischhacker. See Joe Fleischhacker

Flight of the Lindberghs, The (*Der Flug der Lindberghs*). *See Flight over the Ocean, The*

Flight over the Ocean, The (*Der Ozeanflug*), 174, 179, 185, 191–92, 204–14, 222

Flood, The (*Die Sintflut*), 101–6, 194, 213, 274

Florida, 102–4, 194, 230

Flüchtlingsgespräche. See Refugee Conversations

Flug der Lindberghs, Der (*The Flight of the Lindbergs*). *See Flight over the Ocean*

"Four Men and a Poker Game or Too Much Luck is Bad Luck" ("Vier Männer und ein Pokerspiel oder Zuviel Glück ist kein Glück"), 200

"Fragen eines lesenden Arbeiters." *See* "Questions of a Reading Worker"

Freedom (*Freiheit*), 12

"Freiwilligen Wächter, Die." *See* "Volunteer Guards, The"

"From a Reader for City Dwellers" ("Aus einem Lesebuch für Städtebewohner"), 90

Furcht und Elend des dritten Reiches. See Private Life of the Master Race, The

Galgei, 83. *See also Man's a Man, A*

Galileo. See Life of Galileo

Garga, 13. *See also In the Jungle of the Cities*

Gary, Elbert H. *See* Tarbell, Ida

"Gedenktafel für 12 Weltmeister." *See* "Memorial Plaque for 12 World Champions"

"Gegen Verführung." *See* "Against Temptation"

"Gehet hinein in die Schlacht. . . . " *See* "Go forth into battle . . . "

German Democratic Republic (GDR), 219, 220, 238, 267, 269

Germany, 6, 7, 10, 168, 180–81, 233, 236, 238, 240, 245, 247–51, 265–66, 269

"Gesang des Soldaten der roten Armee." *See* "Song of the Red Army Soldier"

"Lied der Eisenbahntruppe von Fort Donald, Das." *See* "Song of the Railroad Gang of Fort Donald, The"

Goddess of Victory, The, 235

Goethe, Johann Wolfgang von, 112, 162, 245; *Faust*, 246, 255, 263

"Go forth into battle . . . " ("Gehet hinein in die Schlacht . . . "), 199

Good Person of Sichuan, The (*Der gute Mensch von Sezuan*), 39, 159, 263

Grosz, George, 9, 69

Guilbeaux, Henri, *Vladimir Ilyich Lenin: A Faithful Portrait of His Nature*, 144

Gute Mensch von Sezuan, Der. See Good Person of Sichuan, The

Hamlet of the Wheat Exchange, The (Der Hamlet der Weizenbörse), 235

Happy End (Hauptmann and Brecht), 23, 179, 198–204, 211, 222, 260

Harris, Frank, 145; *My Life and Loves*, 68–69

Harte, Bret, 222; *California Tales*, 38, 194

Hauptmann, Elisabeth, 4, 49, 55, 102, 113, 123, 130, 179, 191, 199–200, 203, 221, 223, 234, 260, 267

Hauptmann, Gerhart, *Rose Bernd*, 158–59

Hauspostille. See Home Devotions

Haymarket Massacre, 54

Hecht, Ben, and Charles MacArthur, *Reporter*, 222

Heilige Johanna der Schlachthöfe, Die. See St. Joan of the Stockyards

Heilsarmee-Stück. See Salvation Army Play

Herr Puntila und sein Knecht Matti. See Mr. Puntila and His Servant Matti

Hill, Joe, 221–22, 269

Hiss, Alger, 270

Hitler, Adolf. *See* National Socialism

Hollywood, 194, 265, 267, 268

"Hollywood," 268

"Hollywood Elegies" ("Hollywood-Elegien"), 268

Home Devotions (Hauspostille), 87, 176, 178, 215, 217

"Hosanna Rockefeller" ("Hosianna Rockefeller"), 250

House Unamerican Activities Committee (HUAC), 172, 269

"Human Migration to the Big Cities" ("Einzug der Menschheit in die großen Städte"), 16, 57, 58, 77, 90–92, 97, 113, 253, 265

"Ich glaube, ich will meinen Hut aufessen. . . . " *See* "I think I'd like to eat my hat up . . . "

Ihering, Herbert, 45–47, 180

Im Dickicht; Im Dickicht der Städte. See In the Jungle of the Cities

"Immer Wieder [in dem Gemetzel]." *See* "Again and Again"

"Inbesitznahme der großen Metro durch die Moskauer Arbeiterschaft am 27. April 1935." *See* "Appropriation of the Great Metro by the Moscow Workers on April 27, 1935"

Indians (American), 99

Industrial Workers of the World (IWW), 221

Inflation (Whores) (Inflation [Mentscher]), 84

"In Praise of the Revolutionary" ("Lob des munismus"), 157–58

"In Priase of the Revolutionary" ("Lob des Revolutionärs"), 258

In the Jungle of the Cities (Im Dickicht der Städte), 12–48, 58, 88, 89, 106, 119, 132, 141, 147, 151–52, 187, 196–97, 209, 251, 256, 261, 271–72, 273

"I think I'd like to eat my hat up . . . " ("Ich glaube, ich will meinen Hut aufessen . . . "), 188

Jasager, Der, und Der Neinsager. See Yea-Sayer, The, and The Nay-Sayer

Jensen, Johannes Vilhelm, 253; *Madame D'Ora*, 27; *The Wheel*, 25–35, 40, 62, 118

Jhering, Herbert. *See* Ihering, Herbert

Joe Fleischhacker, 59, 63, 73, 84, 90, 109, 113–32, 137, 152, 192–93, 206, 234–36, 242, 260–61, 273

Joe Fleischhacker oder ein Brotkönig lernt backen. See King's Bread, The

John Schlachthacker. See Joe Fleischhacker

Jones, Mother, 267

Kalkutta, 4. Mai. See Calcutta, May 4th

Kalte Chicago, Das. See Cold Chicago

"Kantate erster Mai." *See* "May Day Cantata"

Karl der Kühne: Parodie auf den Amerikanismus. See Charles the Bold, Parody of Americanism

"Kaugummi-Song, Der." *See* "Chewing-Gum Song, The"

King's Bread, The (Joe Fleischhacker oder ein Brotkönig lernt backen, [Brecht and Reyher]), 234–35

Kipling, Rudyard, 12

"Kohlen für Mike." *See* "Coals for Mike"

"Komm mit mir nach Georgia." *See* "Come with Me to Georgia"

"Können ihm Essig holen. . . . " *See* "Can bring him vinegar . . . "

Korsch, Karl, 143, 237

KPD. *See* Communist Party of Germany

"Kranlieder." *See* "Crane Songs"

Kriegsfibel. See War Primer

"Landscape of Exile, The" ("Die Landschaft des Exils"), 220

Lane, Dorothy, 199

Lang, Fritz, *Metropolis*, 255

Lania, Leo, *World in Transition*, 50

Lassalle, Ferdinand, 143

Las Vegas, 194–95, 197

Leben Eduards des Zweiten von England. See Life of Edward the Second of England

Leben des Einstein. See Life of Einstein

Leben des Galilei. See Life of Galileo

"Legend of the Origin of the Book Dao De Jing on Lao Ze's Way into Exile" ("Legende von der Entstehung des Buches Taoteking auf dem Weg des Laotse in die Emigration"), 93, 94

Lenin, Vladimir Ilyich, 142–44, 175, 233; *Left-Wing Communism: An Infantile Disorder*, 143; *State and Revolution*, 142–43

Lewinson, Richard (Morus), 130

Liebknecht, Karl, 8, 246

"Lied der Eisenbahntruppe von Fort Donald, Das." *See* "Song of the Railroad Gang of Fort Donald, The"

"Lied der Ströme." *See* "Song of the Rivers"

"Lied des Stückschreibers." *See* "The Playwright's Song"

"Lied einer Familie aus der Savannah." *See* "Song of a Family from the Savannah"

"Lied eines Mannes in San Francisco." *See* "Song of a Man in San Francisco"

"Liefere die Ware!" *See* "Deliver the Goods!"

Life of Edward the Second of England (Leben Eduards des Zweiten von England), 42, 152–53

Life of Einstein (Leben des Einstein), 269

Life of Galileo (Leben des Galilei), 47, 267

Lindbergh, Charles. *See Flight over the Ocean*

"Lob des Communismus." *See* "In Praise of Communism"

"Lob des Revolutionärs." *See* "In Praise of the Revolutionary"

London, Jack, 38, 76–77, 194, 222

Lorimer, George Horace, 65, 112, 127, 253, 255; *Letters from a Self-Made Merchant to His Son*, 39–40

Lump on the Head, The (Die Beule), 174. *See also Threepenny Opera, The*

Luxembourg, Rosa, 8, 246

Mahagonny (name), 154, 184

Mahagonny. See Rise and Fall of the City of Mahagonny

"Mahagonny Song" ("Mahagonny-Gesang"), 1–5, 90, 182–84

Mahagonny Song-Play (Mahagonny Songspiel), 103, 176–88. *See also Rise and Fall of the City of Mahagonny*

Man from Manhattan (Mann aus Manhattan), 95–101, 118, 193, 208

Man's a Man, A (Mann ist Mann), 49, 52, 83–84, 100, 141, 148, 153, 172, 181, 261, 272, 273

Marx, Karl (Marxism). 139–49 passim, 152, 155–60, 164, 170–71, 175, 176, 191, 204, 209, 225–26, 236, 245, 264, 267; *Capital*, 69, 133, 134, 140, 142–44, 157, 195, 220, 244, 247, 248, 255, 263; *The Communist Manifesto* (Marx and Engels), 156

Marxist School for Workers (MASCH, Berlin), 143

"Marxist Studies" ("Marxistische Studien"), 143, 209

Maßnahme, Die. See Measure Taken, The

Masters, Edgar Lee, *Spoon River Anthology*, 38

"May Day Cantata" ("Kantate erster Mai"), 266

May, Karl, 4

Measure Taken, The (Die Maßnahme), 143, 147, 159, 166, 216, 239–40, 260

"Meditating, so I hear, on Hell . . . " ("Nachdenkend, wie ich höre, über die Hölle . . . "), 268

"Memorial Plaque for 12 World Champions" ("Gedenktafel für 12 Weltmeister"), 223

Mendelsohn, Erich, *America: An Architect's Picture Book*, 69–75

Messingkauf, Der. See Buying Brass

Me-Ti, 219

Miami, 230. *See also Flood, The*

Mills, C. Wright, *The Power Elite*, 270

Morgan, J. Pierpont, 56–58, 81, 255

Morley, Michael, 39

Mortimer Fleischhacker, 97. *See also Joe Fleischhacker*

Morus. *See* Lewinson, Richard

Mother, The (*Die Mutter*), 157, 166, 207, 222, 239, 241, 244, 256, 261–63, 274, 276

Mother Courage (*Mutter Courage*), 256, 276

Mr. Puntila and His Servant Matti (*Herr Puntila und sein Knecht Matti*), 235, 263, 267

Mühsam, Erich, *Sacco and Vanzetti*, 222

Myers, Gustavus, 253, 255; *History of the Great American Fortunes*, 79–83

"Nachdenkend, wie ich höre, über die Hölle. . . . " *See* "Meditating, so I hear, on Hell . . ."

"Nachtlager, Die." *See* "Places to Sleep"

National Socialism (Nazism), 154, 220, 225–26, 237–38, 266, 267, 269

Neher, Caspar (Cas), 13, 26

Neue Sachlichkeit, 8, 28, 70, 74–75, 203, 204

New York City, 70, 72–73, 108, 240, 249–50, 267

New York Times, 270

Norris, Frank, 253, 255–56; *The Epic of Wheat*, 115; *The Grain Exchange*, 116; *The Octopus*, 115–16; *The Pit*, 58–63, 83, 113–16, 122, 128–30, 221, 225, 242, 254; *Wheat*, 116, 128

Nothing Will Come of Nothing (*Aus Nichts wird Nichts*), 174

"Obacht, gib obacht! . . . " *See* "Take care, pay heed! . . . "

"Of Poor B. B." ("Vom armen B. B."), 87–89, 106, 148, 233

"Of the Crushing Weight of the Cities" ("Von der zermalmenden Wucht der Städte"), 89

"On the Drowned Girl" ("Vom ertrunkenen Mädchen"), 87

"On Cities" ("Über die Städte"), 186–87

"On Looking through My Early Plays" ("Bei Durchsicht meiner ersten Stücke"), 25, 39

"On Rhymeless Poetry with Irregular Rhythms" ("Über reimlose Lyrik mit unregelmassigen Rhythmen"), 33

"On the Human Migration to the Big Cities at the Beginning of the Third Millenium"

("Über den Einzug der Menschheit in die großen Städte zu Beginn des dritten Jahrtausends"), 90–92, 97, 113

Oppenheimer, J. Robert, 269

Ozeanflug, Der. See Flight over the Ocean, The

Paquet, Alfons, *Flags*, 50–55

"Parade of the Old New" ("Parade des alten Neuen"), 275

Pastor, Eva, 267

Pauken und Trompeten. See Trumpets and Drums

Piscator, Erwin, 38, 50–53, 165, 221–22

"Places to Sleep" ("Die Nachtlager"), 222, 233, 257, 261

Play of Cold Chicago, The (*Das Stück vom kalten Chicago*), 16

"Playwright's Song, The" ("Lied des stückschreibers"), 257

Plekhanov, Georgi, *The Role of the Individual in History*, 143

Poems Belonging with the Reader for City-Dwellers" ("Zum Lesebuch für Städtebewohner gehörige Gedichte"), 187

Private Life of the Master Race, The (*Furcht und Elend des dritten Reiches*), 267

"Questions of a Reading Worker" ("Fragen eines lesenden Arbeiters"), 94

"Radio—An Antediluvian Invention?" ("Radio—Eine vorsintflutliche Erfindung?"), 213

"Radio Theory" ("Radiotheorie"), 212

Ramthun, Herta, 199

Refugee Conversations (*Flüchtlingsgespräche*), 159, 161, 258

Reich, Bernhard, 202

"Remembering Marie A." ("Erinnerung an die Marie A."), 87

Resistible Rise of Arturo Ui, The (*Der aufhaltsame Aufstieg des Arturo Ui*), 23, 112, 168, 201, 248, 265–66

Reyher, Ferdinand, 223, 234–35, 267–68

Rimbaud, Arthur, 35; *A Season in Hell*, 36

Rise and Fall of the City of Mahagonny (*Aufstieg und Fall der Stadt Mahagonny*), 31, 33, 35, 40, 83, 87, 89, 95, 101–4, 106–7, 119, 165, 176–98, 209–11, 213, 222, 227, 256, 273–74

Robinsonisms in the City (*Robinsonade in der Stadt*), 84

Roundheads and the Peakheads, The (*Die Rundköpfe und die Spitzköpfe*), 168, 239

"Rug Weavers of Kuyan-Bulak Honor Lenin, The" ("Die Teppichweber von Kujan-Bulak ehren Lenin"), 233

Rülicke, Käthe (later Rülicke-Weiler), 247

Rühle, Otto, 144

Ruhrrevue, 211

Rundköpfe und die Spitzköpfe, Die. See Roundheads and the Peakheads, The

Russia (Russian Revolution), 147, 148, 236–37, 275

Sacco, Nicola, and Bartolomeo Vanzetti, 222, 246

St. Joan of the Stockyards (*Die heilige Johanna der Schlachthöfe*), 17, 20, 23, 39, 57–58, 61, 63, 64, 81, 83, 95, 101, 108, 111, 112, 120, 125, 127–28, 129, 159, 160, 197, 198, 201–2, 220, 223, 226, 236, 239–63, 274

Salvation Army, 13, 39, 65, 201–3, 241–44, 246, 259–61, 263

Salvation Army Play (*Heilsarmee-Stück* [Hauptmann]), 199–200, 212

Samson-Körner, Paul, 49, 228

Sandburg, Carl, 38

"Sang der Maschinen." *See* "Song of the Machines"

Saturday Review, 270

Schiller, Friedrich, 112, 162, 245; *Don Carlos*, 17; "The Guarantee," 95–96; *The Maid of Orleans*, 255; *The Robbers*, 43

"Schlechte Zeit für Lyrik." *See* "Bad Time for Poetry"

Schriften zur Politik und Gesellschaft. See Writings on Politics and Society

Schumacher, Ernst, 151–52, 154

"Search for the New and Old" ("Suche nach dem Neuen und Alten"), 275

SED. *See* Socialist Unity Party

Seven Deadly Sins of the Petty Bourgeoisie, The (*Die sieben Todsünden der Kleinbürger*), 119, 191, 263, 265

Shakespeare, William, 145, 162, 245–46, 266; *Hamlet*, 235; *King Lear*, 112; *Macbeth*, 235

Shaw, George Bernard, 65–67; *Major Barbara*, 200, 255; *Saint Joan*, 255

Sieben Todsünden der Kleinbürger, Die.

See Seven Deadly Sins of the Petty Bourgeoisie, The

Sinclair, Upton, 38–39; *The Jungle*, 16–25, 40, 41, 117, 119, 199–200, 252–53; *The Machine*, 39; *Oil!*, 196, 212; *Prince Hagen*, 38; *Singing Jailbirds*, 221–22

Sintflut, Die. See Flood, The

Socialist Party (U.S.A.), 24

Socialist Unity Party of the GDR (SED), 163, 171–72, 237

Sodom und Gomorrah. See Man from Manhattan

"Song of a Family from the Savannah" ("Lied einer Familie aus der Savannah"), 116, 265

"Song of a Man in San Francisco" ("Lied eines Mannes in San Francisco"), 97

"Song of Mandelay, The" ("Der Song von Mandelay"), 188

"Song of the Machines" ("Sang der Maschinen"), 211, 223

"Song of the Railroad Gang of Fort Donald, The" ("Das Lied der Eisenbahntruppe von Fort Donald"), 38, 87, 107

"Song of the Red Army Soldier" ("Gesang des Soldaten der roten Armee"), 86, 87

"Song of the Rivers" ("Lied der Ströme"), 269

Spirit and Face of Bolshevism, 144

Steffens, Lincoln, 82

Sternberg, Fritz, 143, 150, 161, 170, 237

Stück vom kalten Chicago, Das. See Play of Cold Chicago, The

"Suche nach dem Neuen und Alten." *See* "Search for the New and Old"

Svendborg Poems (*Svendborger Gedichte*), 93–94, 215–17, 266

Tahiti, 35, 40, 87, 151, 182–83, 253

"Tahiti," 87, 182, 185

"Take care, pay heed! . . . " ("Obacht, gib obacht! . . . "), 203

Tarbell, Ida, 253, 255; *History of the Standard Oil Company*, 196; *The Life of Elbert H. Gary*, 55–58

"Teppichweber von Kujan-Bulak ehren Lenin, Die." *See* "Rug Weavers of Kuyan-Bulak Honor Lenin, The"

"This Babylonian Confusion" ("Diese babylonische Verwirrung"), 137–38, 169, 217

"Three Hundred Murdered Coolies Report

"Three Hundred . . ." (*Continued*) to an International" (Dreihundert ermordete Kulis berichten an eine Internationale"), 233

Threepenny Opera, The (*Die Dreigroschenoper*), 31, 33, 174, 179–80, 190, 198–99, 201, 203, 223

Three Soldiers, The (*Die drei Soldaten*), 136

"To Those Born After" ("An die Nachgeborenen"), 217–18

Trommeln in der Nacht. See Drums in the Night

Trumpets and Drums (*Pauken und Trompeten*), 269–70

"Überall Freunde." *See* "Everywhere Friends"

"Über den Einzug der Menscheit in die großen Städte zu Beginn des dritten Jahrtausends." *See* "On the Human Migration to the Big Cities at the Beginning of the Third Millenium"

"Über die Städte." *See* "On Cities"

"Über reimlose Lyrik mit unregelmäßigen Rhythmen." *See* "On Rhymeless Poetry with Irregular Rhythms"

United States Steel. *See* Tarbell Ida, *The Life of Elbert H. Gary*

Untergang des Egoisten Johann Fatzer. See Decline of the Egoist Johann Fatzer

Untergang der Paradiesstadt Miami. See Decline of the Paradise City Miami; Flood, The

Untergang der Riesenstadt Miami. See Decline of the Giant City Miami; Flood, The

"Vanished Glory of the Giant City New York" ("Verschollener Ruhm der Riesenstadt New York") 41, 206, 226–34

"Verjagt mit gutem Grund." *See* "Driven Out for Good Reason"

"Verschollener Ruhm der Riesenstadt New York." *See* "Vanished Glory of the Giant City New York"

"Vier Männer und ein Pokerspiel oder Zuviel Glück ist kein Glück." *See* "Four Men and a Poker Game or Too Much Luck Is Bad Luck"

"Volunteer Guards, The" ("Die freiwilligen Wächter"), 268

"Vom armen B. B." *See* "Of Poor B. B."

"Vom ertrunkenen Mädchen." See "On the Drowned Girl"

"Von der zermalmenden Wucht der Städte." See "Of the Crushing Weight of the Cities"

Wagner, Richard, 190

Walcher, Jakob, *Ford or Marx: The Practical Solution to the Social Question*, 143–44

Waley, Arthur, 191

Wall Street, 73, 108, 225–26, 233, 236, 247

War Primer (*Kriegsfibel*), 258

Weimar Republic, 249

Weigel, Helene, 27, 38, 49, 63, 79, 116

Weill, Kurt, 177–79, 182, 188–91 passim, 196

Weizen. See Wheat

"We Nineteen" ("Wir Neunzehn"), 269

Wheat (*Weizen*), 136. *See also Joe Fleischhacker*

"When I years ago . . . " ("Als ich vor Jahren . . . "), 132–33, 138, 213

White, Bouck, 253; *The Book of Daniel Drew*, 63–65, 83, 107–12, 130

Whitman, Walt, 35–38, 58; *Crossing Brooklyn Ferry*, 37; *Leaves of Grass*, 37

"Wir Neunzehn." *See* "We Nineteen"

World War I, 33, 85, 150

World War II, 235

Writings on Politics and Society (*Schriften zur Politik und Gesellschaft*), 67, 143

Yea-Sayer, The, and The Nay-Sayer (*Der Jasager und Der Neinsager*), 166

"Zum Lesebuch für Städtebewohner gehörige Gedichte." *See* "Poems Belonging with the Reader for City-Dwellers"